OVERSEAS CHINESE BUSINESS NETWORKS IN ASIA

EAST ASIA ANALYTICAL UNIT

DEPARTMENT OF FOREIGN AFFAIRS AND TRADE

The National Library of Australia Cataloguing-in-Publication data:

Overseas Chinese Business Networks in Asia

Bibliography.
Includes index.
ISBN 0 642 22960 0

1. Commerce - Asia. 2. Chinese - Asia.
3. Businessmen - Asia. 4. Entrepeneurship - Asia.
5. Businessmen - Social networks - Asia.
I. Australia. East Asia Analytical Unit.

338.04095

Design, typesetting and printing by Green Advertising #6187
Distributed by AGPS Press

FOREWORD

Just as Asian economies are increasingly important to Australia, so are the region's leading business entrepreneurs. This study, commissioned by the Australian Government's *Standing Committee of Deputy Secretaries on East Asia*, represents the most comprehensive attempt to date to document the remarkable success of the overseas Chinese business community in the economies of the Asian region. It aims to encourage and assist Australian business to link up with overseas Chinese business networks that increasingly draw the region's economies together. The role of Australia's community of Chinese entrepreneurs in enhancing our economic integration with Asia is highlighted.

Face-to-face interviews were the main research tool used in the study. Prominent Chinese business people, politicians, academics and officials were interviewed over a series of visits to countries of the region, including Malaysia, Indonesia, Myanmar (formerly Burma), Thailand, Singapore, Taiwan and Hong Kong, in the latter half of 1994 and early 1995. Further interviews were conducted in Australia. A list of interviewees appears in Appendix 1.

An extensive literature survey also was undertaken, using both primary and secondary sources. Surveys were commissioned in the Chinese provinces of Guangdong, Fujian, and Jiangsu, where overseas Chinese are the major foreign investors. A number of Australian Chinese business organisations also were surveyed.

The overseas Chinese business community is itself enormously diverse and complex. It is changing rapidly as the economies and societies of Asia evolve. Ethnic Chinese companies are among the largest, and the smallest, businesses in the region. They are represented in every area of commerce and industry and their business methods range from the most traditional to the most modern.

In researching this book, the authors were very conscious of the risk of losing the sense of this diversity in writing a readable account. They were equally aware that it is virtually impossible to produce any useful analysis from such research without making some generalisations. The authors also recognised that the individual characteristics identified in the study were not unique to overseas Chinese business, but could quite easily apply to other business communities. In an effort to address these fundamental analytical problems, the study canvasses a wide range of views on the nature and extent of overseas Chinese business networks. None of the views expressed in the study, however, should be understood as representing, necessarily, attitudes or policies of the Australian Government, the Department of Foreign Affairs and Trade, the East Asia Analytical Unit, or the contributors.

While the authors have tried to ensure that the vast amount of material presented is accurate some factual inaccuracies may have occurred. The Australian Government, the Department of Foreign Affairs and Trade, the East Asia Analytical Unit and the contributors to the study accept no liability for the accuracy of the contents.

ACKNOWLEDGMENTS

Michael Backman, Executive Officer with the East Asia Analytical Unit, was the principal researcher and author of this study.

At various stages Dr Meredith Borthwick, Phillip Stonehouse, David Binns, Joseph Tsang and Pauline Adobor, all of the East Asia Analytical Unit, and the head of the unit, Dr Frances Perkins, all contributed with editorial inputs, comments and other assistance. Other officers of the Department of Foreign Affairs and Trade and other agencies commented on earlier drafts.

The Federal Government's Standing Committee of Deputy Secretaries on East Asia also provided valuable input.

Some of the research for the study drew on input from consultants Noel Tracy and Dr Constance Lever-Tracy of the Flinders University of South Australia (particularly on investment in China by foreign Chinese - Chapter 10, and the outline of the conglomerates in Appendix 7), and Professor Pookong Kee, Director of the Centre for Asia-Pacific Studies, Victoria University of Technology (particularly on Australian Chinese and their associations - Appendix 5). Professional editing was undertaken by Ann Duffy.

The study has benefited from useful suggestions and advice from Fiona Hu, formerly Director of Research and Publications, Singapore Chinese Chamber of Commerce and Industry; Professor Wolfgang Kasper, University of New South Wales (ADFA campus); and David Ch'ng, Swinburne University of Technology.

The unit is particularly grateful to the many business people, officials and academics in Australia and Asia who consented to be interviewed for this study. They are listed in Appendix 1.

TABLE OF CONTENTS

Executive Summary And Overview		1
	Migration and Settlement	1
	The Importance of Dialect	2
	Traditional Business Profile	3
	Modernisation of Ethnic Chinese Businesses	3
	The Conglomerates	4
	Success Factors	5
	Investment Role in East Asia	6
	Investment Role in China	6
	Investment Beyond the Region	7
	The Networks and 'Outsiders'	8
	Linking Up with the Networks: Selecting A Partner	8
	Governments as Facilitators	10
A Note on Nomenclature		12
Chapter 1	Migration and Settlement	13
	Migration From China	13
	Early Settlement Experiences in South-East Asia	15
	Formation of Chinese Associations	16
	Assimilation	17
Chapter 2	The Importance of Dialect	19
	Dialects: An Overview	19
	Dialect and Occupation Links	26
	International Dialect Links as 'Networks'	32
	Formal International Dialect Linkages	33
Chapter 3	South-East Asia, Indochina and Beyond	34
	Brunei	34
	Cambodia	35
	Indonesia	37
	Laos	47
	Malaysia	48
	Myanmar (Burma)	60
	The Philippines	64
	Singapore	69
	Thailand	73
	Vietnam	80
	Ethnic Chinese in Other Selected Countries	86

TABLE OF CONTENTS

Chapter 4	Hong Kong, Macau and Taiwan	90
	Hong Kong	90
	Macau	99
	Taiwan	100
Chapter 5	An Overview of The Australian Chinese Community	110
	Early History	111
	Recent Arrivals	112
	Australia's Chinese in Commerce	117
	Australia's Chinese - Providing Links to the Regional Economy	118
Chapter 6	Explaining the Success of Ethnic Chinese Business	119
	The Ethnic Chinese on Their Success	119
	Culture and other Institutions	121
	Many Factors for Success	130
Chapter 7	Traditional Chinese Business Practice	131
	Traditional Ways of Doing Business	131
	The Transformation of Ethnic Chinese Business	141
Chapter 8	The Conglomerates	153
	Conglomeration of Ethnic Chinese Business	153
	Some Aspects of Conglomerates' Behaviour	158
	Colleagues and Not Competitors at the Top	161
	Case Study - The Salim Group	163
Chapter 9	Connections and Investment Across Borders	176
	International Linkages of Asia's Ethnic Chinese Communities	179
	International Linkages Between Chinese Communities	180
	The Internet - A New Way to Network	193
Chapter 10	The Role of Foreign-Chinese in the Transformation of China	194
	Overview of Foreign Investment in China	194
	Foreign Investment in China Since 1979	195
	Foreign-Chinese Investment in China	197
	Why Have the Ethnic Chinese Dominated Foreign Investment in China?	203
	The Role of Foreign-Chinese in China's International Trade	205
	The Transformation of the South-East	206

TABLE OF CONTENTS

	Changing Investment Patterns: New Destinations for Foreign-Chinese Investment in China	214
	Employment Consequences of Foreign-Chinese Investment	217
	Annex	219
Chapter 11	South-East Asian Chinese Investment in China	235
	Investment in China from Selected South-East Asian Countries	235
Chapter 12	The Networks and Western Business at Home and Abroad	244
	Linking Up with Outsiders at Home	244
	The Expansion of Ethnic Chinese Business Beyond Asia	247
Chapter 13	Australia and the Networks	251
	Investment in Real Estate	252
	Other Investment	253
	Australian Companies Linking Up with the Networks To Invest and Trade Abroad	256
	Case Study: The Road to China - Linking Up with Australia's Chinese	262
	Annex	266
	Recent Significant Real Estate Acquisitions by Ethnic Chinese from the Region	266
Chapter 14	Linking Up with the Networks: Selecting A Partner	273
	The Right Partner	273
	Governments as Facilitators	278
Appendix 1	Interviewees	280
Appendix 2	Transliteration of Chinese Place Names	287
Appendix 3	Chinese Chambers of Commerce in East Asia	288
Appendix 4	Chinese Business Organisations in Australia	291
Appendix 5	Australian Chinese Organisations: An Overview	294
	Analysing Australia's Chinese Organisations	295
	An Overview of Some of Australia's Main Chinese Chambers of Commerce	297
	Other Leading Chinese Organisations	301
Appendix 6	A Note on *Feng Shui* and Lucky Numbers	310
	Feng Shui	310
	Luck, Lucky Numbers and Symbols	311

TABLE OF CONTENTS

Appendix 7	The Conglomerates - Eight Case Studies	313
	Wu Family	313
	Li Family	315
	Pao/Woo Family	317
	Tomei	319
	Sophonpanich Family	320
	Chearavanont Family	323
	Robert Kuok	327
	Quek/Kwek Family	331
Appendix 8	An Overview of Malaysia's New Economic Policy	334
Appendix 9	List of Acronyms Used	336
Bibliography		340
Index		351

LIST OF ILLUSTRATIONS

Figure 2.1	Origins in China of the Main Dialects and Subdialects of the Overseas Chinese	20
Figure 3.1	Cross-shareholdings and Family Linkages Between Selected Indonesian Conglomerates	43
Figure 4.1	Far Eastern Group	105
Figure 7.1	The Evolution of an Ethnic Chinese Firm	144
Figure 8.1	Overview of the Salim Group: Structure and Key Companies	173
Figure 10.1	China - Special Economic Zones	196

EXECUTIVE SUMMARY AND OVERVIEW

Overseas Chinese business entrepreneurs are at the very heart of East Asia's economic boom.[1] Though relatively few in number, they are economically pre-eminent, and are one of the main forces driving the dynamic growth that characterises the region as a whole, and many of the economies in it.

The 50 million or so ethnic Chinese resident in East Asia outside China generate an estimated GDP equivalent of about US$450 billion. This is almost on a par with China's GDP of approximately US$500 billion, which is generated by more than twenty times the number of people.[2]

Although they are fewer than ten per cent of the population of South-East Asia, ethnic Chinese make up 86 per cent of its billionaires. They control much of the region's non-land capital and its retail trade, and are major stakeholders in most of the region's economies.

In broad terms, this information indicates the importance of understanding the role and *modus operandi* of the ethnic Chinese business community in the economies of East Asia. For Australian companies, such an understanding brings with it the prospect of linking up with the extensive business networks controlled by the community, which stitch together the economies of the region, and link them to the burgeoning China market.

Australia's links through the networks to East Asia, including China, are set to increase in importance - and value - as Australia's community of Chinese entrepreneurs engages more fully in a bridging role.

MIGRATION AND SETTLEMENT

Migration from China to other parts of East Asia has a long history. By the early fifteenth century, there were permanent ethnic Chinese settlements at a number of locations in Asia. The most important waves of migration, in terms of the effect on the current socio-economic landscape of the region, occurred during the nineteenth and early twentieth centuries, normally in conjunction with periods of famine or political upheaval in China.

Almost all of those who left China during this period were from southern coastal provinces, principally Guangdong, Fujian and Hainan. They represented a wide

1 Throughout this study, the term 'ethnic Chinese', rather than the inaccurate expression 'overseas Chinese', has been generally used to denote Chinese in Asia living outside the current administration of the People's Republic of China. For a fuller explanation of this and other terminology used in this study, see the section *A Note on Nomenclature.*

2 The figures are for 1990 and are sourced from *The Economist,* 'The Overseas Chinese: A Driving Force', 18 July 1992.

spectrum of dialects of spoken Chinese, the main ones being Hokkien, Teochiu, Cantonese, Hakka and Hainanese. These remain the main dialects spoken by the ethnic Chinese of East Asia outside China.

Migration was not random, but usually occurred in 'chains', with relatives and neighbours tending to follow each other to particular locations throughout the region. This phenomenon explains the relative concentration of one or more dialect groups in different parts of East Asia today.

An important phenomenon accompanying the waves of migration from China was the formation of mutual help societies in each place of settlement. These were based on either kinship (clan), place of origin in China, dialect or sub-dialect, craft, or a combination of these factors. Mutual help societies assisted new arrivals to settle and lent money to members for specific purposes. Many Chinese entrepreneurs were given their start in business in this manner. Other organisations regulated the different aspects of ethnic Chinese life in the new settlements.

In this manner, the ethnic Chinese created a cohesive web of interlocking organisations and relationships that provided a firm and stable framework within which traditional society could be recreated, maintained and developed and whose individual members could prosper far from home. This characteristic of Chinese settlement in East Asia significantly underpinned the ethnic Chinese business community's later commercial ascendancy.

THE IMPORTANCE OF DIALECT

Like other immigrant communities, the overseas community of ethnic Chinese is not homogeneous. Even today, ethnic Chinese may differentiate among themselves according to dialect, sub-dialect, clan and family, all of which are linked to their place of ancestral origin in China, as well as by country of birth, or of current residence, outside China. The degree to which these differentiators are considered important varies from individual to individual, but ethnic Chinese networks, whether they are for purely social or for business purposes, always comprise individuals who share one or more of these characteristics.

Understanding the importance of dialects and their distribution across East Asia is central to an understanding of how ethnic Chinese business networks operated in the past, and operate in the present. Who did business with whom and what was traded often could be explained, at least in part, by the dialect and sub-dialect spoken by those involved. Today, many sectors of South-East Asia's food trade, for example, are still largely in the hands of Teochiu speakers. Similarly, it is more than coincidence that two of the region's most successful and prominent ethnic Chinese entrepreneurs, Malaysia's Robert Kuok and Indonesia's Liem Sioe Liong, who share an enduring corporate partnership, both speak the Fuzhou/Hokchia sub-dialect, reflecting a common ancestral origin in the north of China's Fujian Province.

A growing trend is to form international clan associations based on dialect. An impetus has been the economic transformation of China. Among other things, international clan associations can provide an excellent basis for borderless commercial networking.

TRADITIONAL BUSINESS PROFILE

The vast majority of ethnic Chinese businesses in East Asia today are small to medium sized, and these, typically, are family owned. Even the large, ethnic Chinese-controlled conglomerates of the region are often groupings of sometimes hundreds of much smaller companies.

Other common characteristics of traditionally-run ethnic Chinese businesses, large and small, appear to be[3]:

- highly centralised decision making
- low margin and high volume as a means of penetrating markets
- rigorous control of inventory to achieve low capital investment and high rates of stock turnover
- reduction of 'transaction costs' (ie the costs of doing business) through a preference for doing business within ethnic Chinese networks
- preference for internal financing
- tendency to undervalue services and other intangibles, such as legal and other advice and R&D (and a preference to internalise these costs, where possible).

MODERNISATION OF ETHNIC CHINESE BUSINESSES

Management and organisational structures that were efficient and effective in smaller ethnic Chinese firms become increasingly inefficient as these firms grow. In recent years, many larger ethnic Chinese enterprises in the region have modernised, shedding many of their more traditional characteristics. This process is continuing. With the economies of the region becoming increasingly integrated, and with Asian companies facing increasing competition from outside the region, many larger firms and groups have had little choice but to bring their management structures more in line with those of other large international companies. Operating responsibility, for example, which in the past was concentrated at the top of the management structure, now is delegated more and more to lower levels.

Nevertheless, today many of these businesses, even the largest of the regional conglomerates, continue to reflect a family-oriented structure, including an essentially patriarchal style of top-level management in which individual members of the controlling family still play a key role. A number of large enterprises, for example, manage the transition from a traditional to a relatively modern business structure by installing the MBA-educated sons and daughters of the controlling family at the head of separate divisions. In this way, the family retains ultimate control but applies modern Western management techniques to improve the company.

---

3 These characteristics are not, of course, individually unique to ethnic Chinese-controlled businesses.

Over time, as ethnic Chinese enterprises continue to expand, such enterprises will evolve increasingly to Western patterns of management. On the other hand, most 'modernising' ethnic Chinese businesses have been careful not to become over-bureaucratised. Despite their size, the major ethnic Chinese enterprises in the region remain, for the most part, entrepreneurial and agile, with the ultimate head, no matter how large the enterprise, staying close to the market, and remaining sensitive to shifts in market conditions.

As financial markets across Asia develop, the traditional reliance by ethnic Chinese firms on retained earnings, or relatives or business associates, as sources of either start-up or expansion capital is waning. The largest ethnic Chinese enterprises increasingly resort to formal methods of raising capital, including share issues in the case of publicly-listed companies, although normally in ways that retain ultimate family control. The clan, however, has remained in some communities an important source of start-up capital, especially for the smaller firms, and retained earnings remain the preferred source of funding for larger firms seeking to expand their operations.

Ethnic Chinese businesses are expanding outside their traditional fields of trading, manufacturing and property development.

THE CONGLOMERATES

Many ethnic Chinese family businesses in East Asia expand by acquiring an ever-increasing number of companies, rather than enlarging existing companies. The resulting business group may be large, but its individual component companies may be relatively small.

In most of the economies of the region, ethnic Chinese entrepreneurs control large, diversified conglomerates. Some of these conglomerates, like Indonesia's Salim Group, encompass hundreds of separate companies spread across a wide range of markets in many countries. These conglomerates imitate the 'footloose' character of other multinationals, operating across economies, identifying niches and drawing together markets.

Almost all of the region's ethnic Chinese conglomerates remain, however, 'family firms' in that they are owned by the members of a single family. Typically, sons and daughters will each be given a division of the conglomerate to manage. Most of the top conglomerates are highly diversified and not centred in a single sector. Almost all either own or are closely associated with one or more private banks, from which they can tap expansion funds. They usually also have links to foreign capital - either through joint ventures with foreign companies or loans from foreign banks. Most have offshore representation, particularly in Singapore and Hong Kong.

As with other ethnic Chinese enterprises in the region, many of the more successful conglomerates are modernised. Typically, their companies are formed into a squat pyramid structure, with a family holding company at the apex, a second tier holding the group's most prized assets (which are usually privately held) and a third tier at the base comprising the group's publicly-listed companies.

In several countries in the region, ethnic Chinese conglomerates are responding to opportunities, as well as spreading political risk, by diversifying outside their home markets. Domestically, the conglomerates also increase interlinkages through cross-shareholdings, cross-directorships and inter-family connections such as marriage. The interlinking of the top Chinese conglomerates not only strengthens the economic position of the ethnic Chinese business community throughout the region, but also its political leverage in the region's individual economies.

SUCCESS FACTORS

All too often, the very high representation of ethnic Chinese business entrepreneurs among the region's economic elite is ascribed to a single factor, even by the entrepreneurs themselves. This is an oversimplification. The reasons for the economic pre-eminence of ethnic Chinese business in the region are many and varied. The study identifies a number of connected elements, varying in their relative significance according to time and place, that in one combination or another partly help explain the ethnic Chinese business community's success.

- An important element underpinning their success is that ethnic Chinese immigrant communities establish their own 'order' by creating a range of informal organisations, the mutual help societies, for example, and networks that support and develop their interests. This ability has made ethnic Chinese business entrepreneurs especially competitive in environments where the legal and administrative infrastructure, the externally imposed 'order', is relatively underdeveloped.
- Through their extensive networks, which often span several countries in the region, ethnic Chinese entrepreneurs tap the latest market intelligence to mobilise capital at short notice and to occupy market niches where the highest profits can be made. Operating to a significant degree within their own networks also enables these entrepreneurs to minimise transactions costs. In such circumstances, the element of 'trust' develops naturally, although it is also underpinned by a powerful enforcement mechanism, the potential loss of business reputation, that is available to, and binds, every member of the network (though not necessarily outsiders).
- The study identifies a number of other elements, but the success of the ethnic Chinese business community in the region has not been all of its own making. Governments have also played an important role in creating a suitable environment for the commercial flair of ethnic Chinese entrepreneurs, backed by their extensive networks of mutual support, to show itself to best advantage. In some cases, their advantage is enhanced through developing symbiotic relations with local indigenous elites. This is natural, given the commercial power wielded by ethnic Chinese business in most of the region's economies and the tendency of ethnic Chinese entrepreneurs to eschew a direct political role for themselves.

INVESTMENT ROLE IN EAST ASIA

The networks that serve ethnic Chinese business entrepreneurs so well in domestic markets are borderless. They link most of East Asia's economies together in a seamless web of connections.

The region's ethnic Chinese business entrepreneurs have created investment flows within East Asia that may exceed flows from the Japanese, normally thought of as the region's largest foreign investors. In particular, the ethnic Chinese-dominated economies of Hong Kong, Taiwan and Singapore are significant net exporters of capital to the region, particularly to the economies of China, Thailand, Indonesia, the Philippines, Vietnam, Cambodia and Myanmar. In this manner, the ethnic Chinese business community of East Asia appears to have taken on a role akin to that of the Japanese in the 1970s and early 1980s, as underwriters of the earlier stages of the region's economic transformation.

INVESTMENT ROLE IN CHINA

Ethnic Chinese entrepreneurs also are the largest source of foreign direct investment in China, and in this way are making a major contribution to China's continuing economic transformation. Their investment role has been critical to the transformation of south-eastern China into an export-oriented economic dynamo.

Conversely, China's opening up to foreign investment has helped to develop the ethnic Chinese business community of the region into an international commercial force. Economic reform in China since 1985 has provided ethnic Chinese entrepreneurs with highly profitable outlets for surplus capital, a means of industrial restructuring and a basis, therefore, for exponential industrial growth.

In 1994 alone, new foreign direct investment in China amounted to US$33.8 billion, of which some 70 per cent, according to official PRC records, came from Hong Kong[4] and Macau, and a further eight per cent from Taiwan[5]. By the end of 1993, ethnic Chinese investment in China employed an estimated 14 million people. On current trends, this may have increased to 18-20 million in 1995.

Ethnic Chinese entrepreneurs enjoy a considerable comparative advantage over non-Chinese competitors. Their language, cultural and paramount skills in making connections and networking give them ready access to market information and an ability to negotiate their way through 'the system' to apply their market knowledge to best advantage.

Their investment in China continues to be largely concentrated in the coastal regions, but is beginning to shift inland as labour and land costs rise. Ethnic

4 Hong Kong is over represented in China's official investment statistics as it functions as both a major investor in its own right and the major entrepot for ethnic Chinese investment from elsewhere in the region, and indeed, non-Chinese investment.

5 This almost certainly understates the true value of Taiwanese investment in China. One Taiwan-based source estimated the actual figure to be at least 20 per cent of the total.

Chinese entrepreneurs normally expand their investment by increasing the number of enterprises they control, rather than by making large investments in new enterprises. This is done to ensure that new investments remain below the threshold of direct central government regulation, and within the purview of local governments, with whom good working relations are more easily established.

A new trend is investment in China by holding companies belonging to South-East Asian ethnic Chinese clan associations. Much of the investment is going into the regions of ancestral origin of clan members, using personal connections and cultural empathies. This phenomenon, incidentally, is providing renewed vigour to many clan associations, as the members' old links to China become commercially valuable.

Singapore Chinese entrepreneurs, on the other hand, tend to focus away from those provinces in which most Singapore Chinese have their ancestral origins. Singaporean investment in China, which is significant, appears to be based more on government-to-government ties than traditional network links. While Singapore is a potential 'gateway to China' for Australian companies, the means of access will not usually be network-based.

INVESTMENT BEYOND THE REGION

The region's ethnic Chinese businesses are significant investors beyond East Asia, but to date their efforts have met with mixed success. This may be explained in part by the more limited opportunities and very different operating conditions in the mature, low-growth economies of Europe, compared with those applying in the high-growth East Asian economies where the ethnic Chinese business community is successful. Ethnic Chinese businesses established in the maturing economies of Hong Kong, Singapore and Taiwan maintained their high growth by diversifying towards the high-growth developing economies of Malaysia, Vietnam, the Philippines, China, and Indonesia. There they are among the leading investors.

Investment by ethnic Chinese entrepreneurs from East Asia in the Australian property market has been enormous in recent years. Much of this appears to be network-based. Australia appears to be favoured for its safe and politically stable investment environment, which complements the higher risks but higher returns of the East Asian market.

While most ethnic Chinese investment in Australia from the region is in hotels and office buildings, the retail and manufacturing sectors are also beginning to attract attention. Much of this investment is from, for example, Singapore Chinese, who are used to doing business in a highly structured environment like Australia's, or others who have become so acculturated in their countries of residence that they are no longer well linked into international ethnic Chinese business networks. This group's interest in investing in Australia may be attributed partly to a lack of special advantage in investing elsewhere in the region. Investment in Australia by the region's ethnic Chinese is also of course linked in many cases to migration plans.

THE NETWORKS AND 'OUTSIDERS'

The pre-eminence of East Asia's ethnic Chinese entrepreneurs in specific markets, as well as entire economies and to a significant degree in the aggregated economies of the region as a whole, renders them highly valuable as business partners. Not only can they provide preferred entree to their own domestic markets, but their ability to treat the entire region as a single market, and their pre-eminent role in the transformation of south-eastern China, where they have a paramount advantage, make them an appropriate partner for Australian companies seeking joint venture access to third country markets.

For their part, and despite a preference for doing business within the networks they control, ethnic Chinese entrepreneurs in the region are willing to link up with non-Chinese partners. Since the end of World War II, Japanese manufacturers have made a concerted and highly successful effort to join forces with ethnic Chinese entrepreneurs in South-East Asia, who have taken on the role of distributors and local partners in manufacturing. Today, partners from outside the region provide access to new technology, marketing and organisational expertise, as well as entry to their domestic markets.

Increasingly, Western firms are recognising the benefits of establishing joint ventures with ethnic Chinese entrepreneurs in East Asia, either to develop their business interests in the region, or, more specifically, to gain preferred entree to the China market. One recent example of such a pairing is an agreement between the large US Walmart retail chain and Thailand's Charoen Phokphand Group to open a chain of discount stores in China.

An increasing number of Australian companies, large and small, also are recognising the benefits of forming strategic partnerships with well-connected ethnic Chinese entrepreneurs from the region to gain access either to their home markets, or other regional markets including China. In addition, Australian companies have begun to tap the potential bound up in the Australian Chinese community, many of whose members possess valuable entrepreneurial skills and links with the regional economies, particularly China.

LINKING UP WITH THE NETWORKS: SELECTING A PARTNER

Selecting the Right Partner Is the Key

Given the degree of heterogeneity in the ethnic Chinese community, or perhaps more accurately communities, of East Asia and Australia, Australian companies will need to take care ensuring that their choice of partner is appropriate to the market or markets they seek to enter. Dialect, country of origin and current residence, and the extent of family or other networks in targeted markets are all issues that bear on appropriateness.

In many cases, the choice may be a matter of commonsense, for example the selection of an ethnic Chinese from Taiwan as a partner in the Taiwan market. Where Singapore is to be used as the 'gateway to China', on the other hand, the choice may be considerably more difficult. Moreover, many ethnic Chinese living outside China, Hong Kong or Taiwan do not speak, read or write any Chinese dialect at all.

Australian Chinese as Partners

The best choice of partner often will be a local one in the targeted market. Alternatively, Australian companies may need to look no further than Australia's own ethnic Chinese community to select a business partner for East Asia.

Australia's ethnic Chinese community is one of the most diverse in the world, with links to every country in the region. An attempt in 1992 to list Australia's ethnic organisations identified 80 of ethnic Chinese origin, although today, 200 is probably closer to the mark. Community organisations include Chinese chambers of commerce, mutual help societies and various vocational, professional and informal business organisations.

Many of these organisations have an international trade and investment orientation, and are a useful starting point, therefore, in the search for an appropriate partner. The great diversity of Australia's ethnic Chinese community means that the chances of locating a potential partner for practically any East Asian market are high. The Sino-Vietnamese community, for example, would be well placed to supply partners for operations in Ho Chi Minh City and other parts of southern Vietnam. Similarly, the large community of relatively recent immigrants from China is being tapped by Australian companies seeking to enter China's market.

Third Country Markets

Connections in third markets in the region also may be prospective. Indonesia will be the best place to link up with Sino-Indonesian business entrepreneurs, but for an Australian company already operating there, Hong Kong also may be a good place to locate Sino-Indonesians to target the Indonesian market, or to seek partners for ventures in south-eastern China. Similarly Taiwan, with its linguistic and cultural ties to China's Fujian Province, is a good place to link up with partners for investment in Fujian.

The presence in Singapore of large numbers of Sino-Burmese, who are leading Singapore's business drive into their former homeland, and the Singapore Government's concurrent investment push into China and Vietnam, make that country a source of possible partners for those and other regional markets.

This is recognised implicitly in the *strategic business linkages initiative* that both the Australian and Singapore Governments are pursuing. The initiative aims to bring businesses of the two countries together to explore jointly opportunities in third country markets in the region. China, Indonesia, India and Vietnam have been identified as offering the best prospects.

At the same time, and as has been noted above, the choice of a Singapore Chinese partner in China is complicated by the fact that most of Singapore's investment there has not been in the geographical areas where the overwhelming majority of Singapore Chinese have their ancestral origins.

Ethnic Chinese Organisations as Source of Partners

The Chinese chambers of commerce and other ethnic Chinese business organisations in the region are a worthwhile first stop in the search for an appropriate partner, particularly a local one. Many compile directories of local ethnic Chinese businesses.

GOVERNMENTS AS FACILITATORS

This study aims to provide an educative rather than a prescriptive tool for Australian business.

Federal, state and territory governments can help to intensify Australia's links with the region's ethnic Chinese networks chiefly by facilitating a greater international business role for Australia's own ethnic Chinese entrepreneurs. Its very diversity is perhaps the Australian Chinese business community's greatest strength, and the community as a result is well placed to tap into a wide range of networks and markets.

Federal, state and territory governments, and indeed the private sector, have each recognised this potential in a number of initiatives aimed at forging closer cooperation between the mainstream and the various ethnic business communities in Australia. The private sector-sponsored *East Meets West* functions, Austrade's pilot *Export Development through Ethnic Communities Program*, and the *Productive Diversity* programs of the Office of Multicultural Affairs within the Department of the Prime Minister and Cabinet are examples.

Governments should give continuing support to initiatives of this sort, with a view to encouraging a more integrated approach to offshore business by mainstream and ethnic Chinese business organisations. The facilitating role of governments is, however, necessarily limited. Ultimately, it is up to the business organisations themselves to formalise their relations, create and maintain databases and to carry out a 'matchmaking' function between their respective members.

The role of the Australian Government may be greater, on the other hand, in the forging of overseas 'strategic business alliances' along the lines of the Singapore-Australia *Strategic Linkages Initiative*. Depending on the success of this venture, the Government should give consideration to extending the initiative to link up with other major concentrations of ethnic Chinese business entrepreneurs in the region, for example Thailand, for third country business. In this same connection, Australia's trade promotion bodies should seek closer ties with individual Chinese chambers of commerce in the region as a means of facilitating the formation of business pairings and consortia.

Governments should encourage the Australian Chinese community's endeavours to host in Australia a forthcoming World Chinese Entrepreneurs' Convention, an annual event bringing together more than one thousand of the world's most successful ethnic Chinese business people.

A NOTE ON NOMENCLATURE

'Overseas Chinese' or 'Ethnic Chinese'?

Strictly speaking, the term 'overseas Chinese' should not be applied to most people of Chinese descent living outside China. 'Overseas Chinese' is a translation of the term *Hua-qiao* ('sojourner') and suggests that those so described are temporarily resident outside China and intend to return to China. This carries the implication that the sovereign and political loyalties of 'overseas Chinese' lie not with their country of residence but with China. Today, the vast majority of the so-called 'overseas Chinese' were not born in China and are citizens of the countries in which they reside. For most, 'returning' to reside in China would be virtually unthinkable. Nevertheless, over time, the term 'overseas Chinese' has been used widely to embrace all Chinese living outside China, whether or not they intend to 'return' to live there. The term as it now is normally used, therefore, has moved on from the original meaning of *Hua-qiao*.

Today, the vast majority of ethnic Chinese living in Indonesia consider themselves as Indonesians, almost all ethnic Chinese living in Malaysia regard themselves as Malaysians and so on. It is for this reason that in this study, the Chinese of Indonesia, for example, are referred to as 'Indonesian Chinese', 'Sino-Indonesians' or simply as 'ethnic Chinese'. Generally, when the term 'ethnic Chinese' appears in the text it refers to individuals of substantial Chinese ancestry who do not live in China.[1]

The Chinese of Hong Kong, Macau and Taiwan are included in the scope of this study as Chinese currently living outside the administration of the Peoples' Republic of China. As such, their business structures and activities set them apart from those in China.

Myanmar or Burma?

In 1989, Burma's name was changed officially to Myanmar by its current Government. In this study, 'Burma' is used to refer to events before 1989, and 'Myanmar' to post 1989 developments. The Government also changed the official English rendering of place names in Myanmar to bring them more into line with Burmese pronunciation. Thus, 'Rangoon' is used to refer to events before 1989 and 'Yangon' to post 1989 events. For simplicity, however, the term 'Burmese' has been retained to denote ethnicity (for example, 'Sino-Burmese') and language.

Chinese Names: Wade-Giles or Pinyin?

In accordance with the usual practice elsewhere, province names in the People's Republic of China have been rendered in Pinyin. (For a comparative chart of commonly used names, see Appendix 2.)

The spelling of other Chinese names often varies considerably. The convention followed in this study has been to adopt the spelling most commonly used by ethnic Chinese outside China. Hence, 'Teochiu', for example, is preferred over 'Chiuchow', 'Teochew', or 'Chaozhou'. The rendering of personal names follows the practice of the individuals themselves.

---

1 'Ethnic Chinese', or *Hua-ren* in Chinese, has been selected as an essentially neutral descriptive term.

Chapter 1

MIGRATION AND SETTLEMENT

Most ethnic Chinese living outside the People's Republic of China reside in other parts of Asia where they have a presence, albeit sometimes small, in every country. (See Table 1.1.) The largest concentrations are in Hong Kong, Macau, and Taiwan, and in the countries of South-East Asia.

Table 1.1

Distribution of Ethnic Chinese Outside PRC

	NUMBER (millions)	PER CENT OF ETHNIC CHINESE POPULATION
Asia	50.3	91.3
Americas	3.4	6.3
Europe	0.6	1.1
Africa	0.1	0.2
Oceania (including Australia)	0.6	1.1
Total	55.0	100.0

Source: Ch'ng, D., *The Overseas Chinese Entrepreneurs in East Asia: Background, Business Practices and International Networks*, CEDA Monograph M100, 1993, p. 26.

MIGRATION FROM CHINA

Trade between the markets of what we call South-East and North-East Asia is not new. For centuries, merchant ships from China traversed the South China Sea, and traders did not consider East Asia to have two parts.

Migration from China to other parts of Asia has a similarly long history. By the early fifteenth century, Chinese communities were established at a number of locations in South-East and North-East Asia. Some of these are mentioned in the records of visits to the region by Admiral Cheng Ho, who made several voyages between 1404 and 1433, travelling as far as Africa to seek tribute for the Chinese emperor.[1]

The descendants of these earlier Chinese settlers throughout Asia now are so assimilated with indigenous populations that few vestiges of their distinctive

1 To this day there are Chinese temples and shrines dedicated to Cheng Ho across South-East Asia, for example, in Malacca on peninsular Malaysia, and another in Semarang on the north coast of Java in Indonesia.

'Chineseness' (their traditional Chinese culture and language) remain. For those Chinese living outside China who are still identifiably Chinese, however, the important waves of migration occurred during the nineteenth and early twentieth centuries.

Periods of heavy migration usually coincided with particularly poor conditions at home. During the latter part of China's Qing Dynasty, political stability deteriorated markedly. Concurrently, during major famines around 1846, 1849 and 1877, more than two million people perished. Another 60 million people were estimated to have died subsequently, during the rebellions that spanned the 1840s and the 1870s. The Treaty of Nanking in 1842, under which the Qing-Manchu Court ceded control of Hong Kong to Britain and opened five ports for trade with Western powers, contributed to this flood of people leaving China. From that time on, the Chinese authorities could not control the movement of their nationals in and out of the country.[2] Emigrants at that time became known as the *Nanyang hua-qiao*, or the 'southern sojourners.'[3]

Almost all those who left China during this period came from the coastal areas of south-eastern China, principally from the areas now covered by the provinces of Guangdong, Fujian and Hainan.[4] As a group, they were linguistically and culturally very different from other Chinese. Within the group, a wide range of dialects are represented; the main ones are Cantonese, Hokkien, Teochiu, Hainanese and Hakka. All of these can be further divided into sub-dialect groups. The main departure points for the Hokkien Chinese who settled in South-East Asia were the port cities of Xiamen (Amoy) and Quanzhou in Fujian. The lower reaches of the Min River near Fuzhou, Putian and Xianyou counties were also important areas of emigration. In Guangdong, emigrants were mostly from the Pearl River delta near Guangzhou, particularly from the counties of Xinhui, Taishan, Kaiping, and Enping, Chaozhou and Shantou (Swatow) along the Han River on the Guangdong-Fujian border, and the Jiaoling area in north-east Guangdong. On Hainan Island, most came from the cities of Haikou and Qiongzhou. Significant numbers of Chinese also came from the provinces of Zhejiang and Jiangsu, and from Taiwan.[5]

Immigration to South-East Asia was not random, but usually occurred in 'chains'. Understandably, relatives and neighbours from towns and villages in China tended to follow one another to particular locations outside, a phenomenon not unique to Chinese migration.

Most south-eastern Chinese dialect groups are represented in most South-East Asian ethnic Chinese communities. However, because of chain migration, differing groups tend to predominate from one community to another. For example, the Fuzhou Hokkien predominate in Sibu in Sarawak, East Malaysia;

---

2 Previously, migration from China had been prohibited by the Qing emperors.

3 See Tran Khanh, *The Ethnic Chinese and Economic Development in Vietnam*, Institute of Southeast Asian Studies, Singapore, 1993, p. 21; and Dobbs-Higginson, M.S., *Asia Pacific: Its role in the New World Order*, William Heinemann Australia, Port Melbourne, 1993, p. 159.

4 Hainan, an island off the coast of Guangdong, was declared a separate province in 1988.

5 See Wu, Y.L. and C.H. Wu, *Economic Development in Southeast Asia: The Chinese Dimension*, Hoover Institute Press, Stanford, 1980, p. 133.

the Teochiu, who come from the nine districts covering the delta of the Han River around Shantou in Guangdong Province dominate the Sino-Thai community; people with origins in Jinmen in Fujian dominate in Brunei; and Cantonese who have their ancestral origins in Taishan in Guangdong dominate in Yangon.[6]

The final wave of migration from China occurred following the communist takeover in 1949. Since then, the exodus from China to South-East Asia has been little more than a trickle.[7] Without a regular wave of Chinese immigrants to wash through the region's ethnic Chinese communities and replenish their 'Chineseness', the existing communities are becoming increasingly acculturated with local communities. The distinctions between the indigenous and ethnic Chinese communities are becoming blurred, although for most countries, complete assimilation is still a long way off.

EARLY SETTLEMENT EXPERIENCES IN SOUTH-EAST ASIA

The Chinese who left China last century and earlier generally did so in quest of better economic opportunities.

In Vietnam, they were at first persecuted but then encouraged in their commercial pursuits. Vietnam's largest concentration of Chinese, at Cholon, began as a small village five kilometres from Saigon, when the Chinese fled Saigon to escape the Tay Son rebellion.[8] Many Chinese fled to Cambodia and the eastern seaboard of Thailand. During the subsequent Tay Son regime, there was a massacre of Chinese at Cholon in 1792. In 1802, the Tay Son dynasty was overthrown by Nguyen Anh who established the Nguyen dynasty (1802-1945). This dynasty used Chinese merchants to collect taxes, set up shipyards and build ships, acquire land and establish social and commercial organisations. In some sectors, the Nguyen dynasty even discriminated in favour of the Chinese, with the result that they faced less constraining regulations than did the ethnic Vietnamese.[9]

Tax 'farming' was an early occupation of Thailand's Chinese. In the nineteenth century, the Chinese, especially the Teochiu, frequently bought the rights from the King or his agents to levy produce taxes.[10] Chinese merchants would bid for the right to tax and trade in products of a particular 'farm'.[11] In the twentieth

6 Chain migration is usually observed in poorer groups. Today, among wealthier ethnic Chinese, particularly those in Hong Kong, there is usually a reverse tendency. Families will often attempt to have family members as geographically dispersed as possible, to diversify the family's business risk and to assist in building up a worldwide network to promote the family's business interests.

7 Indeed, after 1949, there was significant migration from South-East Asia to China as Chinese particularly from Indonesia, the Philippines and Burma resettled in China during the 1950s and 1960s.

8 'Cholon' is derived from the Vietnamese 'cho lon', literally 'big market'.

9 See Tran Khanh, pp. 18-20.

10 The practice did occur prior to the nineteenth century, however. (See Skinner, G.W., *Chinese Society in Thailand: An Analytical History*, Cornell University Press, Ithaca, New York, 1957, p. 19.)

11 Both orchard and vegetable taxes were among such monopoly 'tax farms'. Hafner J.A., 'Market gardening in Thailand: The origins of an ethnic Chinese monopoly', in L.Y.C. Lim and L.A.P. Gosling (eds), *The Chinese in Southeast Asia*, Vol. 1, Maruzen Asia, Singapore, 1983, p. 37.

century, Sino-Thai owned businesses expanded into fishing, ice (which at that time was an important commodity), furniture, yarns and textiles, liquor and bottling, as Thailand's consumer society developed. Many Sino-Thai entrepreneurs also established themselves in the agricultural sector, particularly in milling rice and developing Thailand's primary exports. Others served as traders running import-export houses based in Bangkok.

In the Philippines, commercial opportunities for the Chinese initially evolved around the requirements of the Spanish colonisers. The Chinese were mostly artisans (masons, carpenters, blacksmiths, weavers and printers) bakers, butchers, barbers and traders supplying, incidentally, the silk which formed the basis of the galleon trade between the Philippines and Mexico.

In Indonesia, the Chinese moved quickly to dominate trade and commerce in the major towns and cities. Such was their success that the Government issued regulations to reduce the concentration of ethnic Chinese commercial power between 1955 and 1957. Ownership of rice mills and firms in fifteen other industries was restricted to the *pribumis*, the indigenous Indonesians.[12]

FORMATION OF CHINESE ASSOCIATIONS

A phenomenon accompanying the immigration of Chinese throughout Asia was the creation of mutual help societies, usually based around clans in each place of settlement. These organisations helped subsequent arrivals in settling, and acted as banks through which money could be borrowed, and information traded. Additional societies were set up to regulate other aspects of ethnic Chinese life.

Chinese mutual help societies were formed around one of four principles: kinship, locality, dialect or crafts. (See Table 1.2.) Kinship, clan or surname associations bring together groups of Chinese with a common surname. The same surname does not, however, necessarily imply a common ancestry, although the chances of this are greater if the surname and originating province are the same. Locality associations group Chinese from the same ancestral village or region in China. Often members also will have the same surname. Dialect associations have a relatively broad membership, covering a common ancestral dialect or sub-dialect in each case. They are arguably the most prominent and active ethnic Chinese associations in South-East Asia today. Guild or craft associations bring together the members of one type of occupation. Due to occupational-dialect links brought about by chain migration, the memberships of guild associations usually were confined to a particular dialect or even sub-dialect group (and in some instances, still are). For example, goldsmith guilds in Malaysia, in the past, have been dominated by the Cantonese, while the Singapore bicycle dealer association still is dominated by the Henghua Hokkien.

In addition to these associations, there are general welfare associations, temple committees, school committees, and the all important Chinese chambers of commerce.

---

12 See Ch'ng, D., *The Overseas Chinese Entrepreneurs in East Asia: Background, Business Practices and International Networks*, CEDA Monograph M100, 1993, pp. 28-29.

Table 1.2

Mutual Help Societies

TYPE	ORGANISING PRINCIPLE	EXAMPLE
1. Clan Associations	Kinship by Surname	Lee Clan Association
2. Locality Associations	Locality	See Yap Association
3. Dialect Associations	Dialect or Sub-Dialects	Hokkien Association
4. Guilds	Craft	Goldsmith Association

Adapted from Ch'ng, D., *The Overseas Chinese Entrepreneurs in East Asia: Background, Business Practices and International Networks*, CEDA Monograph M100, 1993, p. 39.

Historically, the clan associations also extended their activities to their home villages, districts, prefectures, provinces and the Government of China. Clan association donations to relieve the plight of their former fellow countrymen reached a peak after the outbreak of the eight-year war following the Japanese invasion of China in 1937.[13] The founder of the Republic of China, Sun Yat Sen, raised money for the revolution which overthrew the Qing Dynasty in 1911, by a direct appeal to overseas Chinese communities. Today, some clan and dialect associations take advantage of China's economic restructuring and their connections and dialects to invest back in their ancestral regions in China. They also often host visiting trade delegations from those regions.

ASSIMILATION

Ethnic Chinese living abroad differ not only according to their ancestral regions in China and the corresponding dialects and sub-dialects they speak, but also according to the length of time they or their forebears have been settled abroad, and the degree of assimilation with the indigenous populations in their countries of residence.

Intermarriage between the Chinese and members of indigenous populations, facilitated by the initial shortage of Chinese females in the early migrant Chinese communities, accelerated the process of integration and assimilation.[14] Where there were religious obstacles to intermarriage, notably in predominantly Moslem Malaya and the Indies, non-Moslems - for example, animists and Christian Batak women from northern Sumatra, and Hindu Balinese women - were often selected. The Chinese who emigrated to the Philippines prior to this century were also usually males who intermarried with indigenous women. By the 1940s, there were about 750 000 mixed Chinese-Filipinos.[15]

....

13 See Cheng, L.K., 'Reflections on the Changing Roles of Chinese Clan Associations in Singapore', *Asian Culture*, April 1990.

14 The emigration of Chinese women to the Malay peninsular only began in the nineteenth century as there was a law of the Manchu government which prohibited the emigration of women from China. (See Tan, C.B., 'Acculturation and the Chinese in Melaka: The Expression of Baba Identity Today' in L.Y.C. Lim and L.A.P. Gosling (eds), Vol 1, p. 59.)

15 Sowell, T., *The Economics and Politics of Race*, Quill, New York, 1983, p. 41.

The Chinese *baba* culture of the Straits Settlements of Singapore, Malacca and Penang originated from the intermarriage of Chinese with indigenous women.[16] Over time, *baba* culture fused Chinese, Malay and British customs. The *babas* reached the peak of their economic power and influence around the turn of the century. They formed an ethnic group distinct from other Chinese - the newly arrived, who were known as the *sinkehs*.[17] Today, few people in Malaysia or Singapore identify as *baba*.[18]

In Indonesia, the Chinese community can be divided into the substantially acculturated descendants of early settlers, the *peranakan*, and those who are not, the later migrants, the *totok*. The *peranakan*, who form perhaps the majority of Indonesia's Sino-Chinese community, have lost much of their 'Chineseness'. Typically, they are unable to read or write Chinese, have few connections with Chinese outside of Indonesia and are often Christian.[19] For them, leaving Indonesia and 'returning' to China would be unthinkable. The *totok*, on the other hand, remain relatively 'Chinese': either they or their parents were born in China; they speak and read Chinese; and they have strong connections to other Chinese in the region. However, the distinction between the *totok* and the *peranakan* is blurring.

Elsewhere, the Chinese have assimilated to varying degrees. In Thailand, the Chinese have assimilated so successfully - assisted by extensive intermarriage - that often it is now difficult to determine who is Chinese. Perhaps for this reason, the Thai-Chinese Chamber chose to open its doors to all Thais, not only Sino-Thais. In lower Myanmar, many ethnic Chinese have assimilated by adopting the local dress and language, although they still form an identifiable community.

---

16 The term *baba* was applied to the menfolk; the women being known as *nonyas*.

17 *Sinkeh* was a term used in Malaya to refer to newly arrived Chinese who had not become acculturated. The *sinkeh* and *baba* Chinese communities generally remained aloof from one another.

18 See Tan, C.B., 'Acculturation and the Chinese in Melaka: The Expression of Baba Identity Today' in L.Y.C. Lim and L.A.P. Gosling (eds), Vol 1, p. 58; Siow, M., 'The Problems of Ethnic Cohesion among the Chinese in Peninsular Malaysia: Intraethnic Divisions and Interethnic Accommodation' in the same volume claims the *baba* population of Malaysia amounts to as much as 15 per cent of the total Chinese population, although this estimate seems very high.

19 The adoption of Malay-style celebrations is another distinguishing feature of the *peranakan*. One study found that the *peranakan* on Java will arrange traditional Indonesian feasts, *selamatans*, on the occasion of the opening of a new building, marriage or birth. (See Raybeck, D., 'Chinese patterns of adaption in Southeast Asia' in L.Y.C. Lim and L.A.P. Gosling (eds), Vol. 2, p. 21.)

Chapter 2

THE IMPORTANCE OF DIALECT

I heard in Kuching that the Hakkas, Cantonese and Hokkiens tend to look down upon the Foochows. But let me tell you, their hard work will pay off one day. They will be the most efficient workers and entrepreneurs.[1]

DIALECTS: AN OVERVIEW

Understanding the importance of Chinese dialects and their distribution across Asia is critical to understanding ethnic Chinese business networks in the region. Dialects and sub-dialects often partly explain who does business with whom and what is traded.

Chinese is a group of languages with a shared script but with many, sometimes mutually unintelligible, spoken varieties. There are literally hundreds of dialects and sub-dialects in China. Table 2.1 shows the main dialect groupings in China.

Table 2.1

Numbers of Speakers of Major Chinese Dialects

(1994 Estimate)

	WITHIN PRC	OUTSIDE PRC
Mandarin	885 million	5 million
Shanghainese (*Wu*)	90 million	-
Hunanese (*Gan*)	42 million	-
Jiangxinese (*Xiang*)	38 million	-
Hokkien (*Min*)	68 million	35 million
Cantonese (*Yue*)	50 million	20 million
Hakka (*Kejia*)	43 million	6 million

Adapted from: Bradley, D., 'Chinese, Thai and other languages of wider communication in the Golden Triangle', a paper delivered to the 'Thailand's Circles of Growth Conference', Chiangmai, Thailand, March 1994.

1 See Ling, A., *Golden Dreams of Borneo*, Singapore, 1993, p. 578. Chapters 51 and 52 of *Golden Dreams* contain detail on early Fuzhou culture in Borneo.

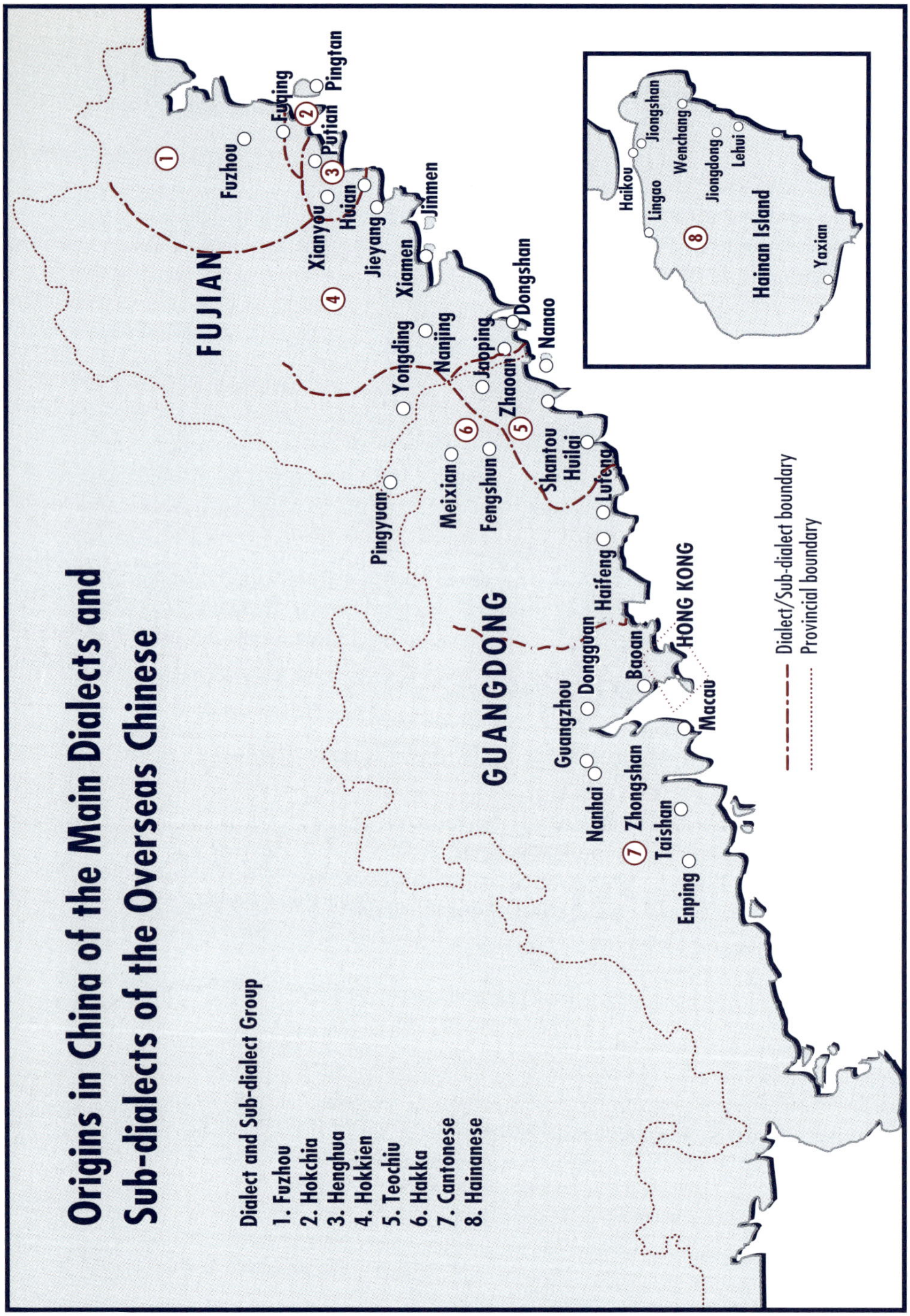

Figure 2.1

Adapted from Chan, K.B. and C. Chiang, *Stepping Out: The Making of Chinese Entrepeneurs*, Prentice Hall, Singapore, 1994.

Most dialects are within the Mandarin grouping, which comprises many sub-dialects based on northern, north-western, southern and south-western sub-groups.[2] The dialects spoken in south-eastern China are very different from Mandarin and are not under the Mandarin 'umbrella'. As most ethnic Chinese outside China have their ancestral origins in the south-eastern provinces, they usually do not have Mandarin as their first language but one of the south-eastern dialects. Generally, throughout China today, Mandarin is the language of government and business, although in the south-eastern provinces, local dialects still may predominate in business.

Modernisation and Dialect Deskilling

As ethnic Chinese communities develop and their members become more 'Westernised', dialect still has an important, although declining, influence in all aspects of community life, including business. Singapore is a case in point.

As Singaporean Chinese businesses expand, they become too large to source all their customers and all their suppliers from the one dialect group. This forces them to operate across dialect divides.

Meanwhile, the Singaporean Government has promoted its 'Speak Mandarin' campaign, promoting Mandarin at the expense of Singapore's main ancestral dialects and sub-dialects such as Hokkien, Teochiu and Hakka. This has encouraged Singapore's Chinese to do business on the basis of a common Chinese heritage, rather than on the basis of ancestral dialects, but there has been a cost: the ability of Singaporeans to do business in south-eastern China has diminished.[3] Moreover, the emphasis on speaking Mandarin rather than reading and writing Chinese has hampered Singaporeans in their business dealings with China. Thus, many can converse effectively with government officials but are not as effective at reading important legal documents, for example.

A good example of a Singaporean business in which ancestral dialect is not important is Tuan Sing Holdings. The main equity holder is a Hokkien family from Indonesia. The CEO is Cantonese and one of the firm's main overseas activities is in Shanghai, where the local dialect is Shanghainese. Like many Singaporean Chinese businesses, Tuan Sing Holdings, in order to expand, has cut across dialect lines.[4]

---

2 The south-western variety spoken in Yunnan, Sichuan, Guizhou, western Guangxi and Hubei, and northern Hunan is used by about 250 million people including nearly all the Chinese in Yunnan. (See Bradley, D., 'Chinese, Thai and other languages of wider communication in the Golden Triangle', a paper delivered to the Thailand's Circles of Growth Conference, Chiangmai, northern Thailand, March 1994.)

3 See Chapter 11 for more details on Singaporean investment in China.

4 Personal communication with Tuan Sing Holdings.

Dialect and sub-dialect are important identifiers among Chinese. They indicate a speaker's ancestral place of origin in China. In the past, dialect differences have signalled a whole range of other social and cultural characteristics, including diet, dress and even social class. Furthermore, the mutual unintelligibility of some dialects and sub-dialects can reinforce dialect and sub-dialect ties. Importantly, however, speakers of different Chinese dialects share a common written language, so literate Chinese with differing dialects can communicate in writing, cumbersome though that may be. This breaks down in cases where Chinese who speak different dialects or sub-dialects are unable to read or write Chinese - a phenomenon common among the 'overseas' communities.

Interestingly, Mandarin is often the *lingua franca* of non-Mandarin dialect associations, because of the mutual unintelligibility of some sub-dialects within the one dialect group. All business of the Federation of Hokkien Associations of Malaysia, for example, is conducted not in Hokkien, but in Mandarin. Similarly, the spoken language of most Chinese chambers of commerce in the region is also Mandarin. The teaching of Mandarin in Chinese schools, where they are permitted in South-East Asia, has facilitated the status of Mandarin as a second language among South-East Asia's Chinese.

Traditionally, ethnic Chinese communities were divided along dialect lines, with a dialect association to guide the dialect grouping. The role of the dialect association in each community was particularly significant: mediating in financial disputes among members; allotting zones of influence in business and trades; and assisting businessmen. Dialect members could pool capital, providing a source of capital normally unavailable to indigenous business people.[5]

For these reasons, dialect continues to be important among ethnic Chinese, and very often, businesses are linked through a mutually shared dialect or sub-dialect. One example of this is the growing trade in vegetables and seafood between Medan in north Sumatra and Penang in Malaysia. The trade has evolved through the common link of the Hokkien dialect spoken by the ethnic Chinese business communities in both places.[6]

The Main Dialect Groups in South-East Asia

Most ethnic Chinese outside China originate from the south-eastern coastal provinces of Fujian and Guangdong (Table 2.2.) A minority come from Hainan Island. Because of this, the dialects of the Chinese diaspora are from south-eastern China - Cantonese, Hokkien, Hakka, Teochiu and Hainanese.

Cantonese

Cantonese is the main dialect of Guangdong Province. Most of Hong Kong's residents are ancestrally from Guangdong and therefore usually speak Cantonese.

5 Tran Khanh, *The Ethnic Chinese and Economic Development in Vietnam*, Institute of Southeast Asian Studies, Singapore, 1993, pp. 34-35.

6 This was indicated by several Penang-based ethnic Chinese businessmen when interviewed for this study.

The Cantonese claim at least six main sub-groups: Siyap, Taishan, Sanwei, Tungkoon, Sun Tuk and Chungshan. These each represent different regional accents or sub-dialects.

Hokkien

Hokkien speakers are ancestrally from China's Fujian Province. Broadly, Hokkien can be divided into two very distinct and mutually unintelligible sub-groupings, northern Hokkien (*Minbei*) and southern Hokkien (*Minnan*). In turn, these are further divided into many sub-dialects. These too can be mutually unintelligible.

Table 2.2

Provincial Origins of Ethnic Chinese, 1991

COUNTRY	NUMBER OF ETHNIC CHINESE (million)	FUJIAN (per cent)	GUANGDONG (per cent)	HAINAN (per cent)
Hong Kong	6.6	2.0	93.2	-
Taiwan	20.3	77	13	-
Singapore	2.7	40	42	-
Malaysia	5.8	30	59	9
Thailand	5.8	10	78	11
Indonesia	7.2	55	45	-
Philippines	0.9	80	20	-
Vietnam	0.7	8	89	2

Adapted from Ch'ng, D., *The Overseas Chinese Entrepreneurs in East Asia: Background, Business Practices and International Networks*, CEDA Monograph M100, 1993, p. 38.

The main Hokkien sub-dialects and regional accents on which the South-East Asian Chinese base their sub-dialect associations are the Hui Aun, Chin Keng, Tong Aun, Cheang Chew, Lung Yen, Hokchia, Foochow (Fuzhou), Aun Khuay, Lam Aun, Eng Teng, Hoi Lam, Hoi Pak, Henghua, Engchoon, and Hock Seong.[7]

Hakka

Unlike other dialect groups, the Hakka do not directly originate from any particular urban or rural centre in China.[8] Their migration to South-East Asia was a continuation of an earlier southward movement within China. Most Hakka

....

7 These names generally follow the names of regions in China's Fujian Province. They are, however, largely expressed in Wade-Giles form, rather than the Pinyin now used in China, as this is the transliteration style that most South-East Asian Chinese know. South-East Asian dialect and sub-dialect based associations nearly always use the Wade-Giles transliteration in their names. It is the Penang Cheang Chew Hokkien Association, rather than the Penang Zhangzhou Hokkien Association, for example.

8 The Hakka are also known as the Khek, particularly by Hokkien Chinese.

today, however, have their roots in Guangdong. There are at least six different types of Hakka: those from Taipu (or Chha Yong), Huizhou, Fengshun, Meixian, Popo (Hoppo or Kityang), and Yongding. The Yongding Hakka comprise the only group of Hokkien Hakka.[9]

Most overseas Hakka are at least bilingual - they speak their own particular Hakka sub-dialect and often the local dialect of their immediate ancestral place of origin in China.[10] Non-Hakka Chinese often can identify the Hakka because they usually speak non-Hakka dialects with a distinctive Hakka accent. Nevertheless, the Hakka cut cross dialect groups, a skill which can help them in business. Thus, Hakka Cantonese and Hakka Hokkien can both operate as Hakka, or respectively as Cantonese and Hokkien, depending on the situation. This can increase their pool of connections.

Traditionally, as a group, the Hakka have been towards the bottom of the socio-economic scale.[11] Hakka women for instance did not bind their feet when foot binding was fashionable.[12] The Hakka specialised in mining and construction. This specialisation is said to have come about because when the Hakka migrated to China's south-eastern provinces, all the valleys were occupied and cultivated, leaving only the hill sides for habitation. Such terrain was not suitable for agriculture but was good for mining and quarrying.

Teochiu (Chiuchow)

The Teochiu have their ancestral origins around Shantou (Swatow), a city at the northern end of China's Guangdong Province. Teochiu and Hokkien (the dialect of nearby Fujian Province) are mutually intelligible.

Hainanese

The Hainanese (also known as the Kengchew or Hailan) have their ancestral origins in Hainan Island, located off the coast of China's Guangdong Province. They speak their own dialect which is similar to southern Hokkien.

More than two million ethnic Chinese of Hainanese origin live in over fifty countries outside China.[13]

Since the 1988 declaration of Hainan Island as a Special Economic Zone and a separate province from Guangdong, the overseas Hainanese have a common

9 See Tan, T.T.W., *Your Chinese Roots: The Overseas Chinese Story*, Times Books International, Singapore, 1986, p. 176. The names of the Hakka regional dialects are in accordance with the forms commonly used among the Hakka of South-East Asia.

10 For example, Alfred Huang, the President of the Chinese Chamber of Commerce of South Australia, is a Hakka who grew up in China's Sichuan Province. He speaks some Hakka but his preferred spoken language is Sichuanese.

11 There have, nonetheless, been many prominent Hakka, including China's paramount leader Deng Xiaoping.

12 This characteristic, was however, more a class one than an ethnic one as Hakka women, by virtue of their economic circumstances, were often involved in physical labour which made foot binding impractical.

13 See Feng, C. and D. Goodman, 'China's Hainan Province: Economic development and investment environment', unpublished paper, University of Technology, Sydney, 1994.

cause, and are becoming re-energised by the economic transformation of their ancestral area. Hainanese community feeling throughout South-East Asia has resurged and many Hainanese associations are forming holding companies to invest in Hainan and exchange business delegations between overseas Hainanese and officials from the province.

Dialect Distribution Across Asia

Chain migration has led to communities of the same ancestral dialect and sub-dialect. Most of the Chinese living on Malaysia's Penang tend to be Hokkien from Xiamen;[14] Yangon's Cantonese typically come from Taishan in Guangdong, as do the Cantonese in San Francisco; the Philippines' Chinese come from Quanzhou, in Fujian; and Los Angeles' Chinese are dominated by the Taiwanese.

Table 2.3 summarises the distribution of dialects in various South-East Asian countries.

Table 2.3

Distribution of Ethnic Chinese in South-East Asia by Country and Ancestral Dialect Group

(By Per Cent)

	HOKKIEN	CANTONESE	TEOCHIU	HAKKA	HAINANESE	OTHER
Thailand	7.0	7.0	56.0	16.0	12.0	2.0
Malaysia	31.7	21.7	12.1	21.8	5.3	7.4
Singapore	40.0	18.0	23.0	9.0	7.0	3.0
Indonesia	50.0	11.5	7.5	16.5	-	14.5
Philippines	85.0	15.0	-	-	-	-
Vietnam	6.0	56.5	34.0	1.5	2.0	-
Cambodia	2.0	10.0	77.0	3.0	8.0	-
Laos	-	15.0	70.0	-	10.0	5.0
Myanmar	30.0	20.0	-	-	-	50.0

Source: various sources, including East Asia Analytical Unit estimates.

The Cohesiveness of Dialect Groups

One further point of difference among the dialect groups outside China is their degree of cohesiveness. During interviews, ethnic Chinese individuals frequently remarked that one dialect group or another was particularly 'clannish'. In several

14 There are more than 350 000 ethnic Chinese outside China with ancestral origins in Xiamen. (See *Business Traveller*, 'Xiamen plays the waiting game', September 1994.)

countries, the Hainanese were cited. One study sampling Hong Kong Chinese identified a common perception of the Hong Kong Teochiu and Shanghainese as especially clan-oriented.[15]

DIALECT AND OCCUPATION LINKS

In the past, dialect and sub-dialect groups have specialised in particular occupations. Thus, if a bicycle dealer in Singapore was Chinese, it was quite likely that he was not just Hokkien but Henghua Hokkien; similarly, a goldsmith in Kuala Lumpur was likely to be Cantonese. This sub-dialect/dialect-occupation linkage reflected the natural tendency to find employment among those who spoke the same language, and also for early Chinese migrants to find employment with relatives and friends who had preceded them. The link between dialect and occupation is, however, breaking down. Today, it is more a historical residual than an ongoing phenomenon, although in some ethnic Chinese communities such linkages are still very much a reality. Table 2.4 features some of the dialect and sub-dialect specialisations that arose in South-East Asia; some are still prevalent today.

> *Hainanese cooks were a special breed, often engaged for their culinary skills by ships, Europeans' houses, Chinese restaurants and most of the social clubs in Malaya, Singapore and Borneo. To them cooking was their pride and dignity....*[16]

Later generations of ethnic Chinese break down these links as they seek employment outside their dialect and sub-dialect group's traditional areas of specialisation. Also, as companies expand, they may be forced to seek custom beyond their usual dialect group. Nonetheless, in some locations, knowledge of links between occupation and dialect and sub-dialects can be of use to outsiders seeking to do business. This is further explored in Chapter 14.

Chinatowns across South-East Asia are often divided into quarters, usually on the basis of dialect or sub-dialect. Bangkok is still considered to have its Cantonese areas and Hokkien areas, although these are becoming less rigidly defined. In the past, Singapore was able to be divided into well defined dialect and sub-dialect areas by block. Areas bounded by streets could be mapped out and designated Henghua Hokkien areas, for example. The combination of geographical dialect areas and sub-dialect/dialect-occupation specialisations gave rise to whole streets dedicated to pawnshops or motor repair shops, for example. This phenomenon is still apparent in more traditional ethnic Chinese communities such as in Penang and the Yaowarat (Chinatown) area of Bangkok.

---

15 So much so that the author concluded that it may be a distinct sub-cultural trait. (See Redding, G.S., *The Spirit of Chinese Capitalism*, Walter de Gruyter and Co., Berlin, 1990, pp. 109-11.) Interviews conducted in Hong Kong for this study also suggested that the Teochiu in particular were perceived by other groups as 'clannish'.

16 See Ling, A., p. 197.

Table 2.4[17]

Common Occupations and Product Lines of Ethnic Chinese Dialect and Sub-Dialect Groups in South-East Asia

Hokkien	grocers and shops; rubber, copra, coffee, pepper, tobacco plantations and business; import-export; rubber and plastics; textiles, knitwear, weaving and garments; glassware; earthenware; gold and jewellery; printing; hotels and entertainment; finance
Henghua Hokkien	bicycle dealers; trishaw drivers; bus and taxi drivers; car and motorcycle spare-parts
Fuzhou Hokkien	coffee shops
Engchoon Hokkien	rubber dealers and shopkeepers
Teochiu	import-export, especially of food; clothing; rice milling and trading; canned food; cosmetics; hardware; jewellery; distilling; publishing; furniture; finance and insurance; shipping; antiques and curios
Cantonese	gold shops; restaurants; machine repair; construction; food and beverage; printing; watches/clocks; sugar; dentistry
Soon Tuck; Tungkoon Cantonese	Domestic servants
Hakka	building and construction; mining, pawnshops; leather and hides, weaving, shoe manufacturing, tailoring and textiles; truck driving; trishaws; herbalists; metal working; carpentry; smithing
Taipu Hakka	pawnshops
Hainanese	cooks; coffee shops; beverages; hotels; pharmacy; furniture; hairdressing; fishing
Yunnanese	jewellery, trade in gems and jade

17 These specialisations have been particularly well defined in Malaysia and Singapore but have been applicable elsewhere in varying degrees. (Various sources, including original research by the East Asia Analytical Unit.)

The Teochiu - Asia's Food Traders

Many sectors of East Asia's food trade tend to be dominated by the Teochiu. In Thailand, Malaysia, Singapore, Laos and Cambodia, the Teochiu are said to 'control' trade in rice.

In Singapore and Malaysia, trade in fresh vegetables, fruit and seafood is significantly in the hands of the Teochiu. Teochiu dominate Bangkok's business community and fresh food imported into Singapore arrives from Thailand via Teochiu dialect links.

Many mini-markets and cold storage facilities in Malaysia and elsewhere are owned by the Teochiu and one of Malaysia's largest food export-import concerns, the Chuan Hauy Group, is controlled by Teochiu interests. Similarly, many of Australia's Teochiu are involved in the food trade, operating small Chinese grocery businesses. The two largest exporters of Australian rice to Hong Kong are companies controlled by the Teochiu.

Much of the Teochiu's prominence in this area has its roots in the Thai Teochiu's early control of the rice trade between Bangkok, Singapore, China and Hong Kong. This gave them the connections in these centres to trade other commodities, and capital to expand and diversify. The Thai Teochiu tended to trade with the Teochiu in other centres, thereby 'exporting' the occupation-dialect link prevalent in Thailand at the time.

Case Study - The Northern Fujian Sub-Dialect Groups

Fuzhou, Hokchia and Henghua are all sub-dialects spoken by people whose origins are in the northern end of China's Fujian Province.[18] The Fuzhou and the Hokchia sub-dialects are broadly similar, but both differ greatly from Henghua. All three are very different from the Hokkien spoken in southern Fujian. The speakers of all three sub-dialects tend to be colocated in northern Fujian. The Henghua, for instance, hail from the old Henghua Prefecture comprising the Putian and Henghua Districts, and the Fuqing District (where most Fuzhou speakers have their origins) which forms part of the Putian Region.[19] The Fuzhou area was divided into ten prefectures. Fuzhou speakers are ancestrally from any one of these areas, and each area produces a different accent. Thus, the Fuzhou sub-dialect can be further broken down into smaller groupings, providing yet another sub-layer of loyalties.[20]

18 There is much debate as to whether Fuzhou, Hokchia and Henghua can be properly regarded as sub-dialects of the Hokkien dialect. Some academics believe that they constitute three separate dialects in their own right. For the purposes of this study, they have been treated as sub-dialects of Hokkien, if only because the Chinese of South-East Asia generally appear to treat them as such. South-East Asian Fuzhou associations are commonly affiliated with Hokkien Federations, for example.

19 Suryadinata, L., 'The Xinghua community in Singapore: A study of the socio-economic adjustment of a minority group', in L. Suryadinata., (ed.), *Chinese Adaption and Diversity: Essays on Society and Literature in Indonesia, Malaysia and Singapore*, Singapore University Press, Singapore, 1993, p. 29.

20 See Ling, A., p. 580 for detail on Fuzhou accents and the attendant loyalties invoked.

The Fuzhou, Hokchia and Henghua were comparatively late arrivals in South-East Asia. There is a large concentration of Fuzhous in Sibu in the Malaysian state of Sarawak.[21] Many of the Fuzhous who arrived in Sibu did so at the behest of the then Rajah of Sarawak, who specifically wanted Fuzhou settlers over other Chinese because they were reputed to be particularly hard working and thrifty. A Fuzhou clansman, Wong Nai Siong, brought 1 118 Fuzhou men to Sibu in three batches, most of whom arrived in 1900 and many of whom were from his own clan.[22] Several thousand more arrived subsequently.

Large numbers of Henghua arrived in Indonesia and other parts of South-East Asia during the 1930s, coinciding with civil unrest in China.[23] The late arrival of the Henghua in South-East Asia might be attributed to the lack of a good oceanic port in the Putian Region and to their lack of commercial contacts in South-East Asia.[24] Before their overseas migration, the Henghua usually engaged in either agriculture or fishing.

The Distribution of the Fuzhou, Hokchia and Henghua in South-East Asia

The Fuzhou, Hokchia and Henghua are numerically very small but are represented in most South-East Asian countries.[25] Around five per cent of Malaysia's 5.2 million ethnic Chinese are Fuzhou. Singapore's Henghua community is relatively small, measuring approximately 0.7 per cent of the Chinese community (or about 14 000 people).[26] The proportion that is Fuzhou is probably higher, but figures are not available. A 1921 census indicated that at that time there were only 3 845 Fuzhous and just 1 659 Henghuas in Singapore.[27] There is also a relatively small Fuzhou community in Bangkok.

Traditional Occupations of the Fuzhou, Hokchia and Henghua

By the time the Fuzhou, Hokchia and Henghua arrived in South-East Asia, very few market niches had not already been filled by other Chinese. They found themselves at the bottom of the economic ladder within the Chinese community, perhaps more so than the Hakka. Many became rickshaw pullers and others became unskilled labourers. On obtaining a little capital, the Henghua entered

21 An estimated 70 per cent of Sibu's 180 000 population have a Fuzhou ancestry. (See *Asian Wall Street Journal*, 'Stamina and success mark Fuzhou Chinese diaspora', 8 June 1994.) Most Fuzhou in Malaysia are Christian, which may be a contributing factor to their disproportionate success. Being Christian would have placed them at a distinct advantage when dealing with colonial administrators and would have given them access to English education and further advancement.

22 See Yong, P., *A Dream of Freedom: The Early Sarawak Chinese*, Pelanduk Publications, Petaling Jaya, p. 37.

23 Suryadinata, L., 'The Xinghua community in Singapore: A study of the socio-economic adjustment of a minority group', in Suryadinata, L. (ed.), p. 33.

24 Suryadinata, L., pp. 34-35.

25 In most accounts of the distribution of the northern Fujian sub-dialects, the Fuzhou and the Hokchia tend to be combined.

26 Suryadinata, L., p. 29.

27 See Tan, T.T.W., p. 177.

the bicycle, car and motorcycle spare-parts trades in Singapore, Malaysia and Indonesia.[28]

This, together with the 'rapid-fire' speech of the Fuzhou in particular and a past reputation for being relatively rural, reinforced the disregard felt for them by other dialect groups and encouraged their preparedness to pursue business in an independent and competitive manner and their intense orientation toward their families.[29] These characteristics help explain the group's success in business and political spheres, particularly in South-East Asia.

The Commercial Success of the Fuzhous

Historically, ethnic Chinese communities could be represented as a series of concentric circles. The innermost circle represents the numerically smallest dialect group. It is kept spatially concentrated by its particularly minority status, and is surrounded by other, larger dialect groups. The next circle represents the second smallest group and so on. The closer to the middle a dialect group is, the more pressure it feels from the surrounding circles, and the greater the imperative, therefore, for its members to struggle to achieve an elevation in social and economic status.

Several small ethnic Chinese dialect groups have this 'minority within a minority' status, and have achieved disproportionate success in their representation in the upper echelons of business and, where possible, politics. The Hakka and Fuzhou claim a considerable number of prominent clansmen who are at the very top in business in the region.[30] Among the Fuzhou/Hokchia are:

- Liem Sioe Liong - Indonesian founder of the Salim Group.
- Liem Oen Kian (Djuhar Sutanto) - Liem Sioe Liong's main business partner.
- Bong Son An (Burhan Uray) - chairman of the Indonesia's timber-based Djajanti Group.
- Tan Tjoe Hing (Hendra Rahardja) - head of Indonesia's Harapan Group.[31]
- Pipat Tantipipatpong (Chen Teh Shu) - head of Bangkok's Pornpat Group, a major shareholder in Bangkok Bank and managing director of Taiwan-based United World Chinese Commercial Bank.
- Datuk Tiong Hiew King - controller of Malaysia's Sibu-based Rimbunan Hijau Group, one of South-East Asia's largest timber concerns. His other interests include several newspapers, finance, shipping and plantations.

---

28 Even the head of the giant Lippo Group, Mochtar Riady, an Indonesian Henghua, conformed to the Henghua-bicycle trades link, reputedly beginning his working life in a Jakarta bicycle shop. (See *Time*, 'The secret weapon', 10 May 1993.)

29 The one thing in their favour was a better than average level of education.

30 This section draws on *Asian Wall Street Journal*, 'Stamina and success mark Fuzhou Chinese diaspora', 8 June 1994. For the purposes of this section, 'Fuzhou' refers to both the Fuzhous and the Hokchia, on account of their similarities.

31 Hendra Rahardja is related to Eddie Tansil, another prominent Fuzhou businessman. Tansil was the controller of Indonesia's Golden Key Group, and was gaoled in 1994 for his part in bribing state bank officials.

- Robert Kuok Hock Nien - controller of the Shangri-La Hotel Group and the *South China Morning Post*. Other interests include sugar and oil palm plantations, flour milling, a television station, and shipping.
- Datuk Wong Tuong Kwang - founder of Malaysia' timber-based WTK Group which has operations in Malaysia, Indonesia and Papua New Guinea.
- Tan Sri Ling Beng Siew - founder of Malaysia's Hock Hua Bank. His other interests include timber and gold mining.
- Hii Yu Peng - controller of Malaysia's Delta Group.
- Datuk Ting Pek Khiing - controller of Malaysia's Ekran Bhd with interests in construction and resorts. Ekran recently won the right to build Malaysia's US$5.8 billion Bakun hydropower project.
- Robbie Sumampouw - holder of 63 per cent of the equity in the A$50 million Christmas Island casino.

The Fuzhou also have been well represented in Malaysia's cabinet. They form five per cent of Malaysia's Chinese population, but account for three of the six Malaysian Chinese members in the last cabinet. Current MCA chairman and Transport Minister, Ling Liong Sik is a Fuzhou, as is the current Minister for Housing and Local Government and the Minister for Science, Technology and the Environment. The Deputy Chief Minister of Sarawak, Wong Soon Kai, is also a Fuzhou.

The International Society of Fuzhous

The Fuzhous have a formal international grouping, the International Society of Fuzhous. The Society met in 1990 (Singapore), 1992 (Sibu) and 1994 (Fuzhou, China). Malaysia, which probably has South-East Asia's largest number of Fuzhous, sent a delegation of approximately 1 000 to the 1994 conference.

The organisation recently formed a formal executive. Robert Kuok and Liem Sioe Liong are on the executive committee and Datuk Tiong Hiew King heads the Malaysian chapter.

Apart from the international society, Fuzhou communities, like other dialect and sub-dialect groups, have numerous local Fuzhou associations across South-East Asia. One of these, the Singapore Futsing Association, attracted a number of Indonesian Fuzhous after most Chinese associations were banned in Indonesia in 1965. For example, Liem Sioe Liong and his long-standing business partner, Liem Oen Kian, are now both lifetime honorary chairmen of the association. [32]

[32] See Sato, Y., 'The Salim Group in Indonesia: The development and behaviour of the largest conglomerate in Southeast Asia', *The Developing Economies*, December 1993.

INTERNATIONAL DIALECT LINKS AS 'NETWORKS'

Usually there will be some common personal link between ethnic Chinese business people who have long-standing, cross-boundary business relationships with one another. The link may be family relationship, shared ancestral village or region in China, same surname, or possibly same school. Perhaps the most common connection, however, is the same sub-dialect, which may suggest other characteristics such as a common ancestral heritage and even possibly, distant blood relations. Often such 'networks' may not be active, but should a business opportunity arise, they can be activated to enable business opportunities to be quickly exploited in an environment of mutual 'trust'.[33]

Case Study: A Sub-Dialect Based Business Network in Operation

One of the most enduring relationships among South-East Asia's senior business people is between Indonesia's Liem Sioe Liong and Malaysia's Robert Kuok.[34] Kuok also has a long and close relationship with fellow Malaysian Khoo Kay Peng and both Liem and Khoo have had business links with Indonesia's Mochtar Riady.

These entrepreneurs are linked because they are Hokkien and ancestrally, they are from the northern part of China's Fujian Province. Khoo is a Hokkien, Liem and Kuok are Fuzhou Hokkien, and Riady is a Henghua, ancestrally from a prefecture which adjoins the Fuzhou area.

During the 1960s, Kuok and Liem set up a sugar planting and milling joint venture in Indonesia, PT Gunang Madu. Now they also have joint shipping and palm oil interests. In 1994, Liem and Kuok planned to enter into a partnership with a prominent Indonesian *pribumi* businessman and an Indonesian armed forces (ABRI) foundation, whereby Liem's Indonesian sugar plantations and mills would be merged with Kuok's trading operations. The proposed entity is expected to invest more than US$1 billion in projects in south Sumatra.

In late 1994, Liem acquired 20 per cent of Malaysia's Kuantan Flour Mills (KFM). Liem's Salim Group is expected to embark on a reverse takeover of KFM, injecting some Salim assets into the company in a move designed to complement Kuok's Malaysian flour milling interests. In early 1995, a consortium headed by the Salim-controlled company, Metro Pacific Corporation, won the right to develop a huge tract of land adjacent to Manila's Makati business district. Another prominent member of the consortium is Kuok Philippines Properties Inc., controlled by Robert Kuok.

....

33 For a full discussion of the role of trust in ethnic Chinese business relationships, see Chapter 7.

34 See *Asiaweek*, 'Hard choice: A China push raises questions in Jakarta', 4 May 1994; *Asian Wall Street Journal*, 'MUI share in SCMP grows with purchase of 5% stake', 19 May 1994; *Asian Wall Street Journal*, 'MUI joins an old associate in Philippine investment', 7 July 1994; *Economic and Business Review Indonesia*, 'Salim: Phones in Manila - flour in Malaysia', 10 December 1994; *Business Times*, 'SCMP deal: Who's doing whom a favour', 22 April 1994; *Asian Wall Street Journal*, 'Metro Pacific Group pays $1.6 billion for Manila site', 9 January 1995; and *South China Morning Post*, 'MUI accepts Lippo explanation', 4 June 1994.

Kuok and Khoo's business relationship first emerged in the 1970s. Both have served as directors of Malaysia's state-linked Bank Bumiputera. In 1980, Kuok helped Khoo take control of Malayan United Manufacturing Bhd, and in 1991, Kuok helped Khoo retain control of his Malayan United Industries (MUI) Group in the face of a hostile takeover bid from another Malaysian Chinese entrepreneur, Vincent Tan. Since Khoo sold his MUI Bank to the Hong Leong Group in 1993, he has acquired a stake in a number of companies controlled by the Kuok family. He purchased significant minority equity in Hong Kong's South China Morning Post (Holdings) Ltd; around 35 per cent of Manila-based Shangri-La Properties Inc; and a 30 per cent stake in Hong Kong-based Kerry Financial Services Ltd.

In December 1993, Khoo's MUI purchased Lippo Ltd's controlling stake in Morning Star Holdings, a Hong Kong-based travel company. Lippo is controlled by Mochtar Riady who was formerly the CEO of Liem's Jakarta-based Bank Central Asia.

These corporate linkages among South-East Asia's top ethnic Chinese entrepreneurs illustrate a common theme. For them, competing against one another in business is something they prefer to avoid, and instead, they prefer to informally accommodate each other, reaping the benefits of combined market power as they do so.

FORMAL INTERNATIONAL DIALECT LINKAGES

The international linkages between ethnic Chinese tend to be informal and dialect or sub-dialect based. Some of these are formalised in international dialect associations, which function partly as social groups and partly as dialect-based international chambers of commerce.

The International Society of Fuzhous is one such example. There is an international Teochiu association which meets every two years and there are international Hakka associations. In September 1994, an international Hokkien association was formed. An inaugural meeting was held in Los Angeles at which an executive was elected. The meeting was sponsored by the Southern-California Fukienese Association which paid for delegates to come from around the world.

The growing wealth of overseas Chinese communities around the world and improvements in international air links mean that such associations may become more prominent in future.

Chapter 3

SOUTH-EAST ASIA, INDOCHINA AND BEYOND

The outstanding feature of the Chinese in South-East Asia and Indochina is their high representation among the commercial elites of the region. Chinese communities throughout the region typically eschew direct involvement in politics in favour of business. In most countries in this region, minority Chinese communities are now the predominant economic force. This chapter profiles their remarkable success as immigrants, along with their sub-ethnic make-up, commercial, political and social position, activities and organisations, in South-East Asia and Indochina.

BRUNEI

History and Demographics

Throughout most of the period of British protection, ethnic Chinese were encouraged to settle in Brunei because of their commercial skills. It was hoped that they would help develop Brunei as a trading centre in the same way they had helped develop Singapore and Malaya.

Around 15 per cent or some 42 800 of Brunei's population of 285 000 people are ethnic Chinese.[1] The ethnic Chinese community is decreasing as a proportion of the total because its growth rate is much lower than that for the Malay and other indigenous communities and all further immigration is prohibited.

The biggest Chinese dialect group in Brunei is the Hokkien, many of whose members originated in Jinmen in China. The Hakka and the Cantonese are also represented, but in relatively small numbers. Most of Brunei's ethnic Chinese are Christian.

Position in Society

Though most of Brunei's Chinese have lived there for more than one generation, and some for several generations, fewer than ten per cent hold Bruneian citizenship. Unless the father is a citizen, a person born in Brunei is not eligible for citizenship. If non-Bruneians seek citizenship, they must pass a Malay language and general knowledge test, and must have lived in Brunei for 20 out of the previous 25 years. In these circumstances, most of Brunei's ethnic Chinese enjoy permanent resident status only, and travel abroad on certificates of identity issued by the Government of Brunei.

1 Based on data from the 1993 *Brunei Statistical Yearbook*.

Commercial Role

Despite their relatively small numbers, Hokkien are prominent in Brunei's private sector. The Brunei Chinese Chamber of Commerce is the main ethnic Chinese community organisation. In many cases, Brunei's ethnic Chinese entrepreneurs have a prominent Malay partner. The ethnic Chinese provides the commercial know how and the Malay partner the entree to government.

The role of the ethnic Chinese in Brunei is not exclusively commercial. A number have entered Brunei's civil service, with the most senior rising to the level of Permanent Secretary.

CAMBODIA

History and Demographics

Cambodia's ethnic Chinese community currently numbers between 200 000 and 300 000. Prior to the 1975 Khmer Rouge takeover, this number stood at around 500 000. Roughly 77 per cent are Teochiu, ten per cent are Cantonese, eight per cent are Hainanese, three per cent are Hakka and two per cent are Hokkien.[2] Most live in the major cities or towns, such as Phnom Penh, Sihanoukville, Battambang and Kampong Cham.

Cambodia's Chinese under Pol Pot

Many of Cambodia's Chinese fled or were killed during the Lon Nol regime (1970-75), the Pol Pot Khmer Rouge regime (1975-79) and the early years of the Vietnamese-backed People's Republic of Kampuchea (PRK) regime. According to one estimate, approximately half of Cambodia's Chinese population perished under the Khmer Rouge, a death toll twice as high as that among the ethnic Khmer urban population. The reason may have been race-based, but probably the predominantly 'middle-class' character of many ethnic Chinese attracted the attention of Pol Pot's forces.[3]

Those who remained, were invariably driven by the Khmer Rouge from Phnom Penh and other cities into the provinces. In recent years, many ethnic Chinese have returned to Phnom Penh to buy back, where possible, their former properties and re-establish their businesses.

2 These figures are for 1962-63. They may still be current if it can be assumed that the exodus of ethnic Chinese in the 1970s and the ongoing return of ethnic Chinese to Cambodia, occurred, and is occurring on a *pro rata* basis. See Willmott, W.E., *The Chinese in Cambodia*, University of British Columbia, Vancouver, 1967, p. 18.

3 Kiernan B., 'Kampuchea's Ethnic Chinese Under Pol Pot', *Journal of Contemporary Asia*, 16.1, 1986.

Position in Society

Historically, Cambodia was one the best examples in the region of the assimilation of ethnic Chinese with indigenous societies.[4] To a large degree, the tolerance accorded the Chinese has returned since the fall of the Khmer Rouge regime. This is due to several factors, including King Sihanouk's long-term association with the Government in Beijing and the tendency of the Khmer to have traditionally shown less preference for Cambodia's minority ethnic Vietnamese community.

In 1990, Cambodia's State Council passed a bill giving ethnic Chinese the same rights as other Cambodians, as well as the right to establish their own associations, temples, and Chinese-language schools and to celebrate Chinese festivals. Subsequently, a formal Chinese Association was formed in 1990, with its headquarters in central Phnom Penh. The association's members are well connected and play an increasingly important role in business. The association also oversees the establishment of Chinese schools; approximately fifty exist. The Chinese Government assists by providing textbooks and other materials.

Commercial Role

Traditionally, the Chinese in Cambodia engaged in trading and, to a lesser extent, construction, small-scale manufacturing (such as textiles) and food processing (such as rice milling). Historically, the rice merchants in Cambodia were ethnic Chinese. Just before the Khmer Rouge takeover, the Chinese comprised about five per cent of the population, but controlled approximately 70 per cent of industrial investment.[5] Ethnic Khmers, on the other hand, traditionally worked in agriculture.

The Phnom Penh Chinese community currently owns most of the city's retail enterprises and imports most consumer goods. Market reforms and other policies sympathetic to ethnic Chinese interests introduced in the mid 1980s and early 1990s, and operations by the United Nations Transitional Authority in Cambodia (UNTAC) during 1992-93 attracted a new generation of wealthy ethnic Chinese business entrepreneurs to Cambodia. They came from many countries including Thailand, Hong Kong, Singapore, Malaysia, Taiwan, the United States and Australia. Most sought opportunities in property development and general trading. Some, particularly the Taiwanese, are involved in small-scale manufacturing.

Political Role

Cambodian Chinese traditionally have not displayed an overt interest in politics, although one of the parties that contested Cambodia's first Parliamentary election in 1946, the Democratic Progressive Party led by Prince Norodom Montana, claimed to represent the interests of Phnom Penh's ethnic Chinese

---

4 See Dobbs-Higginson, M.S., *Asia Pacific: Its role in the New World Order*, William Heinemann Australia, Port Melbourne, 1993, p. 163.

5 Sowell, T., *The Economics and Politics of Race*, Quill, New York, 1983, p. 44.

business community.[6] None of Cambodia's current politicians is fully Chinese, although several have a mixed Chinese heritage.

King Sihanouk's relationship with China helped promote a secure position for the ethnic Chinese community and many of its members have good government contacts.

INDONESIA

Approximately 3.5 per cent of Indonesia's population is of ethnic Chinese descent. The largest concentrations of ethnic Chinese are in Jakarta and Surabaya on Java, but virtually all towns and cities across the Indonesian archipelago have some ethnic Chinese residents and there are long-standing Chinese communities in central Java. About 30 per cent of the northern Sumatran city of Medan's population of 1.5 million is ethnic Chinese.

Most Indonesian Chinese are ancestrally Hokkien although other dialect groups from south-eastern China are represented. Many ethnic Chinese in Sumatra are Hakka, descended from indentured or 'coolie' labourers imported to work in the Sumatran plantations. Also a small number of Hainanese are in Indonesia.

As mentioned in Chapter 1, the Indonesian Chinese can be broadly classified into two groups, the *totok* and the *peranakan*.

The *totoks* usually arrived more recently in Indonesia. They are primarily Buddhist; they speak Chinese; and they follow Chinese customs. Many retain links to ethnic Chinese outside Indonesia. *Totoks* are prominent business leaders in Indonesia. Liem Sioe Liong, Mochtar Riady and Eka Tjipta Widjaja are well-known *totok* businessmen.

The term *peranakan* refers to those ethnic Chinese who have lived in Indonesia for at least several generations and have shed many external aspects of their Chinese heritage. Many have inter-married with indigenous Indonesians. Most cannot speak Chinese, and few have strong links to China or Chinese communities elsewhere.[7] Broadly, the *peranakan* have a history of absorption into the local community akin to that of the *babas* and *nonyas* of Malaysia and Singapore.[8] *Peranakan* Sino-Indonesians either speak local languages at home such as Javanese, or use Indonesian or even Dutch.

Ethnic Chinese in Indonesian Society

While the social, cultural and political position of the ethnic Chinese in Indonesia has been uncertain or tenuous for several centuries, their position economically and legally has been generally firmer. Throughout much of the

6 See Osborne, M., *Sihanouk: Prince of Light; Prince of Darkness*, Allen and Unwin, 1994, p. 59.

7 Several *peranakan* interviewees in Jakarta mentioned they thought they were probably Hokkien but could not be sure. Prominent *peranakans* such as BAKOM-PKB Chairman Kristoforus Sindhunatha and LIPI Senior Researcher Dr Thee Kian Wie speak Dutch in their family homes; whereas, Vice-Chairman of the board of directors of the CSIS Harry Tjan Silalahi speaks Javanese.

8 Like the *babas* of some of the Straits Settlements, some of the *peranakan* spoke their own dialect, known as *Melayu Cina*.

colonial period, foreign Asian residents of the Dutch East Indies (who were overwhelmingly Chinese) were accorded middle level legal status (below Europeans, but above the indigenous population) and had better access to legal protection than did members of the indigenous population. Historically, Chinese migration was inwards; however, periods of social and political discrimination led to an outward flow of Chinese from Indonesia, including to China and thereafter, Hong Kong.

Dutch colonialism in Indonesia helped to entrench a sense that the Chinese community was distinct. The Dutch imported many Chinese as 'coolies' for cheap labour. Chinese businessmen often were used as commercial go-betweens and brokers, and accorded privileges under the colonial administration. Ethnic and racial groups, including the Chinese, were segregated into their own neighbourhoods.

During the turbulent years of the Sukarno Government, following Indonesian independence, the Chinese were subject to official discrimination and hostility. In part, this resulted from their perceived association with the former colonial regime. Many could not become Indonesian citizens. They were the target of a law in 1959 banning 'aliens' from running businesses in rural areas. Although the large Indonesian Communist Party (PKI) attracted a significant Chinese following during the 1950s, the PKI decided not to allow Chinese in the leadership, apparently in response to their perceived unpopularity with the wider community. Many Chinese left Indonesia during this period. In the first three months of 1960, 90 000 departed.[9] In the anti-communist campaign of 1965-66, significant numbers of ethnic Chinese Indonesians were killed, although the number was fewer than has sometimes been suggested, since many Chinese had by then moved to urban areas which were less affected by violence.

The New Order Government which emerged from this period promoted the assimilation of Chinese with the wider community, partly to reduce the potential for inter-communal conflict. All Chinese-language newspapers were banned except the Government-controlled *Harian Indonesia*, as was the open display of Chinese written script and other manifestations of Chinese culture. Chinese were encouraged to take Indonesian names, and many did so.

Many *peranakan* Chinese support Government efforts to assimilate the Chinese community and reduce its distinctiveness. Some blame the conspicuousness and wealth of the *totoks* for the political vulnerability of the wider Chinese community.

About one per cent of Sino-Indonesians have adopted Islam, the religion of most Indonesians. The conversion rate has not always been this low. Ethnic Chinese arriving before the establishment of the Dutch colonial presence often converted to Islam. The social segregation which operated under the Dutch subsequently acted to discourage such conversions. Consequently, Chinese settlers arriving after the Dutch established authority in the Indies (the vast majority of ethnic Chinese in Indonesia) had a very low conversion rate.

---

9 Redding, G.S., *The Spirit of Chinese Capitalism*, Walter de Gruyter and Co., Berlin, 1990, p. 26.

Today, displays of Chinese culture still are banned in many areas. There are few ethnic Chinese in the top levels of government bureaucracy or the military. Chinese ethnicity is indicated on the identity cards which all Indonesian citizens must carry and non-*pribumi* are expected to produce documents to indicate their ethnic background when applying for official positions or entry to school or university.

Of late, the ban on the teaching of Chinese language has eased, a result of Indonesia's growing tourism and trade links with Taiwan, China and other Chinese-speaking countries. The Coordinating Minister for Political Affairs recently announced that the teaching of Chinese would be permitted for the workers in the hospitality and tourist trade. In addition, promotional publications for the tourist trade could be printed in Chinese. The Government also announced that visitors from China would be permitted to enter Indonesia via Surabaya airport in addition to Medan and Jakarta.[10] These concessions are in line with an apparent softening of the application of anti-Chinese script laws in recent years.[11]

Anti-Chinese violence has occasionally recurred, for example in riots in Medan, North Sumatra in April 1994.[12] Such incidents often have been motivated more by economic issues, such as perceived inequitable wealth distribution, than sheer racism. The Medan riots, for example, focused on wage demands and were aimed at local business and factory owners, most of whom were Chinese.

Despite these factors, the New Order Government has produced more stability and security for the Chinese in Indonesia, and now they are more prominent in the business community. The central position of Chinese-controlled companies in the Indonesian economy means that some sections of the Chinese community have attained significant indirect political influence.

Government Policies

During the 1970s, the Government Agency for the Communication of Comprehension of National Unity (BAKOM-PKB) advised on the assimilation of Sino-Indonesians. The agency's objective was to de-Sinify the Chinese and act as a quasi-government body managing potential non-government vested interests. Today, BAKOM-PKB's influence is waning although regional BAKOM-PKB boards remain, each having around 30 members from all ethnic groups. The representatives on the agency's national board include a range of Sino-Indonesians. The agency recently criticised the constraints on ethnic Chinese entry to the civil service and the military, claiming that this reinforces economic segregation.

The Government has generally eschewed adopting racially-based policies like Malaysia's New Economic Policy (NEP) to help non-Chinese business. Indeed,

10 See *The Australian*, 'Indonesia relaxes ban on Chinese language', 4 August 1994.

11 Increasingly, magazines in Chinese or photocopies of such magazines are openly displayed for sale in Jakarta's Chinatown area of Glodok, for example.

12 Medan, Indonesia's fourth largest city is an important industrial and regional centre.

some critics maintain that ethnic Chinese business has succeeded in Indonesia because of favourable government treatment in awarding official contracts, licences and other support. President Soeharto's relationship with some senior ethnic Chinese business figures (the *cukongs*) has been one underlying theme in political debate in Indonesia.[13] Some ministries reportedly seek to redress informally this perceived imbalance by favouring *pribumis* when they award government contracts.

President Soeharto sought to offset potential 'social jealousy' arising from the newly visible wealth of Chinese-owned business conglomerates following financial sector reforms in the late 1980s. In early 1990, he called on the nation's top businessmen, most of whom are ethnic Chinese, to distribute 25 per cent of corporate equity to the cooperatives movement. In March 1991, this call was repeated.[14] The Government's reluctance to push the issue further may be due to concerns about destabilising Indonesia's investment climate.

An outstanding problem for a significant minority of Indonesia's ethnic Chinese (about 300 000 people) is the question of citizenship. Even though many Sino-Indonesians have lived in Indonesia for generations, they still are defined as residents and not citizens. The issue is critical because without citizenship, they cannot obtain passports.

As part of restoring diplomatic relations with the PRC in 1990, Indonesia undertook to resolve the citizenship issue for its resident ethnic Chinese community. In 1993, President Soeharto instructed that the citizenship process for ethnic Chinese be streamlined and hastened. In August 1994, the Government formed an advisory team to investigate ways to improve the citizenship process. The Government hopes that 80-90 per cent of resident ethnic Chinese will become citizens.[15]

Ethnic Chinese Business Interests

During the struggle for Independence, some ethnic Chinese entrepreneurs assisted army units in their battles against the Dutch by providing supplies and credit. At that time, fledgling Sino-Indonesian business people tapped international credit markets (particularly through Bangkok Bank) via their links to other Chinese abroad. Some of these relationships continue to endure.

The economic policies of the New Order Government underpinned a sustained period of economic growth in Indonesia and helped develop large, diversified business conglomerates.[16] Sino-Indonesians control approximately 73 per cent of

....

13 The *cukong* system (*cukong* or *tjukong*, is Hokkien for 'master') refers to the partnership which has been forged between senior Sino-Indonesian business people and members of the *pribumi* power elite.

14 See Sender, H., 'Inside the overseas Chinese network', *Institutional Investor*, August 1991, p. 36.

15 The citizenship drive will reduce the number of ethnic Chinese in Indonesia that the PRC can claim some responsibility towards, thereby negating some of the justification for the PRC to establish consulates in high ethnic Chinese population areas such as Medan, in North Sumatra.

16 Chapter 7 discusses, in part, the modernisation of ethnic Chinese enterprises in Indonesia. Chapter 8 includes discussion on the structure and behaviour of Indonesia's Sino-controlled conglomerates, and includes a detailed discussion of the Sino-Indonesian Salim Group. Chapter 11 includes detail on Sino-Indonesian investment in China.

listed firms by market capitalisation.[17] At the end of 1993, Sino-Indonesians (who constitute just 3.5 per cent of all Indonesians) controlled 68 per cent of the top 300 conglomerates and nine of the top ten private sector groups. The top ten conglomerates appear in Table 3.1.

Table 3.1

Indonesia's Top Ten Business Groups

(As at 1993, by Gross Assets)

GROUP	ASSETS (Rp billion)	ACTIVITIES	ETHNICITY
Salim	30 403.4	Diversified	Sino-Indonesian
Sinar Mas	14 623.7	Diversified	Sino-Indonesian
Bank Danamon	8 682.2	Finance	Sino-Indonesian
Gadjah Tunggal	7 500.0	Tyre Production	Sino-Indonesian
Astra	7 492.0	Car Assembly	Sino-Indonesian
Lippo	7 076.6	Finance, Property	Sino-Indonesian
Dharmala	6 000.0	Agri-industries, Property	Sino-Indonesian
Barito Pacific	5 887.0	Timber, Plywood	Sino-Indonesian
Bimantara	4 560.0	Diversified	*Pribumi*
Ongko	4 200.0	Property	Sino-Indonesian

Source: Pusat Data Business Indonesia, *Conglomeration Indonesia*, 2nd edition, Jakarta, 1994.

Table 3.2

Ethnicity of Indonesia's Top 300 Conglomerates

(As at 1993, by Gross Assets)

ETHNICITY	1988 NUMBER	1988 TOTAL ASSETS (per cent)	1993 NUMBER	1993 TOTAL ASSETS (per cent)
Sino-Indonesian	191	74.6	204	80.1
Pribumi	98	23.4	81	16.4
Joint *Pribumi*/ Sino-Indonesian	11	2.0	15	3.6

Source: Pusat Data Business Indonesia, *Conglomeration Indonesia*, 2nd ed., Jakarta, 1994.

....

17 Control by market capitalisation has been determined after listed firms controlled by governments or foreigners are discounted. (See Yamaguchi, M., 'The emerging Chinese business sphere', *Nomura Asian Perspectives*, Vol. 11, No. 2, July 1993, Nomura Research Institute.)

In recent years, businesses controlled by Sino-Indonesians have grown more rapidly than other businesses. As shown in Table 3.2, Sino-Indonesians controlled 191 of the top 300 conglomerates in 1988. This amounted to control of 74.6 per cent of the assets of the top 300. By 1993, this had grown and 204 of the top 300 were Sino-Indonesian controlled, amounting to 80.1 per cent by assets.

A striking feature of the Indonesian corporate landscape is how many major conglomerates are interlinked. (See Figure 3.1.) Apart from the Bakrie, Sudwikatmono, Humpuss, Bimantara, Citra Lamtoro Gung, Hanurata and Mercu Buana Groups which are controlled by *pribumi* business people, the remaining 33 conglomerates shown are controlled by Sino-Indonesians. In recent years, interlinkages occurred through cross-shareholdings and directorships, joint ventures between conglomerates and family links such as marriage between the major business families. Sino-Indonesian controlled conglomerates linked by family connections include: the Lippo Group and the Myapada Group, the Lippo Group and Panin Bank, the Gadjah Tunggal Group and the Ometraco Group, the Gunung Sewu Group and the Dharmala Group, and the Gemala Group and the Danamon Group.[18]

The recent rush of interlinkages has turned potential competitors into colleagues, allowing market share to be maintained and new sources of capital to be accessed. One by-product of the interlinkages, however, is the management of the political risk inherent in an uncertain successor to the current political regime. The interlinkages mean that if one conglomerate is adversely affected during the transition, this will flow on to most other major conglomerates, so each conglomerate has a vested interest to maintain all the others' interests. Future political leaders therefore may be unlikely to challenge the economic position of the conglomerates for fear of the widespread economic implications of such actions. In this way, the conglomerates may be seen to a degree as having responded to possible future political uncertainty by arraying themselves as if they are inter-dependent dominos.

Some conglomerates are linked to companies controlled by members of the Soeharto family, particularly the sons and daughters of President Soeharto. These conglomerates have been very successful, and have grown rapidly in recent years. An example of one such linkage is a US$1 billion pulp mill in southern Sumatra, planned as a joint venture between companies controlled by Sino-Indonesian Prajogo Pangestu, and President Soeharto's eldest daughter, Siti Hardiyanti Rukmana, together with two Japanese partners.[19] Well connected *pribumi* partners usually bring political capital to a joint venture. They are useful in negotiating bureaucratic or regulatory obstacles. In this way, many contribute only small amounts of equity to joint ventures but achieve a high proportion of the profits, thus earning a return on their political capital.

---

18 There is also a family link between Indonesia's Matahari Department Store chain and Ong Tjoe Kim's Metro Department Store chain in Singapore. Ong is a Sino-Indonesian now resident in Singapore.

19 See *Far Eastern Economic Review*, 'Business briefing', 21 April 1994.

Figure 3.1

Cross-shareholdings and Family Linkages Between Selected Indonesian Conglomerates

The Government has provided explicit support to some of the major Indonesian conglomerates. In 1985, the Government took a 35 per cent stake in a Salim Group-controlled company, Indocement, at a cost of US$330 million, saving the company from probable collapse. In 1989, the Government took over the Salim Group's 40 per cent share in the loss-making PT Cold Rolling Mill Indonesia Utama. The company is now a fully-owned unit within the state-owned PT Krakatau Steel.[20]

Many large Sino-Indonesian concerns either have *pribumi* partners or a *pribumi* chairman. For example, the chairman of Lippobank is Hasjim Ning, an indigenous Indonesian; whereas, the controller of the bank is vice-chairman Mochtar Riady, a Sino-Indonesian.[21] Liem Sioe Liong, the controller of the giant Salim Group has two other ethnic Chinese partners, but also two *pribumi* partners. This pattern, common among Sino-controlled conglomerates, is known as an 'ali-baba' arrangement.[22]

The Peranakan in Business

Indonesia's *peranakan* Chinese have less contact with ethnic Chinese networks, both domestically and internationally, than their prominent *totok* counterparts. As a result, such networks have not played a major role in their success.

The Gemala Group is controlled by the *peranakan* Wanandi family, headed by Sofyan Wanandi. Although ethnically Chinese, the family, originally from Padang in Sumatra, is Catholic and educated in the United States, Switzerland and Australia. The family does not speak Chinese and does not have good links with cross-border ethnic Chinese networks. It therefore has looked to expand its operations in the West, in the United Kingdom, the United States and Australia.[23]

Another *peranakan* businessman is William Soeryadjaya (Tjia Kian Liong).[24] Soeryadjaya was born in West Java in 1922 and although ethnically Chinese, cannot speak Chinese and is a devout Christian. He went into business aged 19, selling used papers and then agricultural products. In 1947, he went to the Netherlands for vocational training, returning in 1949. He set up a leather business which failed, as he was unable to compete with his *totok* competitors who controlled the leather business.

In 1952, he moved into the export-import business, dealing in a range of commodities. In 1957, he established PT Astra International Inc. with his younger brother Drs Tjia Kian Tie and an associate, Liem Peng Hong. Initially PT Astra marketed soft drinks and exported agricultural products. At one time, PT

20 See *The Asian Wall Street Journal*, 'Salim group steels itself for life after Suharto', 25-26 February 1994.

21 See Lippobank, *Annual Report 1993*, Jakarta, 1994.

22 The 'ali' refers to the *pribumi* partner and the 'baba' refers to the ethnic Chinese partner.

23 Personal communication with Gemala.

24 Information on the Soeryadjaya family has been sourced from: Suryadinata, L., 'Chinese Economic Elites in Indonesia: A preliminary Study', in J.W. Cushman and Wang Gungwu, *Changing Identities of the Southeast Asian Chinese since World War II*, Hong Kong University Press, 1988.

Astra was affiliated with General Ibnu Sutowo, the *pribumi* director general of Pertamina. Under Soeryadjaya's leadership, PT Astra became the largest automobile and motorcycle assembler in Indonesia with almost 50 affiliated companies. Unlike many other Chinese-controlled companies, PT Astra employed many *pribumi* at the management level and was considered a good example of an 'assimilated company'.

At the beginning of 1992, Soeryadjaya's business fortunes faltered. Bank Summa, part of a financial group owned by his son, Edward, collapsed under heavy debt. The Government was finally forced to order the bank's closure. To meet the outstanding obligations of Bank Summa, Soeryadjaya had to sell his family's interests in Astra. On-going speculation about the implications of a Soeryadjaya divestment from Astra, the suspension of Summa's banking licence but not share trading in Astra, and William's hesitancy in selling his shares, caused Astra's share price to collapse. Soeryadjaya's competitors, who were mostly *totoks*, took advantage of the underpriced shares to take control of Astra.

The *totok* businessman Prajogo Pangestu is now the largest single and controlling shareholder in PT Astra. He and the other businessmen who bought Astra shares in the aftermath of the collapse of Bank Summa have since made massive capital profits on their investments. Although probably *ex poste* rationalisation, some see the involvement of *totok* businessmen in Soeryadjaya's difficulties as symptomatic of wider competition between *totok* and *peranakan* business interests.

Community, Business and Academic Organisations

Unlike some other Chinese communities in South-East Asia, there are few social organisations for Chinese Indonesians based on common regional heritage in China. One important factor against the formation of dialect associations is that most of Indonesia's ethnic Chinese are *peranakan*, and cannot speak any Chinese dialect.

There are several traditional surname associations in Jakarta's Kota area. These associations have a largely *peranakan* membership and are quite old. There are also some surname associations in Semarang on Java's north coast. They are largely social and welfare organisations, but might also function to a small degree as *de facto* chambers of commerce. Unlike their counterparts in Singapore, they have not amassed significant real estate holdings.

Although Chinese are not strongly represented in government, Chinese individuals and Chinese-supported institutions influence policy and play a role in national affairs. The ethnic Chinese business community funds the Centre for Strategic and International Studies (CSIS), and the Prasetiya Mulya Foundation. Several senior ethnic Chinese business people such as Liem Sioe Liong's son, Anthony Salim, and Bob Hasan have been appointed to the Majelis Perwakilan Rakyat (MPR), the forum of 920 electors which meets to elect the president.

CSIS was established in the 1960s by the Sino-Indonesian Wanandi brothers in cooperation with leading military figures who were close to President Soeharto, specifically Ali Murtopo and Sudjono Humardani. Most of its members are ethnic Chinese. It has acted as a think-tank for government. In the past, members of CSIS were appointed to the MPR which elected the president.

The Prasetiya Mulya Foundation, which was set up ostensibly to perform good social works, also operates as an informal lobby group for senior members of the ethnic Chinese business community, as well as a *de facto* Chinese chamber of commerce. The foundation provides services such as management training for small- and medium-sized enterprises, most of which tend to be *pribumi*. The foundation's current chairman is Liem Sioe Liong. Other executive members include Sino-Indonesian entrepreneurs: Eka Tjipta Widjaja (Sinar Mas Group), Prajogo Pangestu (Barito Group), The Ning King (Argo Manunggal Group) and Rachman Halim (Gudang Garam Group). The foundation also has links to the CSIS.[25]

LAOS

Demographics

About 50 000 ethnic Chinese live in Laos, accounting for about 1.3 per cent of the population. As many as 70 per cent are Teochiu; the bulk of the remainder are Cantonese, then Hainanese. Most live in the capital Vientiane, or in Savannakhet.

Laos' northern provinces bordering China (Luang Namtha, Oudomsai and Phongsali) are home to an ethnic Chinese minority known as the Ho (or Haw).

Position in Society

There is little current friction between the majority Lao and ethnic Chinese communities, although in the past, sometimes the relationship was uneasy. What little friction there is arises out of resentment towards labourers from China coming to work in northern Laos. Apart from this, there is little discernible disquiet at the commercial success of the ethnic Chinese in Laos. Intermarriage between the two communities is common. Most of Laos' ethnic Chinese have resident status but carry PRC or third country passports. Chinese, like other ethnic groups, are free to apply for Lao citizenship. Several prominent Lao politicians have either an ethnic Chinese or part-Chinese heritage; one is the current foreign minister, Somsavad Lengsavath.

The Commercial Involvement of Laos' Ethnic Chinese

Many of Laos' ethnic Chinese fled during the communist takeover in 1975.[26] Nonetheless, ethnic Chinese are still prominent today in Laos' commercial sector, where they specialise in retail and repair shops, restaurants, and hotels.

25 *Prospek*, 'Mereka Bukan Shang Hui', 16 January 1994.

26 Many fled to West, but also to Thailand and particularly Bangkok, where Teochiu is spoken by most of the local Chinese.

MALAYSIA

Historical Background

Malaysia's ethnic Chinese form a well defined group within Malaysian society. They have not attempted to acculturate. Past governments encouraged economic integration and promoted ethnic harmony through means other than acculturation.

It is uncertain when the first Chinese settlers came to the Malay peninsular, although fifteenth century Chinese records appear to indicate Chinese were present then in Malacca.[27] However, most descend from Chinese who came to Malaya under the British colonial administration. The Chinese were employed as 'coolie' labour (many of whom were indentured) in the tin mines of northern Malaysia. The Hakka were among the poorest people in China at the time of the 'coolie' trade and consequently offered themselves for labour in the colonies. This accounts for the relatively high proportion of Hakka in Malaysia today.

Alongside the recently arrived Chinese, the *sinkeh*, lived the Straits Chinese or the *baba*, although the two communities had little to do with one another. *Baba* culture had three centres, Penang, Malacca and Singapore, although the Singapore *babas* tended to be an offshoot of the Malacca *babas*. Nearly all Singapore *baba* families had their roots in Malacca.[28]

With considerable rubber and tin mining interests, many *baba* families became very wealthy during the commodities boom early this century. The *baba* tended to identify more with the British colonialists, so much so they became known as the 'King's Chinese'. In contrast, the *sinkeh* retained their Chinese ways; and followed more traditional pursuits such as working as coolies, trading or operating small shops.

There are relatively few *baba* Chinese in Malaysia today, and those that remain are a relatively insignificant force in Malaysian society.[29] Descendants of Malaysia's *baba* families have profoundly influenced modern-day Singapore, however.[30]

Generally, the position of Malaysia's Chinese has been significantly influenced by the Malaysian Government's attitude to China and the threat of communism. In the early years after Malaysia's Independence in 1957, remnants of the Chinese-dominated Malayan Communist Party (MCP) were still waging their armed

---

27 See Tan, C.B., 'Acculturation and the Chinese in Melaka: The Expression of Baba Identity Today' in L.Y.C. Lim and L.A.P. Gosling (eds), *The Chinese in Southeast Asia*, Vol. 1, Maruzen Asia, Singapore, 1983, p. 59.

28 See Chia, F., *The Babas Revisited*, Heinemann Asia, Singapore, 1994, p. 11. Former MCA President and Finance Minister, Tun Tan Siew Sin, was a Malacca-born *baba*.

29 There are about 5 000 *Babas* in the State of Malacca, or about 3 per cent of the State's ethnic Chinese population and there are a few ethnic Chinese in Penang who still identify themselves as *baba*. (See Tan, C.B., in L.Y.C. Lim and L.A.P. Gosling (eds), Vol. 1, p. 58). The acculturation of the *babas* is now such that several *baba* associations have fought to have their members granted indigenous or *bumiputera* status by the Government - something which the Government has agreed to consider on a case by case basis.

30 See the discussion on Singapore later in this Chapter for a detailed discussion on this.

struggle from the Perak-Thai border area against the Government. China was suspected of assisting the insurgents which tended to cast a pall over the wider Malaysian Chinese community.[31]

Relations between Malaysia and China began to thaw in 1985 with a visit to China by Prime Minister Mahathir and in 1988, travel restrictions on Malaysians wanting to visit China were lifted. Further high level visits have been made to China.[32] Now, diplomatic relations between the two countries are restored; bilateral investment and trade is expanding; and the domestic position of Malaysia's Chinese is improving.

Demographics

Approximately 29 per cent of Malaysia's population is of ethnic Chinese descent.[33] This minority is estimated to control 61 per cent of share capital in Malaysia by market capitalisation.[34] Similarly, the Chinese continue to make up the bulk of the professional class, accounting for around 60 per cent of all private sector administrative and managerial positions.

An important division among Malaysia's Chinese follows the language used in education, either Chinese or English.[35] Those educated in Chinese tend to be relatively traditional in outlook and generally less commercially successful than their English educated counterparts. The Chinese educated, however, now are beginning to come into their own as their language and cultural skills increasingly are called upon to promote and manage Malaysia's expanding trade and investment links with China and Taiwan.

As elsewhere, Malaysia's ethnic Chinese community comprises a multiplicity of dialects. The main dialect communities are the Hokkien (approximately 32 per cent), the Teochiu (approximately 12 per cent), the Cantonese (approximately 22 per cent), the Hakka (approximately 22 per cent) and the Hainanese (approximately 5 per cent).[36] Each dialect is further divided into sub-dialect groups.

As a result of chain migration, the various dialects and sub-dialects are not distributed randomly around Malaysia. Kuala Lumpur is known as a 'Cantonese town'; Johor Baru, located across the causeway from Singapore, is known as a 'Teochiu town'. More generally, the Chinese of the northern regions of

---

31 See Pandey, B.N., *South and South-East Asia 1945-1979: Problems and Policies*, Macmillan, London, 1980, p. 59.

32 See Chapter 11 for further details.

33 The 1992 census found that there were 5.4 million Malaysian Chinese out of a total of 18.6 million Malaysians.

34 See Yamaguchi, M., 'The emerging Chinese business sphere', *Nomura Asian Perspectives*, Vol. 11, No. 2, July 1993, Nomura Research Institute; and Suryadinata, L., 'Introduction' in L. Suryadinata (ed.) *The Ethnic Chinese in the ASEAN States: Biographical Essays*, ISEAS, Singapore, 1989 p. 1. Control by market capitalisation has been determined after listed firms controlled by governments or foreigners are discounted.

35 This is similar to the case in Singapore, discussed later.

36 See Wu, Y.L. and C.H. Wu, *Economic Development in Southeast Asia: The Chinese Dimension*, Hoover Institute Press, Stanford, 1980, p. 135.

peninsular Malaysia tend to be Hokkien and Teochiu, the central region Cantonese and Hakka, and the southern region Hokkien and Teochiu. The ethnic Chinese living around Malaysia's coast, in cities like Malacca and Georgetown, tend to be Hokkien. Historically, the newly arrived Hokkien often were traders for whom access to ports was essential. The ethnic Chinese in the New Villages, the towns formed during the early 1960s to resettle Malaysia's poorer citizens, are mostly Hakka, as are the Chinese in Sabah.[37] The ethnic Chinese community in Sarawak, especially in Sibu, is predominantly Fuzhou Hokkien.

Traditional and Other Chinese Social Structures in Malaysia

Traditional Structures

Given that the pressures for assimilation have been comparatively weak, traditional social structures among the ethnic Chinese in Malaysia are still relatively strong. There are more than 4 000 Chinese associations in Malaysia. Among these are the surname, dialect and locality associations discussed in Chapter 1. These associations are still important, especially among the Chinese educated. Some occupational guilds and traders' associations are also still prominent. Traditional ethnic Chinese social structures probably are best observed in Penang, where the Chinese form most of the population and tend to be more traditional than, for example, their Kuala Lumpur counterparts.

Some of the main surnames in Penang which form the basis for some of the stronger surname associations, the *kongsi*, are Khoo, Cheah, Yeoh, Lim and Tan. The Khoo Kongsi is particularly prominent and is one of the wealthiest, being a large property holder in Georgetown. Many kongsi have clan temples for worshipping ancestors.[38]

There are at least fourteen sub-dialects among the Penang Hokkien. Each has its own district/dialect association which functions primarily as a welfare and social organisation, and an informal chamber of commerce.[39] These associations typically control considerable property and other assets. Members of the Hui Aun

---

37 In Sabah, 16 per cent of the population is ethnically Chinese, and 70 per cent of these are Hakka.

38 The most prominent among Penang's surname associations are the Lee Si Chong Soo, the Khoo Kongsi, the Cheah Si Ching Soo, the Yuoh Si Har Yong Tong (who tend to be English educated), the Lim Si Kew Leong Tong, the Tan Si Eng Chuan Tong, the Yeap Si Ching Soo, the Teoh Si Chong Soo, the Saw Khaw Lean Chong Soo (which covers several surnames), the Sin Quah Chuah Chong Soo (also covers several surnames), the Ooi Si Keng Har Tong, the Chew Si Chong Soo, the Loh Si Tong Chong Seah, the Neoh Si Ching Soo, and the Eu Si Chong Soo. These surname associations are all for Hokkiens, although other dialects may have the same surname. Non-Hokkien wives of Hokkien husbands are now permitted to belong to their husband's Hokkien surname association.

39 They are the Hui Aun Association, the Chin Keng Association, the Tong Aun Kin Har Association, the Cheang Chew Association (its membership is mostly English educated, was among the first to come to Penang, and includes many prominent people), the Lung Yen Association, the Hokchia (Fuzhou) Association, the Aun Khauy Association, the Lam Aun Haoy Kuan, the Eng Teng Association, the Hoi Lam Haoy Kuan, the Hoi Pak Haoy Kuan, the Hinuah Haoy Kuan, the Engchoon Haoy Kuan and the Hock Seong Kong Haoy.

association are said to be among the most influential people in Penang. The late Tan Sri Loh Boon Siew, one of Malaysia's most successful business people (and a significant investor in Australian property), was a Penang Hui Aun Hokkien.[40]

Another important traditional Chinese social organisation is the Chinese cemetery committee. As elsewhere in South-East Asia, Chinese cemeteries are differentiated on the basis of dialect. There are, for example, separate Hokkien, Teochiu and Cantonese cemeteries, many of which have considerable and increasingly valuable land holdings.[41] In Penang, the most important Chinese cemetery committee is the United Hokkien Cemetery Committee, which controls five cemeteries, each exclusively for Hokkien.[42]

Guilds were very strong in Penang, stronger than elsewhere in Malaysia, although their influence is declining. One of the most prevalent guilds today consists of Penang's taxi drivers who combine to set fares for destinations all over the island.[43]

Dialect-occupation linkages where most of those in a particular business speak the same dialect, are diminishing in importance in Penang, as they are elsewhere in Malaysia. Some, however, are still significant. Because of these links, the memberships of some guild and dialect associations overlap, such as in the Penang Fuzhou Association and the Coffee Shop Traders Association. This is because most of Penang's coffee shops still are run by the Fuzhou Hokkien.

Malaysia's traditional Chinese social organisations still have an important but diminishing role. Many also control considerable property assets. Since earlier restrictions on interaction with China were relaxed, the older generation of Malaysian Chinese now can travel to China to visit ancestral regions. The re-established links with China generate, particularly in older Malaysian Chinese, a renewed pride in their clan and other aspects of their Chinese roots. Additionally, Malaysia's current robust economy has generated funds within the ethnic Chinese community for welfare works, banquets and religious activities. These conditions provide further impetus to renew clan consciousness.

Chinese schools are still very important in Malaysia. Like other 'mother-tongue' schools, the Chinese schools only recently attracted government funding.[44] Around three quarters of Malaysian Chinese students at primary level attend Chinese schools. For secondary schooling, however, most go to government

40 Loh died in 1995.

41 Land set aside for cemeteries may occasionally be sold - but only if the land has not already been used as a cemetry. For the Chinese, building over or near graves is poor *feng shui* and therefore unthinkable. (For a description of *feng shui*, see Appendix 6)

42 The five cemeteries are: Batu Lanchang Cemetery, Batu Gantong Cemetery, Mount Erskine Cemetery, Paya Ternborg Cemetery and Telok Bahang Cemetery.

43 This has grown out of a traditional Chinese association, but is now no longer restricted to Chinese. The taxi industry on Penang is also heavily regulated by the State Government.

44 The Chinese schools are largely funded by donors from within the Chinese community, although in February 1994, the Federal Government set an important precedent by allocating M$2 million for independent Chinese high schools in Sabah and M$6 million for renovations to partially-aided Chinese schools in Penang.

Bahasa Malaysia schools, although there are at least sixty independent Chinese secondary schools.[45]

Political Role

As in most economies, Malaysian politics and commerce are inextricably entwined. The Government, through its frequent interventions in the market, is a prominent player in the economy. Any analysis of the commercially successful ethnic Chinese in Malaysia would be incomplete without mention of the role played by politics and government. In Malaysia, the Chinese have not avoided direct political involvement as they have elsewhere, but have played a full and active role.

Historical Involvement of Malaysia's Chinese

Historically, political affiliations among Malaysia's Chinese broadly followed dialect lines. For example, the Hokkien tended to support the Malaysian Chinese Association (MCA); the Hakkas generally lined up behind 'leftist' opposition parties (for example, the Democratic Action Party), although there may be a new trend to the MCA; the Hainanese were leftward leaning, but now support the MCA; and the Cantonese were said to be 'fence-sitters'.[46] However, these tendencies were not so much based on dialect as class, reflecting the socio-economic stratification of the Malaysian Chinese community on dialect lines.

Malaysia's Ethnic Chinese and Party Politics

Malaysia's main political parties are ethnically based.[47] The United Malays National Organisation (UMNO) is the main Malay political party. The Malaysian Indian Congress (MIC) is the main Indian party. The largest party purporting to represent the interests of Malaysia's ethnic Chinese is the Malaysian Chinese Association (MCA), although it has only ever attracted around 30 per cent of the Chinese vote. Together with a range of smaller parties, these three parties form the ruling coalition government, the *Barisan Nasional* (National Front). Two other Malaysian political parties are Chinese dominated, although open to all ethnic groups. They are *Gerakan Rakyat Malaysia* (or *Gerakan*), which belongs to the *Barisan Nasional*, and the Democratic Action Party (DAP), Malaysia's main opposition party.

Historically, the Chinese-educated dominated the MCA. However, with the emerging trade between Malaysia and China, those with strong Chinese language skills have moved away from politics to business, leaving a hiatus which the English-educated Chinese are filling. During the 1960s and early 1970s, the MCA was a powerful partner in the *Barisan Nasional.* This influence began to recede after 1974, when the MCA lost control of the Ministry of Finance and the Ministry of Trade and Industry. With the MCA's reduced level of influence, the

---

45 *The Straits Times*, 'MCA may follow UMNO's move to curb money politics', 21 June 1994.

46 Siow M., in L.Y.C Lim and L.A.P. Gosling (eds), Vol. 1, p. 173.

47 Malaysians of non-Malay descent are actually prohibited from joining UMNO. Similarly, non-Chinese cannot join the MCA. See *Far Eastern Economic Review*, 'Malaysian first', 14 July 1994.

Associated Chinese Chambers of Commerce and Industry Malaysia attempted to fill the vacuum by becoming more vocal in representing Chinese business concerns, but its influence was limited.[48]

Gerakan receives much of its support not from ethnic Chinese business people but from Chinese professionals, such as lawyers and doctors. Traditionally, the DAP has sought to represent Malaysians in lower socio-economic groups, particularly the Chinese of the New Villages, although of late, its supporters increasingly are urban middle class.[49]

Commercial Role

Malaysia's Chinese play a major role in the economy.[50] They are less dominant than the Chinese in Thailand, although their per capita income is much higher. Generally, as the importance of foreign, particularly British, capital has declined in Malaysia, Malaysian Chinese and *bumiputera* interests have increased.[51]

The New Economic Policy (NEP)

The NEP was inaugurated in 1971 in response to perceived inequities in wealth distribution, largely between the Chinese and the poorer Malays. These inequities contributed to anti-Chinese unrest and rioting in May 1969.[52]

The NEP did not impose any divestment laws on the Chinese, but sought to expand the economy, allowing the *bumiputeras* a bigger share of a bigger cake. Although the source of much disquiet within the Malaysian Chinese business community, the NEP ultimately proved remarkably successful by the time it formally ceased and was replaced by the National Development Policy in 1991. It achieved a better distribution of economic power. There has been no repeat of the May 1969 riots. Today, ethnicity is no longer the socio-economic class identifier that it once was, although many NEP regulations are still in force.

The NEP had a profound effect on the Chinese business community. Given the unequal distribution of wealth among Malaysia's ethnic groups, the Government

48 See Jesudason, J. V., *Ethnicity and the Economy: The State, Chinese Business, and Multinationals in Malaysia*, Oxford University Press, Singapore, 1989, pp. 131-33.

49 The DAP has claimed that one of the main problems in the New Villages has been uncertainty over land titles. This uncertainty has hampered the attempts of poorer Malaysian Chinese to use land as collateral.

50 See also Chapter 9 for the international links of Malaysia's Chinese, Chapter 11 for Malaysian Chinese investment in China, and Chapter 13 for Malaysian Chinese investment in Australia (investment which is largely centred on real estate).

51 The *bumiputeras* (literally, 'sons of the soil') are the indigenous Malaysians.

52 Another factor was a perception of growing Chinese political power, particularly after the 1960 elections when Chinese parties made significant gains.

clearly had an imperative to act in the interests of national cohesion.[53] To give Malays a greater stake in the economy, it introduced wide-ranging measures that had the character of 'affirmative action', in a commercial sense, in favour of Malays.[54] For example, in 1975, the Government introduced the Industrial Coordination Act (ICA) requiring every manufacturing firm with shareholders' funds in excess of M$250 000 or employing more than 25 full-time workers to apply for a manufacturing licence. The Act specified that firms covered must organise to further the 'national interest', which was subsequently defined by regulation, giving the responsible Minister enormous powers to regulate all aspects of firms' operations. Regulations thus imposed have included requiring respondent firms to put aside at least 30 per cent of their equity for Malay interests; requiring non-Malay firms to employ and train Malaysian citizens to reflect the multi-racial composition of the country's population in all grades of appointment up to managerial level; and requiring firms to adopt real measures over a reasonable period of time to use Malay distributors to the maximum extent possible, the minimum being 30 per cent of turnover.[55] The Government also introduced national targets for increasing corporate equity in the hands of *bumiputeras*. Over the NEP period (1970-90), *bumiputera* share in corporate stock was to increase from 1.5 per cent to 30 per cent. Non-Chinese were to hold 40 per cent, and foreigners, the remaining 30 per cent.[56]

Overall, Malaysia's Chinese business community complained bitterly about what it saw as NEP-promoted discrimination. In 1985, twenty-four Chinese federations, assembly halls and other associations endorsed a declaration by the Chinese Guilds and Associations of Malaysia calling for the repeal of the ICA and the abolition of the distinction between *bumiputera* and non-*bumiputera*.[57]

Not surprisingly, methods were devised to get around many of the NEP's more onerous stipulations. One common method was the previously mentioned 'ali-baba' arrangement, which involved the use of *bumiputera* fronts to act on behalf of Chinese interests. Other Chinese business people deliberately chose to keep their interests small or to split their interests into seemingly unconnected units to avoid coming within the purview of the ICA. Overall, however, such

53 The relative position of the *bumiputeras* at the time of the introduction of the NEP was very poor indeed. With few exceptions, the *bumiputeras* lived on small rural plots and were mostly involved in agricultural pursuits. In 1970 in terms of employment, the Chinese dominated almost all non-agricultural occupations. 72.1 per cent of construction workers, 66 per cent of mining and quarrying, 65.4 per cent of manufacturing and 65.3 per cent of commerce workers were Chinese. In terms of ownership, 75.6 per cent of retail trade, 55.0 per cent of wholesale trade and 70.6 per cent of haulage transport was controlled by Malaysia's Chinese. The banking sector was also dominated by the Chinese. Of the 16 local banks in 1970 all but one (which was state-owned) were in Chinese hands. The distribution of government contracts also favoured the Chinese, particularly those with MCA patronage. By 1970, 85 per cent of construction contracts worth in excess of M$100 000 went to Chinese firms, 11.6 per cent went to foreign firms and just 2.5 per cent to Malay firms.

54 The main aspects of the NEP are listed in Appendix 8.

55 See Jesudason, J. V., pp. 136-37.

56 These targets were met with some success. By 1990, the proportion of corporate equity (by par value) in *bumiputera* hands had grown to 20.3 per cent, and the Chinese share had increased from 22.8 percent to 44.9 per cent.

57 See Kua, K.S. (ed.), *Polarisation in Malaysia: The Root Causes*, K.Das Ink, Petaling Jaya, 1987, Appendix.

arrangements suited low technology and small operations, and were not readily available to larger enterprises. In any event, as a skilled Malay middle class gradually evolved under the auspices of the NEP, quotas and other pro-Malay arrangements became less onerous for the Chinese and the incentive to avoid them diminished.

Chinese Business Structures in Malaysia Today

Business mergers between Chinese and *bumiputeras* which were forced by the NEP now occur spontaneously; the Government's role as marriage broker is increasingly redundant. *Bumiputeras* and Chinese are getting together by choice, and mutual resentment is being replaced by mutual interest. As a result, now very few medium- to large-sized Malaysian firms are solely Chinese. Most have at least some *bumiputera* employees, equity, management and, occasionally, directors, and all listed companies must have *bumiputera* equity and directors. Many small Chinese firms also now include a prominent *bumiputera*, such as an ex-bureaucrat or politician, on their boards.

Most small- and medium-sized enterprises however are still Chinese-owned. Typically, they are family-owned. Most capital for these businesses comes from retained earnings, as they often face difficulties raising loans from banks due in some cases to their inadequate accounting systems. Most of these enterprises are involved in foundry, import-export, and plantations. Unlike in Indonesia, there are relatively few conglomerates in Malaysia. Larger Malaysian Chinese companies tend to concentrate on one or two core businesses.

Although most Malaysians have a good knowledge of English, Mandarin helps outsiders attempting to access the Chinese business community. In Kuala Lumpur, where Chinese of Cantonese background dominate the Chinese business community, Cantonese is helpful.

Decision-making in many of the larger Chinese-controlled groups still is largely the preserve of the founding patriarch. For example, the head of MUI Group, Khoo Kay Peng, is reputed to make most of the Group's decisions and he has no core of senior executives to take this role. Hong Leong (M) Group is reputed to have a good base of managers but major decisions are still reserved for the controlling family. This pattern is common among Malaysian Chinese businesses as with Chinese firms elsewhere.

The Growing Partnership Between Malaysia's Chinese Entrepreneurs and the Government

In the past, strong ties between Malaysia's Chinese business community and the Malay political leadership existed only at the apex of Malaysian society. This made the position of the Chinese vulnerable whenever the Malay leadership changed. Tan Siew Sin, former MCA President (1961-74), sensed this vulnerability and urged the Chinese community to forge closer links with the Malays, especially in business joint ventures.[58] In recent years, many senior ethnic Chinese business people appear to have heeded Tan's advice.

---

58 See Jesudason, J. V., p. 129. That Tan should have urged this is not surprising, particularly given his *baba* status.

Many of Malaysia's more prominent Chinese entrepreneurs tend to voice their concerns direct to senior UMNO figures, reducing the role of the MCA. As in many countries, 'know who' as well as 'know how' has become important in determining business success.[59] Many of Malaysia's new Chinese millionaires who emerged or became more prominent during the 1980s are personally acquainted with leading Malay and Chinese politicians.[60] Some of Malaysia's more established Chinese entrepreneurs also forged important alliances with senior Malay figures. Robert Kuok, for example, chose early on to support - actively and prominently - the Government's *bumiputera* advancement program. He became a founding director of Bank Bumiputera Malaysia which provided credit to ethnic Malays.

Malaysia's main parties have business interests which allow them to reduce their reliance on membership dues. Many Chinese business groups have invested in businesses associated with the MCA, but some also invested in UMNO-related interests. The Quek family is one example. In April 1989, the Quek-controlled Hong Leong Co (M) Bhd announced that its publicly-listed Hume Industries had won a M$500 million supplies contract from the UMNO-owned United Engineers (M) Bhd. Hong Leong then announced a rights issue for Hume Industries. The new shares were taken up by Jaguh Mutiara Bhd, giving it a large stake in Hume Industries. The following April, UMNO's main investment arm acquired Jaguh Mutiara.[61] In this way, Malay political and business interests merged with Chinese business interests[62].

Several ethnic Chinese entrepreneurs also bought formerly government-held assets as they were privatised. For example, Malaysia's lottery operation, Sports Toto, was controlled until 1985 by the Ministry of Finance, but was sold to interests associated with entrepreneur Datuk Vincent Tan Chee Yioun.[63] In 1993, the Government also awarded a consortium led by Vincent Tan the right to develop a M$6 billion national waste disposal project.

The Corporate Involvement of the MCA

Most major political parties in Malaysia are directly involved in business. UMNO was the first, thus ensuring it did not depend financially on the MCA. UMNO's corporate investments, together with Government's large *bumiputera* holding companies that acquired shares on behalf of the *bumiputeras*, led the MCA

59 See Jomo, K. S., 'Is Chinese capital in Malaysia 'progressive'?', Unpublished paper, 1994.

60 Mackie, J.A.C., 'The Ethnic Chinese Economy in Southeast Asia', paper presented to the International Conference on Southeast Asian Chinese Culture, Economy and Society, Singapore, 21-23 January 1994.

61 See Gomez, E. T., *Money Politics in the Barisan Nasional*, Forum, Kuala Lumpur, 1991, p. 8.

62 Close co-operation between the Government and the private sector or 'Malaysia Inc' is an important aspect of the Government's economic policy agenda. This approach is apparent in the range of government/private sector consultative mechanisms, including annual dialogue processes between business and the Ministries of Finance and International Trade and Industry, and meetings of the Malaysian Business Council in which key government and private sector interests are represented. It is also evident in the Government's emphasis on the role of the private sector in the development and management of public utilities as part of its privatisation masterplan.

63 See Gomez, E. T., *Money Politics in the Barisan Nasional*, p. 5.

leadership in the early 1980s to believe that the Chinese would need to form large business organisations if they were to compete effectively with government-controlled agencies and foreign corporations.[64]

Then MCA President Tan Koon Swan subsequently set about building an MCA-controlled, non-profit cooperative, Multi-Purpose Holdings Bhd (MPHB), and a subsidiary, Koperatitif Serbaguna (M) Bhd (KSM), into two of Malaysia's largest cooperatives. Membership of MPHB was open to MCA members only. MPHB initially performed well, and the MCA attracted many new members who simply wanted to access MPHB.[65]

The MCA's involvement in business ultimately proved disastrous. MPHB came close to bankruptcy in the mid 1980s, a result of fraud and mismanagement.[66] After the 1986 elections, the new MCA president, Ling Liong Sik, subsequently removed MPHB's five-seat board of directors and replaced them with non-politicians. The new board was chaired by prominent Malaysian businessman Robert Kuok. By mid 1988, Kuok was able to resign having restored MPHB to profitability.[67] The MCA now has largely divested itself of direct involvement in business, opting instead for portfolio investment.

The coverage of ethnically-based unit trusts is to be extended in Malaysia. Each Malaysian State is soon to introduce its own *bumiputera* unit trust. In response, the MCA may back corresponding Chinese unit trusts at the State level, or push for access to existing unit trusts for all low income people, not only *bumiputeras*. MCA-backed trusts are unlikely to mirror the MCA's corporate involvement of the 1980s; instead, they will be comparatively modest investment vehicles to shore up the position of lower-income Chinese.

Chinese Capital Raising in Malaysia

Banks have supplanted traditional sources for business capital within the Chinese community. Even small Chinese-owned businesses now raise money from financial institutions rather than from other members of the 'network'.[68] The exception appears in Penang, where many traditional Chinese business practices continue to flourish. In Penang, business still raises capital through the 'tontine' system, whereby a group of, say, twenty Chinese businesses in one area might contribute M$5 000 each to a pool of funds which one member each month either wins or buys the right to access at nominal rates of interest.

64 By 1990, UMNO-linked Renong Bhd had become the second largest conglomerate in Malaysia, second only to Sime Darby Bhd. (See Gomez, E. T., *Money Politics in the Barisan Nasional*, p. vii.)

65 At the time, cooperatives were a significant form of ethnic Chinese business in Malaysia. By the mid-1980s there were approximately 3 500 cooperatives of various types, of which 34 were deposit-taking and held deposits of almost M$4 billion. (See Gomez, E. T., *Money Politics in the Barisan Nasional*, pp. 50-51.)

66 See Gomez, E. T., *Money Politics in the Barisan Nasional*, pp. 5-6; and Gomez, E.T., *Political Business: Corporate Involvement of Malaysian Political Parties*, James Cook University of North Queensland, Townsville, 1994, p. 209.

67 See Gomez, E.T., *Political Business: Corporate Involvement of Malaysian Political Parties*, p. 209.

68 The smallest operators however, still must rely on retained earnings or occasionally the illegal money lenders operating in the New Villages.

Credit cooperatives once played an important role in the Chinese community. These are non-profit, deposit-taking institutions usually managed by a clan or some other form of Chinese association.[69] In 1986, the Government froze 24 deposit-taking cooperatives (DTCs). Around 588 000 mostly Chinese Malaysians had deposited collectively M$1.4 billion in them. Subsequent investigations found that apart from suffering from mismanagement and fraud, many of the cooperatives did not act as non-profit managers of deposits but acted as profit seekers and share speculators. Ten of the DTCs were taken over by other financial institutions at the urging of the Government. The episode damaged the reputation of the DTCs as financial institutions, and consequently, their importance has declined.[70]

Chinese-owned banks with a dialect-based clientele were once prominent, but now are largely a thing of the past. Only one bank, the Hock Hua Bank has a largely dialect-based customer base. It is still regarded as almost exclusively the preserve of the Fuzhou Hokkien community.[71] Until recently, the Kong Lee Bank (now the Pacific Bank) was a Cantonese bank, and the Penang-based Ban Hin Lee Bank was a Hokkien bank.

Increasingly, Malaysian Chinese have turned to the stock market to fund their rapid business expansion. In recent years, the Kuala Lumpur Stock Exchange has been one of the region's most buoyant.[72]

The Clans in Business

As in Singapore, Malaysia's clan associations hold significant real estate and consequently, are becoming increasingly wealthy. The push by the MCA for the conglomeration of Chinese business encouraged some of the associations and clans to form their own holding companies to pursue business opportunities. The Penang-based Khoo Kongsi, for example, currently is developing real estate outside Georgetown. One of the Kuala Lumpur Hakka associations set up a holding company, Kayin Holdings in 1980, to administer the association's investments in Malaysia. The Kuala Lumpur-based Federation of Hokkien Associations of Malaysia (see Box) owns a holding company, Hoklian Holdings (established in 1981), which administers the federation's property interests in Kuala Lumpur, Negri Sembilan and Malacca and has recently signed an agreement to build a hotel in China. The national association of Hainanese has also formed a holding company to invest in China's Hainan Province. Among the

69 Examples of clan- and dialect-based deposit taking cooperatives included the Koperasi Sepadu Bhd, which was started by the Eurasian and Hakka communities; and Koperasi Jasa Rakyat Bhd (Kojasa) which was formed by the youth movement of the Federation of Hokkien Associations of Malaysia. (See Gomez, E. T., *Money Politics in the Barisan Nasional*, p. 71, 74.)

70 See Gomez, E. T., *Money Politics in the Barisan Nasional*, pp. 50-64.

71 Non-Fuzhous are able to bank with the Hock Hua Bank but it is suspected that the Fuzhous get better terms when borrowing. It is centred in Sarawak and Sabah where there is a high concentration of Fuzhous, but it also has branches in Peninsular Malaysia, including in Kuala Lumpur.

72 Many larger Chinese family controlled companies have listed on the KLSE. A practice has been to list on the KLSE, achieve a huge premium and then 'stag' the shares down to a bare majority shareholding, leaving the controlling family with large realised capital gains although retaining majority control of the company.

dialect federations, the Cantonese Federation of Malaysia reputedly has the biggest investment portfolio. Some of the Chinese temple committees have substantial property holdings and many Chinese cemetery committees are also relatively wealthy.

Chinese Chambers of Commerce

Chinese chambers of commerce and similar organisations throughout Malaysia mostly are represented in the Associated Chinese Chambers of Commerce and Industry of Malaysia (ACCCIM), which is a first stop for those seeking business opportunities in Malaysia. Like many other Chinese chambers, clan and dialect associations, the chamber has significant business interests in property, credit and leasing; these are grouped under Unico Holdings Bhd.

An important regional chamber is the Kuala Lumpur and Selangor Chinese Chamber of Commerce and Industry. This chamber has 2 300 members, of which 65 are guilds. There are also corporate and individual members. The chamber is in turn a member of ACCCIM. It has a number of divisions dealing with welfare, industrial, commercial, financial and legal matters. In the past, the chamber focused on welfare issues, but with the Government introducing policies to promote the economic advancement of the *bumiputeras*, it has turned its attention to economics and business. Funding is from donations and subscriptions. The chamber has no other significant sources of income. Consequently, it is building new offices, several floors of which will be rented out to provide a more steady stream of income. The chamber is not organised along dialect lines and is steadfastly apolitical, although the MCA did at one stage unsuccessfully run candidates for the board. The chamber organises seminars and dinners and occasionally makes representations to Ministers.[73]

Modern Chinese Organisations

As the popularity of traditional Chinese organisations wanes, new structures take their place. In Kuala Lumpur, classmate and alumni associations are popular.

Increasingly, Malaysian-Chinese business people opt to join business organisations that are not Chinese, but are often dominated by an ethnic Chinese membership. Members of the Federation of Malaysian Manufacturers (FMM) are mostly Chinese, but some are Malay or foreign.[74] Another is the Master Builders Association Malaysia (MBAM), where 25 out of 27 office bearers and council members are ethnic Chinese.[75] While not dominated by Malaysian Chinese-controlled firms, the Malaysian International Chamber of Commerce and Industry (MICCI) has recently elected its first Malaysian Chinese president. Organisations like these operate like Chinese chambers of commerce, but their unrestricted membership enables the predominantly Chinese membership access to a wider network.

---

73 Another important regional chamber is the Penang Chinese Chamber of Commerce which functions in a similar fashion. Its secretariat is located in Penang's large Chinese Town Hall, to which all of Penang's Chinese associations belong.

74 See Jesudason, J. V., p. 139.

75 See Master Builders Association Malaysia, *Master Builders*, 2nd Quarter 1994.

The Federation of Hokkien Associations of Malaysia

The Federation of Hokkien Associations of Malaysia is one of Malaysia's pre-eminent dialect federations. It is the peak body of Hokkien associations in Malaysia and some of Malaysia's most prominent businessmen serve on its executive committee. They include Lim Goh Tong, head of the Genting Group, and Tiong Hiew King, controller of the Rimbunan Hijau timber and logging company. The late Loh Boon Siew, controller of the Boon Siew Group, was also a member.[76] The federation has 138 affiliated associations. Most of the members tend to be relatively traditional in outlook and Chinese-educated. Despite its Hokkien membership, the federation conducts its business in Mandarin because many Hokkien sub-dialects are mutually unintelligible.

The federation is active in business and formed Hoklian Holdings, its business arm, fourteen years ago. Apart from its Malaysian investments, the company recently agreed with Anxi sub-province in Fujian to build a hotel, and is considering other investments there. Anxi was chosen as it is the ancestral region of many federation senior executives.[77] The federation receives regular visits from Anxi business delegations.

In 1995, the federation will send delegations to visit Hokkien associations in the Philippines, Hong Kong, Macau and Taiwan, and in September 1994, it was represented at the inaugural World Hokkien Association meeting in Los Angeles. In 1996, it will host the Second Meeting of the World Hokkien Association.

MYANMAR (BURMA)

In Myanmar, like China, legal and other 'soft' infrastructures are still being developed, and good connections are essential for doing business.[78] The ethnic Chinese have social and business structures which operate well in the absence of sound legal and other structures; they have a propensity for developing international connections. They are therefore at their most competitive in countries such as Myanmar.[79] It is likely that as Myanmar opens to foreign

---

76 See The Federation of Hokkien Associations of Malaysia, *Handbook, 1993*, Kuala Lumpur, 1993.

77 Most of the Federations' general membership is not, however, ancestrally from Anxi. (Personal communication with the Federation.)

78 'Soft' infrastructures are those formal and informal rules which govern how markets work.

79 The personalised nature of doing business in Myanmar was emphasised in a recent interview with Set Maung, Financial Adviser to Myanmar's current Government, whose advice to prospective foreign investors concerned at difficulties in repatriating profits and other regulations was, 'If you come here and talk to us, you can get around everything.' (See *Asian Wall Street Journal*, 'The Asian Economist', 26 January, 1995.)

investment, the ethnic Chinese will thrive on their comparative advantage until conditions allow all investors to compete on an equal footing.

Myanmar's Chinese have been careful not just to network with each other but to forge relationships with senior government figures. Several senior business people in Yangon reported that having a good relationship with the Government was essential to doing business.[80] The golf course is a very important venue for business, as senior members of the government (and the military) are avid golfers. Like others seeking to do business in Myanmar, many ethnic Chinese businessmen have become keen golfers.[81]

Historical Background

Chinese emigrants arrived in Burma from Guangdong and Fujian in the Song (960-1279AD) and Ming (1368-1644AD) Dynasties. Few Chinese took up residence in Burma, however, until the Yuan (1271-1368AD) Dynasty when Chinese business activities expanded beyond seasonal visits. At the turn of the twentieth century, many came to Burma from Malaya; both countries had a common colonial administration at the time.[82] Many also came from China, some as emigrants in search of a better life and others as employees of the KMT Government to work on infrastructure development.

Demographics

Reliable estimates of the proportion of Myanmar's population who are of Chinese or largely Chinese descent are difficult to find, but estimates range up to 15-20 per cent.

Myanmar is divided into two parts so far as its ethnic Chinese are concerned: upper and lower Myanmar. The ethnic Chinese community of upper Myanmar is dominated by the Yunnanese, with significant numbers of Hokkien in Mandalay (Myanmar's second biggest city and something of a boom town) and a concentration of Hakka in the northern town of Lashio.[83] There is also the Kokang, an ethnic Chinese minority. The Kokang live along the Yunnanese border and speak Mandarin. Some of their leaders have been and still are prominent in the cross-border narcotics trade.

The ethnic Chinese community of lower Myanmar centres on Yangon and is dominated by the Hokkien (perhaps 60 per cent) and Cantonese (most of the remainder). These Cantonese largely have their ancestral origins in Taishan and therefore are relatively homogeneous. The Hokkien, on the other hand, are divided into sub-dialects, with Fuzhou being prominent.

80 To the extent that military officials are involved in business, it is indirect, as they are not allowed to serve as directors on company boards or to have direct business dealings.

81 One interviewee remarked that when he was engaged by a large Japanese company to be its representative in Yangon, he was actually paid overtime for the time he spent playing golf.

82 See Wu, Y.L. and C.H. Wu, p. 81.

83 One Mandalay-based Fuzhou Hokkien estimated on the basis of the membership of dialect associations that there are as many as 5 000 Fuzhous living in Mandalay.

Perhaps 20 per cent of Myanmar's ethnic Chinese live in Yangon, with another 20 per cent in the Shan States, and 13 per cent in each of the Bago and Ayeyarwady regions. Mandalay and Tenantharyi account for the rest.[84]

Social Position

Partly in response to the perceived threat of the Cultural Revolution, serious anti-Chinese rioting broke out in Burma during 1967. This resulted in substantial property damage to Chinese shop-houses and businesses. The Government responded by banning many of the traditional Chinese associations and Chinese schools.[85]

The ethnic Chinese in the north are not well assimilated, and most non-Chinese Burmese distinguish between them and the ethnic Chinese of the south. Indeed, the Chinese in the north are the object of considerable resentment among non-Chinese Burmese. This may be partly due to the conspicuous wealth of many northern ethnic Chinese; typically, non-Chinese Burmese in the north are much poorer. The wealth of the northern Chinese has grown rapidly in recent years because of the legal and illegal border trade with China. Chinese in the north, although not Myanmar citizens, often have Myanmar passports and National Registration Cards (NRCs), allegedly through bribing local officials. Many non-Chinese Burmese believe the northern ethnic Chinese, particularly the Yunnanese, are 'agents' for the PRC, a belief that was boosted when in early 1994, a large, new Chinese consulate was opened in Mandalay.

The growing wealth of the northern Chinese has allowed them to purchase large tracts of real estate in the northern cities and towns of Mandalay, Lashio and Thazi.[86] They also are acquiring land in the important tourist centre of Bagan (Pagan).

On the other hand, the ethnic Chinese of lower Myanmar tend to be relatively well integrated and assimilated into Myanmar society.[87] They usually can speak Burmese (some of the current generation speak only Burmese), have adopted Burmese names for use outside the ethnic Chinese community and Burmese dress, and like most Burmese, generally are Buddhist.[88]

....

84 See Wu, Y.L. and C.H. Wu, p. 81.

85 Chinese schools are still banned but many ethnic Chinese families engage private tutors to teach their children Chinese or send their children to Chinese schools in Singapore and elsewhere.

86 Central Mandalay suffered two devastating fires in 1981 and 1984. When many Burmese were unable to finance the rebuilding of their houses and shops, ethnic Chinese business people bought up the land in what has been described as 'the Chinese takeover of Mandalay.' Mandalay has become a thriving centre with modern homes, hotels, shops, and high rise buildings which are largely occupied by ethnic Chinese, and a series of new satellite towns on the outskirts which are occupied by other Burmese. (See Mya Maung, 'On the road to Mandalay', *Asian Survey*, May 1994. p. 455.)

87 Ne Win, who seized power in a coup in 1962 and ruled until 1988, is of part Hakka ancestry. (See Courtland, C., *Collins Illustrated Guide to Burma*, William Collins Sons & Co. Ltd, 1988, p. 42.)

88 Notwithstanding this, the non-Chinese Burmese differentiate between the Cantonese and the Hokkien, referring to the latter as the 'long sleeves' and the former as the 'short sleeves', apparent references to the ethnic dress traditionally worn by Cantonese and Hokkien women.

Assimilation of Chinese in Yangon seems to have reached a particularly high level. One (ethnic Chinese) interviewee remarked that he had on occasion concluded business deals with individuals in Yangon and only discovered later that they were also of ethnic Chinese origin. Several ethnic Chinese interviewees remarked that the Government did not differentiate between Burmese citizens of Chinese origin and other Burmese, or between their respective companies, in employment policies or purchasing requirements.

Traditional Ethnic Chinese Social Structures in Myanmar

Before 1967, six Chinese chambers of commerce operated in Burma, but after the racial unrest, all but one were closed. The remaining chamber, the Myanmar Chinese Chamber of Commerce (MCCC), founded in 1910, operates today with only *de facto* consent from the authorities. Despite its ambiguous legal status, the MCCC has an elected executive; holds annual meetings; and has property holdings. The Hokkien who operate small-to medium-sized family enterprises in timber product exports, rice, bean and legume trading, and cooking oil production, dominate it.

In Mandalay, no Chinese chamber operates, but dialect associations are very strong. These tend to operate as *de facto* Chinese chambers of commerce.[89]

Surname associations are still popular within Myanmar's Chinese community. They tend to focus on welfare and social activities. In Yangon, the two largest clans are the Hokkien Tans and the Lims. At one stage, guilds were common, but they were outlawed in 1967 and since then, have been replaced by several large, government-sponsored associations open to all Burmese regardless of ethnicity. The Yunnanese are reputedly the most clan conscious, although they are outnumbered by the Hokkien and the Cantonese in Yangon. There and in Mandalay, where Yunnanese are numerous, they have their own associations.

Commercial Role

Historically, the Hokkien were the dominant business force among the Chinese in Yangon, particularly the Fuzhou Hokkien. Yangon's Cantonese community traditionally was involved in the small-scale manufacturing of handicrafts and similar products.

After 1962 when Ne Win came to power, Burma embraced socialism, and private factories and commercial establishments were nationalised. Chinese economic activity was seriously curtailed. For those who chose not to emigrate, opportunities were limited to some service industries, small cottage industries or the black market, which burgeoned.[90]

---

89 Mandalay also has some very large Chinese restaurants which have recently been opened atop some of the taller office buildings. These provide important venues for ethnic Chinese business gatherings.

90 See Wu, Y.L. and C.H. Wu, pp. 82-83.

Today, Myanmar's ethnic Chinese are at the forefront of the opening up of the country's economy.[91] Much of the foreign investment now entering Myanmar is channelled through ethnic Chinese networks.[92] In the north, ethnic Chinese, including groups prominent in the Shan State and eastern border regions since 1949, are becoming a dominant economic force in Mandalay and other significant commercial centres in upper Burma.

Yangon's 'Daily Commercial News'

The production of a daily newsletter attests to the current vibrancy of Yangon's ethnic Chinese business community. It contains the prices for the day's trading in the main commodities traded in Yangon - items such as cooking oil and rice. Several interviewees in Yangon reported that a group of businessmen who meet early each morning near the Shwedagon Pagoda fix prices, and then publish them in the newsletter which is hand delivered to subscribers. This acts as the community's financial newspaper.

Members of Myanmar's ethnic Chinese business community often act as agents (or fronts) for ethnic Chinese investors outside Myanmar. This role, explored further in Chapter 9, is played by ethnic Chinese both in the north and south, but for different clientele.

THE PHILIPPINES

Legal and other 'soft' infrastructures are also still being developed in the Philippines, so connections are particularly important in business. In such an environment, ethnic Chinese business people have been particularly successful.

History

Almost all Filipino Chinese have their ancestral origins in Fujian, a result of the Philippines' close proximity to Fujian and Taiwan, and the steady flow from these areas to the Philippines. The massacres of Chinese in the Philippines in 1662, 1663, 1686 and 1762 did not deter the flow.[93] Immigration from China to the Philippines continues and illegal Chinese immigrants pose a major policy problem for the Philippines Government.

---

91 Some ethnic Chinese business people had a head start in taking advantage of Myanmar's more open economy because their past involvement in the narcotics, timber and gemstones trade allowed them the capital to branch out into formal sectors. It also meant early access to international distribution networks.

92 Chapter 9 discusses, in part, the role of ethnic Chinese in Myanmar's international trade and investment.

93 See Wu, Y.L. and C.H. Wu, p. 73.

Demographics

The ethnic Chinese community is one of the most economically influential groups in the Philippines today. It is prosperous in business, well assimilated, has strong community and clan associations, and tends to be concentrated in the metropolitan areas.

The community of about 1.2 million (or about two per cent of the total population) controls between 50 and 60 per cent of share capital by market capitalisation.[94] Also about 35 per cent of sales in the Philippines can be attributed to firms controlled by ethnic Chinese.[95] Approximately ten per cent of the Filipino Chinese community was born outside the Philippines (China, Taiwan or Hong Kong) and approximately 85 per cent are ancestrally Hokkien. Around 50 per cent live in metropolitan Manila and the rest are concentrated in Cebu, Iloilo and Davao City. Of those in Manila, about half live in Manila's Chinatown district which encompasses the areas of Binondo, Tondo, Santa Cruz and Quiapo. Most of the poorer Chinese live in the Chinatowns.[96]

Position in Society

Chinese Filipinos are relatively well integrated into national life, although there is still some residual resentment towards them. They have adopted some local customs. Thus, on the day that the strongly Catholic ethnic Filipinos celebrate All Saints Day (1 November), Manila's ethnic Chinese community takes the opportunity to visit Manila's Chinese Cemetery to pay homage to its ancestors.

Intermarriage between ethnic Chinese and ethnic Filipinos is widespread. Some leading business families have ethnic Chinese ancestors, although are not normally considered as ethnic Chinese. An example is the Cojuangco family - whose name is a Filipino version of a Chinese name - a prominent member of which is former President Corazon Aquino. Two other examples of prominent business families with Filipinised Chinese names are the Sycip and Gokongwei families. The Archbishop of Manila, Cardinal Sin, is also of largely ethnic Chinese ancestry.

Citizenship is an important issue for the ethnic Chinese community. Before the Marcos Presidency, it was extremely difficult for Chinese Filipinos, even those born in the country, to obtain citizenship. President Marcos, in preparing to normalise relations with China in 1975, issued a decree in 1974 enabling Chinese Filipinos to take out citizenship.

---

94 Control by market capitalisation has been determined after listed firms controlled by governments or foreigners are discounted. (See Yamaguchi, M.; and Dobbs-Higginson, M.S., *Asia Pacific: Its role in the New World Order*, William Heinemann Australia, Port Melbourne, 1993, p. 160.) The Chinese population in the Philippines is smaller than what it would otherwise be, because the American Administration restricted Chinese immigration to prevent the Chinese from using the Philippines as a gateway to the United States. (For this, see Kunio, Y., *The Rise of Ersatz Capitalism in South-East Asia*, Oxford University Press, Singapore, 1988, p. 55.) There are, however, many more Filipinos with part-Chinese heritage.

95 The study also found that 34 per cent of sales were attributable to foreign-owned firms, and 31 per cent to firms owned by ethnic Filipinos. (See Redding, G.S., 1990, p. 28.)

96 Mackie, J.A.C., 'The Ethnic Chinese Economy in Southeast Asia'.

Most Chinese Filipinos took out citizenship before the 1975 deadline. However, when Corazon Aquino came to power, there were around nine thousand unresolved applications for citizenship.

Traditional Ethnic Chinese Social Structures in the Philippines

Since Spanish times, ethnic Chinese in the Philippines have had a strong structure of community associations. The first were family and clan associations which served as mutual help societies to protect the social and economic interests of members. Towards the end of the nineteenth century, an increased sense of Chinese cultural identity resulted in the establishment of Chinese schools. One of the first, the Anglo-Chinese school, was established in 1899. Earlier in 1888, the first Chinese newspaper was established.

In the nineteenth and twentieth centuries, Chinese trade associations proliferated. The Filipino Chinese General Chamber of Commerce (FCGCC) was formed in 1902 and the Federation of Filipino Chinese Chambers of Commerce (FFCCC) was set up in 1954. Both organisations promoted the economic interests of the community, although the FFCCC became prominent because it campaigned against planned retail nationalisation laws and other similar measures. The FCGCC joined the FFCCC in 1978, but separated from it in 1991.

These two organisations remain the Philippines' most powerful Chinese community associations. Although the FFCCC generally is regarded as more politically influential, the FCGCC has considerable business interests, including the Philippine Chinese Charitable Association, the Chinese General Hospital and the Chinese Cemetery. It is considered more liberal and has stronger links (through trade and investment) to China. The FFCCC, on the other hand, generally is regarded as representing the 'older generation' conservative Chinese elite. In recent times, there has been considerable rivalry between the two organisations.

Although surname, hometown, school and fire prevention associations remain prominent, their influence and popularity among ethnic Chinese are declining.

Commercial Role

The Regulation and Diversification of Chinese Commercial Interests

Throughout the Spanish and American periods, the ethnic Chinese prospered in wholesale and retail trade. During the 1950s, however, they began to move into other areas of economic activity, particularly after the enactment of the Retail Trade Nationalisation law in 1954. This act required non-Philippine citizens with retail trade businesses to liquidate their assets, either within ten years or upon the death of the owner of the business, whichever came first. The law affected more than 80 per cent of ethnic Chinese-owned businesses. The passage of similar laws nationalising the rice and corn trades during this period also adversely affected the ethnic Chinese business community.

Paradoxically, and in line with the experience of ethnic Chinese communities elsewhere in South-East Asia, the impact of this essentially anti-Chinese legislation was to strengthen the economic base of the community. Since obtaining Philippine citizenship was difficult, many Chinese moved out of the retail sector into areas such as manufacturing and textiles. As a result, the Chinese business community was at the forefront of post-war Philippine industrialisation.

Table 3.3

Philippine Banks in Which Ethnic Chinese Have a Controlling Interest

BANK	MAIN EQUITY HOLDER
Metro Bank	George Ty
Rizal Commercial Banking Corporation	Alfonso Yuchengco
Equitable Bank	Peter Go Pailian
Allied Banking Corporation	Lucio Tan
China Banking Corporation	Gilbert and Peter Dee
Security Bank and Trust	WT Lee
PB Com	Ralph Nubla
Philippine Trust	Emilio T Yap
Philippine Banking Corporation	Domingo Lee
Producers Bank	Co Bun Chun

Source: Ch'ng, D., *The Overseas Chinese Entrepreneurs in East Asia: Background, Business Practices and International Networks*, CEDA Monograph M100, 1993, p. 34.

In a further move against the Chinese influence in the economy, the Government enacted the Republic Act No. 3018 of 1960, stipulating that all alien-operated businesses in the retail and wholesale trade, cultivation, and transportation sectors were to cease operating within two years, and mills and warehouses within three years. The Chinese channelled the liquefied funds from these businesses into foreign trade, manufacturing and banking. In 1956, there were only four Chinese-controlled banks in the Philippines; by 1971, there were nine; and by 1974, there were sixteen. In 1991, Filipino Chinese had majority shareholdings in ten out of 26 private commercial banks.[97] These banks are listed in Table 3.3.

The Commercial Interests of the Filipino Chinese Today

Apart from banking, ethnic Chinese interests also dominate in coconut products (coconut oil, in particular), food processing (for example, bakery products and

97 See Ch'ng, D., *The Overseas Chinese Entrepreneurs in East Asia: Background, Business Practices and International Networks*, CEDA Monograph M100, 1993, p. 33.

seasoning), tobacco, textiles (especially hosiery and knitting), plastics, footwear, glass and some metal products (such as tubes and pipes, wire rods, nails and bolts, and containers). The ethnic Chinese also have significant interests in wholesale and merchandise trade, especially exporting, and control the major department store chains.

Filipino Chinese who are members of the Philippine economic elite include Lucio Tan, John Gokongwei, Andrew Gotianum, Henry Sy, George Ty, and Alfonso Yuchengco.[98]

Increasingly, senior Filipino Chinese business interests are asserting themselves over established local Spanish-descent Filipino interests. In 1995, a consortium of Filipino and other Chinese bid successfully for the right to develop a huge tract of land adjacent to Manila's Makati business district. The consortium, which bid an unprecedented US$1.6 billion, is headed by the Metro Pacific Corporation which is ultimately controlled by the Sino-Indonesian, Liem Sioe Liong. Other members included companies controlled by Malaysian Chinese Robert Kuok, and Filipino Chinese Andrew Gotianum, Henry Sy, George Ty and Lucio Tan.[99]

Filipino Ethnic Chinese and Politics

Traditionally, the Filipino Chinese community has maintained a relatively low political profile. This is partly due to its preference for business rather than politics, and partly due to the fear of persecution from anti-Chinese elements. In elections, the Chinese have tended to hedge their bets by supporting several candidates in the one race.

A few ethnic Chinese became very wealthy during the Marcos years, benefiting from close links with the Marcos administration. Lucio Tan was the most prominent of these. Another was Jose Campos. Six or more very successful Chinese entrepreneurs have emerged since the Marcos period.

In recent years, the Filipino Chinese community has needed to deal with a spate of kidnappings for ransom. Since 1991, there have been over two hundred such kidnappings, several of which resulted in the deaths of those kidnapped.[100] In metropolitan Manila, at least seventeen kidnap gangs operate; two are the Red Scorpion Group and the Omar Ring. Some of the organisations behind these groups have their roots in Hong Kong or Taiwan. Some in the Chinese Filipino community are concerned that the relevant authorities have not treated the kidnappings with the urgency they feel is warranted.

98 The interests of the six encompass tobacco companies, airlines, banking, breweries, department store chains, insurance companies, travel companies and export-import. This group of businessmen was recently persuaded by President Ramos to invest a total of P600 million (US$21.9 million) in a consortium to undertake infrastructure projects in the Philippines. The move was prompted by concerns of heavy Filipino Chinese investment into China at the expense of the Philippines. The main project the consortium will embark on is the modernisation of Manila's Ninoy Aquino International Airport. Other possible projects are the construction of a road linking Manila and the Subic Bay free port, an alternative international airport at the former Clark Air Base, and the construction of a 1,200 megawatt coal-fired power station in Pangasinan.

99 See *Asian Wall Street Journal*, 'Metro Pacific Group pays $1.6 billion for Manila site', 9 January 1995.

100 See *Far Eastern Economic Review*, 'Victims of success', 8 December 1994.

SINGAPORE

Demographics

The Chinese account for 77 per cent of Singapore's 2.7 million population and are estimated to control 81 per cent of Singapore's listed companies by market capitalisation.[101] Over 40 per cent of Singapore's Chinese have their ancestral roots in Fujian Province and 40 per cent in Guangdong Province.[102] In terms of dialect, 40 per cent are ancestrally Hokkien speakers; 18 per cent are Cantonese; 23 per cent are Teochiu; 9 per cent are Hakka; 7 per cent are Hainanese; and the remainder are an assortment of other dialects.[103] In terms of language abilities, around 20 per cent of Singaporean Chinese speak English as their preferred language. These tend to be the political, bureaucratic and professional elite. A further 65 per cent speak English adequately, but prefer to speak in Mandarin or some other dialect. The remaining 15 per cent cannot speak English or speak it only poorly.[104]

Notwithstanding this ethnic diversity, the Hokkien followed by the Teochiu dominate business. Most of the senior office bearers in the Singapore Chinese Chamber of Commerce and Industry (SCCCI) tend to be either Hokkien or Teochiu.

Unlike in other South-East Asian countries, the Chinese are the overwhelming majority in Singapore. They and their country are prosperous and secure. These conditions create the values and culture of Singapore's Chinese which increasingly diverge from those of ethnic Chinese elsewhere in South-East Asia.[105]

The government sector plays a very significant role in encouraging, directing and cajoling the private sector. A range of so-called 'government-linked' companies often play an important role in leading the way, particularly in foreign investment. Private sector firms find they can prosper more if they can enter into partnerships with these companies, as it gives them access to government-sponsored projects, particularly in China.

Singapore as a Modern State with Baba Influences

Some aspects of how Singapore is structured today and how it relates to China have their genesis in the outlook of the Straits Chinese, the *baba* and *nonya* community, of Singapore at Independence.

....

101 See Far Eastern Economic Review, *All Asia Travel Guide*, 16th edition, Review Publishing Co. Ltd, Hong Kong, 1993, p. 107; and Yamaguchi, M. Control by market capitalisation has been determined after listed firms controlled by governments or foreigners are discounted.

102 Ch'ng, D., p. 38.

103 This data is based on a survey undertaken in 1963, the results of which are found in Wu, Y.L. and C.H. Wu, p. 135, and data obtained in Yamaguchi, M. While only 40 per cent of Singaporean Chinese can claim a Hokkien heritage, it is likely that many more can speak it. Before Mandarin usage became widespread in Singapore, Hokkien was the *lingua franca* of the Chinese community.

104 Personal communication with Associate Professor Choi Kwai Keong, Chinese Language and Research Centre, National University of Singapore.

105 Redding, G.S., p. 35.

Many Malacca *babas* migrated to Singapore, where they continued their eclectic Chinese/Malay/English lifestyle. From the London-educated *baba* elite came Singapore's first politicians. Lee Kuan Yew, whose mother was a *nonya*, was the country's first and longest serving prime minister. This group also included Lim Kim San, an early cabinet minister, and Goh Keng Swee, a finance minister and ultimately a first deputy prime minister.[106] Along with the British during the colonial period, they shaped the institutions that have made Singapore what it is today.

These men regarded traditional Chinese ways as outdated and superfluous to the task of modern nation building. Rather, they set about building on the institutional legacy left by the British, further displacing traditional Chinese structures with a British-style public administration, albeit with some local characteristics. Thus, the role of the Chinese chambers of commerce in Singapore has been taken over to a degree by the Government's Economic Development Board (EDB) and Trade Development Board (TDB). Similarly, government-linked banks such as the Development Bank of Singapore (DBS) replaced the clans as providers of business capital. Clan social functions are no longer important venues where young people can meet; instead, the Government's Social Development Unit has attempted to fill this role. Indeed, traditional clan associations have largely been supplanted by the various government boards or by the governing People's Action Party (PAP). Senior positions in either of these bring kudos; senior positions in clan associations do not.

In a similar fashion, the Government moved to phase out education in Chinese and promote education in English. This was done to check Communist influence among students of Chinese and promote integration into Singapore's multiracial society. At the same time, it signalled to Singapore's neighbours a readiness to identify with the South-East Asian region rather than with China. English education, however, did not dominate completely until the 1980s. Today, most literate Singaporeans aged over forty were educated in Chinese, and regard English-educated Singaporeans as quite different from themselves. This tendency is particularly notable in graduates from Singapore's privately-founded Nanyang University, the only Chinese language university in the region. The university switched to English in the 1970s and was subsequently subsumed into other educational institutions, but its graduates still form a cohesive subset in Singapore society. As Nanyang degrees initially were not recognised and later not greatly valued by the Government, many graduates advanced in the private sector rather than the public service.

Over time, these non-traditional institutions - party and government-run associations and English educational institutions - have tended to diminish the traditional Chinese cultural affiliations of Singapore's Chinese population, despite the vast majority coming from traditional Chinese rather than *baba* backgrounds.

....

106 Goh Keng Swee's cousin was Tan Siew Sin.

Singapore today can be seen as a modern state with some *baba* characteristics, in the sense that it is the English educated, with their *baba* antecedents, who dominated the running and shaping of Singapore's institutions during the years after Independence. This has had a significant impact on how Singaporeans relate to other Chinese communities in Asia, and invest in China, aspects of which will be discussed in chapter 11.

Traditional Chinese Institutions in Singapore

For those Chinese pursuing traditional lifestyles, clan and dialect were, until recently, quite important. Singapore's Chinese community is relatively heterogeneous, being differentiated primarily by dialects. Mutual unintelligibility of dialects and strong locality consciousness resulted in 'strong xenophobia' within each dialect group. The end result was a dialect-structured society, characterised until recently by dialect groups concentrated in specific neighbourhoods in the city area and trade specialisations.[107]

Traditional Associations

Traditional associations in Singapore are organised along four main lines. First, are those based on kinship and identified by a surname. Second, are those defined by area of origin in China. Third, are those which perpetuate a dialect, and, fourth, are those based on occupations or crafts reminiscent of the guilds of traditional China.[108]

Around 200 surname associations cover 96 surnames. These function to provide mutual help, bursaries, loans, and scholarships for the children of members.[109]

In recent years, clan and dialect associations have been losing favour among Singapore's Chinese; some associations now exist in name only. Many clan strongholds have been broken up with the process of urban renewal and their replacement by Housing Development Board high-rise housing complexes. Also the initial rationale for many clan associations has declined with the growing affluence of Singapore and the cessation of migration from China.

....

107 Suryadinata, L., 'The Xinghua community in Singapore: A study of the socio-economic adjustment of a minority group', in Suryadinata, L., (ed.), *Chinese Adaption and Diversity: Essays on Society and Literature in Indonesia, Malaysia and Singapore*, Singapore University Press, Singapore, 1993, p. 28.

108 Redding, G.S., p. 56.

109 See Cheng, L.K., 'Reflections on the Changing Roles of Chinese Clan Associations in Singapore', *Asian Culture*, April 1990.

In 1986, the Singapore Federation of Chinese Clan Associations (SFCCA) was formed in a move designed partly to resuscitate the flagging fortunes of the clans. The federation focuses on cultural events, leaving the SCCCI to concentrate on business and economic matters.[110]

Structurally, the SFCCA is made up of 146 institution members. The SFCCA has seven founder members representing seven dialect groups.[111]

Of late, interest in clan associations is reviving. Many of these associations hold valuable real estate and on the strength of this, are re-energising. The Ngee Ann Kongsi was founded last century by twelve families who paid $175 for 75 acres of land alongside which now runs Singapore's Orchard Road, a major shopping and tourist precinct.[112] The Kongsi recently built the Ngee Ann City complex, one of Singapore's newest and largest shopping centres on its land in a joint venture with Japan's Takashimaya. Future net revenues from the project probably will be used to fund schools and other charitable works of the clan.

Clans are re-energising by developing their ancestral areas of China. Several Singapore-based clan associations have formed holding companies through which clansmen can invest in China using their ancestral links. This phenomenon is explored further in Chapter 11.

Singapore Chinese Chamber of Commerce and Industry (SCCCI)

Perhaps the most significant traditional Chinese organisation in Singapore today is the Singapore Chinese Chamber of Commerce and Industry (SCCCI), which was founded in 1906.[113] Until recently, the structure of the chamber was based on seven dialect-based *bangs* representing six dialect groups.[114] The *bang*-based structure was abolished at the chamber's annual meeting in August 1993. The Hokkien dominate the SCCCI today, although there was a time when it was the Teochiu.[115]

....

110 The objects of the SFCCA are as follows:

(a) To promote, foster and encourage better and closer relationship, coordination, cooperation and understanding among the various Chinese Clan Associations in Singapore;

(b) To promote, organise, or finance educational, cultural, social and other activities for greater awareness, understanding and appreciation of the Chinese language, culture and traditions;

(c) To encourage, finance or undertake research related to the Chinese language, culture and traditions;

(d) To promote better relationships, understanding and cooperation between the Federation and other organisations in the public and private sectors;

(e) To organise, participate, or help in comminuting and welfare services;

(f) To promote and protect the interests and welfare of the members; and

(g) To do all such other things as are incidental or conducive to the above objects or any of them.

See Cheng, L.K., 'Reflections on the Changing Roles of Chinese Clan Associations in Singapore', *Asian Culture*, April 1990.

111 See Cheng, L.K., 1990.

112 See Kraar, L., 'The wealth and power of the Overseas Chinese', *Fortune*, March 1971.

113 See SCCCI, *Singapore Chinese Chamber of Commerce and Industry: Directory of Members of the 47th Council*, March 1993 - March 1995, Singapore, 1993.

114 See Cheng, L.K., p. 59.

115 In 1941, the Teochiu head of the Overseas Union Bank, Lien Ying Chow, was elected the Chamber's president, for example. (See Kraar, L.)

The chamber currently has around 5 190 members.[116] Members must be Singapore registered companies of Chinese origin. Membership is not open to individuals or to those who are largely non-Chinese.[117] Non-Chinese cannot become associate members. Of the chamber's 117 trade association members, the most prominent are in textiles, garments, real estate and timber processing.

The chamber operates a library and a small, but active research team. One of the most important functions of the chamber, however, is to organise delegations for business missions abroad, and to receive visiting delegations. During 1993, the chamber received 231 overseas delegations, most from China.[118] The chamber also holds regular seminars for its members on diverse topics such as trade and investment opportunities in the various countries of the region, real estate laws in China and political risk insurance.[119]

The SCCCI maintains good relations with most Chinese chambers in the region, especially those of Kuala Lumpur, Bangkok, Hong Kong and Brunei.

THAILAND

History

The Chinese have a long presence in Thailand: in 1660, approximately 10 000 Chinese lived there and by 1855, they were almost 200 000, or roughly two-thirds of the total population of Bangkok.[120] Significant numbers of Hokkien Chinese arrived in the early to mid nineteenth century.[121] They are still concentrated in the southern provinces of Thailand, and traditionally have dominated the rubber, spice and tin sectors there. Subsequent waves were dominated by the Teochiu, who lived by the coast and were expert sailors, traders and fishermen. Their migration from China, like that of other Chinese, was initially forbidden by the Qing emperors, but when it was discovered that Thailand could be an abundant source of rice and commodities, the policy changed and the junk trade between Thailand and China was encouraged.[122] Frequent natural disasters, famine and epidemics soon turned these trade flows to immigration flows. The final wave accompanied the communist takeover of mainland China in 1949. Many of the families who already had a presence in Thailand emigrated and settled permanently.

....

116 See SCCCI, *Singapore Chinese Chamber of Commerce and Industry: Directory of Members of the 47th Council.*

117 There are some individuals who are members, but these joined prior to 1968 when individuals were able to join. Subsequent to the rule change, they were allowed to keep their membership status, but no new individual memberships were granted.

118 See SCCCI, *Singapore Chinese Chamber of Commerce and Industry Annual Report '93*, Singapore, 1994, p. 4.

119 See SCCCI, *Singapore Chinese Chamber of Commerce and Industry Annual Report '93*, p. 33.

120 Hafner, J.A., 'Market gardening in Thailand: The origins of an ethnic Chinese monopoly', in L.Y.C. Lim and L.A.P. Gosling (eds), Vol. 1, p. 36.

121 Like the Teochiu, the Hokkien did have a presence in Thailand long before this, however.

122 See Chantavanich, S., 'From Gonsi to Business Corporatism: Socio-Cultural and Political Conditions of Ethnic Chinese Big Business Families' Success', a paper presented to the Fifth International Conference on Thai Studies, School of Oriental and African Studies, London, 1993.

Demographics

It is difficult to estimate the number of Chinese in Thailand due to their high degree of assimilation and decades of intermarriage with ethnic Thais. Ten per cent is most commonly used, although it is difficult to verify and could well be a serious under-estimate. On the basis of ten per cent, there are approximately 5.8 million Sino-Thais. Around 56 per cent are of Teochiu origin. The next largest group is the Hakka, followed by the Hokkien and the Cantonese.[123] There is also a significant Yunnanese Chinese community, particularly in the northern provinces. As in other South-East Asian countries, the Chinese in Thailand are based in the larger towns, and particularly in Bangkok.

The Sino-Thai community has played an important role developing Thailand's private sector. Indeed, it is estimated to control 81 per cent of listed companies by market capitalisation.[124] As in other South-East Asian countries, the role and influence of the Chinese has been particularly important in the post World War II era. The Sino-Thai community is, or has been active, in virtually all sectors, including agriculture (rubber, sugar, maize, vegetables, but rarely rice), manufacturing, banking and finance, construction and real estate, and retail and wholesale trading.[125]

Social Position

An important feature of ethnic Chinese in Thailand, compared with the Chinese of other South-East Asian societies, is the extent of their assimilation. Many senior Thai military officials and politicians are now either ethnic Chinese or have a mixed Thai-Chinese heritage.[126] As intermarriage is common, there is considerable blurring between those who are ethnically Thai and those who are ethnically Chinese, particularly in Bangkok. Assimilation is not, however, complete; Chamlong Srimuang, popular former governor of Bangkok, former leader of the Palang Dharma Party and former deputy prime minister, faced a smear campaign in Thailand's general elections in 1992 over his 'Chineseness'. Although some underlying tension exists, particularly in rural areas, racially-motivated violence against ethnic Chinese in Thailand is virtually unheard of.[127]

The high degree of acceptance of Sino-Thais in Thai society is partly due to the exploits of the half-Chinese Phaya Taksin (Chao Teh Sin). Taksin was instrumental in reuniting Thailand after the Burmese invaded in 1767, and in founding the new Thai capital of Thonburi directly across the Chaophaya River

---

123 See Yamaguchi, M.

124 See Yamaguchi, M. Control by market capitalisation has been determined after listed firms controlled by governments or foreigners are discounted.

125 Mackie, J.A.C., 'The Ethnic Chinese Economy in Southeast Asia'.

126 Among these is Chuan Leekpai, Prime Minister from 1992 to 1995, whose father's ancestors originated in China's Fujian Province. Chuan is from Thailand's south, where Thailand's Hokkien Chinese are concentrated. Until recently, there have been barriers against Chinese entering the senior levels of the military. Chinese were prevented from entering Chulachomklao Military Academy until the 1970s, although thereafter, discrimination was on a *de facto* basis.

127 See *Sydney Morning Herald*, 'Hidden side of the resurgent dragon', 28 April 1993.

from Bangkok.[128] Taksin subsequently had himself crowned king. Taksin's exploits led to the Teochiu being known as the 'Royal Chinese' in the Thonburi period.[129]

In the earlier part of this century, Thai rulers made a concerted effort to avert serious anti-Chinese sentiment. In 1907, King Rama V proclaimed that he regarded the Chinese not as foreigners but as part of his country and thus entitled to share in the fruits of the country's prosperity. Rama VI initiated nationalist programs, but these focussed on assimilation rather than discrimination policies. Thus a law was passed in 1918 requiring all students in private schools to be taught in the Thai language and instructed in Thai history and geography. Furthermore, non-ethnic Thais born in Thailand were eligible for Thai citizenship.

In the mid twentieth century, the Thai Government tried to promote Thai entrepreneurship, partly to counter the paramount commercial position of the Chinese. By then, however, Sino-Thais so dominated financial and trading institutions that ethnic Thais found it difficult to launch commercial or industrial ventures. This in part spurred on the development of state enterprises, such as the Electricity Generating Authority of Thailand, under the control of ethnic Thai bureaucrats.

In the post war era of nationalist ruler Phibunsongkhraam, the development of a Thai national identity took on a more strident tone. Ethnic Chinese were encouraged to adopt Thai citizenship and Thai names, and attend Thai schools and universities, through the use of an annual Alien Registration Tax. Access to the public service (including the military) was restricted for those with Chinese names. Chinese language newspapers and instruction were banned. Only in the early 1970s could Chinese retailers once again use Chinese characters on shop hoardings.

In spite of these policies, Thailand has generally led the way amongst South-East Asian countries in fostering a culture of tolerance towards the ethnic Chinese. The period 1973-76 saw a resurgence of democracy in Thailand. Concern at perceived connections Sino-Thais might have with communist China declined. This change in the domestic political scene contributed to the switching of ethnic Chinese policy from one of restriction and control to one of assimilation in 1973.[130]

Over the years, the Sino-Thai community has worked assiduously to develop its ties with ethnic Thais, particularly in Bangkok social circles and with the extended royal family. A strong feature in Bangkok social life has been the intermarriage between ethnic Thai and Chinese families (business acumen, hard work and money complementing status, position and land).[131]

The ethnic Chinese community has worked to forge ties with ethnic Thais through Sino-Thai welfare organisations. The Huachiew Foundation is the largest Chinese welfare foundation in Bangkok. It is fully funded by wealthy Sino-

128 See Wu, Y.L. and C.H. Wu, p. 136.

129 See Chantavanich, S.

130 See Ch'ng, D., p. 31.

131 A recent example was the marriage of the eldest son of the Chirathivat family (which controls the Central Group) to the Queen's niece.

Thai business people and operates schools, hospitals and the recently opened Huachiew Chalermprakiet University, all of which are open to all Thais regardless of ethnicity. This sets the foundation and similar bodies in Thailand apart from most other equivalent organisations in other parts of South-East Asia.

Integration Through Good Works

The Huachiew Foundation offers a corpse collection service. Prior to this service, no organisation was charged with collecting the bodies of the deceased from accidents and the like in Bangkok - an omission possibly derived from ethnic Thais' profound superstition regarding death. The foundation fills this gap by collecting the bodies of all Thais, regardless of their ethnicity, and thus performs a very valuable social service.

The relative acculturation of the Sino-Thais has been a factor in their assimilation.[132] Most share the same religion (Buddhism) and are prepared to learn the Thai language. Thai monks often bless new Chinese enterprises, and photographs showing the clan patriarch or matriarch prostrate before members of the Thai Royal Family are prominently and proudly displayed in many Sino-Thai offices.[133] The current issue of the Thai Chinese Chamber of Commerce's directory shows 16 of the 51 senior office holders and executive committee members not in business suits but in formal Thai dress complete with royal awards and honours.[134]

Over time, popular Thai perceptions of the ethnic Chinese have developed to the point where it is now acceptable for Thais to claim Chinese ancestry.

Involvement in Politics

For much of this century, Sino-Thais have bolstered up their dominant position in industry and commerce by cultivating high level government and military connections. As civilian government becomes more accepted and permanent, the need to include a senior military figure on company boards will diminish, but the appointment of at least one well-connected figure will continue to be a sensible practice. Members of the extended Thai Royal Family, senior politicians and military officers, and elite technocrats often fulfil this role.

As the political process has become more central to decision making, Sino-Thai business people have acted more directly in party politics. Nowadays, Thais of either part- or full-Chinese heritage form most of the Thai Parliament. The leaders of all the major political parties have either a part- or full-Chinese

....

132 The acculturation has worked both ways - some ethnic Thai businesses are increasingly using the principles of *feng shui* alongside their own beliefs to design their buildings and shops.

133 See Sender, H., 'Inside the overseas Chinese network', *Institutional Investor*, August 1991, p. 32.

134 See Thai-Chinese Chamber of Commerce, *14th Board Executive Committee 1994-1995 of Thai-Chinese Chamber of Commerce, Bangkok, Thailand,* Bangkok, 1994.

heritage.[135] Apart from Chuan Leekpai, other recent Thai prime ministers with a Sino-Thai background include Chatichai Choonhavan, Kukrit Pramoj, and Anand Panyarachun. An informal grouping of Sino-Thai opposition politicians (the Group of 16) also has emerged recently.

Most of the major political parties receive much of their backing from major Sino-Thai controlled conglomerates. Several prominent Sino-Thai business families have subsequently groomed individuals from within their ranks to play a role in government. Former Deputy Prime Minister Amnuay Viravan, for example, was a former executive chairman of the Bangkok Bank, owned by the Sophonpanich family. Another former deputy prime minister, Boonchu Rojanasatien, was also formerly of Bangkok Bank. The Srifeungfung family has, in the past, been well connected to the Chart Thai political party as well as to various political leaders.[136] The former Minister for Transport and Communications, Vichit Suraphongchai, is a former president of Bangkok Bank.

Business organisations also influence public decision making. The more powerful of the Sino-Thai organisations and business families tend to represent the ethnic Chinese community to the Thai elite. Two examples of these bodies are the Thai-Chinese Chamber of Commerce and the Group of 55, an informal grouping of influential business people. In addition, those business bodies not specific to the Chinese community (such as the Federation of Thai Industries) are invariably dominated by Sino-Thai business people.

The Role of Clans in Thailand

While Thai is now the first, if not the only, language of many of the new generation of Sino-Thais, several interviewees in Bangkok remarked that there was still a fair degree of 'clan consciousness', particularly when it came to special clan celebrations and funerals.

The various clan associations in Bangkok operate schools, hospitals and temples. Once important as sources of capital, they largely were supplanted in this function by the development of a fully-fledged conventional banking system in Thailand. They continue to provide start-up capital to members where bank finance is unavailable and assist members when their small businesses experience liquidity problems.

Unlike clans in Singapore and Malaysia, Bangkok-based clan associations do not form holding companies to pursue clan-based investment in ancestral areas in China. Nevertheless, clan business is still big business. The clans are major property holders in Bangkok, as are the Chinese-operated schools. They usually operate on a non-profit basis, or any profits tend to be re-invested, further adding to the clan's wealth.[137]

....

135 For example: Chuan Leekpai (Democrat Party), Amnuay Viravan (Nam Thai Party), Chavalit Yongchaiyudh (New Aspiration Party), Chatichai Choonavan (Chart Pattana Party) and Banharn Silpa-archa (Chart Thai Party).

136 See Chantavanich, S.

137 People also donate their time to clan temples and schools, thereby cutting costs and further adding to these institutions' wealth.

The Thai-Chinese Chamber of Commerce (TCCC)

The TCCC was founded in Bangkok in 1909. It is not structured along dialect lines. Indeed, the chamber accepts members of any ethnicity. The only requirements are that members be Thai residents and have domestic business interests. All positions are open to any member, but it is commonly believed that the president is always reserved for a Teochiu.[138] The chamber has only ever had one non-Teochiu president. The current president, Dr Boonsong Srifeungfung, is a prominent billionaire businessman and patriarch of one of Bangkok's major Sino-Thai business families.

Currently 48 business associations or guilds belong to the chamber as well as individual and corporate members. Given the multi-dialect nature of the chamber, business generally is conducted in Mandarin.

Historically, the TCCC had a close relationship with China; this continues today. For some of the period when Thailand and China did not have diplomatic relations, the chamber operated as a *de facto* consulate for China. Today, the chamber maintains a 'close' relationship with the Chinese Embassy in Bangkok.[139] The chamber receives visiting business delegations, including hundreds each year from China. In a single morning in 1994, the chamber received ten separate delegations from China.[140]

It is not clear what the future will hold for the TCCC. At present, it is a very active organisation with many members. However, as the Chinese become further assimilated, it will be difficult to determine who is Chinese and who is not.[141] One businessman in Bangkok commented at interview that the TCCC was really 'for the older generation' and young Sino-Thai business people were more attracted to the Thai Chamber of Commerce. This is probably so, but clearly the TCCC is still an important venue for business.

Commercial Role

The Thai economy is unique in South-East Asia because no class of indigenous big business entrepreneurs exists.[142] Even smaller businesses in Bangkok, especially in retailing, are mostly owned and operated by Sino-Thais. Also the original founding families dominate the private sector, both owning and operating most major enterprises.

In large Sino-Thai controlled companies, control passes to the children of the family business founder. Daughters, as well as sons, often hold very senior and visible positions in industry and commerce. Furthermore, the eldest child may not be the heir to whom control passes. Among the current generation of the five

....

138 The Teochiu of Bangkok are not particularly exclusive, but several interviewees in Bangkok mentioned that there are two positions in Bangkok that the Teochiu always try to hold. They are the Presidency of the Chamber and the Chairmanship of the Huachiew Foundation.

139 Personal communication with Dr Boonsong Srifeungfung, President of the Chamber.

140 Personal communication with Dr Boonsong Srifeungfung.

141 This probably is the main reason why the Chamber accepts members of any ethnicity - discriminating between ethnic Thais and Chinese is in many instances impossible.

142 Mackie, J.A.C., 'The Ethnic Chinese Economy in Southeast Asia'.

major Sino-Thai business families, the second sons of the Wang-lee, Sophonpanich and Chearavanont families head or headed their respective family businesses.[143]

The big Sino-Thai business groups have grown, forming companies encompassing new areas of business but allowing the founding family to continue to retain ultimate control. Invariably these companies overlap and often compete with one another, reflecting sometimes complex and shifting intra-family politics.

Many of the big Chinese families in Bangkok have grown large from providing services such as banking. Many started in the international rice trade which largely operated on credit. The quadrangle trade consisted of rice flows between Bangkok, China, Singapore and Hong Kong. The rice flows generated credit flows; the credit was tapped in four countries. With credit being such a significant part of the trade, many families found it easy and logical to start a bank. Once the banks grew, the families diversified into transport and other areas. This is the way most of Thailand's big conglomerates were formed. Many also branched out into property, a fortuitous move given recent rapidly-inflating Bangkok property prices.[144]

The big four private banks in Thailand (Bangkok Bank, Thai Farmers Bank, Bank of Ayudha and the Bangkok Commercial Bank) are Sino-Thai family concerns.[145] They also control significant commercial, manufacturing and property investments.[146]

The five key families in Thailand's business community are Teochiu with ancestral origins in Shantou, China. They are the:[147]

- Wang-lee or Chen family from the Chenghai District, near Shantou
- Sophonpanich or Chen family from the Chaoyang District
- Tejaphaibul or Zheng family from the Chaoyang District
- Srifeungfung or Zheng family from Fengsun District
- Chearavanont or Xie family from the Chenghai District.

All five families have children in key positions in the family business, although professional managers also ensure modernisation.[148]

If anything, the trend for large businesses to be family controlled is increasing. One study found that in 1979, among the top private, listed companies in Thailand (most of which were Sino-Thai controlled and owned), 33 per cent had top stockholders that were either members of the same family, individuals or

....

143 See Chantavanich, S.. Suvit Wang-lee was a second son who rose to head the Wang-lee family's business interests, but he died in a plane crash in Thailand in mid 1994.

144 See Sender, H., p. 40.

145 As, indeed, are most other privately-owned banks.

146 Mackie, J.A.C., 'The Ethnic Chinese Economy in Southeast Asia'.

147 See Chantavanich, S. One other prominent Bangkok Chinese family is the Lamsam family, whose assets include the Thai Farmers Bank. The Lamsams are unusual for a prominent Sino-Thai business family in that they are ancestrally Hakka.

148 See Chantavanich, S.

companies affiliated with the same family, or a corporation directly owned by the same family. By 1988, this figure had risen to 45 per cent. The study concluded that very few CEOs in large Thai-owned corporations were appointed only on the basis of their specialised managerial skills; generally, they had some family connection.[149]

Sino-Thai Business in the 1990s

The biggest challenge Sino-Thai business families faced in recent years was increased international competition. Sino-Thai families traditionally were reluctant to relinquish ownership and management of their companies though many depended on foreign loan capital and technology. This characteristic made it difficult for all but the most prominent families to raise funds for offshore expansion, which normally would be achieved by way of public listing. Generally, the larger Sino-Thai family conglomerates have listed some of their assets, but currently, the preferred way to raise capital is by way of loans or offshore bond issue taking advantage of the current high, real differential between domestic and international interest rates.[150]

Inefficient corporate structures gradually are being remodelled, although some families have resisted this. Some Sino-Thai business families tend to hold on to corporate assets long after the optimal time. However, such attitudes are beginning to change.[151]

VIETNAM

History

The Cantonese dominate the Sino-Vietnamese community. The first significant wave of Chinese into Vietnam occurred as long ago as the third century BC when the first Chinese emperor of the Qin dynasty conquered the area which forms northern Vietnam today. During the subsequent ten centuries of Chinese colonisation, Vietnam received enormous numbers of Chinese migrants, which continued until the middle of the twentieth century. Between 1923 and 1951, as many as 1.2 million Chinese emigrated from China to Vietnam.[152]

Demographics

At least 54 ethnic minority groups account for 13 per cent of Vietnam's population. The ethnic Chinese, known as the *Hoa*, constitute the third largest group, making up 12 per cent of the minority population, or around one million

....

149 See Suehiro, A., 'Family business reassessed: Corporate structure and late-starting industrialization in Thailand', *The Developing Economies*, December 1994.

150 Some of the companies that have been partially floated in recent years have been members of the Charoen Phokphand Group, Saha-Union, the Dusit Thani Group, and Unicord.

151 Chapter 7 includes further discussion on the attempts by large Sino-Thai business concerns to modernise.

152 See Tran Khanh, *The Ethnic Chinese and Economic Development in Vietnam*, Institute of Southeast Asian Studies, Singapore, 1993, pp. 14, 22.

out of a total population of approximately 72 million. Most ethnic Chinese live in the south, particularly in the metropolitan area of Ho Chi Minh City, and less than one per cent live in the north.[153]

The ethnic Chinese have had a disproportionate impact on the Vietnamese economy. The enforced socialisation of the South's economy following the communist victory effectively curtailed much of this influence; however, the commercial role of the ethnic Chinese community in Ho Chi Minh City has quickly rebounded since *doi moi* (economic renovation), though not to the same level as before 1975.[154]

There are two loose groupings of *Hoa* in Vietnam: the increasingly prosperous and commercially-oriented Chinese community in Ho Chi Minh City; and the population scattered over other major centres. Political change and events since 1975 have affected the distribution and relative concentrations of the *Hoa*. Table 3.4, derived from data obtained during the 1989 census, shows the five territories with the greatest concentrations of ethnic Chinese.

The major concentration of ethnic Chinese is in Ho Chi Minh City's inner district of Cholon. This group is traditionally heavily business oriented. Before 1975, the *Hoa* operated a virtually autonomous social system including hospitals, schools and business, centred on Cholon. In recent years, the Government has allowed the Chinese in Cholon to re-establish some of these institutions, though in a more controlled form than previously.

Although most Vietnamese Chinese are fluent in Vietnamese, they can be divided according to their ancestral dialects, as Table 3.5 shows.

Apart from the main dialect groups, several other ethnic Chinese groups reside in Vietnam. They are the Ngai, Sandiu and the Tudi who are culturally similar to the people of China's neighbouring Guangxi Province.[155] These groups do not have the commercial significance of other ethnic Chinese groups.

Another group of ethnic Chinese, the Minh Huong like the *peranakan* of Indonesia and the *babas* of Singapore and Malaysia, have ancestors who migrated from China as early as the seventeenth century. Over time, they have become acculturated. Many are of mixed heritage and rather than belong to either or both groups,they form a category of their own.

---

153 The 1989 census found the number of individuals who identified themselves as ethnic Chinese to be 960 000. Also, see Wu, Y.L. and C.H. Wu, p. 132.

154 One study concluded, for example, that during the decade 1965-1975, the proportion of commercial and industrial activity in South Vietnam controlled by the ethnic Chinese was 70-80 per cent and yet at that time, they accounted for less than 10 per cent of the population. (See Barton C.A., 'Trust and credit: Some observations regarding business strategies of overseas Chinese traders in South Vietnam' in L.Y.C Lim and L.A.P. Gosling (eds), Vol. 1, p. 48.)

155 See Tran Khanh, pp. 30-31.

Table 3.4

Areas of Vietnam in which the Ethnic Chinese are Most Concentrated

TERRITORY	CHINESE POPULATION	PER CENT OF CHINESE POPULATION	PER CENT OF TOTAL POPULATION
Ho Chi Minh City	524 000	54.4	13.3
Dong Nai	85 000	8.8	4.2
Hau Giang	102 000	10.6	3.8
Song Be	32 000	3.3	3.4
Minh Hai	40 000	4.2	2.5

Source: Tran Khanh, *The Ethnic Chinese and Economic Development in Vietnam*, Institute of Southeast Asian Studies, Singapore, 1993, p. 26.

Table 3.5

Dialect Distribution in Southern Vietnam, 1989

(Percentage of the Chinese Population)

CANTONESE	TEOCHIU	HOKKIEN	HAINANESE	HAKKA
56.5	34.0	6.0	2.0	1.5

Source: Tran Khanh, *The Ethnic Chinese and Economic Development in Vietnam*, Institute of Southeast Asian Studies, Singapore, 1993, p. 31.

Position in Society

Vietnamese history, language, religion, culture and social and administrative structures owe much to more than two thousand years of contact with China, including almost one thousand years of Chinese political domination. In these circumstances, the *Hoa* should have assimilated easily and naturally with mainstream Vietnamese society. On the contrary, the *Hoa* continue to form a distinct community in Vietnam. At the same time, some *Hoa* have merged with the majority ethnic Vietnamese (or *Kinh* as they refer to themselves) through intermarriage or other means. Nevertheless, even relatively assimilated *Hoa* are often discernible, for example by certain elements in the Vietnamese names they have adopted.

During the fifteenth century, the Dai Viet rulers sought to enforce an assimilation policy on Chinese living in Vietnam. This included forcing the Chinese to adopt Vietnamese dress. However, by the seventeenth century, a critical mass of ethnic Chinese in Vietnam allowed Chinatowns to sprout in or alongside almost every big city or town. It was at this time that the Chinese also began to congregate on the basis of their dialect groups. Chinese chambers of commerce also emerged to regulate business activity.[156]

The authorities further attempted to assimilate the ethnic Chinese community. In 1956, President Ngo Dinh Diem of South Vietnam declared all ethnic Chinese born in Vietnam to be Vietnamese citizens. All other Chinese were aliens and needed to apply for residential permits which had to be renewed periodically. Subsequently, another decree was issued which required all Vietnamese citizens to adopt Vietnamese names within six months or pay a heavy fine. One further decree listed eleven trades which aliens could not engage in; at that time, all eleven were heavily dominated by ethnic Chinese. Aliens plying those trades had six months to liquidate or transfer their businesses to Vietnamese citizens.[157] These new laws did not generally operate too punitively against the Chinese community. Many simply became Vietnamese citizens or passed their businesses to sons or daughters who were born in Vietnam. The message to the ethnic Chinese, however, was clear. The Government wanted them to assimilate as quickly as possible. There was further evidence of this in the Diem regime's banning of dialect associations in 1960. Notwithstanding this, the ethnic Chinese maintained their traditional social structures at least until the communist victory in 1975.

After May 1975, the activities of the dialect associations and the Chinese Chamber of Commerce were prohibited and their assets transferred to the state.[158]

Traditional Ethnic Chinese Structures

As with ethnic Chinese communities elsewhere in South-East Asia, dialect and occupation are closely associated. The Cantonese handled most rice trade in Vietnam as well as the manufacture of metal household goods. The Hokkien specialised in trading, import-export, ship building and ocean shipping, intermediary business, hotels and restaurants, and the manufacture of rubber products. They also owned most large enterprises and were the second most commercially powerful dialect group. The Teochius were the second largest dialect group, but the third most powerful economically. They specialised in rice trading and handicrafts but were not as advanced in these areas as the Cantonese. Most Teochiu worked as labourers, porters, and tradesmen. The Hakka specialised in handicrafts. The Hainanese were mostly fishermen and plantation workers.[159]

More formal, traditional ethnic Chinese organisations were based on one or several of the following characteristics: dialect group, surname, business type, recreational interests, religion and charitable functions. From the late nineteenth century, each dialect group had its own financial investment organisations,

---

156 See Tran Khanh, p. 16.

157 See Tran Khanh, pp. 28-29.

158 See Tran Khanh, p. 36.

159 See Tran Khanh, pp. 30-31.

conducted its own commerce, regulated the business dealings of its members, and funded schools, clinics, religious houses and recreation clubs.[160]

The Chinese After 1975

In 1974, the Government of North Vietnam estimated that the ethnic Chinese in South Vietnam controlled more than 80 per cent of the food, textile, chemical, metallurgical, engineering and electric industries; held virtual monopolies in the wholesale and import-export trades; and controlled over 50 per cent of retail trade. They also owned 42 of the 60 biggest companies.[161]

Shortly after the communist victory in 1975, many senior South Vietnamese Chinese business people were arrested as 'comprador bourgeoisie'.[162] New restrictions were placed on the ability of ethnic Chinese to acquire Vietnamese nationality and on their participation in certain business sectors.[163]

The Government's 'socialist transformation' campaign of 1978-79 stopped much of the independent business and social activity of the *Hoa* community and virtually all businesses closed down. This coincided with the worsening of Vietnam's relations with China and the rising suspicion of the *Hoa* as 'fifth columnists', and culminated in the Chinese border incursion of 1979, in response to the Vietnamese invasion of Cambodia. The subsequent exodus depleted dramatically Vietnam's ethnic Chinese population.

Beginning in 1978, around 230 000 ethnic Chinese left Vietnam for China and another 220 000 left for South-East Asia by boat. From a population of 1 236 000 in 1976, the ethnic Chinese population had shrunk to 935 000 by 1979. By 1989, it had increased slightly to 961 702 but as a proportion of the overall population, it had fallen to 1.5 per cent.[164]

Although the new regime attempted to control the economy, there was still a lively, though contracted commercial sector. One reason for this was the corrupt and badly managed state sector. Also, over time, the new regime nationalised the external trade sector, which diverted ethnic Chinese capital into manufacturing, in joint ventures with local governments or state enterprises.[165] Thus, while conditions in Vietnam after 1975 were bad for ethnic Chinese business people, some options remained possible.

---

160 See Tran Khanh, p. 34.

161 See Ch'ng, D., p. 35. An example of one of the more successful South Vietnamese ethnic Chinese at the time of the collapse of the Republic of Vietnam, was Ly Long Than. Ly controlled 23 different enterprises, including enterprises such as Vietnatexco and Vinafilco textile factories, Vinatefinco cloth dyeing and printing mill, Viunica and Vicasa steel factories, Nakydaco edible oil factory, Rang Dong sea transport, Saigon-Singapore shipping companies, Lubico biscuits and sweets factory, a real estate company, the Thien Hong hotel and restaurant, Nam Do Bank, and Trung Nam Bank. (See Tran Khanh, p. 80.)

162 Of those so deemed, 117 out of 159, or around 70 per cent were ethnic Chinese. (See Tran Khanh, p. 81.)

163 See Dobbs-Higginson, M.S., *Asia Pacific: Its role in the New World Order*, William Heinemann Australia, Port Melbourne, 1993, p. 163.

164 See Tran Khanh, p. 25.

165 See Tran Khanh, p. 88.

The Chinese Under Doi Moi

Since the early 1980s, the Government has gradually reintegrated the *Hoa* into mainstream economic development. By 1982, the Vietnamese Communist Party had issued a directive acknowledging that their policies had operated unduly harshly on the *Hoa*, and that the group should no longer be treated as reactionaries. However, it was not until the introduction of *doi moi* in 1986 that the Chinese were actively encouraged to take part in economic development. In the 1990s, their influence is again substantial. The Chinese business community takes full advantage of the *doi moi* reform process, which aims to increase living standards and establish strong business links with regional neighbours.

With the promulgation of private business laws in 1989 and company laws in 1990, the number of private sector businesses has expanded. At the end of 1992, there were 420 private enterprises registered in Ho Chi Minh City alone, of which 200 businesses or 45 per cent were ethnic Chinese-owned. These included several large enterprises such as the Viet-Hoa Construction Company, Minh Phung Garment Factory, Chien Thang Agricultural Processing Company, Viet Huong Instant Noodle Processing Company, Thang Loi Machine Rice Mills Factory and Son Hoa Plastics Enterprise.[166] Vietnam's largest producer and exporter of footwear, the Binh Tien Imex Corporation, a large, private sector company also is controlled by a Sino-Vietnamese businessman, Vuu Khai Thanh. The company's expansion has been partially funded by Taiwanese investors. Thanh's brothers and sisters, who left Vietnam as 'boat people' during the late 1970s, intend opening representative offices for the company in New York and Los Angeles.[167] Enterprises such as these, using international Chinese-Vietnamese networks, are likely to become increasingly common.[168]

Since 1992, private banks have been allowed to set up in Vietnam. By February 1993, ten private domestic banks operated and now there are many more. Several of these have ethnic Chinese shareholders and attract an ethnic Chinese clientele. The Viet-Hoa Bank, for example, started in December 1992 by 53 shareholders, most of whom are ethnic Chinese, is one of Cholon's largest business groups. About 60 per cent of the bank's customers are ethnic Chinese. Before 1975, there were eleven private, domestic banks with ethnic Chinese shareholders, so there is potential for expansion.[169]

Vietnam's ethnic Chinese business community is resurging. Over 700 goldsmith shops have opened in Ho Chi Minh City since private trading in gold was permitted in early 1989, and the new five-storey US$5 million An Dong shopping centre in Cholon was funded by a group of local Chinese business people.[170]

Despite all this activity, Vietnam's ethnic Chinese are still cautious. Mindful of the 1978 crackdown, they prefer to invest in medium-sized, rather than large

166 See Tran Khanh, p. 94.

167 See *Far Eastern Economic Review*, 'Giant steps', 8 July 1993.

168 Chapter 9 examines the trade and investment international links of the Sino-Vietnamese.

169 See *Far Eastern Economic Review*, 'Do it yourself', 31 March 1994; and Tran Khanh, p. 91.

170 See Tran Khanh, pp. 90-91.

projects. Further confidence was instilled by the National Assembly's approval in 1994 of a law on domestic investment.[171]

ETHNIC CHINESE IN OTHER SELECTED COUNTRIES

South Korea

Over the centuries, Korea maintained a close relationship with China and the Chinese influenced markedly Korea's culture and politics. Korea nevertheless maintained its independence and identity. Following the Korean war, the Chinese community suffered from official discrimination. Many Chinese left South Korea, mainly for North America. Approximately 20 000 ethnic Chinese currently reside in South Korea; 90 per cent of these are ancestrally from China's Shandong Province. South Korea's ethnic Chinese face a range of discriminatory measures, though as aliens rather than as Chinese *per se*. As a result, they are not well assimilated into Korean society. Korea's ethnic Chinese are not significant in the commercial sector, although they run about 1 000 restaurants.[172] They maintain close links with Taiwan. Indeed, almost all hold Taiwanese passports and about 75 per cent of those who undertake higher education outside of South Korea do so in Taiwan.[173]

Canada

The Canadian Government's 1991 census found that 5.1 per cent of Canada's population are of Asian origin. A growing proportion of these are ethnic Chinese. Of the 231 000 new migrants arriving in Canada in 1991, 8.9 per cent were born in China and 7.1 per cent came from Hong Kong. Hong Kong has since become Canada's most significant source of immigrants.[174]

Canada's large ethnic Chinese community is concentrated in its west, particularly in Vancouver and Toronto. The spending power of the community is around Can$1.4 billion annually. The prominence of the Vancouver community is also attested to by three daily Chinese newspapers.[175]

The rapid expansion of Canadian Chinese commercial influence in Vancouver has caused some concern in the wider community. Chinese investment is criticised for being largely in existing real estate and not in areas likely to lead to new and broader trading links with Asia. Furthermore, Vancouver's Chinese community is generally not involved in mainstream Canadian business activities

171 See *Far Eastern Economic Review*, 'Do it yourself', 31 March 1994.

172 See Tseng, Y.L., 'Survival of the persistent', *Free China Review*, July 1989.

173 See Chang, C., 'Aliens in their adopted land', *Free China Review*, July 1989.

174 See *British Columbia Business*, 'Two Solitudes', April 1994.

175 The size of Vancouver's Chinese communities warrants Hong Kong Cantonese pop stars making the trip out from Hong Kong for performances. In November 1993, Hong Kong singer Jackie Cheung gave two sold out performances in Vancouver for which tickets were priced up to Can$128 each. (See *British Columbia Business*, 'Two Solitudes'.)

through, for example, membership of local chambers of commerce. Instead it maintains its own Chinese business associations.[176]

Canadian Steps Towards Better Using its Ethnic Chinese Community

Canada is well placed to take advantage of the potential its large and affluent Chinese community provides for opening doors in Asia. Until recently, however, there was no program to facilitate the interlinkages between the Chinese and non-Chinese business communities in Canada.

However, the Asia Pacific Foundation of Canada has held five roundtables across Canada bringing together Asian and non-Asian Canadian business people to examine ways in which Asian Canadians could provide Canada with a greater competitive advantage in the Asia Pacific region. The results of the roundtables were then distilled into a report released at the end of 1994. The study concluded that there was a clear limit as to what the Government could do to encourage the two groups to mix. Nonetheless, the roundtables generated a series of recommendations.[177] Among them were:

- An annual roundtable could be convened at either a provincial or national level to highlight trade and investment opportunities in the Asia Pacific region and to feature Asian Canadian firms that had used their links to the region to increase their business with the region. The event would be organised by business for business.
- Asian Centres could be established to offer business-related information to newly-arriving Asian Canadians and to match their opportunities, interests, contacts and skills with the needs of local businesses.
- Small- and medium-sized enterprises should be encouraged to explore opportunities for developing strategic alliances in Asian markets. This would allow them to bid on larger contracts requiring a broader range of services. Asian Canadian businesses may make ideal partners given their linguistic and cultural familiarity with the region.

It is not clear yet which of the report's recommendations will be pursued. Meanwhile the Canadian Government has undertaken several other steps to better integrate the Asian and non-Asian business communities. One is to compile a directory of ethnic business contacts. The Department of Canadian Heritage directory lists Canada's ethnic business associations and other useful business contact points for linking up with the ethnic business community.[178] Another important step is the Chretien Government's appointment of Raymond Chan, an ethnic Chinese, as Secretary of State for Asia Pacific. Chan has made a

---

176 Some people have blamed the emergence of seemingly mutually exclusive Chinese and non-Chinese economies in Vancouver on Federal multicultural policies. See *British Columbia Business*, 'Two Solitudes'.

177 See Asia Pacific Foundation of Canada, *Asian Canadians: Canada's Hidden Advantage*, 1994.

178 See The Federal Department of Multiculturalism and Citizenship Canada, *Multiculturalism means Business 1993: A Directory of Business Contacts*, Minister of Supply and Services Canada, 1993. The Federal Department of Multiculturalism and Citizenship Canada has been renamed the Department of Canadian Heritage.

number of high profile visits to the Asian region seeking greater trade and investment links, and has unofficially visited Taiwan. Several other senior political figures at both federal and state levels have led large trade missions to China and Hong Kong.

India

India's ethnic Chinese community is not significant either in numbers or commercial influence and faces perpetual uncertainty given the rivalry between India and China. During the Sino-Indian conflict in 1962, for example, several thousand Indian Chinese were interned, deported and deprived of their citizenship.[179] There are some pockets of ethnic Chinese commercial influence. One is the 8 000 to 10 000 mostly Hakka Chinese who live in Calcutta (out of a total population of around ten million). This small minority dominates the city's leather industry, owning and operating around 300 tanneries.[180] There are also Shanghainese and Cantonese, and some of Calcutta's Chinese came from Burma in the 1960s. In addition to tanneries, the Chinese are prominent in restaurants and dry cleaning. [181]

Papua New Guinea

Papua New Guinea's ethnic Chinese population is fewer than 3 000, or less than 0.2 per cent of the total population. Nonetheless, ethnic Chinese have been prominent in PNG's commercial sector, typically owning shops and operating as traders. The father of current Prime Minister, Sir Julius Chan, was a prominent PNG Chinese merchant and plantation owner.[182] A former speaker of the House of Assembly, Perry Kwan, was also part-Chinese. Most of PNG's ethnic Chinese live in either Port Moresby, Lae or Rabaul. Approximately 90 per cent are Cantonese (the next largest group is the Hakka); most are locally born; and a large proportion are Christian.[183]

United States

California has roughly one million Chinese residents, representing the largest Chinese community outside Asia.[184] The Los Angeles Chinese community is dominated by the Taiwanese and that of San Francisco is dominated by the Taishan Cantonese. The Chinese were first attracted to the United States in large numbers by the Californian gold rush which preceded Australia's. Subsequent liberal immigration laws saw the Chinese population steadily rise, until it

....

179 See Basu, E.O., 'Profit, Loss and Fate: The Entrepreneurial Ethic and the Practice of Gambling in an Overseas Chinese Community', *Modern China*, Vol. 17, No. 2, April 1991, p. 234.

180 See Basu, E.O.

181 *Asiaweek*, 'Calcutta's fading Chinese enclave', 22 June 1978.

182 See Pan, L., *Sons of the Yellow Emperor: The Story of the Overseas Chinese*, Mandarin, 1991, p. 75.

183 See Wu, David Y.H., *The Chinese in Papua New Guinea: 1880-1980*, The Chinese University Press, Hong Kong, 1982.

184 Viviano, F., 'Pacific Giants: The Overseas Chinese', *San Francisco Chronicle*, 27 May 1987, in Kotkin, J., *Tribes*, Random House, New York, 1993, p. 168.

experienced another dramatic surge post 1949, in the wake of the nationalists' defeat in China by the communists.

US Steps Towards Better Using its Ethnic Chinese Community

As in Canada, the Chinese and non-Chinese business communities in the United States are not well integrated. To a large degree, the Chinese business community is self reliant and has little need to form strong links with non-Chinese business. A significant proportion of the Chinese business community is of Taiwanese origin and is heavily involved in direct trade and investment between the United States and Taiwan.

Despite the sizeable Chinese community in the United States, the Federal Administration does not currently have any programs or activities to facilitate linkages between the Chinese and non-Chinese business communities. The US Department of Commerce does, however, maintain a listing of ethnic Chinese business organisations that operate in the United States, which it makes available to non-Chinese American business seeking to link up with local Chinese partners.

Japan

The first significant group of ethnic Chinese immigrants to Japan arrived shortly before World War II, when emigrants from China's Guangdong and Fujian Provinces and Shanghai settled in Nagasaki, Kobe and Yohohama, looking for business opportunities. After the war, another group arrived, fleeing communist repression at home. Now more than 110 000 ethnic Chinese live in Japan. Japan's Chinese do not play a significant commercial role in Japan. About one third are involved in many of the estimated 6 000 Chinese restaurants scattered across Japan and a small number are involved in trade between Japan and China.[185]

In the January 1995 Kobe earthquake, much of the Kobe Chinatown was destroyed and there were significant numbers of casualties among its inhabitants.

Former USSR

There are many ethnic Chinese minorities in the former USSR, particularly in those republics that adjoin China. Of the 17 million people in Kazakhstan, almost 500 000 are ethnically Chinese.[186]

Pacific and Indian Ocean Island States

Most island countries in the Pacific and Indian Oceans have significant Chinese communities. Fiji, for example, has a largely Cantonese Chinese community, Mauritius has a Chinese community of about 40 000 which is dominated by the Hakka, and Tahiti has a significant Chinese community, 85 per cent of which is Hakka. These communities generally are prominent in retail sectors.

---

185 See Chong, C., 'Making it in Japan', *Free China Review*, July 1989.

186 See Far Eastern Economic Review, *All Asia Travel Guide*, 16th edition, Review Publishing Co. Ltd, Hong Kong, 1993, p. 166.

Chapter 4

HONG KONG, MACAU AND TAIWAN

The Chinese of Hong Kong and Taiwan are qualitatively different from the Chinese of China or South-East Asia, particularly in their business practices. Consequently, they cannot be considered as overseas Chinese or as mainland Chinese. They form a category of their own. Their business methods are quite different to those of the Chinese in China, particularly given the very different rules and institutions under which the Hong Kong and Taiwan business communities have developed. Yet, the Hong Kong and Taiwan Chinese remain very China-focused and most of their investment abroad goes into China.

HONG KONG

Demographics

Hong Kong grew dramatically after the 1949 communist victory in China. In 1945, Hong Kong's population was around 600 000 but by 1951, it was over two million.[1] By 1956, it was 2.6 million.[2] Today, Hong Kong has a population of around 6.3 million, around 98 per cent of whom are ethnic Chinese.

Most of Hong Kong's Chinese are Cantonese (approximately 90 per cent) with their ancestral origins in China's neighbouring Guangdong Province. Many other dialect groups, however, are represented: 2 per cent of the population is Hokkien, 1.6 per cent is Hakka, 0.7 per cent is Shanghainese, 1.4 per cent is Teochiu (Chiuchow) and at least 1.1 per cent is Putonghua (Mandarin speakers who originate from central and northern China). Some senior business people are ancestrally non-Cantonese but speak Cantonese.[3]

The Cantonese are perhaps the major business group in Hong Kong in general, and the Shanghainese are possibly the most prominent in manufacturing. After the Cantonese, the Teochiu are the most prominent in business. They also are said to be the most 'clan conscious': they have their own Teochiu chamber of commerce under which various Teochiu community associations and eight separate Teochiu county associations are organised.[4] Also the international Teochiu organisation, the Teochiu Alliance Association, has an active chapter in Hong Kong which will host the biennial meeting of the association in late 1995.

....

1 See Wong, S.L., *Emigrant Entrepreneurs: Shanghai Industrialists in Hong Kong*, Oxford University Press, Hong Kong, 1988, p. 3.

2 See Ch'ng, D., *The Overseas Chinese Entrepreneurs in East Asia: Background, Business Practices and International Networks*, CEDA Monograph M100, 1993, p. 35.

3 Prominent non-Cantonese business people include Li Ka-shing, and the Ma publishing family who are Teochius, and the Tsang (Goldlion ties) family which is Hakka. Ethnicity is also not a basis for election to Hong Kong's Legislative Council, but an ability to speak Cantonese is important as it is the language used in the Council.

4 One of the most prominent members of the Teochiu chamber of commerce is Li Ka-shing. Li has also fully funded Shantou's only university; the Shantou region being the ancestral home of the Teochius.

Most Hong Kong Teochiu are not ancestrally from Shantou but from the surrounding counties. Many Teochiu are Christian due to the work of Presbyterian missionaries who operated in Shantou during the nineteenth century.

As in many parts of South-East Asia and Indochina, the Teochiu still are very prominent in importing rice into Hong Kong.[5] Furthermore, several small banks in Hong Kong cater to a largely Teochiu clientele. One, the Commercial Bank (which was merged with Asia Finance in 1990 to form Asia Financial), controlled by Robin Chan of the Thai-Teochiu Sophonpanich (Chen) family specialises in financing Hong Kong-Thailand trade. Hong Kong's Teochiu community does not appear to be a substantial investor in Shantou; instead, it invests more in South-East Asia.

The sizeable Hakka population which mostly resides in the New Territories, like the Hakka elsewhere, traditionally were concentrated at the lower end of the socio-economic scale, for example as construction industry labourers. In recent years, the lot of the Hakka has improved: rural land holders have benefited from Hong Kong's buoyant real estate market; and many benefit from stable employment due to Hong Kong's enduring construction boom. Today, there are at least six formal Hakka community associations.

'Returnee' Sub-Groups

The Chinese community in Hong Kong features sub-groups of ethnic Chinese from South-East Asia who have settled in Hong Kong. They have come from Indonesia, Myanmar, the Philippines and Vietnam and formed small enclaves in Hong Kong.

Indonesian Chinese make up possibly two per cent of the Hong Kong Chinese population.[6] The impetus for many of Hong Kong's Indonesian Chinese to leave Indonesia was the passing of anti-Chinese legislation in 1959, and subsequent political and ethnic unrest. Most went first to China. After 1979, when China's emigration rules were loosened, many left China for Hong Kong. Around 70 per cent of the Indonesian Chinese who went to China now reside in Hong Kong.

Hong Kong's Indonesian Chinese have their own association, with several hundred members. The Indonesian Chinese community is not particularly prominent in Hong Kong's business sector, although some members facilitate trade links between Hong Kong and Indonesia, particularly in timber, plywood, and manufactured foods. The community is still to fully assimilate. This is probably due to its numbers; the largely Hokkien ancestral background; the lack of Cantonese proficiency of its members; and for many, their *peranakan* character, that is, their relative lack of 'Chineseness'. Today, the Indonesian Chinese are concentrated in the areas of North Point and Kowloon Bay.

Many *Burmese Chinese* left Burma in the wake of the Government's nationalisation program which began in 1962, and in the face of anti-Chinese

5 The two largest Hong Kong importers of Australian rice, Lui Hing Hop Company and Yuen Long, are each headed by Hong Kong Teochiu businessmen, both of whom hold Australian citizenship.

6 Also see Chapter 9 for detail on the Indonesian Chinese living in Hong Kong.

riots in 1967. Of those now in Hong Kong, some went directly and others settled briefly in China. Generally, the Burmese Cantonese ultimately settled in Hong Kong and the Burmese Hokkien in Singapore.

The Burmese Chinese in Hong Kong are almost fully assimilated and have no organisation or chamber of commerce of their own. Rather than business people, they are in the professions. One of the most prominent Burmese Chinese in Hong Kong is Sally Aw Sian from the Tiger Balm family, currently proprietor of the *Hongkong Standard* and the *Sing Tao Daily*. Another is the honorary chairman of *The Mirror*, Xu Xi Min. Anticipating 1997, many Burmese Chinese have left Hong Kong for the United States, Canada and Australia. As professionals, they are relatively mobile.

As many as 80 000 *Philippines Chinese* live in Hong Kong. Mostly they are of Hokkien descent, and are concentrated in North Point and Kuntong. This group imports Philippine food, beverages and other items, catering to the thousands of ethnic Filipina maids who are temporarily employed in Hong Kong.

Relatively few *Vietnamese Chinese* currently live freely in Hong Kong. This is largely due to Hong Kong's recent restrictions on immigration. Those Sino-Vietnamese settled in Hong Kong are believed to be active in investing back into southern Vietnam. Some have freely resettled there to take advantage of Vietnam's economic transformation. Although a relatively new group in Hong Kong, the Sino-Vietnamese are likely to assimilate relatively well with their largely Cantonese background.

Traditional Chinese Organisations in Hong Kong

Hundreds of traditional Chinese associations in Hong Kong cover the whole range of organisations discussed in Chapter 1. Apart from Cantonese associations, there are Teochiu, Hakka and Hokkien community associations. Some of the smaller birthplace associations own small restaurants serving their regional cuisine, largely for their members. Traditional Chinese associations are complemented and being possibly displaced by new types of associations such as graduation class groupings, university alumni groups, Lions and Rotary.

The Chinese General Chamber

The Chinese General Chamber, founded in 1900, is one of the oldest, largest and financially best-resourced chambers of commerce in Hong Kong.[7] The chamber has around 6 000 members, including 3 500 companies, 2 200 individuals, and 90 associations and guilds, and is very trade-focused. Of its members, 47.5 per cent are in export, import and re-export; 28.6 per cent are involved in services, retail and wholesale; and 4.3 per cent are in manufacturing and processing. Membership is restricted to ethnic Chinese or companies largely controlled by ethnic Chinese. The chamber describes its membership as largely 'pro-China'.

....

[7] Information on the Chinese General Chamber has been sourced from personal communications; *The Chinese General Chamber of Commerce*, Hong Kong 1990 (Chamber pamphlet); and The Chinese General Chamber of Commerce, *1993 Annual Report*, Hong Kong, 1994.

The chamber purports to represent Hong Kong Chinese business interests and is directly represented on Hong Kong's Legislative Council and on the boards and committees of various statutory bodies. It also acts as an intermediary in cases of trade complaints or trade disputes between members, or members and overseas firms. It receives hundreds of business delegations from China each year and also provides some consular services on behalf of the PRC.

The chamber's monthly newsletter, *Business Info*, contains enquiries from local and overseas importers and exporters, and information on manufacturers and distributors.

Since 1982, each year the chamber has run around five, six-week courses for officials from China with forty officials per course. The courses expose participants to the workings of Hong Kong's capitalist system. While in Hong Kong, the officials' expenses are covered by the chamber. The program benefits both sides: the officials better understand how Hong Kong functions, and the chamber's members develop new, and presumably sympathetic, connections in China.

Hong Kong's Business Community

Business in Hong Kong has a largely Western veneer. Several powerful and well-funded government regulatory bodies oversee it. In recent years, they have embarked on a series of high-profile investigations in an attempt to ensure that the modest parameters placed on Hong Kong's business community are enforced. Much of the territory's big business community is modern and Westernised, but small- and medium-sized businesses tend to be more traditionally Chinese. Typically, they are family owned and operated, and lack Western-style management structures.

As with many ethnic Chinese businesses elsewhere, many small and medium Hong Kong Chinese businesses appear to undervalue services as production inputs.[8] However, Hong Kong's business people have not shied away from borrowing large sums from Western banks. Borrowing from external sources means some of the risk associated with large projects can be passed on to banks, compared with using only internal financing.[9] Some of Hong Kong's biggest companies, such as Gordon Wu's Hopewell Holdings and Li Ka-shing's Cheung Kong, are some of the city's biggest borrowers.

Many large Hong Kong business groups appear to be Western in style but are family controlled. As late as 1988, ten family groups controlled 54 per cent of Hong Kong's stock market capitalisation. Seven of these were ethnic Chinese, and three were British.[10]

---

8 This aspect of ethnic Chinese business is elaborated on in Chapter 7.

9 This is more so, if initial returns can be distributed to companies related to the borrower, leaving the borrower comparatively asset poor and unable to cover its loans to external borrowers.

10 See Ch'ng, D., p. 36.

Due Diligence

Due diligence investigation is a thriving industry in Hong Kong. Potential business partners are investigated to ensure that they have a sound corporate history and are likely to meet their side of any agreements and contracts. In Hong Kong, US companies are the biggest users of external due diligence advice, usually in relation to prospective partners in south-eastern China and occasionally in relation to potential Hong Kong partners. Such investigations are particularly valuable for Western firms intending to operate in China, where embryonic or poorly enforced business regulations mean that attempting to recover losses from unsatisfactory or fraudulent partners may be extremely difficult. One prominent accounting firm is said to have 200 to 300 full-time staff working in China on due diligence work.

Activity on the part of organised crime gangs or triads is a factor in Hong Kong, although its level of influence is difficult to gauge. It is most likely restricted to small business (particularly nightclubs, gambling houses, and minibus services) and the construction sector.

There is little evidence of excessive in-house borrowing among diversified Hong Kong diversified companies with financial arms. However, one often-heard complaint centres on the shifting of funds between listed and private or unlisted companies: this masks the performance of the listed companies, disguises the overall performance of the group and avoids government regulations.

Some listed companies in Hong Kong announce frequent rights issues, requiring shareholders continually to take up new scrip or have their equity diluted. This has particularly been the case in Hong Kong's escalating property market and the overheating southern China economy, both of which have demanded that companies raise ever-increasing amounts of capital. Some family-controlled companies, including those at the top end of the business scale, may have been over zealous in their demands on minority shareholders attracting criticism for unfairly frequent rights issues.[11]

Business and Sub-Ethnic Groups

Today, the Cantonese dominate commerce in Hong Kong, particularly at the level of small- and medium-sized enterprises. Most of these firms are family owned and managed.[12] They have been responsible for much of Hong Kong's investment in Guangdong, setting up thousands of small manufacturing plants, as wage, land

....

11 Chapter 7 details at length the business practices of companies controlled by ethnic Chinese families across Asia.

12 98 per cent of manufacturing establishments in Hong Kong employ fewer than 200 people. (See Ch'ng, D., p. 14.) In this respect, small- and medium-sized businesses in Hong Kong are broadly similar to ethnic Chinese businesses elsewhere. See Chapter 7 for further detail on traditional Chinese businesses and their structures.

and other costs in Hong Kong have risen and the economy of China becomes more open.[13]

At the upper echelons of Hong Kong business, other dialect groups become more important. These three broad groups are: the Shanghainese, established senior Hong Kong Chinese business people, and the South-East Asian Chinese. The three have different methods of doing business.

The Shanghainese

The term 'Shanghainese' loosely refers to Chinese people who are ancestrally from the core areas of the Lower Yangze Delta region in China. The region incorporates areas from three Provinces: the southern parts of Jiangsu and Anhui, and the northern part of Zhejiang. The main cities in this area include Ningbo, Hangzhou, Wuxi, Nanjing, Suzhou and Shanghai itself. The common dialect is Wu, or more broadly, Shanghainese.

The Shanghainese in Hong Kong, or their forebears, came to Hong Kong in 1949 or soon after. Many were qualitatively different from other migrants, being well-educated members of Shanghai's former business elite. Consequently, their influence over the Hong Kong economy has greatly outweighed their numbers.

When they arrived, they found little manufacturing industry. Conditions were, however, conducive to business, and they were able to recreate their manufacturing base with what little funds, plant and equipment they were able to salvage from Shanghai. The Hong Kong and Shanghai Bank was the main source of capital and the rush of migrants provided a large employment base.

The Shanghainese focused on textiles and cotton spinning. A recent survey of Hong Kong's cotton spinning mills suggested that around 80 per cent of the mills had majority Shanghainese ownership.[14] The predominance of the Shanghainese in the industry is such that the Hong Kong Cotton Spinners' Association can be considered as a Shanghainese association. Apart from this association, there is no Shanghai Chinese chamber of commerce or similar body, possibly reflecting the essentially cosmopolitan character of the Shanghainese when compared to other ethnic Chinese immigrant communities.[15]

Generally, Hong Kong's Shanghainese so far have been relatively cautious in investing in Shanghai, Ningbo and surrounding areas. Much of their investment there has involved buying back enterprises they owned before the communist takeover, setting up some new manufacturing enterprises and developing infrastructure.[16] Many Shanghainese entrepreneurs have directed their external investment to South-East Asia where labour costs are similarly low, but the

---

13 See Chapter 10 for more detail on Hong Kong investment in Guangdong. Also, the case study of the Tomei Group in Appendix 7 provides a brief account of the expansion of one medium-sized Hong Kong manufacturer into Guangdong.

14 See Wong, S.L., p. 13.

15 There are however some Shanghainese associations in Hong Kong that have a geographic basis.

16 One example of a Hong Kong Shanghainese company which has re-acquired expropriated assets in Shanghai is the Winsor textile group. Another investor is the Wharf Group, whose founder, Y.K. Pao, was born in Ningbo, has participated in port development there.

domestic political and business environment appears more stable and output is less likely to be subject to possible US trade sanctions.

In the past, Hong Kong Shanghainese-controlled firms had a high concentration of Shanghainese management staff. To a lesser degree, this practice is still evident today. Also some well established banks in Hong Kong largely cater to a Shanghainese clientele, such as the First Chekiang Bank and Shanghai Commercial. Most senior Shanghainese-controlled firms, however, raise funds in the same way as other Western-style companies - from bond and stock markets and from larger, international banks.

The Shanghainese are still a dominant force in the Hong Kong manufacturing sector. Prominent Shanghainese and *Ningbobang* business people include Peter Woo, the son-in-law of the late Y.K. Pao (founder of the World International Group); Sir Run Run Shaw, of the TVB Group; Henry Tang of the Winsor Textile Group; the Chao family, owners of the Wah Kwong Shipping Holdings; Frank Tsao of International Maritime Carriers; Frederick Chao (Exco); Lydia Dunn; T.K. Ann; Cha Chi Ming; Y.C. Chow; G.T. Chow; and Larry Yung.[17]

Senior Cantonese and Other Business People

This group comprises most of Hong Kong's senior traders and property developers. Many were originally refugees from Guangdong. Their business focus is largely Hong Kong and China; only in recent years, have they sought to diversify outside these two markets. Prominent among this group are Li Ka-shing (Cheung Kong and Hutchisons), Gordon Wu (Hopewell Holdings and CEPA) and the Kwok Brothers (Sun Hung Kai Group).[18]

This group's investment in China is largely in infrastructure development such as ports, highways and power stations. The risk of a long-term commitment in the mainland means that much of this investment is designed to achieve the bulk of returns in the construction phase, rather than over the life of the project. Some of the huge China projects announced have also failed to materialise and others appear to have been somewhat exaggerated. Some overly optimistic accounts of planned investments have attracted favourable media coverage and enabled funds to be raised more easily and the companies' share prices to appreciate. It has been claimed that some of the funds sought for investment in China have been diverted to the Hong Kong real estate market.

Hong Kong-Based South-East Asian Chinese Business

Several large Hong Kong companies are the arms of South-East Asian Chinese-controlled conglomerates. These firms have expanded rapidly in recent times.

....

17 *Ningbobang* literally means the 'group from Ningbo'. The Ningbo Economic and Technical Development Zone claims there are some 300 000 people outside of China who are ancestrally from Ningbo, for example. Many of the big investors into Ningbo are of Ningbo descent. (See Ningbo Economic and Technical Development Zone, *Investment Guide to Ningbo Economic and Technical Development Zone,* Ningbo, 1995.) See also Appendix 7 for an account of the Pao Group.

18 See Appendix 7 for a description of the business activities of the Li Ka-shing and Gordon Wu Groups.

Their business focus generally differs from Hong Kong Chinese-controlled firms in that they concentrate on all parts of South-East Asia, as well as China and Hong Kong. They are often used to doing business in less structured environments, so some have earned reputations for testing the limits of Hong Kong's regulatory framework and being somewhat cavalier.

South-East Asian Chinese entrepreneurs with a significant presence in Hong Kong include Malaysia's Robert Kuok through his Kerry Group, Indonesia's Oei Hong Leong through China Strategic Holdings, Indonesia's Mochtar Riady through Lippo Group, and the Philippines' Frank Chan (brother of Lucio Tan) through Eton Properties. Indonesia's Salim Group's stake in Hong Kong is substantial through a US$400 million or 35 per cent holding in First Pacific Company Ltd.

Many South-East Asian Chinese entrepreneurs have sought a presence in Hong Kong as a base for securing a foothold in China. However, some interviewees in Hong Kong believed that many were treading relatively carefully in China. For example, the Sino-Indonesian Lippo Group reportedly has plans to invest as much as US$10 billion in China, but to date, has invested 10 per cent or less of this sum.[19]

Hong Kong Services to Chinese Communities Worldwide

The Hong Kong Chinese business community's efforts to diversify offshore involved, among other things, developing operations to service Chinese communities elsewhere in the world. Lippobank (HK), has Lippo Finance Australia in Sydney to provide trade financing for Sydney's Asian community, and banks in Los Angeles and San Francisco to service local Chinese communities there.

Similarly, Hong Kong-based Sing Tao Holdings, publisher of some of Hong Kong's leading newspapers, has sought to serve Chinese communities around the world with its Chinese-language newspapers. Its newspapers are established in Toronto, Vancouver, Alberta, New York, San Francisco, Los Angeles, London, Sydney and Auckland. The group is also investigating the feasibility of either publishing local editions of its newspapers, or establishing newspapers in Taiwan and Vietnam. There are also plans for a small newspaper in Shenzhen in China's Guangdong Province. This will serve the indigenous Chinese population and the many ethnic Chinese expatriates living in the Special Economic Zone.

Another Hong Kong-based company, the Kuok-controlled Shangri-la Asia, seeks to open Shangri-la Hotels in strategic 'gateways to Asia' and other places where there are significant ethnic Chinese communities. There are already Shangri-la Hotels in Bangkok, Jakarta, Kuala Lumpur, Manila, Penang, Singapore, Vancouver and China.

19 Personal communication with the Lippo Group.

Australian Chinese Association of Hong Kong

The Australian Chinese Association of Hong Kong (ACAHK) was set up in 1993. The 330 members are largely Hong Kong Chinese residents holding Australian citizenship. (Overall, there are about 30-40 000 Australian passport holders who reside in Hong Kong.) The membership covers professionals as well as business people.

The association intends to set up a business chapter soon. This will facilitate and streamline members' business activities between Australia and Hong Kong. Examples of how the association has furthered Hong Kong-Australia trade and investment include:

- A member who had sourced wool from New Zealand for processing in his China-based factories was encouraged by other association members to buy wool from Australia instead. He now buys US$5-7 million worth of wool annually from Australia rather than from New Zealand.
- The association is assisting a large Melbourne-based paper and cardboard manufacturer to find a partner in China.
- In 1994, the association's president led five business delegations to Australia; three came from China and two from Hong Kong.
- To promote Australian wine in Hong Kong, the association has held two Australian wine tasting functions.

The association intends to affiliate with the Hong Kong Club in Melbourne and is already affiliated with the Sydney-based Australian Chinese Community Association. Affiliations such as these mean that ACAHK members can go to Sydney or Melbourne and be assured of assistance. The association also has a close relationship with the Australian Chamber of Commerce in Hong Kong (which has more than 1 000 members). The two have an overlapping membership and frequently hold joint functions.

Hong Kong Post 1997

From 1 July 1997, Hong Kong will be administered as a Special Administrative Region of China. The Sino-British Joint Declaration of 1984 states that Hong Kong will retain its current social, economic and legal systems for fifty years after 1997. In 1990, Beijing issued *The Basic Law of Hong Kong*, detailing those systems.

The uneasiness felt by the Hong Kong business community about the impending changeover seems to come in waves. There has not been a wholesale move out of Hong Kong by business, but a number of precautions have been taken.

Many Hong Kong Chinese have citizenship in Britain, the United States, Canada or Australia, but continue to live in Hong Kong. Most Hong Kong companies have registered in international tax havens such as Bermuda and the Cayman Islands, reasoning that while they still may have significant assets in

Hong Kong, international expropriation laws may offer some protection. Many larger companies have diversified their assets out of Hong Kong, investing in Canada and the United States. One means of protection, especially among Hong Kong's senior business people, is to forge business and other ties with senior cadres in China. Many have sought to become advisers to Beijing on Hong Kong affairs. Some have gone into joint ventures with senior Chinese officials or their children, the so-called 'princelings', although recent developments in Beijing suggest that this strategy has its own dangers.[20]

So far, Singapore has not attracted significant investment from Hong Kong Chinese, although several Hong Kong companies have listed on the Singapore Stock Exchange. The single largest Hong Kong investment in Singapore to date is the Singapore World Trade Centre. Senior Hong Kong businessmen including Li Ka-shing and Sir Run Run Shaw invested in it, as a result of encouragement by the Singapore Government rather than a flight of capital. Generally, Chinese interviewed in Hong Kong saw Singapore as a relatively unattractive place for Hong Kong businesses to relocate because of its relatively highly structured business environment.

The current attitude of the Hong Kong Chinese business community to 1997 seems to be one of cautious optimism. In this light, much of the current flow of investment out of Hong Kong reflects the maturing of Hong Kong's economy with its manufacturers seeking cheaper labour offshore, rather than merely hedging against uncertainties post 1997. In the past decade, around 75 per cent of Hong Kong's manufacturing has been relocated to south-eastern China. Hong Kong is the largest investor in China. The Hong Kong-China relationship is mutually reinforcing with Hong Kong investment in China possibly totalling as much as US$75 billion by the end of 1993, and considerable investment by China in Hong Kong.

MACAU

Around 97 per cent of the 460 000-strong population of the Portuguese territory of Macau is ethnic Chinese.[21] The majority are Cantonese. Also, there are significant numbers of Burmese and Indonesian Chinese who had sought, unsuccessfully, to gain entry to Hong Kong from China after Hong Kong's entry rules were tightened. Most are in small business.

Tourism and gambling, along with exporting (mainly textiles) are the major industries. Hong Kong entrepreneurs are prominent, especially in hotels and ferries between Macau and Hong Kong.

---

20 Li Ka-shing's association with the Beijing municipal government is an example. Some officials in the government were recently removed over allegations of corruption.

21 See Far Eastern Economic Review, *All Asia Travel Guide*, 16th edition, Review Publishing Co. Ltd, Hong Kong, 1993, p. 316.

TAIWAN

Like the Chinese of Hong Kong and Macau, the Chinese of Taiwan are not overseas Chinese. Also, their history and business environment make them quite separate from the mainland Chinese.

Taiwan was ceded to Japan in 1895 by the Treaty of Shimonoseki at the conclusion of the Sino-Japanese war of 1894-95. The Japanese went on to rule Taiwan until 1945. Between 1945 and 1949, Taiwan came under the control of the Nationalist Chinese (KMT) Government of Chiang Kai-shek. With the communist takeover of the mainland in December 1949, the KMT Government, its forces and sympathisers fled to Taiwan, in all, about 1.5 million people. Taiwan was to be used as the base from which China would be recaptured from the communists.[22] This did not happen; instead, Taiwan's economy was transformed. In 1951, per capita GNP was US$145; by 1993, it was US$10 566.[23]

Today, Taiwan's Chinese have strong ethnic links to markets outside Taiwan. Taiwan is one of the biggest sources of investment into China, and is strongly connected to the United States with its sizeable Taiwanese community, particularly in Los Angeles. To the extent that international Chinese networks are used, Taiwan business people tend to use family rather than clan links. Taiwanese business families tend to locate close family members around the world to extend their business networks. The use of clan connections for this purpose is essentially a foreign concept to most Taiwanese.

Demographics

Around 97 per cent of Taiwan's population of 21 million is ethnically Chinese. The Chinese are overwhelmingly of Hokkien ancestry and at least 85 per cent can be considered 'native Taiwanese', meaning that their families lived in Taiwan prior to the arrival of the KMT. Over 85 per cent of Taiwan's population speak Taiwanese (a variant of southern Hokkien) as a first or second language, including as many as ten per cent of the population who are ancestrally Hakka.

Taiwan has not attracted 'returnees' from South-East Asia in significant numbers, compared with Hong Kong. There are some Burmese Chinese resident in Taiwan, almost no Indonesian Chinese, and only a small number of Sino-Vietnamese.[24]

Chinese who arrived in Taiwan in the wake of the 1949 defeat of the KMT came from provinces all over China, but particularly from Jiangsu, Zhejiang and Shanghai (the commercial and administrative bases for the KMT regime); Sichuan and Shandong (catchment areas for the KMT's foot soldiers); and Guangdong and Fujian (whence escape was relatively easy).

Although there are significant entrepreneurial Shanghainese families in both Taiwan and Hong Kong, they rarely go into business together. They are not as

....

22 Far Eastern Economic Review, *All Asia Travel Guide*, p. 347.

23 See Chinese National Federation of Industries, *Chinese National Federation of Industries 1994-1996*, Taipei, (promotional brochure), p. 10.

24 The Taiwan Government did send a 'rescue' ship to Vietnam in 1975 to pick up some Vietnamese Chinese who had been helpful to the Taiwan Government.

cohesive as other ethnic Chinese groups which share a common language and place of origin. This may be because Shanghainese settlers in Taiwan after 1949 were KMT sympathisers; whereas, those who settled in Hong Kong were sometimes not. Taiwan's Shanghainese do not appear to be substantial investors in Shanghai. When they do invest, this is often because of Shanghai's relatively good infrastructure, location and growth potential rather than any familial or other ties to the city or region.

Structure of Business

History

The unusual structure of Taiwan's business sector today has its antecedents in the regulations applied by the Japanese administrators during the period of Japanese occupation (1895-1945). From 1912 to 1923, Taiwanese firms without Japanese participants were prohibited from using the word *kaisha* ('company' or 'corporation') in their names. As a result, most Taiwanese businesses remained small independent shops or partnerships.

For big business, an important turning point in Taiwan's postwar corporate economy was the Land Reform of 1949-53, which privatised four state-owned corporations (Taiwan Cement, Taiwan Agricultural and Forestry Products, Taiwan Industrial Machinery and Mining, and Taiwan Pulp and Paper) and gave their shares to former landlords as compensation for their land titles. The government now controls a few sizeable key industries and public utilities.[25] In 1962, the Taiwan Stock Exchange (TSE) was opened. Although relatively old, the TSE is not tightly regulated. It is commonly believed to be prone to insider trading and wild swings, usually blamed on the presence of many small investors and the corresponding absence of major institutional investors.

Structures Today

Today, at least 95 per cent of Taiwan's enterprises are small- to medium-sized and are family owned and managed. There are several enormous companies, such as Acer, Evergreen and Formosa Plastics, but these too are family controlled with various family members playing key roles in management.

There are no holding companies in Taiwan as they are prohibited by law. Instead, related companies seek to arrange themselves through cross-shareholdings into the type of group structures permitted elsewhere. Business groups in Taiwan tend to consist of a range of closely related horizontally and vertically integrated companies. Members of the group are related through interlocking directorships and cross-shareholdings. Typically, smaller companies will be arranged around a nuclear or core company, with the larger company contracting work to the smaller ones. Such a structure allows for flexibility in the face of cyclical product demand.

---

25 Numazaki, I., 'Networks of Taiwanese Big Business: A Preliminary Analysis', *Modern China*, Vol. 12, No. 4, October 1986, pp. 489-91.

One study has identified three basic models of ownership among Taiwan's business groups:[26]

- *The sister type*: When partners X and Y jointly invest in companies A, B and C, the three companies are said to be in a 'sister' relationship.
- *The mother-child type*: When partners X and Y jointly invest in a company A, which in turn holds shares of companies B and C, company A then stands as 'mother' to 'children' B and C.
- *The marriage type*: When partners X and Y invest in a company A, while Y and Z invest in another company B, the two companies are related to each other by virtue of a sharing of a common investor Y. This type of relationship is usually formed when one of two partners independently invites a third party to set up a new company as part of an expansion drive.

These three types of business group formation are not mutually exclusive.

The connections of the directors of companies which form a business group can also be summarised:

- *The immediate family type*: This refers to those business groups whose core owner-managers consist of a father and his son(s) or siblings (usually brothers) without a father.
- *The descent type*: This is when core owner-managers of a business group consist of members of a patrilineal lineage (*zu*) beyond any one immediate family.
- *The native-place alliance type*: This is a unique pattern of partnership. The relationship between two or more families that constitute core owner-managers of a business group stems from the families sharing a common native place. The best known example of this in Taiwan is the *Tainanbang*.

The management of individual companies in Taiwan is unusual. Management normally consists of two separate levels: the board of directors and auditors who set broad corporate policies, and the group of managers who carry out daily management activities. The overlap of management within the business group occurs at the level of the board of directors and auditors alone. Managers, by contrast, are responsible for a specific division or a single corporation. Unusually, company auditors often sit on the board of directors and are close associates or relatives of the dominant members of the board, rather than being independent.[27]

Taiwan's larger companies tend to be well structured, particularly as access to government R&D and other incentive programs is contingent on good accounting methods. Often the fact that a company is listed on the Taipei Stock Exchange is accepted as sufficient evidence that it is well organised, and therefore eligible for special government assistance. Few business groups in Taiwan

26 Numazaki, I., p. 493.

27 See Numazaki, I., 'The Tainanbang: The rise and growth of a banana-bunch-shaped business group in Taiwan', *The Developing Economies*, December 1993, p. 501f.

encompass a finance arm. Subsequently, excessive in-house lending is not common. In any event, stringently applied government regulations constrain the practice. Government officials are also generally prohibited from serving as directors on the boards of private companies, although a sizeable sector consists of state-owned firms or firms owned by the KMT.[28]

Today, many Taiwan companies have joint ventures in Taiwan with Japanese interests. Japanese firms are favoured because Japan is geographically close; shipment times between the two markets are comparatively quick; and because of historical factors many Taiwanese are fluent in Japanese.

In recent years, there has been a substantial 'hollowing out' of Taiwan's industrial sector, as much manufacturing has shifted offshore as labour costs rise. A common phenomenon has been for several members of a business group or cluster with complementary production to move offshore together, recreating the cluster in places like Shenzhen, Fujian and Malaysia.

Taiwanese and Mainlanders in Business

The main division in Taiwanese society and commerce is between the native Taiwanese and those who came from China after 1949.

Most enterprises in Taiwan are owned and operated by native Taiwanese, including most of Taiwan's largest companies. Overall, the success of the mainlanders in Taiwan's business sector is not disproportionate to their numbers. As elsewhere in Asia, those who have owned land in metropolitan areas have done extremely well and branched out into other fields of business. In Taiwan, the land holders have generally been the native Taiwanese. The mainlanders, initially at least, expected to return home and therefore did not acquire land in Taiwan. The end result was that when Taiwan's economic 'miracle' and the subsequent boom in the property market occurred, the huge capital gains made by native Taiwanese passed by most resident mainlanders.

Today, rather than being well off, many ex-KMT soldiers are relatively poor, surviving on little more than modest government pensions. Other mainlanders with senior business positions are usually in state-owned or KMT-owned enterprises, such as textiles and shoe manufacturing. Since the KMT was effectively the only political party permitted to operate legally until 1986, there was little need to distinguish between state and party ownership of enterprises. The two gradually are being separated, but resident mainlanders remain prominent in both.

Successful mainlanders in the private sector form a relatively distinct group. Linguistic differences between mainlanders and native Taiwanese, and the authoritarian rule of the transposed KMT government, have contributed to a separation of Taiwanese from mainlanders.[29] Shanghainese-controlled companies

---

28 Many of these are in the process of being privatised, although there is still some government ownership in the manufacturing sector, as well as in the more usual spheres of government ownership such as the public utilities.

29 Numazaki, I., 'Networks of Taiwanese Big Business: A Preliminary Analysis', *Modern China*, Vol. 12, No. 4, October 1986, p. 516, 520.

still tend to favour Shanghainese in senior management positions (but not exclusively), and native Taiwanese companies tend to favour those speaking Taiwanese. Mainlanders from the north have had to acquire these skills.

Although mainlanders came from all parts of China, those who stand out in business today came from Shanghai, Sichuan and Shandong. As in Hong Kong, the Shanghainese who arrived in Taiwan after 1949 represented Shanghai's business elite. They tended to set up textiles and cotton spinning factories in much the same way as the Shanghainese did in Hong Kong.

Case Study: Far Eastern Group

The Far Eastern Group, formed in 1942 in Shanghai, initially operated in knitting and commodities trading.[30] In 1949, the controlling Hsu family fled Shanghai with some of their knitting machines. In Taiwan, the family, like many others, got their start-up capital from the Central Trust of China, a KMT government-run bank.

The Far Eastern Group has a structure typical of many larger Taiwanese groups of companies. The group's structure perhaps best fits the 'mother-child' model, and its ownership, the 'immediate family' type. As Figure 4.1 shows, a government prohibition on holding companies means that achieving a coherent group structure must be done via cross-shareholdings. These are arranged around the core or 'mother' company, Far Eastern Textile Ltd. The founding Hsu family maintains control of the group through these cross-shareholdings. Altogether, the group comprises 80 companies.

Today, the group has a gross turnover of around US$4.8 billion, gross assets of around US$10 billion and 21 000 employees. It is the third largest manufacturing group in Taiwan and the biggest exporter of textiles. Four of its companies are listed on the TSE. The group has joint ventures in Taiwan with German, French, US and Japanese interests, and has invested in Canada, the Philippines, Malaysia, Singapore, Thailand and Hong Kong. To date, the group has little investment in China.[31] Its size, visibility and the perceived risk of investing in China in the past account for this.

30 Information for this section is sourced from Far Eastern Textile Ltd, *Annual Report 1993*, Taipei, 1994; Asia Cement Corporation, *An Introduction to the Hualien Plant of Asia Cement Corporation*, Taipei, 1994; and personal communication with the Far Eastern Group.

31 Although a US$30 million textile plant to be constructed in Shanghai was announced in early 1995.

Far Eastern Group

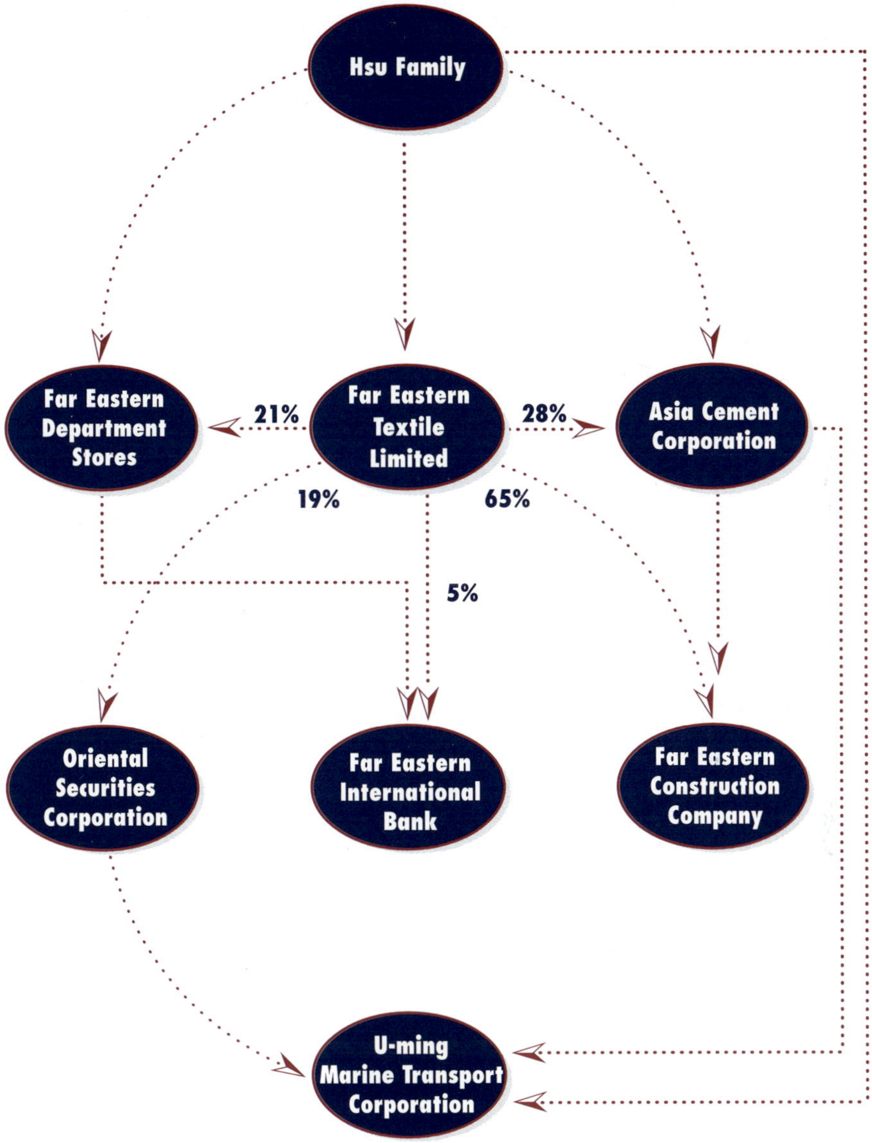

Figure 4.1

Sources: Ch'ng, D., *The Overseas Entrepeneurs in East Asia: Background, Business Practices and International Networks*, CEDA Monograph M100, 1993; and *Far Eastern Textiles Ltd, Annual Report 1993*, Taipei, 1994.

Chinese Business Organisations in Taiwan

In Taiwan, unlike South-East Asia and Hong Kong, traditional Chinese organisations are generally not based on dialect or sub-dialect. There are, however, some business groupings based on a common birthplace and birth year. Much of the networking among Taiwanese business people tends to be through high school or university classmates, community service groups such as Rotary and Lions, or business and trade associations.

The Tainanbang and the Taipeibang

Two informal but relatively powerful groupings of native Taiwanese heads of enterprises in Taiwan, are based on 'birthplace kinship'.[32] Their influence is more residual than enduring. They are the *Tainanbang*, whose members are from the Tainan district in southern Taiwan, and the *Taipeibang*, whose members are from the Taipei area. The *Tainanbang* is the more prominent of the two. Although informal in structure, it is a relatively tight-knit grouping of business people representing at least twenty-seven different enterprises, including the large President Enterprise, Tainan Spinning, and Prince Garments Manufacturing. Most of the members are connected by a common regional heritage and through the cross-shareholdings and overlapping directorships of their companies. One prominent member of the *Tainanbang*, Kao Chin-yuan, the head of the President Group, is chairman of the Chinese National Federation of Industries, one of Taiwan's most powerful peak industry bodies.[33]

The Chinese National Federation of Industries

The Chinese National Federation of Industries (CNFI) established in 1942, is a non-profit organisation consisting of 136 trade associations representing more than 80 000 manufacturing enterprises.[34] Like other trade organisations, the CNFI is required by law to assist the Government in implementing economic policies and industrial laws; cooperate in the drafting of business regulations; communicate government policy to its members; organise trade missions to be sent abroad; and provide a range of other services to members. The CNFI also produces a monthly newsletter for members.

In addition to Kao Chin-yuan, CNFI's executive includes some of Taiwan's most successful entrepreneurs, including the heads of Taiwan Cement Corporation, Tatung Company, Formosa Plastics, and the Prince Motors Group.

---

32 This section draws on Numazaki, I., 'The Tainanbang: The rise and growth of a banana-bunch-shaped business group in Taiwan', and from interviews conducted in Taiwan during February 1995.

33 Fu Hsien-ta, who emigrated to Australia in 1991 and acquired at least six Queensland shopping centres, also originated from Tainan. Fu still holds substantial assets there and in Taiwan more generally, including the Sun Smile Chicken fast food chain. (See *Business Review Weekly*, 22 May 1995, and Chapter 5 of this study.)

34 Information for this section is sourced from Chinese National Federation of Industries, *Chinese National Federation of Industries 1994-1996*, Taipei, and from personal communication with the CNFI.

Trade and Industry Associations

Taiwan's trade and industry associations tend to be government-sponsored rather than spontaneously created, private organisations.[35] Each trade association usually has a board of 20-30 of the top business people in the field. A survey of a Taiwan trade directory yielded at least 228 active trade and industry associations covering almost every conceivable trade item.[36] The associations tend to be quite specific. For example, there are the Taipei Stainless Kitchen Utensil Association, the Taipei Teeth-Model Manufacturers' Association, the Taiwan Eel Exporters Association, and the Taiwan Maize Powder Association.

Access to these associations is essential for outsiders wanting to do business in Taiwan. Most companies in Taiwan belong to at least one association and most associations compile useful handbooks of members' names, addresses and areas of business.

The Tongnian

Tongnian are groupings of individuals born in the same lunar year. Such groupings cut across dialect and birthplace lines. They tend to be informally organised, meeting, say, once a month. One Taiwan *tongnian* brings together several of Taiwan's most prominent business people, including Wang Yong-qing, the founder of Formosa Plastics, Cai Wanchun of the Cathay Group, Lin Yijia of the Taiwan Glass Group, and Tu Yong-liang of Wan Yuan Textile, as well as several senior government members. The group presents a useful forum for staying in touch and exchanging business news.[37]

The Overseas Chinese Affairs Commission

The Overseas Chinese Affairs Commission was established in 1926 and reconstituted in Taiwan after 1949.[38] The commission is directly responsible to the Legislative Yuan (Taiwan's Parliament) and in theory is charged with 'administering' the 'overseas Chinese'.[39] In practice, the commission compiles statistics on the overseas Chinese and provides financial and other assistance to Chinese organisations and schools abroad. The commission however, does claim to have provided financial assistance to some 500 000 Sino-Vietnamese after 1975, assisting them to make their way from Vietnam to the United States.

The commission claims to have contact with 3 000 of the more than 9 000 Chinese organisations abroad. It distributes text books to some 2 000 out of the almost 4 000 Chinese schools worldwide, and provides assistance to Taiwanese

---

35 The Government also tends to informally approve the heads of each association.

36 Yellow Pages Corporation, *1995 Taiwan Yellow Pages*, Taipei, 1994.

37 Numazaki, I., 'The Tainanbang: The rise and growth of a banana-bunch-shaped business group in Taiwan', p. 505.

38 Information for this section is sourced from Overseas Chinese Affairs Commission, *We Always Stay Together*, Taipei, June 1991; and from personal communication with the commission.

39 This involves promoting Taiwan among Chinese outside of China, for example.

alumni organisations.[40] The commission has assisted in establishing 78 Taiwan alumni associations in Chinese communities around the world; these have formed into a peak association.

In the past, the commission attempted to attract 'overseas Chinese' investment to Taiwan. Appeals were made to the patriotism of the 'overseas Chinese' to encourage their assistance in developing Taiwan. This role has ceased. Investment flows have reversed and Taiwan is now a major net offshore investor.

The commission plays a direct, though relatively minor, role in the investment flows from Taiwan by administering the Overseas Chinese Credit Guarantee Fund. This fund was incorporated in 1988 with NT$1 billion (about A$50 million) and offers credit guarantees to approved 'overseas Chinese' businesses in the United States, Singapore, Thailand and parts of Europe. The service is handled by overseas branches of Taiwan's banks or overseas Chinese banks under contract.

The role of the commission is diminishing. As ethnic Chinese outside China assimilate with local populations, the number of true 'overseas Chinese' (*Hua-qiao*) declines. A shift in domestic political sentiment has also seen a questioning of the role of the commission. Increasingly, the commission focuses more on the interests of Taiwan-born 'overseas Chinese' communities than the more general 'overseas Chinese'.

Taiwanese Companies in China

Taiwanese companies are major investors in China: the reported level of Taiwanese investment in China may be as little as one quarter to a third of the actual total.[41] Official figures suggest investment of US$4.7 billion to date in 20 000 factories, but actual investment is more likely to be of the order of US$20 billion.[42] Typically, Taiwanese entrepreneurs create a low cost 'paper' company in Hong Kong to use as a transhipment point for goods and services between Taiwan and China.[43]

The Taiwan Shoe Association, for example estimates that up to 80 per cent of Taiwan's shoe companies have moved to China in search of labour cost advantages.[44] The Shenzhen Special Economic Zone was an earlier, favoured destination for Taiwan's investment, but there is now a shift away from the zone because of rising costs. Taiwanese are now the largest source of outside

....

40 Many ethnic Chinese, particularly from South-East Asia, go to Taiwan for university education. This tends to be more for pragmatic reasons such as relatively cheaper tuition fees, than for political reasons. To date, more than 60 000 'overseas' Chinese have graduated from high schools, colleges and universities in Taiwan.

41 See Chapter 10 for further detail on Taiwanese investment in China.

42 Personal communication with the Chung Hua Institute of Economic Research, Taipei.

43 See Kao, J., 'The worldwide web of Chinese business', *Harvard Business Review*, March-April 1993, p. 34.

44 See Kao, J., p. 34.

investment in Fujian Province. As a result, provincial governments in China commonly provide tax and other incentives to attract investment from Taiwan.[45]

The President Group, with thirty-five projects currently underway in China, is thought to be the largest and certainly the most dynamic Taiwanese investor. The group competes directly with the Sino-Thai conglomerate, Charoen Pokphand, which is one of the single largest foreign investors in China.

45 A number of smaller Taiwan firms have also been able to negotiate with municipal authorities to increase their investment in town areas in return for permission to be granted for their relatives in China to move from rural areas into the towns and cities. Some of the small, discrete investments by smaller Taiwanese firms into China of say, around US$100 000, may be explained in this way.

Chapter 5

AN OVERVIEW OF THE AUSTRALIAN CHINESE COMMUNITY

Australia's Chinese population is very diverse. All of Asia's various Chinese communities are represented in Australia.

Chinese first began emigrating to Australia in the nineteenth century, mainly to the gold fields.[1] More recently, Australia has attracted substantial numbers of Chinese from China and South-East Asia (particularly Malaysia) to take advantage of the high quality of its educational institutions. Australia's proximity also meant that many Indochinese refugees (a high proportion of whom were ethnic Chinese) made their way to Australia. Many successful Hong Kong and Taiwanese Chinese business people also have been attracted to Australia's stability and quality of life. Significant numbers of Chinese also have emigrated to Australia from the Pacific, including Papua New Guinea.

According to the 1986 Census, 1.3 per cent of Australia's population claimed a Chinese ancestry. The 1991 Census found that 1.6 per cent of Australia's population spoke Chinese at home and in metropolitan Sydney, Chinese was the most commonly spoken language after English.[2] These figures indicate broadly the number of Australians with a Chinese background. The actual number of Australian Chinese is likely to be more than 300 000. Most have migrated within the last decade from various countries in Asia.[3] Table 5.1 shows the birthplaces of those ethnic Chinese who were not born in Australia.

One study estimated that in 1981, in addition to Chinese from China, Hong Kong, Taiwan and Malaysia living in Australia, there were 3 000 Chinese people from Singapore, 2 500 from Papua New Guinea, 6 000 from Timor, and 30 000 from Indochina.[4]

1 The commonly used Australian expression 'fair dinkum?' which is used to question the reliabilty of what one is being told, is an expression likely to have arisen in the gold fields during this time. 'Dinkum' is a corruption of the Cantonese for 'true gold'.

2 Both these figures will tend to underestimate the proportion of Australia's population which is ethnically Chinese, however. Many South-East Asian Chinese might claim a Vietnamese or Malaysian ancestry rather than a Chinese one, and many Chinese, particularly in Australia, may not speak Chinese as a first language.

3 Ip, D. and C. Lever-Tracy, 'Trailblazing into China: Networks and Linkages of Smaller Diaspora Firms', Unpublished paper, 1993.

4 See Crimson, L., G. Beattie and J. Selby, 'The Segmentation and Integration of the Chinese in Brisbane, Australia', *Journal of Comparative Family Studies*, 16 (2), Summer 1985.

Table 5.1

People in Australia of Chinese Ancestry by Birthplace

(Based on Census Data)

BIRTHPLACE	1986	1991 (ESTIMATED)
China	28 500 (26.1 per cent)	60 000 (31.1 per cent)
Hong Kong	23 900 (21.9 per cent)	50 100 (26.0 per cent)
Malaysia	29 000 (26.6 per cent)	44 200 (22.9 per cent)
Vietnam	27 800 (25.5 per cent)	38 400 (19.9 per cent)

Source: Ip, D. and C. Lever-Tracy, 'Trailblazing into China: Networks and Linkages of Smaller Diaspora Firms', unpublished paper, 1993.

EARLY HISTORY

The few Chinese living in Australia before the gold rush years were largely market gardeners and retail traders in urban areas.[5] Around 1850, gold deposits were found near Bathurst, Bendigo and Ballarat. Chinese subsequently came to Australia from the See Yap districts (Ning Yung, Lung Kong, Hoi Ping and Yun Ping) on the Pearl River Delta in Guangdong Province.[6] Although Cantonese, they had divided loyalties according to village, county and district. These were asserted in the form of various traditional associations. Many of these Chinese had contracts with creditors in China who had paid for their voyage to Australia. In return, they were required to pay some or all of the gold they found in the fields during their first year's prospecting.

Since the discovery of gold in Australia coincided with the decline of gold fever in California, some Chinese came directly to Australia from California. By 1859, there were 42 000 Chinese in Victoria compared with 25 000 in 1854. Efforts were made by the Victorian Parliament to restrict Chinese immigration and a £10 poll tax was charged on Chinese coming ashore in Victoria. Subsequently, many Chinese landed near Robe, a coastal town in South Australia, and walked to the Victorian goldfields rather than pay the poll tax. Between 1856 and 1858, some 16 500 Chinese made their way in this fashion.[7]

In 1901, the Commonwealth Immigration Restriction Act was introduced. The Act required subsequent entrants to Australia to take a dictation test. Just before this, China had been second to Britain and Ireland as a source of immigration. By 1911, emigration and few new entrants contributed to the Chinese population in

---

5 This section draws in part on, Tan, T.T.W., *Your Chinese Roots: The Overseas Chinese Story*, Times Books International, Singapore, 1986.

6 Wade-Giles transliterations have been used here for the See Yap districts as this is the form by which they are generally known by overseas Cantonese.

7 Old Chinese coins are still unearthed around Robe to this day.

Australia falling from a peak of around 50 000 to 20 775. By 1947, the figure was 6 404.

RECENT ARRIVALS

The easing of Australia's restrictive immigration rules in the mid 1960s and the abolition of the 'White Australia Policy' in 1973 allowed the Chinese to resume their importance as a major immigrant community in Australia.

This development was accelerated when the Australian Government decided in the 1980s to sharpen the economic focus of its immigration policy, a policy trend also reflected in the immigrant intakes of the United States and Canada. This policy has allowed the migration of people with high skills, professional qualifications and wealth. Malaysia, Hong Kong and Singapore are now important sources of doctors, engineers, accountants, and computer specialists who trained in Australia and whose qualifications and experience are readily recognised in this country. By the early 1990s, Hong Kong was the single largest source of skilled and professional immigrants to Australia. Hong Kong and Taiwan are the most important source of business migrants.[8]

The high socio-economic and occupational profile of Australia's Chinese who were largely from the former British colonies, was changed in the late 1970s, as refugees arrived from Indochina and later East Timor. Many of those immigrants born in Vietnam have some degree of Chinese ancestry, but they and other new arrivals typically lacked English language skills, tertiary qualifications and work experience readily recognised in Australia. More recently, around 40 000 PRC nationals were given residency in Australia after the June 1989 Tiananmen incident and this has further diversified Australia's growing Chinese community.

Malaysian Chinese in Australia

Approximately 100 000 Malaysians have permanent resident status in Australia. Another 10 000 Malaysian students temporarily live in Australia, undertaking secondary and tertiary studies. Many are Malaysian Chinese.

Malaysian Chinese with permanent resident status in Australia tend to be tertiary educated and concentrated in the professions. They also reflect the dialect distribution found in Malaysia, speaking Cantonese, Hokkien, Hakka, Hainanese and Teochiu. For some, their presence in Australia enables them to relay local business information to their families in Malaysia, allowing investment advice to be sourced from within the family network, rather than from outside the family.

Vietnamese Chinese in Australia

During the late 1970s and early 1980s, there was a large influx of people from Vietnam. At the beginning of 1975, only 940 Vietnamese lived in Australia,

[8] Many Hong Kong Chinese have settled in Sydney, including in and around the suburb of Chatswood. Taiwanese migrants tend to prefer Brisbane, although significant numbers also settle in Sydney.

including students and diplomats. By 1986, there were 83 049.[9] At least one third of the Vietnamese now living in Australia are of ethnic Chinese origin (the *Hoa*) and most are Cantonese, followed by Teochiu.[10]

To date, the Australian Vietnamese Chinese community has remained fairly self-contained. There has been little organisational interaction between Vietnamese Cantonese and other Cantonese speakers, for example. Rather than joining existing organisations in which the Cantonese are dominant, the Sino-Vietnamese tend to set up their own organisations. Members of the community maintain close ties with Vietnam, and as much as 90 per cent of the investment being made in Ho Chi Minh City by Australia's Vietnamese community is of *Hoa* origin.

Hong Kong Chinese in Australia

Hong Kong Chinese are the largest Chinese community in Australia, as well as one of the most affluent.[11] Like Canada, the United States and Europe, Australia is a favoured destination. In 1993-94, 3 652 Hong Kong-born people permanently settled in Australia.[12] Also, many China-born are from Hong Kong. Most Hong Kong immigrants arrive under the Federal Government's skills program (business skills, employer nomination and independent entrant). Several prominent Hong Kong business people have taken out Australian citizenship, including C.K. Ma of the Oriental Press Publishing Group.[13] Reflecting the dialect make-up of Hong Kong, most Hong Kong immigrants in Australia are Cantonese, possibly followed by the Teochiu.

In Australia, Sydney is a favoured destination. This is partly reflected in the significant property purchases by Hong Kong Chinese in Sydney, mentioned in Chapter 13. After having obtained Australian citizenship, some Hong Kong business people return to Hong Kong to resume business - the so-called 'astronaut effect', observed in Hong Kong Chinese communities in Canada and elsewhere.[14]

---

9 See Tran Khanh, *The Ethnic Chinese and Economic Development in Vietnam*, Institute of Southeast Asian Studies, Singapore, 1993, p. 98.

10 Most of the refugees taken in by Australia came from southern Vietnam where most of Vietnam's ethnic Chinese resided. Members of the northern Vietnam Chinese community who left Vietnam tended to flee to southern China, especially to Behai in southern Guangdong Province. There many attempted to leave for Australia on boats in late 1994.

11 The 1991 Census found that 58 955 people identified themselves as having been born in Hong Kong, 55 per cent of whom were residing in New South Wales. On the basis of subsequent immigration flows, it is likely that the Hong Kong-born population in Australia measured around 82 000 at the end of 1994. This, however, tends to underestimate the number of people living in Australia who could be considered as part of the Australian Hong Kong community. Many Hong Kong people were not born there but in Guangdong and other Chinese provinces and emigrated to Hong Kong during the aftermath of the 1949 communist victory.

12 Hong Kong-born represented 4.7 per cent of total immigrants in 1993-94. (See Bureau of Immigration, Multicultural and Population Research, *Immigration Update*, December Quarter 1994.)

13 As mentioned in Chapter 13, C.K. Ma purchased the Sydney Hilton.

14 The 'astronaut' phenomenon refers to those people who migrate from Hong Kong but who then return, often leaving behind their families in their new countries of residence. Many of the so-called 'astronauts' return to Hong Kong after having found the business environments of their new destinations too unfamiliar.

The Taiwanese in Australia

The Taiwanese Chinese community is currently Australia's most rapidly growing community.[15] Almost all its members arrived with considerable wealth and under the Federal Government's independent business skills program. Australia's Taiwanese Chinese are concentrated particularly in Brisbane, largely due to chain migration. The Brisbane Taiwanese community generally has come from southern Taiwan, rather than from around the Taipei (northern) area. Members of the group are significant purchasers and developers of shopping centres, particularly in Queensland, as well as exporters to Taiwan of primary produce, mainly seafood, fruits, and vegetables.[16] Others import a range of manufactured goods. Immigrant Taiwanese investment in the Chinese print media in Australia is having an impact on the ethnic Chinese media. The new, quality *Independent Daily* is owned by a group of Taiwanese business migrants and *The Chinese Herald*, founded by Vietnamese Chinese publishers, recently was purchased by another Taiwanese interest.

Like the Hong Kong Chinese, the Taiwanese find Australia safe and secure. However, some wealthy Taiwanese settlers find it difficult to start and run a business in Australia. Common difficulties relate to their lack of English skills, inadequate knowledge of the Australian economy and society, low familiarity with Australian taxation laws and poor local contacts due to their recent arrival. Taiwan's economic dynamism will be a strong pull to these Taiwanese whose wealth was generated as part of Taiwan's rapid economic transformation. Like the 'astronauts' of Hong Kong, some return to do business and live in Taiwan, leaving children and at times spouses, in Australia.

Mainland Chinese in Australia

Recent large intakes of mainland Chinese have increased the diversity of Australia's existing Chinese communities, and replenished their stock of Chinese language, business and cultural skills. As well as the 48 637 people, most of whom are Chinese students, who applied for residence after the Tiananmen incident,[17] a significant number of new immigrants who are Chinese-born arrive in Australia each year to settle permanently. In 1993-94, for example, 2 944 did so.[18] There are significant implications of this migration for Australia's economic links to the region.

....

15 The 1991 Census identified 13 025 Taiwan-born people residing in Australia. The largest proportion (39.3 per cent) were residing in New South Wales and the second largest (32.1 per cent) in Queensland. In 1993-94, 814 Taiwan-born immigrants arrived to permanently settle in Australia, although in 1985-86, the figure was as high as 2 056. (See Department of Immigration and Ethnic Affairs, 'Community Information Summary: Chinese in Australia', November 1994; and Bureau of Immigration, Multicultural and Population Research, *Immigration Update*, December Quarter 1994.)

16 The most prominent Taiwanese acquirer of Queensland shopping centres has been Fu Hsien-ta who left Taiwan for Brisbane in 1991. Since his arrival, Fu has spent almost A$142 million acquiring six Queensland shopping centres and a one third interest in one other. (See *Australian Financial Review*, 'The new Mandarins', 29 April 1994.)

17 See Department of Immigration and Ethnic Affairs, 'Community Information Summary: Chinese in Australia', November 1994.

18 See Bureau of Immigration, Multicultural and Population Research, *Immigration Update*.

Table 5.2

Provincial Origins of Former Chinese Students

(From a Sample of 1 018)

PROVINCE	NUMBER	PER CENT
Shanghai	404	39.7
Guangdong	279	27.4
Fujian	77	7.6
Beijing	75	7.4
Liaoning	19	1.9
Shandong	18	1.8
Zhejiang	15	1.5
Hubei	14	1.4
Sichuan	11	1.1
Shanxi	9	0.9
Jiangsu	8	0.8
Anhui	7	0.7
Jiangxi	7	0.7
Hebei	6	0.6
Guangxi	5	0.5
Heilongjiang	5	0.5
Henan	4	0.4
Yunnan	3	0.3
Hunan	3	0.3
Jilin	2	0.2
Gansu	1	0.1
Ningxia	0	0.0
Shaanxi	0	0.0
Guizhou	0	0.0
Ningxia	0	0.0
Xizang (Tibet)	0	0.0
Others (including Xingjiang)	16	1.6

Source: Australian Government

Like the Taiwanese, the former students from the PRC are recent arrivals. Most of the students are sourced from parts of China that are not traditional sources of Chinese migrants. This and the number of students who have been or are likely to be granted permission to stay in Australia is changing the nature and structure of Australia's Chinese population. A sample of 1 018 of the former students showed that an estimated 47 per cent of the recent migrants to Australia from the PRC were from Shanghai and Beijing, but only 36 per cent were from the south-eastern provinces, the traditional source of Chinese migrants. (See Table 5.2.)

With chain migration, the 40 000 PRC nationals now living in Australia as a result of the Tiananmen incident may attract a further 60 000 new Chinese migrants. Most of the former students have settled in New South Wales, as shown in Table 5.3.[19]

Table 5.3

Distribution of Former Chinese Students in Australia

STATE OR TERRITORY	TOTAL	PER CENT
NSW	19,203	66.15
Vic	7,244	24.95
Qld	950	3.27
WA	808	2.78
SA	378	1.30
ACT	327	1.13
NT	50	0.17
Tas	41	0.14
Not specified	30	0.11
Total	29,031	100.00

Source: Australian Government

The lack of English language skills and qualifications recognised in Australia may persuade some of the former students to look for economic opportunities elsewhere. China's booming regional economies offer a great attraction, especially as many of the former students come from Guangdong and Shanghai. Anecdotal evidence suggests that many who have secured Australian passports have returned to invest in small businesses in China using the capital saved when enrolled as students. Those who have not, are still able to do business in China, using friends and relatives in China as proxies. Also many have formed small businesses in Australia and are active in the newer chambers of commerce and business groups discussed in Appendix 5.

---

19 The figures relate to those who lodged applications for permanent residence prior to 1 November 1994. Dependents of applicants are not included.

AUSTRALIA'S CHINESE IN COMMERCE

Australia's Chinese are involved in all sectors and many are professionals. Traditionally, however, the Chinese have operated small businesses such as restaurants and shops. Many such businesses have grown into export and import concerns. Several Chinese families in Melbourne who began as restaurateurs have branched out into seafood exports to Asia, for example.

Among recent arrivals, there is some degree of occupation specialisation. Many new settlers from China have small consultancy companies which facilitate trade and investment between Australia and China. Many Sino-Vietnamese have small shops, particularly bakeries; the Teochiu Vietnamese also appear to be concentrated in Asian groceries; and Cantonese Vietnamese frequently start in jewellery and goldshops. Many Hong Kong Chinese are involved in real estate, as well as the professions, particularly dentistry. A survey of Taiwanese business migrants found that 46 per cent who had established businesses after their arrival in Australia were in service industries and 36 per cent were in export.[20]

Some recent Chinese migrants to Australia use informal methods of raising business capital. Anecdotal evidence suggests that informal banks operate in some communities. The tontine system described in Chapter 3 also operates: a number of individuals regularly contribute an equal amount to a pool of funds and then bid for the right to use the funds. Overwhelmingly, however, Australia's Chinese business community raises funds from banks. To take advantage of this, Australia's major banks employ Chinese staff in those branches closest to concentrations of Chinese businesses.

Among long-term resident Australian Chinese entrepreneurs, two of the most successful are Bernard Chan and Daniel Chen; both are based in Sydney.[21] Chan came to Australia during the 1960s from Rabaul in Papua New Guinea where he had set up a general store and invested in coconut and cocoa plantations.[22] In Australia, the Chan family has concentrated on property-related interests. Chen is a Teochiu and was born in Shantou, China. He arrived in Australia during the 1930s and set up as a clothing and textile wholesaler. Chen also is involved in export-import; owns two supermarkets, one in Sydney's Chinatown and the other in Chatswood; has winery interests; and has a substantial property portfolio, including a A$100 million 26-level tower in Sydney currently being developed.

....

20 A survey of Taiwan business migrants to Australia found they have a below average rate of business establishment after arrival, compared with other groups. After two years in Australia, only 48 per cent of those surveyed were in business. Poor English-language skills and problems in adapting to a very different business environment appeared to have been the main reasons for the slow rate of business establishment. (See Department of Immigration and Ethnic Affairs, 'Community Information Summary: Chinese in Australia', November 1994.)

21 Information on the two entrepreneurs has been sourced from *Business Review Weekly*, 'Rich 200', 21 May 1993, and 22 May 1995.

22 Rabaul, along with Port Moresby and Lae, have historically had significant Chinese populations, 90 per cent of whom are Cantonese.

AUSTRALIA'S CHINESE - PROVIDING LINKS TO THE REGIONAL ECONOMY

The diverse and growing Chinese community in Australia can contribute significantly to Australia's economic well-being domestically, regionally and internationally. Compared to the Chinese communities in South-East Asia, the United States, Canada, Europe, and elsewhere, Australia's Chinese community is one of the most diverse. This diversity means that in many instances, non-Chinese Australian entrepreneurs looking to do business with Asia can first approach Australia's Chinese for possible connections.

The diverse origins, as reflected in dialects, language, professional and business skills, and experiences, allow these communities to assist non-Chinese Australian businesses to trade with and invest in China, Taiwan, Hong Kong, and other regional economies where the ethnic Chinese are important as suppliers, consumers, financiers or intermediaries.[23]

---

23 Chapter 13 looks at mainstream Australian companies linking up with local Chinese business people to do business in Asia, and Chapter 14 provides advice on selecting the right partner.

Chapter 6

EXPLAINING THE SUCCESS OF ETHNIC CHINESE BUSINESS

Remember that you are responsible to your ancestors, not just to yourself. Our ancestors are not honoured by compromise; they are honoured by responsible behaviour and hard work.[1]

By any measure, the ethnic Chinese outside China have been phenomenally successful in business. Numbering about 50 million worldwide, they dominate, and in a sense drive, commerce throughout much of South-East Asia, controlling, for example, up to two thirds of the region's retail trade with less than ten per cent of the population. As detailed in Chapter 3, in most South-East Asian countries, the ethnic Chinese usually form only a small minority, yet they tend to control much and sometimes most of the non-land capital. Of South-East Asia's billionaires, 86 per cent are ethnic Chinese. (See Table 6.1.) Also the investment flows within East Asia attributed to the region's ethnic Chinese, are estimated to be greater than those from the Japanese.[2]

All too often the success of ethnic Chinese business people is ascribed to a single characteristic. However, the reasons are varied and many, and no single factor is especially dominant. Rather, connected elements vary in their significance from time to time and place to place. No single factor is unique to the ethnic Chinese; it is the range of factors and their interaction which has contributed to ethnic Chinese commercial success.

THE ETHNIC CHINESE ON THEIR SUCCESS

Interestingly, when the ethnic Chinese business people interviewed for this study nominated three reasons for the relative success of ethnic Chinese in business, most proffered reasons within a narrow range: a propensity for hard work, good connections, and an ability to keep business expenses low. Others were: having wealth in the first place which affords a relatively high level of education which in turn generates more wealth; honesty; good business acumen; a preference for long term investments rather than quick short-term profits; feelings of insecurity; and a cultural (or even as one interviewee steadfastly claimed, a 'genetic') disposition for industriousness. Most of these factors are undoubtedly important, but only partially explain the commercial success of ethnic Chinese.

....

1 Tan Suang U to his son in Botan, *Letters from Thailand*, translated by S. Fulop, Editions Duang Kamol, Bangkok, 1991, p. 205.

2 See SyCip, W., 'Role and prospects for developing countries in East Asia', unpublished paper.

Table 6.1

Asia's Ethnic Chinese Billionaires[3]

PLACE	PRINCIPAL(S)	ESTIMATED NET WORTH (US$ billion)	MAIN COMPANY
Hong Kong	Lee Shau Kee	6.5	Henderson Land Co.
	Kwok Brothers	6.4	Sun Hung Kai Properties
	Li Ka-shing	5.8	Hutchison Whampoa
	Pao Family	3.3	Wheelock & Co.
	Cheng Yu-tung	3.3	New World Development
	Ng Teng Fong and Robert Ng	3.0	Sinoland and Far Eastern Organisation
	Stanley Ho	2.1	Shan Tuk Holdings
	Hon Chiu Lee	1.8	Hsyan Development
	Gordon Wu	1.7	Hopewell Holdings
	Ronnie Chan	1.2	Hang Lung Development Co.
	Lo Ying Shek	1.1	Great Eagle Co.
Thailand	Chearavanont family	5.3	Charoen Pokphand Group
	Sophonpanich family	2.4	Bangkok Bank
	Lamsam family	1.8	Thai Farmers Bank
	Mongkol Kanjanapas	1.6	Tanayong and Bangkok Land
	Ratanarak family	1.0	Bank of Ayudhya
Philippines	Lucio Tan	1.7	Fortune Tobacco
	Henry Sy	1.1	SM Prime Holdings
	John Gokongwei	1.0	JG Summit Holdings
Indonesia	Liem Sioe Liong	3.0	Salim Group
	Eka Tjipta Widjaja	2.7	Sinar Mas Group
	Prajogo Pangestu	2.5	Barito Pacific Group
	Wonowidjojo family	1.8	Gudang Garam
Singapore	Kwek family	2.0	Hong Leong Group
	Khoo Teck Puat	1.6	Malayan Banking Corporation
	Lee family	1.3	Oversea-Banking Chinese Corporation
Malaysia	Quek family	2.1	Hong Leong Group
	Lim Goh Ting	2.1	Genting Bhd
	Robert Kuok	2.1	Kerry Group
Taiwan	Tsai family	7.5	Cathay Life Insurance
	Yue-Chee Wang	2.1	Formosa Plastics
	Wu family	2.1	Shin Kong Life Insurance
	Koo family	2.0	China-trust Commercial Bank
	Chang Yung-fa	1.1	Evergreen Group and EVA Airways
	Huang Shi Hue	1.1	Ching Fong Group

3 Adapted from *Forbes*, 'Billionaires in the making', 18 July 1994.

CULTURE AND OTHER INSTITUTIONS

When it comes to doing business, culture matters. In this sense, culture can be said to be a business input - other things being equal, a business-friendly culture leads to higher levels of production. The values of an ethnic group are part of its culture, and when these values are compatible with current opportunities, the chances of business success are heightened. Unfortunately, factors of production such as 'culture' and 'values' cannot be bought and sold. Communities come to possess such factors through societal evolution. The 'cultural capital' of ethnic Chinese allows them to prosper throughout Asia.

If cultural capital is to remain in its optimal form to ensure the survival and prosperity of a community, then the community must be open to alternative cultures and concepts.[4] So it has been with the ethnic Chinese. They have shown themselves to be highly adaptable in order to ensure their prosperity, de-emphasising, for example, those aspects of their culture likely to create serious friction with indigenous populations, and acquiring new cultural attributes superior to their own. This cultural smorgasbord has enriched Chinese business communities throughout South-East Asia and elsewhere with a range of cultural syntheses, varying from place to place.

Common or core characteristics are shared by the various ethnic Chinese communities of South-East Asia, but overlaid on these are cultural differences tempered by their divergent histories. The *baba* culture of the Straits Settlements of Penang, Malacca and Singapore is perhaps the best example of the evolution of a Chinese community into one with Chinese, Malay and British characteristics. The *baba* adopted English outdoor dress, Malay language and many Malay eating habits, but remained Buddhist.

New Frameworks for Commercial Organisation

One of those core characteristics that identifies many ethnic Chinese business people, is an ability to transplant and adapt their own framework of social and community organisation and interact with new environments. This allows Chinese communities to thrive, particularly in countries where rules and institutions are relatively undeveloped, and often gives them a considerable advantage over indigenous populations.

This framework for commercial organisation and interaction originated in China, where the state has not traditionally maintained order by jurisdiction. Historically, the ruling Chinese elite was small, scattered over a vast land and only interested in taxation as a means to fund its own spending. Civil law was not greatly developed. Private substitutes for the otherwise state-provided protection of private property, provision of infrastructure and creation and enforcement of a legal code had to be found. To this end, informal institutions evolved. These included the kin and family networks prevalent today among many ethnic

....

4 Kasper, W., 'Cultural Community, Liberty and Prosperity: Twelve Hypotheses', Unpublished paper, December 1993, p. 4.

Chinese.[5] Thus, the ethnic Chinese have a long history of ordering themselves, rather than relying on a central authority to do it for them.

Outside China, the propensity of the Chinese to create 'order out of chaos' manifested itself in the establishment of mutual help societies to house, clothe, feed and resettle new migrants; chambers of commerce to regulate business activity; craft guilds to regulate specific occupations; welfare and temple committees to undertake charitable works and run schools and hospitals; and dialect and clan associations to organise cultural activities and provide small-scale credit to members. Organisations such as these continued to operate in parallel with state-sponsored regulatory bodies where gaps existed in the state's regulatory coverage or where the rules of the state were not enforced. Today, these associations may still be important in countries where legal and other soft infrastructure are underdeveloped.

Confucianism

Confucianism is not without influence. It is, however, only one of many factors that propel the ethnic Chinese to the forefront of Asian business. Confucianism consists of a set of ethical rules allowing for the harmonious, efficient interaction of people and constraining erratic and opportunistic behaviour. The importance of education and the family are emphasised. Confucianism gives precedence to vertical relationships in society, rather than horizontal ones. Of prime importance is the relationship between father and son, and the loyalty family members give to the head of the family.[6]

An important aspect of Confucianism is that its precepts are vague enough to allow flexible interpretation. Thus, behaviour can be modified in the face of changing circumstances without running up against a rigid Confucian constraint.

---

5 See Jones, E., et al, *Coming Full Circle: An Economic History of the Pacific Rim*, Oxford University Press Australia, Oxford, 1993, p. 33; and Redding, G.S., *The Spirit of Chinese Capitalism*, Walter de Gruyter and Co., Berlin, 1990, p. 45.

6 See Ch'ng, D., *The Overseas Chinese Entrepreneurs in East Asia: Background, Business Practices and International Networks*, CEDA Monograph M100, 1993, p. 42.

CONFUCIANISM

Confucianism[7] is not a religion but a set of pragmatic rules for daily life. The following are the key principles of Confucian teaching:

1. The stability of society is based on unequal relationships between people. The junior partner in any social relationship owes the senior partner respect and obedience; the senior owes the junior partner protection and consideration.

2. The family is the prototype of all social organisations. A person is not primarily an individual; instead, he or she is a member of a family.

3. One should treat others as one would like to be treated oneself.

4. Virtue with regard to one's tasks in life consists of trying to acquire skills and education, working hard, not spending more than necessary, being patient, and persevering. Moderation is necessary in all activities, as is keeping face.

5. Venerate things past and hence respect one's elders as sources of wisdom and guidance.

The Central Role of Trust and Transactions Costs

In many Asian countries, business activity occurs where economic and legal institutions are either embryonic or not fully effective. Because of this, the costs of doing business, 'transaction costs', are relatively high. In modern economies, transport and transactions costs tend to absorb at least 40 per cent of the national product.[8] Clearly, with transactions costs making up such a significant proportion of output, those communities with cultural arrangements leading to relatively lower transactions costs will be more successful in the marketplace. Successful ethnic Chinese businesses minimise transactions costs.

This is achieved in the first instance by choosing primarily to do business with one another. Most ethnic Chinese are culturally empathetic with one another, write the same language and have a range of community mechanisms to further enforce contractual obligations without needing recourse to authority or institutions outside that community.

There is a high correlation between low transactions costs and a high degree of community cohesion. As discussed previously, probably because of their status as minorities within the Chinese immigrant population, certain groups such as the Teochiu and the Fuzhou regard themselves as particularly conscious of their clan

....

7 See Hofstede, G. and M.H. Bond, 'The Confucius Connection: From Cultural Roots to Economic Growth', *Organizational Dynamics*; and Redding, G.S., p. 51.

8 See North, D.C., 'Transactions costs, institutions and economic performance', Occasional Paper no. 30, San Francisco, International Centre for Economic Growth, 1992 in Kasper, W., 'Global Competition, Institutions and the East-Asian Ascendancy', unpublished paper, 1993.

group. Interestingly, these two groups are notably prominent among successful ethnic Chinese business people in the region. (See Chapter 2.)

Common group membership creates among members a presumption of trust. What helps make this presumption a reality is an enforcement mechanism. Among many ethnic Chinese business people of Asia, an individual's word is his bond. This is assisted by the fact that if one breaks one's word, news of this will be quickly disseminated among the business community, leaving that person out of all future business opportunities. 'Trust' in this instance is underpinned by a powerful enforcement mechanism.[9]

The ethnic Chinese have several institutions to facilitate the enforcement of contracts between them. One is the flow of 'business gossip' that allows them to be familiar not only with the business affairs of their competitors, but also those of their friends. This flow is facilitated by frequent banquets and community gatherings. The most important institution for the free flow of business information is the Chinese chamber of commerce. Most towns and cities in South-East Asia with a sizeable Chinese business community have one.

A tangible example of the importance of trust and the attendant enforcement mechanisms is found in a study of the ethnic Chinese in the former South Vietnam.[10] The study found that on average, the interest charges incurred by ethnic Chinese merchants in Saigon from ethnic Chinese money lenders were about half those paid by ethnic Vietnamese. This enabled the Chinese to monopolise wholesale trade where gross profit margins were low and average turnover periods long. Involvement in wholesale trade was impossible for Vietnamese merchants, who instead, clustered in lower level retail operations where gross margins were higher. On the face of it, the interest rate differential looks like a clear cut example of discrimination, but in reality it simply reflected the differing levels of risk and availability of enforcement mechanisms. If an ethnic Chinese merchant defaulted on his loan, this was reported to the local Chinese chamber of commerce. If an ethnic Vietnamese did so, there was no similar enforcement procedure.

The Effect of Being a Minority Culture

Like many ethnic minorities, particularly commercially successful ones, the ethnic Chinese have faced varying degrees of persecution, discrimination or political repression in most of the countries in which they have settled. One survey of more than 150 ethnic Chinese entrepreneurs both inside and outside China found that 90 per cent of those who were first-generation emigrants had experienced war; 40 per cent had gone through a political disaster like the Cultural Revolution; 32 per cent had lost a home; and 28 per cent had weathered

---

9 This is little different to more formally structured societies. In the West, 'trust' in business transactions is underpinned by legal sanctions.

10 See Barton, C.A., 'Trust and credit: Some observations regarding business strategies of overseas Chinese traders in South Vietnam' in L.Y.C Lim and L.A.P. Gosling (eds), *The Chinese in Southeast Asia*, Vol. 1, , Maruzen Asia, Singapore, 1983, p. 62.

economic disaster resulting in a significant loss of wealth.[11] Experiences like these have encouraged many Chinese business people overseas to develop various strategies to hedge against uncertainty. Thriftiness and an emphasis on education are two such examples. Accumulating wealth brings a measure of certainty and security, and education is easily transported.

Self Selection

Another factor contributing to the commercial success of the ethnic Chinese may well be that those who left China were generally more able, more entrepreneurial, and less averse to taking risks than the remaining population. This is a characteristic of most immigrant groups.

It is not necessarily that the ethnic Chinese have an inherent capacity for hard work. Rather, those who migrated to South-East Asia may have 'selected themselves' on the basis of their capacity for hard work, which in the early days of migration to many countries in the region meant coolie labour. Therefore, it is reasonable to surmise that the Chinese who left for South-East Asia were particularly hard working.

The Benefits of a Low Profile

Although some ethnic Chinese entrepreneurs deliberately court publicity, many avoid it.

Measures which reduce visibility include not listing companies on the stock market unless absolutely necessary, thus obviating the need to produce annual reports and alerting competitors to corporate success, and not becoming directly involved in politics. The acculturation of ethnic Chinese, including their adoption of local eating habits and dress also makes them less visible. Partly because of an undervaluation of services such as marketing and partly as another manifestation of the desire for relative anonymity, ethnic Chinese manufacturers tend not to use their own brand names, or at least, not to promote them. Until recently, there have been few ethnic Chinese equivalents of Chanel, General Electric, or Sony.[12] Measures like this have been helpful in preserving the wealth of the ethnic Chinese.

Risk Diversification Through Dispersion of Capital

Indigenous families tend to be relatively geographically concentrated, and accordingly, the economic fate of a single family can rise or fall through the operation of a single factor. Chinese extended families in South-East Asia are frequently geographically dispersed, and therefore able to spread risk to preserve their capital. Hence, an indigenous family is more likely to have all its wealth wiped out than an ethnic Chinese family.

Spreading wealth across borders in this way helps to diversify 'country risk'.

....

11 See Kao, J., 'The worldwide web of Chinese business', *Harvard Business Review*, March-April 1993, p. 25.

12 See Redding, G.S.

The Family as an Input For Ethnic Chinese Success

Most ethnic Chinese have close-knit families. A child growing up in such a family is subjected to extensive socialisation, not just from immediate parents, but from siblings and the entire extended family. As eighteenth century economist Adam Smith observed in his *Theory of Moral Sentiments*, families are an important institution for constraining behaviour so that the outcomes of self-seeking behaviour accord with the community good. Such a strong socialising framework can ensure the replication of traits such as thrift, studiousness and industriousness.

The strong attachment ethnic Chinese have to their families also contributes to their acceptance of relatively long time horizons before investments generate returns. Ethnic Chinese families are very vertical, patriarchal (sometimes matriarchal) and have obligations to ancestors and future generations. The economic unit is not the individual but the extended household. In conventional attempts to model a 'household' consumption function, consumption is presumed to have a finite period in which to occur; it ends with the death of the individual. With the ethnic Chinese, however, since the economic unit, the household, is infinitely long-lived, so is the consumption period. In such a case, if an investment project will generate returns into the next generation and beyond, then it is a good investment as all gains do not have to be realised before the demise of the investing individual.

The importance of preserving family, rather than simply individual, honour cannot be overstated. Families will go to great lengths to ensure that all family members are good debtors. The family name can be used as a simple screen for credit worthiness. If one family member proves a poor debtor, all other members may be tarnished with a bad reputation, something which may inhibit their access to capital and raise the risk premium on loans, but also cause them considerable disquiet.

The Ethnic Chinese as the Fillers of Market Niches

Ethnic Chinese entrepreneurs could be characterised as fillers of economic potholes on the road to development. Developing markets are imperfect and incomplete, giving rise to market niches and opportunities to make higher than normal profits.[13]

The ethnic Chinese specialise in markets where competition is not atomistic, and where their products benefit from a degree of market power, (such as traded manufactures). This allows them to accrue oligopolistic rents, *ie* higher than normal profits. Because indigenous people have historically tended to operate in markets where competition is relatively atomistic and homogenous (such as in agricultural production) they do not benefit from any such oligopolistic power.

Raising funds relatively easily and quickly, and networking across markets, ethnic Chinese business people are able to identify market niches as they arise, and to

....

13 The most usual reason for such niches is the uneven distribution of information. It follows that those who can quickly and cheaply access information will be those most able to identify market niches and fill them.

move quickly into niche opportunities. They are often also sensitive to changes in demand, able to respond quickly, and are innovative (or at least use innovations from elsewhere). These qualities assist them in preserving and expanding their market niches.

Market niches arise not only in embryonic markets but in markets constrained by external factors. Government regulation is one such constraint. Others are local customs which prevent indigenous people from engaging in certain types of enterprise, leaving the way open for those not so constrained. Neither dietary restrictions nor usury prohibitions limit the sectors in which most ethnic Chinese business people can operate, allowing them to fill the niches left by others.

For example, the dominance of Calcutta's Hakka community in leather tanning, mentioned in Chapter 3, is attributed to the shunning by higher caste Hindus of tanning. Another example is the Sino-Thai Bangkok Bank, which in the 1960s and 1970s lent to ethnic Chinese businesses, filling a niche across South-East Asia left by Western banks who would not lend to many ethnic Chinese entrepreneurs, citing as the reason their often unsatisfactory book-keeping practices.

The Importance of Property

Many ethnic minorities are more influential than their numbers suggest. What has elevated ethnic Chinese business people to being super successful has been their holdings of property. As Asia has boomed in recent years, so have Asian property markets. Most big ethnic Chinese-controlled conglomerates have property divisions, and indeed, this is how many of them have been able to branch out into other fields, using their increasingly valuable property to secure loans for further investment.

Cross-Border Connections

Given the wide dispersion of ethnic Chinese across South-East Asia and the relatively narrow area of China from which most have come, many ethnic Chinese there have friends or relatives living in other countries. Where these are lacking, clan, sub-dialect or similar connections normally can be tapped. Other connections include classmate linkages and religious (particularly Christian) networks.[14] This phenomenon was summarised by an ethnic Chinese businessman who, when interviewed in Yangon, said that he had been successful in business because wherever he went in South-East Asia, there was always someone there with whom he had some sort of connection and who was ready to help.[15]

14 Christian linkages among the ethnic Chinese are particularly prominent among overseas Teochiu. In the past, Christian missionaries operated in Swatow (now Shantou) and a substantial number of Teochiu are now Christian.

15 Chapter 9 provides much more detail on these kinds of connections across borders.

Another advantage of these 'networks' is that investment advice can be internalised within the network, a relatively cheap source of information. Thus, ethnic Chinese entrepreneurs engage in knowledge arbitrage across the markets in which they operate. Such networks mean that market niches can be quickly identified and exploited and deficiencies in one market can be matched to excesses in others, allowing dispersed markets to be integrated.[16] Cross-border connections enable the Chinese to bypass often cumbersome official channels, saving on time, regulations and other costs. All this is made possible by the many thousands of interconnecting ethnic Chinese networks that cover much of Asia.

To a degree, the trade and investment that occurs between ethnic Chinese communities in different countries may look like a borderless ethnic Chinese economy, although this probably overstates the case. Most ethnic Chinese are firmly rooted in their countries of residence - a Malaysian Chinese in many respects is more Malaysian than Chinese, for instance. However for many ethnic Chinese entrepreneurs the choice of residence, work and investment remain pragmatic considerations. As south-eastern China's economy has taken off, many senior ethnic Chinese business people from South-East Asia have chosen to live in Hong Kong, where they are better able to oversee their China investments. For most, however, it is enough simply to know ethnic Chinese in other markets, to call on them, and trade and invest with them.

Access To Capital

Historically, ethnic Chinese business people have been able to call on friends, relatives and particularly the clan for capital. The enforcement mechanisms helped guarantee the money was repaid. As a result, funds flowed freely. In places where the banking system was either embryonic or non-existent, such sources of capital were crucial. This meant that ethnic Chinese business people were able to seize opportunities quickly, whereas non-Chinese who did not have similar access to capital could not. Many older ethnic Chinese business people interviewed in South-East Asia discussed the ability of either themselves or their parents to get a start in business because of the availability of funds through the informal networks. Often, the funds came from relatives living elsewhere, particularly in Hong Kong.

Where capital markets are poorly developed, such as Myanmar, traditional ways of raising capital are followed. In Singapore, Malaysia and Thailand, traditional sources may still be important for smaller business people for start-up capital, but generally, now banks and other formal types of financial institutions are favoured.

Political Linkages

Developing a close relationship with the local indigenous elite is crucial to the continuing success of the ethnic Chinese in South-East Asia. In the nineteenth century, some of the wealthier Chinese traders and financiers in South-East Asia

---

16 Ethnic Chinese entrepreneurs tend to integrate markets which have not been integrated because of prohibitive transactions costs. They have a comparative advantage when it comes to transactions costs because they often are able to internalise them.

made themselves indispensable to local rulers or officials by providing financial skills and funds.[17] The Chinese were favoured for this role as it was unlikely they would ever become political rivals to the court; whereas, indigenous courtiers always posed that risk.[18]

Today, the connections between the political elite and the ethnic Chinese business community have changed, but they are still very important. In all countries, a relationship with the government can be invaluable for accessing information, government contracts and other privileges. As discussed in Chapter 7, many senior ethnic Chinese business people have benefited from good political connections.

The Role of Sound Government

The success of ethnic Chinese business people has not been all their own making. The business-friendly character of South-East Asian governments has made a considerable difference to the opportunities enjoyed by ethnic Chinese.

Aspects of government in South-East Asia which particularly benefit entrepreneurs, ethnic Chinese or otherwise include:[19]

- Relatively weak labour unions which are enterprise orientated;
- Flexible labour markets and the participation of women in the labour force, increasing the potential supply of labour. As a result, labour supply bottlenecks are few and labour costs are relatively low;
- Relatively low levels of rent seeking (the seeking of higher than normal profits with the benefit of government patronage and regulation). Domestic markets generally are exposed to external competition. *De jure* protection certainly exists but is often poorly enforced;
- Most Asian countries have experienced a move towards regulatory liberalisation, encouraging entrepreneurs to keep innovating to remain competitive;
- The recognition by East Asian governments that their economies were initially on the periphery of world trade, (meaning that their exports faced higher transactions costs than otherwise) and their preparedness to keep local production factors (such as tax rates, wage costs and land rents) lower to compensate for these higher transactions costs;

---

17 See Mackie, J.A.C., 'Overseas Chinese Entrepreneurship', *Asian-Pacific Economic Literature*, May 1992, p. 44.

18 In some South-East Asian countries, senior ethnic Chinese business people are still to a degree fulfilling this role - staying close to the indigenous elite, supplying them with financial advice and capital, but without posing a direct political threat.

19 This section draws in part upon: Kasper, W., 'Global Competition, Institutions and the East-Asian Ascendancy', Draft Paper, 1993; and Kasper, W., 'Accelerated Industrial Evolution in East Asia: Some Lessons', Economics and Management Discussion Paper, Department of Economics and Management, University College, The University of New South Wales, Australian Defence Force Academy, July 1989, p. 10.

emphasising centralised decision making. They normally focus on one product market. The owner/manager is usually close to the market that the firm serves and is sensitive to matters of cost and efficiency.[3]

A study of 250 of the largest ethnic Chinese companies in the Philippines found these common operating principles:[4]

- Low margin and a high volume to penetrate markets and guarantee a steady flow of profit.
- Rigorous control of inventory to achieve low capital investment and high rates of stock turnover.
- Reduction of transactions costs by use of networking within the Chinese community.

Management and Decision Making

A frequently noted, although not unique, characteristic of smaller Chinese firms is the high degree of centralised decision making. Non-Chinese, family-owned and run firms in Australia and elsewhere feature many characteristics normally ascribed to traditional ethnic Chinese firms. Typically there will be little consultation by managers prior to decision-making and subordinates are encouraged to be loyal and dependent. However, operating decisions are frequently delegated to lower management in larger Chinese firms, just as in Western firms. In larger firms, the Chinese rely on highly centralised finance and budget decision making, and on personnel practices which enhance trust and control. Recruitment decisions in ethnic Chinese firms appear to emphasise trustworthiness and loyalty to a far greater degree than in Western firms. In addition, top managers retain control over employees through bonuses and pay increases, personal loans to employees and involvement in formal social activities off the job. Thus while operating responsibility may be delegated to lower level managers, effective control of employees is still retained at the higher levels.[5]

The tendency for centralised decision-making in ethnic Chinese firms may not be an identifying characteristic, but a function of such firms usually being family owned and managed. Such firms do not separate ownership and management and thus, managers have an even greater personal stake in the firm's prospects than otherwise. An example of a non-Chinese Australian family-owned firm with similar characteristics is the Moran Group which has its head office in Sydney. The group is Australia's largest private hospital and nursing home enterprise

....

3 One common method for the owner/manager to stay in touch is to regularly eat lunch with his employees, bosses and employees all mixed together. Anthony Salim, a senior executive with Indonesia's largest conglomerate, the Salim Group, and son of founding patriarch, Liem Sioe Liong, has the reputation for being willing to listen to any of the group's thousands of employees, no matter how junior, to hear their ideas on how the business can be improved.

4 The study is quoted in Redding, G.S., *The Spirit of Chinese Capitalism*, Walter de Gruyter and Co., Berlin, 1990, p. 170.

5 See Deyo, F.C. 'Chinese Management Practices and Work Commitment in Comparative Perspective' in L.Y.C Lim and L.A.P. Gosling (eds), *The Chinese in Southeast Asia*, Vol. 2, Maruzen Asia, Singapore, 1983, p. 126.

founded by Doug Moran in whom, along with other family members, most major decision making is vested.[6]

Several characteristics of Chinese firms assist fast decision making:

- Centralised control.
- Flexible technology: a bauxite smelter has only one purpose, a sewing machine can make clothing, curtains or hang gliders as marketing opportunities dictate.[7]
- When it is present book keeping is kept simple: often this is a simple balance sheet so that the owner always knows the financial position of the firm and can decide quickly to exploit opportunities.[8]

All these characteristics combine to make ethnic Chinese business concerns efficient, effective and fast moving. Australians doing business with such firms will usually not have to wait long for decisions to be made, or potential agreements to be mulled over, as commonly, decisions can be made on the spot.

One consequence of the preference for centralised decision making is that many ethnic Chinese businesses elect not to operate in sectors where decentralised decision-making is necessary, such as complex manufacturing and service industries. On the other hand, real estate development, a business where management is easily centralised, is an area where ethnic Chinese business people are active, if not predominant, in Asia.

Employer-Employee Relations

Typically, management in the ethnic Chinese firm follows a paternal pattern. Most structures encourage strong loyalty to the firm by employees. Financial support to educate employees' children, payment of hospital bills, soft loans, and subsidised food in the workplace all cut down employee turnover, thus reducing hiring and training costs.[9] During economic downturns, ethnic Chinese firms prefer to retain employees rather than treat them as a variable cost to be added and subtracted with the vicissitudes of the economic environment. This further underscores the long-term attachment ethnic Chinese employers and employees have. The loyalty ethnic Chinese firms show to their employees and the loyalty expected of employees is furthered by the common practice of promotion through seniority.

Another way ethnic Chinese firms ensure that the interests of their employees match those of the firm is to remunerate employees with a basic wage but to add potentially huge bonuses, that are linked to the fortunes of the firm. A bonus of six month's or a year's pay is not unusual for firms that are doing well. Bonus

6 See Chapter 13 for further detail on the Moran Group.

7 Redding, G.S., p. 221.

8 This contrasts with the more complex accounting practices of many Western firms, where the decision makers are usually not immediately aware of the firm's cash position and are therefore unable to move as quickly.

9 See Redding, G.S., p. 215.

payments usually are determined by the manager, and in large firms, the top manager will decide on the bonuses for his executives, who in turn decide the bonuses for their subordinates. Discretionary bonuses such as these can be considered a form of profit sharing. Middle and senior staff of Robert Kuok's group of companies, for example, are known to be handsomely rewarded, often with substantial tranches of non-voting deferred shares in Kuok companies.[10]

A Preference for Internal Financing

As ethnic Chinese businesses become larger and more sophisticated, raising capital from clan sources or from friends and relatives increasingly is becoming a thing of the past as financial markets become more developed across Asia. Nonetheless, traditional ways to raise funds still may be important for small enterprises starting out. The clan is, for some, an important source for start-up capital. Several Sino-Thais interviewed mentioned that this was still the case in Bangkok. Elsewhere, the 'tontine' system is used.[11] Most of the venture capital in Taiwan is sourced from friends and relatives, largely because Taiwan's commercial sector is dominated by small-scale entrepreneurial concerns, still operating on a traditional basis.[12]

For larger ethnic Chinese firms, retained earnings fund expansion, largely because internally generated funds are cheap and present no risk of surrendering control of the firm to outsiders, as equity or debt financing could do.

Singapore's Tuan Sing Holdings, a medium-sized property developer with operations in Singapore and China, is typical of ethnic Chinese concerns when it comes to raising funds. When interviewed, the firm's CEO, Peter Sung, indicated that the company preferred to raise cash for expansion first from retained earnings, then by borrowing and finally, from issuing stock.

Ethnic Chinese conglomerates typically use a mixture of all three methods to raise funds, although when it comes to debt financing, this often may mean raising loans from a financial arm associated with the conglomerate, rather than going to an outside source.

Thus when it comes to raising funds, ethnic Chinese businesses of whatever size generally opt for sources least likely to dilute the owner's control. Traditional, more personalised ways of raising capital are being replaced by more formal methods even for smaller enterprises and for larger ones almost all funds are raised from formal sources.

---

10 See Studwell, J., 'Sweet and sour times for a sugar king', *Asia, Inc.*, December 1994.

11 The tontine system is explained in Chapter 3.

12 Biggart, N.W. and G.G. Hamilton, 'On the limits of a firm-based theory to explain business networks: The Western Bias of NeoClassical Economics', Unpublished paper, Research Program in East Asian Business and Development, Institute of Governmental Affairs, University of California, Davis, 1990, p. 5.

The Treatment of Services as Business Inputs

Many ethnic Chinese entrepreneurs tend to undervalue services and intangibles as business inputs.[13] Many prefer to minimise payments outside the firm for legal, financial or marketing advice, R&D, intellectual property, design or any other service or intangible. Such businesses often prefer to either internalise the costs for such services by having them provided in-house; borrow them in the case of new technology; or simply to forego them. Thus, intangible production inputs are given a low priority, often to the detriment of the firm. Generally only as ethnic Chinese firms expand and are forced to pay a higher regard to intangible and service inputs, do they do so. Some firms leave it almost too late to seek outside advice on restructuring, going to the brink of collapse before calling outside experts to assist. In interviews, some Chinese chambers of commerce in the region commented that even they occasionally have difficulties getting their members to pay for the services they provide. Even some Australian Chinese businesses may try to avoid legal contracts and prefer instead to sign agency agreements and memoranda of understanding with local partners. This underscores a preference for personalised exchange and a dislike by some of engaging external legal advice for the drawing up of formal contracts.

Aw Boon Haw, creator of Tiger Balm internalised the cost of many of the business services he required. Aw recognised the necessity of marketing his product and became one of the region's consummate marketeers. Rather than contract outsiders to promote his product, he did it all himself. The Haw Par pavilion theme parks were set up to promote Tiger Balm. Also, rather than pay others to advertise in their newspapers, Aw started his own newspapers.[14]

Where payment for outside assistance is unavoidable, ethnic Chinese business people may offer equity in a planned project in lieu of the requisite fee. In Australia, this can cause a mismatch, as Australian legal and accounting firms normally prefer to collect fees rather than become joint-venture partners. Nonetheless, the practice of offering equity for services rendered diversifies the risks of projects, and can ensure that the services provided are of a high quality. Perhaps, the most spectacular example of this practice was Liem Sioe Liong's successful enticement of Mochtar Riady to become the CEO of Indonesia's Bank Central Asia (BCA) by offering him 17.5 per cent of BCA's shares.[15]

A consequence of undervaluing services and intangibles is that many smaller ethnic Chinese companies typically report only on tangibles in their business plans. Estimated costs for proceeding with a project often will include equipment and hardware but ignore the cost of services. A business plan to construct a factory might, for example, detail the costs of the bricks, mortar and roofing, but exclude the cost of employing builders and electricians.[16]

---

13 This was a constant theme of interviews with ethnic Chinese business people across Asia.

14 See Pan, L., *Sons of the Yellow Emperor: The Story of the Overseas Chinese*, Mandarin, 1991, p. 178.

15 The share deal is described in Ch'ng, D., p. 114.

16 Business plans also tend to neglect to mention the competition.

Inheritance

Traditionally, Chinese families have valued sons very highly as it is the role of sons to honour the ancestors, including deceased parents. Some elderly Chinese with daughters but no sons have adopted on their deathbed a son with full inheritance rights, who will carry out the filial duty.[17] Others pass on control of the family's businesses to a son-in-law. Hong Kong billionaire Sir Y.K. Pao died leaving only daughters. None assumed control of Pao's businesses. Subsequently, the family's property, transport, communications, financial services and retailing interests were passed to son-in-law Peter Woo and the shipping interests were passed to son-in-law Helmut Sohmen.[18]

Arising from the wish to be appropriately mourned after death is the desire to leave the son with a sizeable inheritance to continue to show necessary honour to the ancestors. The son's duty is to ensure that the inheritance is maintained and built up to honour the ancestors who contributed to it. Running the family's businesses into the ground would bring great dishonour to the ancestors.

Traditionally, each son received an equal share of his father's estate; the inheritance was partible and patrilineal, with the eldest son assuming control of the family's business interests.[19] A variant on this was to give the eldest son half the estate and divide the other half between the remaining sons. This accounts in part for traditional ethnic Chinese firms being of small to medium size, even though a family's combined wealth may be quite considerable. It still is usual for control, but not necessarily full ownership of the family's business interests to pass to a son.[20]

There are some significant exceptions to the eldest son 'rule'. Anthony Salim, who is currently running the Salim Group on a day-to-day basis, is Liem Sioe Liong's youngest son. The heir apparent to Alfonso Yuchenko, the founder of a Philippines' conglomerate of more than seventy companies involved in banking, finance, insurance, trading, farming, oil exploration, construction, timber, cement and manufacturing, is his eldest daughter.[21] Eka Tjipta Widjaja, the founding patriarch of Indonesia's giant Sinar Mas Group appears to have passed over the five sons of his first wife, by installing a daughter, Sukmawati Widjaja, as vice chairman and CEO of the group. Eka Tjipta Widjaja has retained the chairmanship for himself. Henry Sy, the controller of one of the Philippines' largest retailing groups, is understood to have selected one of his daughters, Teresita Sy, as his successor, passing over four sons and another daughter.[22]

....

17 For some anecdotes on this, see Chia, F., *The Babas Revisited*, Heinemann Asia, Singapore, 1994, pp. 40-41.

18 See *Forbes*, 'Billionaires in the making', 18 July 1994.

19 See Hamilton, G.G., 'Overseas Chinese Capitalism', Working Paper 42, Research Program in East Asian Business and Development, Institute of Governmental Affairs, University of California, January 1992.

20 This may not always be in the best interests of the family's businesses.

21 See Ch'ng, D.

22 See *Far Eastern Economic Review*, 'Strength in numbers', 21 July 1994.

Some ethnic Chinese business families, particularly in Thailand, set up family trusts. On the death of the family patriarch, the family business is not divided among the family members or inherited by just one person. All family members have a share in the family trust. Profits from the business are distributed to the family members. With such a structure it is not clear which family members own various parts of the business, often leading to family squabbles and protracted management problems.

This diffuse ownership by family members of family-held assets is sometimes a major problem. Unravelling corporate problems resulting from such inheritance practices and resultant family disagreements has become a thriving business for Bangkok based consultants who restructure family business groups around the complexities of intra-family politics.

However, the conglomerates are restructuring slowly to avert such destructive feuding. Increasingly when companies are handed from one generation to another they are divided among the children. Often, each child is given a company and the other siblings each have a minority shareholding and are represented on that company's board.

The Centrality of the Family

A central theme running through many traditional ethnic Chinese businesses is the desire to keep the family together. Often newly arrived Chinese in Australia who start a small business will involve the whole family in the enterprise, even if it means over-staffing and underemployment. As ethnic Chinese firms grow larger, the imperative to keep the family together may come more from pragmatic reasons than from traditional social ones. The Hong Leong Group spread across Singapore and Malaysia, for example, consists of complex cross-shareholdings that make it difficult for any single family member to disengage from the group. All the sons and daughters of Eka Tjipta Widjaja's first wife are involved in the management of Sinar Mas.[23] At least twelve Kwok family members hold executive positions in the Kwoks' Hong Kong-based, retail, real estate and financial services Wing On Group, and reportedly only family members or family friends achieve senior management positions in the Taiwanese Chung Shing Textile Group.[24] These examples of family involvement in business are symptomatic of a wider preference by ethnic Chinese entrepreneurs to maintain the family's business interests intact.

....

23 See Sinar Mas, *Sinar Mas Group* (promotional brochure).

24 See *Washington Post*, 'Relative success story', 11 September 1994.

The Marco Polo Pacific Dynasty Fund

Hong Kong-based Kerry Investment Management Ltd, a member of the Robert Kuok Group, has, with a Swiss firm, set up the Marco Polo Dynasty Fund for investors.[25] The Fund only invests in publicly listed, family-controlled companies in the region. Kerry Investment Management found that between 1986 and 1991, the average growth in the earnings per share for the top ten family-controlled companies listed on the exchanges of Singapore, Thailand, Malaysia, and Hong Kong outstripped the earnings growth for the top ten general stocks and top ten government-linked stocks by factors of three or more.

The fund has identified a range of possible family-controlled stocks on exchanges in Hong Kong, Singapore, Malaysia, Thailand, Indonesia and the Philippines.

Investment is not restricted to companies which are controlled by ethnic Chinese, but most of the companies tend to be controlled by ethnic Chinese. The fund believes that family-owned companies perform so well because they tend to be the most entrepreneurial, and generally they restrict their operations to the fast growing Asian region.

Corporate Family Friction

The fact that most ethnic Chinese businesses are family owned has its costs. When ownership and control are vested in different members of one family and that family splits, the implications for its business interests can be profound. Two recent examples of ethnic Chinese family infighting which have spilled over to the corporate arena are the Bangkok-based Tejaphaibul family, and the Singapore- and Malaysia-based Yeo family.

The Tejaphaibul family controls the Bangkok Metropolitan Bank, Bangkok's World Trade Centre, property and other interests. The second generation became embroiled in family conflicts which led to one part of the family in control of the Bank severing short-term credit lines to another part in control of the family's Kloster Beer interests. Resultant cash flow problems harmed the beer interests.[26] Bangkok Metropolitan Bank also has made in-house loans to companies owned by the family. Many of these loans are now non-performing, making sale of the bank difficult. Investment in the World Trade Centre, which features one of Bangkok's largest shopping malls, has brought the family more problems. The complex was widely understood to have made substantial cumulative losses, although it now may be profitable.

25 Information has been sourced from Marco Polo Pacific Dynasty Fund (prospectus summary), Hong Kong, and personal communication with Kerry Investment Management Ltd.

26 See Sender, H., 'Inside the overseas Chinese network', *Institutional Investor*, August 1991, p. 40.

The Yeo family consists of six separate but related Yeo families and controls the Singapore-based Yeo Hiap Seng Ltd, a food and beverages group with an annual turnover of S$266.5 million in 1993.[27] By 1994, several Yeo families wanted to withdraw from the family holding company, Yeo Hiap Seng Holdings, to go their separate ways. The wider Yeo family subsequently split into two camps, leading to complicated and lengthy court proceedings.[28]

Public airings of internal family problems are unusual for ethnic Chinese business families. They prefer to keep their disagreements private and present a united front to the outside world.

Trading Favours

Ethnic Chinese business people in the region appear to operate with an implicit balance sheet of favours of very long duration. There are numerous examples of favours done by the major ethnic Chinese entrepreneurs for one another. The favours are almost always returned, sometimes years later. Often big corporate moves today can be explained in terms of favours done years ago. The giver and receiver of a particular favour will often share some link, such as a common dialect, educational institution or church group.

A good example is the relationship between Robert Kuok and Khoo Kay Peng, both Malaysian Hokkien Chinese. As detailed in Chapter 2, Khoo, the controller of Malaysia's MUI Group sold his MUI Bank in 1993 and spent much of the proceeds on buying equity in assets controlled by Kuok.[29] Far from being only a recent relationship, the pairing has its antecedents before the late 1980s when Kuok saved MUI from a hostile takeover bid from Malaysian entrepreneur Vincent Tan. Enduring relationships such as this underscore the personalised nature of ethnic Chinese business.

Links with Property

Nearly all the ethnic Chinese entrepreneurs interviewed stated that real estate was their preferred investment. Singapore property was particularly prized. In a recent *Far Eastern Economic Review* survey of the preferred investments of various personalities in the region, of the eight ethnic Chinese surveyed, six reported that either the most profitable investment they had made so far, or wished to make, was in property.[30]

Property is tangible; it can be readily used as security for raising additional capital; and to date, it has proven an exceptional investment.

....

27 See Yeo Hiap Seng Ltd, *YHS: Annual Report 1993*, Singapore, 1994.

28 The court cases surrounding the Yeo family's disagreements received extensive media coverage in Singapore. See for instance *The Straits Times*, 'Alan Yeo begins court bid to wind up YHS Holdings', 21 June 1994; 'Keppel Corp was to take 49% of YHS Holdings, Alan Yeo tells court', 22 June 1994; 'Judge takes witness to task for contradicting affidavit', 24 June 1994; and 'Respondents 'unfamiliar with assertions in joint affidavit' ', 25 June 1994; *The Straits Times Weekly Edition*, 'Three senior execs leave YHS, and 'more changes forthcoming' ', 8 October 1994.

29 See *Asian Wall Street Journal*, 'MUI joins an old associate in Philippine investment', 7 July 1994; and 'MUI share in SCMP grows with purchase of 5% stake', 19 May 1994.

30 See *Far Eastern Economic Review*, 'If only I had bought...', 24 November 1994.

Much of the wealth of ethnic Chinese business people across Asia is now tied up in considerable real estate holdings, and, as previously discussed, the fast capital appreciation of real estate in many East Asian cities is responsible for the rapid accumulation of wealth of many ethnic Chinese families. Many of the larger ethnic Chinese-controlled business groups in the region have also pioneered integrated industrial and residential estates, particularly in China.

Most ethnic Chinese conglomerates have a property arm and some of Asia's leading ethnic Chinese entrepeneurs are involved principally in real estate development and speculation. The Singaporean and Malaysian Hong Leong Group is a big investor in property.[31] Hong Kong's wealthiest individual, Lee Shau-kee, has made most of his wealth through his Hong Kong-based Henderson Land.[32] Mochtar Riady's Lippo Group is a significant property developer and manager in Indonesia, Hong Kong and China. One of Bangkok's largest property companies is Bangkok Land, owned by the Sino-Thai Kanjanapas family, and Singapore's biggest land developer is Singapore Land, controlled by Indonesia's Liem Sioe Liong through UIC. Among the top 500 ethnic Chinese controlled companies in the region, the most common core competence was in land and property development, as Table 7.2 indicates.

The Role of Dialect and Sub-Dialect in Banking

Ethnic Chinese set up most of South-East Asia's private banks to service their trading interests. As a result, in the early years, South-East Asia's banks closely followed the dialect cleavages of the Chinese communities. Particular banks were seen as Cantonese or Teochiu, servicing the clients of a particular speech group almost exclusively. Servicing just one dialect or even sub-dialect group was an efficient response as little information could be gathered on potential borrowers other than by word of mouth. Credit worthiness was determined by name as much as anything else, and outside a dialect group, a person's financial situation generally would not be known, particularly given the strong link between occupation and dialect then prevalent.

Most of Singapore's banks arose out of a specific dialect client base.[33] United Overseas Bank (UOB) started as a bank serving a Hokkien clientele. It expanded its client base by acquiring two other banks which served different dialect groups. One had a Cantonese clientele, the other mostly Hakka. Another Singaporean bank, Overseas Union Bank (OUB) was initially a Teochiu bank. Its founder Lien Ying Chow was a prominent Singaporean Teochiu.[34]

---

31 For instance, it was the buyer of the New Zealand High Commission site in Hong Kong. (See *Australian Financial Review*, 'Developer buys site for $59m', 3 November 1994.)

32 See *South China Morning Post*, 'The making of HK's top tycoon', 30 July 1994.

33 Chew R., 'Local Chinese banks in Singapore' in L. Suryadinata, (ed.), *Chinese Adaption and Diversity: Essays on Society and Literature in Indonesia, Malaysia and Singapore*, Singapore University Press, Singapore, 1993, p. 58.

34 In the early days, Lien canvassed for depositors among the Teochiu communities in Thailand, Hong Kong, Vietnam and other parts of South-East Asia. Lien's Teochiu connections with Thailand assisted in the promotion of Thailand's maize trade, leading to his being decorated by the Thai Government in 1965. (See Kraar, L., 'The wealth and power of the Overseas Chinese', *Fortune*, March 1971.)

Today, some banks still can be classed as dialect based, although drawing on only one dialect group means impeding the rate at which a bank can expand. As has been mentioned, the Hock Hua Bank is Malaysia's only remaining dialect bank and serves the Fuzhou community. It accepts non-Fuzhou customers, although Fuzhous are widely believed to be able to achieve better conditions for borrowing. The Kong Lee Bank (now the Pacific Bank) still has a residual Cantonese client base but has reached out to non-Cantonese customers in recent years. Similarly, the Penang-centred Ban Hin Lee Bank has expanded beyond its traditional Hokkien customers, although the bank still is majority owned and controlled by Penang's Yeap family and largely serves the Penang Chinese community which is Hokkien dominated.[35] Several Hong Kong banks draw their clientele from specific dialect groups. One, the Commercial Bank (now a component of Asia Financial) controlled by Robin Chan of the Teochiu-Thai Sophonpanich family, has a largely Teochiu client base.

THE TRANSFORMATION OF ETHNIC CHINESE BUSINESS

Inefficient Business Structures

Ethnic Chinese firms organised in a traditional way can run into problems if they attempt to expand beyond the limits of family control. Management and organisational structures which were efficient for smaller firms become increasingly inefficient as firms grow. Old practices suddenly may become a disadvantage. Such problems are exacerbated when many ethnic Chinese entrepreneurs are reluctant to seek outside assistance to restructure and streamline. Ethnic Chinese companies that have grown quite large tend to maintain immature organisational structures; for example, management 'spokes' around a powerful founder 'hub', or a management structure of just two layers. One survey of over 150 ethnic Chinese entrepreneurs found that 70 per cent still operated around one of these two simple structures.[36] Boundaries between companies in a group are often ill-defined and holding companies are rare; this makes management inefficient.

Some groups of companies grow to encompass too many members spread across too many sectors. The best known example of a large, highly diversified ethnic Chinese conglomerate is Indonesia's Salim Group, which has acquired over 400 separate companies.[37] Such expansion can arise when ethnic Chinese entrepreneurs retain assets long after it is optimal to do so, often because selling a company may be seen as an admission of failure.[38] However, the goodwill and the prospects for realised capital gain of ethnic Chinese firms are linked to the trust in, and good reputation of, the current owners. If the owners choose to sell, much

35 See *Asian Wall Street Journal*, 'UMG to acquire a sizeable stake in Ban Hin Lee', 19 August 1994.

36 See Kao, J., 'The worldwide web of Chinese business', *Harvard Business Review*, March-April 1993, p. 26.

37 Anthony Salim, the son of Group patriarch Liem Sioe Liong, is now currently trying to streamline the Group, disposing of companies not related to core activities.

38 See Chu, T.C. and T. MacMurray, p. 124.

of the goodwill disappears. Furthermore, the sale of a company may raise questions about the viability and credit worthiness of the current owner's other businesses.

> *The leaders of Asia's top groups are enormously energetic and entrepreneurial and have remarkable business judgement. However, their organisations are creaking at the seams. Many of the basic improvements needed here are fairly clear, better information systems, increased training and more sophisticated human resource management. The real challenge, however, lies in the management ranks. Middle management is often thin, senior management overloaded, and decision making too centralised in the hands of too few. Growth puts an enormous burden on this kind of management structure.*[39]

Often, the head of a conglomerate will be the chairman or president-director (in the case of Indonesia) of one member of the group and chairman of the group itself. This can appear a vague role, since often the group will have no formal structure, such as being grouped under the umbrella of an overall holding company. A lack of a formal structure has advantaged the region's large Sino-business families in the past. Outsiders have been unable to determine accurately what the family controls. However, the costs of having no formal organisation may begin to exceed the benefits. Sales are not consolidated, nor is group profit or debt, making potential lenders and investors wary and presenting an obstacle to corporate financing from outside sources.

Restructuring ethnic Chinese enterprises is a growth industry. Legal and accounting firms, and banks provide management expertise. Some companies have specialised in taking over ethnic Chinese firms that have failed due to poor management but have sound assets. Several Indonesian companies rescue ailing companies by setting up consortia to take them over and restructure them. Zeta Holdings, controlled by Johannes Kotjo, formerly a senior executive with the Salim Group, does this. Zeta Holdings now has interests in 52 firms.[40]

Modern Business Structures

Over recent years, much of the larger, ethnic Chinese-controlled corporate sector across Asia has been transformed rapidly. As the economies of the region become integrated and companies face greater competition, many large companies and groups have modernised their management structures.

As traditionally run ethnic Chinese firms expand, they need to adapt to the pressures of size and complexity. Unlike the centralised decision making often found in the small Chinese family firm, operating decisions in these larger

39 See Chu, T.C. and T. MacMurray, 'The Road Ahead for Asia's Leading Conglomerates' *The McKinsey Quarterly*, Number 3, 1993.

40 See *Asiaweek*, 'Jakarta's corporate doctor', 9 November 1994.

modern Chinese enterprises are increasingly delegated to lower level management, as is the case in non-Chinese enterprises. However, top management in the Chinese firms retains effective power over workers (in decisions relating to pay, discipline, and so on), and decisions on finance and personnel recruitment remain highly centralised and personalised, rather than relying on formal rules and written procedures, as in more bureaucratic Western firms.[41]

Conceivably, as ethnic Chinese businesses expand, they will evolve from a traditional structure to a more modern (Western) one. It has been postulated that ethnic Chinese businesses lose their traditional character when they enter modern, technologically based industries oriented to the world market. To the extent that they are different, it has been argued that their differences create economic weaknesses, not strengths, and must be overcome if they are to survive in a competitive world industry.[42] This may be overstating the case.

The evolution of an ethnic Chinese firm could be represented as a continuum with one end point representing a small, traditionally-run, family firm, and the other, a large, modern, Western-style corporation. The graduations between either end mark approximate points or stages where traditional characteristics are successively shed or displaced. One such continuum appears in Figure 7.1.

An important transition is the separation of ownership and control, when the owner/founder accepts outsiders as managers. The evolution from 'ownership control' to 'management control' often may accelerate change.[43] Other aspects of this diminution of traditional character include taking on outsiders as employees, re-assessing the value of service inputs and acquiring them, accepting outside ownership, hiring Western-trained management, and floating some part of the company on a stock exchange, exposing the company not only to outside ownership but to new and more stringent reporting requirements.

At some point in their growth, large ethnic Chinese firms might find it more efficient to approach formal financial institutions than to rely on traditional networks for capital. Traditional networks may not be able to bear the risk of say, a US$1 million loan. For the network to source such a loan, a 'syndicate' would be needed, and the risk premium would rise. However, with a large wholesale bank, the risk premium might be lower (the losses might be more withstandable), as may the organisation costs of putting together the loan. Thus, there will be a marginal dollar of debt at which the firm finds it cheaper to use a bank than more traditional sources of capital.

Alternatively, equity markets can be tapped for funds, an increasingly common practice. In Indonesia, there has been a spate of listings by ethnic Chinese firms. Among those conglomerates which have listed, the ten largest raisers of capital on the JSE appear in Table 7.1. All but the Bakrie Group and Semen Cibinong are Sino-Indonesian controlled.

....

41 See Deyo, F.C.

42 Lim, L.Y.C., 'Chinese business, multinationals and the state: Manufacturing for export in Malaysia and Singapore' in L.Y.C Lim and L.A.P. Gosling (eds), *The Chinese in Southeast Asia*, Vol. 1, Maruzen Asia, Singapore, 1983, p. 254.

43 See Suehiro, A., 'Family business reassessed: Corporate structure and late-starting industrialization in Thailand', *The Developing Economies*, December 1994, for the genesis of these terms.

The Evolution of an Ethnic Chinese Firm

WHERE:

A ~ Expertise from outside the immediate family but within the clan is brought into the firm.

B ~ Senior management control weakens as the firm expands and one or two middle managers are brought in.

C ~ Capital is raised from sources outside the clan network – perhaps from a bank.

D ~ The firm begins to seek closer relations with the political elite.

E ~ Outside, professional managers are brought in.

F ~ The firm is restructured and streamlined.

G ~ The firm may list on the local stock exchange; capital may be raised on international bond markets.

H ~ The family sells down its stock to a bare majority holding.

Figure 7.1

Table 7.1

The Ten Biggest Raisers of Capital on the JSE

(As at August 1994)

BUSINESS GROUP		NUMBER OF SUBSIDIARIES TO HAVE LISTED	TOTAL FUNDS RAISED
1	Gadjah Tunggal Group	6	Rp 1 867.68 billion
2	Sinar Mas Group	4	Rp 1 157.22 billion
3	Astra Group	4	Rp 1 502.26 billion
4	Bakrie Group	4	Rp 1 446.23 billion
5	Dharmala Group	9	Rp 1 131.80 billion
6	Ometraco Group	6	Rp 999.73 billion
7	Salim Group	5	Rp 932.57 billion
8	Semen Cibinong	1	Rp 730.86 billion
9	Lippo Group	7	Rp 659.49 billion
10	Barito Group	1	Rp 659.49 billion

Source: *Republika*, 'Peraup dana publik terbesar (The biggest holders of public funds)', 10 August 1994.

The modernisation of ethnic Chinese businesses does not always require compromises regarding ownership and control. Many ethnic Chinese business families are reluctant to fill senior management positions with outsiders, so they send family members abroad for Western training. Thus management remains in the hands of insiders but at the same time, much-needed Western management skills are brought into the organisation.

A traditional ethnic Chinese business which has modernised is Bangkok Bank. In the past, the bank was well known for lending to clients on the basis of their connection to the bank's founder Chin Sophonpanich. Lending was often done on trust or by reciprocating a favour. The bank supplied liquidity to the ethnic Chinese across South-East Asia. By the 1980s, the bank had become very Westernised. Chin Sophonpanich was no longer accessible to old contacts and personalised lending became a thing of the past. Chin's son, Chatri, who became the bank's CEO, was born outside China and is Western educated. He is not as linked in with ethnic Chinese networks as was his father. As a result, Bangkok Bank now is growing more slowly than in the past, although it probably is more prudent and solid. It has all the trappings of a Western-style bank - a public relations/corporate affairs division, a research division, formally-trained staff and it is now a public company. An older ethnic Chinese businessman based in Yangon, summarised the transformation of Bangkok Bank. He remarked that he had received his start in business with a loan from Chin Sophonpanich, whom he knew, to set up several factories. If he were starting out today, Bangkok Bank would inevitably demand to see well kept business records, accounts, and a detailed business plan before it would lend even a modest amount.

Hiring or poaching staff from Western companies is increasingly common. Western multinational companies send professionals to their Asian branches to find that they are lost to local Chinese companies starved of professional management skills. Hong Kong-based entrepreneurs, Robert Kuok and Li Ka-shing, for example, are reputed to recruit the best management staff available, regardless of their ethnicity. In 1990, Singapore's Hong Leong Group hired the then local head of IBM to be the group managing director. Hong Kong's Sun Hung Kai Properties also is now in the hands of professionally-trained managers, including the three Western educated sons of the founder.[44]

Many Sino-Indonesian companies have been restructured in recent years, usually by grouping disparate companies under one or several holding companies and streamlining non-core assets. Only one Sino-Indonesian conglomerate has been fully consolidated. This is the Astra Group, which has been brought under PT Astra International, a holding company controlled by Prajogo Pangestu. The 1990 consolidation brought together over sixty companies formerly controlled by the Soeryadjaya family. Other restructured conglomerates either have been gathered under a series of holding companies, or have some parts that have been consolidated. In some instances, consolidation reveals corporate problems within Sino-Indonesian conglomerates, as such moves allow greater transparency.[45]

Sinar Mas, for example, has been restructured recently. Sinar Mas now consists of four holding companies structured around four separate lines of business. Some Sinar Mas companies also have been listed on the Jakarta Stock Exchange. Although each of the children of the founder has a distinct area to oversee, much of Sinar Mas now is managed by Western-trained professionals, many of whom are not ethnic Chinese. The group general manager is Filipino and many of the Sinar Mas-controlled Bank International Indonesia executives have come from Western banks, particularly Chase Manhattan. The founder is less active, overseeing the Group from a distance rather than being involved in its day-to-day management, and now meeting with his family to discuss business once a week.[46] Its methods of raising funds also are growing in sophistication. In 1994, the Group raised US$875 million on bond markets to invest in its pulp and paper companies.[47] The Group also has been involved in exchange rate and interest rate swaps.[48] Perhaps the most overt sign of Sinar Mas restructuring is its recent establishment of a corporate communications and public relations division. Ethnic Chinese firms in the past usually were not concerned about corporate image. Indeed, they preferred to have little or no 'image'.

Sinar Mas is not the only ethnic Chinese-controlled group using sophisticated ways to raise funds to expand. In Bangkok, large Sino-Thai business groups use bond markets and offshore banks to take advantage of the current interest rate differential between funds raised in Bangkok and those raised outside Thailand.

....

44 See Sender, H., p. 40.

45 See Shari, M., 'Selling family secrets', *Asia, Inc.*, December 1994.

46 Personal communication with Sinar Mas.

47 Bonds are preferred to issuing shares as the family's equity is not diluted.

48 The swaps have to date been of mixed success. In May 1994, PT Indah Kiat, a Sinar Mas company closed on several swaps losing US$25.6 million. Curiously, the Widjaja family covered the entire amount, reimbursing it out of their own funds. Another Sinar Mas company, PT Tjiwi Kimia lost a further US$12.5 million on an exchange rate swap. (See *Far Eastern Economic Review*, 'Don't look now', 8 December 1994.)

Indonesia's Salim Group also raises much of its funding from international capital markets by issuing convertible bonds in Luxembourg and Germany.[49]

Sino-Indonesian Mochtar Riady's Lippo Group has long preferred to hire Western-trained professionals. The managing director of the Indonesian-based Lippoland is a non-Chinese American.[50] Despite Lippo's stable of professionals, major decisions still rest with Mochtar and sons, Stephen and James.[51] Increasingly, Mochtar is assuming the role of 'elderly patriarch', withdrawing from day-to-day involvement. However, he still is relied upon for his excellent connections. Group expansion generally follows those connections. Also, Lippo spends considerable resources on marketing, although this is unusual for an ethnic Chinese-controlled group.

Although ethnic Chinese businesses increasingly take on Western characteristics as they expand, most seem careful not to become over-bureaucratised. They retain their status as 'light travellers', largely substituting skeletal professional management for skeletal family management. Thus major decisions are reserved for the owner/controller, with the ultimate group head staying close to the market, remaining sensitive to changes in market conditions. Despite their size, the major Sino-controlled companies in the region remain, for the most part, entrepreneurial and agile, and willing to experiment with new business opportunities as new markets open up. [52]

49 See *Republika*, 'Peraup dana publik terbesar (The biggest holders of public funds)', 10 August 1994.

50 See *Australian Financial Review*, 'Stake in centre in Indonesia', 4 November 1994.

51 Personal Communication with the Lippo Group. Nonetheless, Mochtar, Stephen and James are all professionally trained. Mochtar is the current head of the Asian Bankers' Association.

52 See Chu, T.C. and T. MacMurray.

Corporate Modernisation: Panin Bank

PT Pan Indonesia (Panin) Bank is Indonesia's eighth largest publicly-listed bank. It is not part of a wider conglomerate.[53]

Panin was formed in 1971 when three banks merged. Four more banks were acquired later. Four Sino-Indonesians, Mu'min Ali Gunawan, Gunadi Gunawan, Titjan Ananto and Mulyadi Kusumo established Panin. Prominent Sino-Indonesian businessman Jan Darmadi also became a shareholder in 1988, but has since reduced his shareholding to less than two per cent. Early on, Sino-Indonesian Mochtar Riady managed Panin. Riady left in 1975 to join Liem Sioe Liong's Bank Central Asia (BCA) taking some senior management and clients with him.

In 1982, Panin became the first Indonesian bank to issue shares to the public. The Gunawan family now controls 44 per cent of Panin's shares; the remaining 56 per cent belong to the public. The bank is run by a professional management team. Chandra Gunawan, the eldest Gunawan son was appointed as a Deputy President on the Board of Directors in 1993, but he is US-trained, holding an MBA and having prior banking experience. Panin recently introduced new products such as currency swaps, interest rate swaps and forward trading in its drive to boost fee-based income. It also has a number of foreign joint ventures, one with Australia's ANZ Bank.

All Sectors Preferred

Nowadays ethnic Chinese businesses are spread across all sectors; Table 7.2 lists the core competencies of the 500 biggest ethnic Chinese-controlled firms in the Asian region. Perhaps the only reason why ethnic Chinese business people are not significantly active in some areas is that those areas are not profitable. Traditionally, ethnic Chinese have not been greatly involved in the agricultural sector, often because they were prohibited from owning land in many South-East Asian countries. Today, however, the region's biggest agribusiness conglomerate, Thailand's Charoen Pokphand, is ethnic Chinese-controlled.

In the past, some ethnic Chinese business people preferred moveable assets. For example, several Shanghainese entrepreneurs who fled after 1949 and settled in Hong Kong and Taiwan moved into shipping. Ships can be moved easily from one place to another. Similarly, education (human capital) is another mobile asset. The satellite is a modern mobile asset and some larger ethnic Chinese concerns have moved into communications involving satellites and satellite technology.

53 Information for this section has been largely derived from Panin Bank, *1993 Annual Report*, Jakarta, 1994.

Table 7.2

Main Business Areas of the Top 500 Ethnic Chinese-Controlled Public Companies in Asia[54]

CORE COMPETENCY	NUMBER OF FIRMS	PERCENTAGE OF THE TOTAL
Land and Property Development	119	20.8
Banking	37	6.5
Hotel	37	6.5
Engineering and Construction	33	5.8
Textiles and fibres	28	4.9
Finance	24	4.2
Computers, Semi-Conductors	19	3.3
Food	19	3.3
Consumer Electronics	16	2.8
Chemicals	15	2.6
Insurance	12	2.1
Telecommunications	12	2.1
Beverages	11	1.9
Gaming	11	1.9
Clothing	10	1.7
Leisure, Tourism, Entertainment	10	1.7
Plantations	10	1.7
Cement Manufacturing	10	1.7
Steel Manufacturing	9	1.6
Retailing	8	1.4
Shipping	8	1.4
Machinery	7	1.2
Paper Manufacturing	7	1.2
Automobile	6	1.0
Energy Supply	6	1.0
Publishing	6	1.0
Electric Wire and Cable	5	0.9
Ceramics and Glass	5	0.9
Feedmill	5	0.9
Trading	5	0.9
Pharmaceuticals	5	0.9
Public Transport	4	0.7
Tyres	4	0.7
Mining	4	0.7
Agri-Industry	4	0.7
Timber	3	0.5
Toys	3	0.5
Tobacco	3	0.5
Metal Cans	3	0.5
Broadcasting	3	0.5
Pre-Mixed Concrete	2	0.3
Consumer Goods (Cosmetics, etc)	2	0.3
Movie Making	2	0.3
Batteries	2	0.3
Jewellery	2	0.3
Sporting Equipment	2	0.3
Forestry	2	0.3
Photography Services	1	0.2
Shoe Manufacturing	1	0.2
Watches and Eye Frames	1	0.2
Lifts and Escalators	1	0.2
Ferry Services	1	0.2
Education	1	0.2
Ship Repair	1	0.2
Road Haulage	1	0.2

Source: Personal communication with David Ch'ng, Swinburne University of Technology.

54 The number of core competencies exceeds 500 because several firms have more than one core competency.

Traditionally, the ethnic Chinese occupied market niches, where competitors were few and higher than normal profits could be earned. So it is today. The region's ethnic Chinese business people are moving rapidly into emerging sectors, positioning themselves to capture the benefits of being there first.

Singapore's Ong Beng Seng - Building a Middle Class Multinational

As the region's middle class broadens and deepens, Singaporean entrepreneur Ong Beng Seng is fast developing possibly Asia's first diversified international conglomerate based almost exclusively on leisure industries.[55] He is a partner in Yangon's Narawat Hotel which was opened in 1994. Ong also has acquired Australia's Brash Holdings, with its record and hi-fi chain; Singapore-based Travel Bug Holidays; the Haagen-Daas icecream franchises in Singapore and Hong Kong; the Hard Rock Cafe franchise for most of South-East Asia; Planet Hollywood in Asia; interests in the Four Seasons Hotels group; the Singapore Hilton; the Parkroyal and Townhouse hotels in Perth; the Chevron Hotel site in Surfers Paradise; and Melbourne's Banks Hotel.

The group also is a big player in the designer fashion industry. It operates a DKNY boutique in London and several Giorgio Armani and Bulgari stores worldwide. In April 1995, the group announced it had signed a S$21 million agreement to invest in Donna Karan Japan and to develop and operate 29 Donna Karan and DKNY retail stores and boutiques across Asia, over five years. Ong's group has announced plans to convert Region Air, its air charter service, into Singapore's third airline to service holiday destinations in South-East Asia.

In all, Ong's operations are borderless, capitalising on the trend towards growing consumer disposable income and growing Asian middle-class brand consciousness.

Rent-Seeking

Part of the transformation of ethnic Chinese business has involved the active courting of government. As ethnic Chinese business concerns grow, an alliance with the state becomes inevitable, either to sustain the size of business holdings,

[55] See *Bangkok Post*, 'S'pore to get third airline', 23 September 1994; *Australian Financial Review*, 'Surfers Chevron sale first in forecast property surge', 1 November 1994; *Australian Financial Review*, 'Better times in bad old Burma', 23 November 1994; Sender, H., 'Inside the overseas Chinese network', *Institutional Investor*, August 1991, p. 43; *Australian Financial Review*, 'Singapore developer emerges as preferred buyer for Brash', 23 June 1994; *The Straits Times*, 'Ong Beng Seng's Brash swoop stuns observers, angers lobbyists', 24 June 1994; *Australian Financial Review*, 'Donna Karan to lift Asian profile', 27 April 1995.

expand them, or protect them. Initially, governments may grant privileges enabling businesses to grow bigger and faster than they otherwise would. Ethnic Chinese entrepreneurs have accessed officially-sanctioned monopolies, protection from competition from abroad, soft loans and the like from governments across Asia. Such privileges also allow traditionally-run, large ethnic Chinese concerns to survive despite inefficient traditional management. For modernised ethnic Chinese firms, government patronage can mean easier access to government contracts and privatisations, and freedom from otherwise applicable regulations. Not to form a close alliance with the political elite may be unwise. Such was the case with Sino-Indonesian William Soeryadjaya who was assiduously independent of government. When his Bank Summa was collapsing, the government made little effort to assist, hastening Summa's demise.

The new generation of ethnic Chinese entrepreneurs have good relationships with the political elites in their countries and other countries. The Sino-Indonesian controller of the Lippo Group, Mochtar Riady, often is cited as a consummate networker. He is said to have good relations with the political elite in Beijing and is known to be friendly with US President Clinton and Mrs Clinton, a relationship which developed when Riady took over an Arkansas bank when President Clinton was Arkansas State Governor.[56] In late 1994, President Clinton appointed John Huang, Vice Chairman of Lippo Group US Operations, as Principal Deputy Assistant Secretary of the US Department of Commerce.[57]

In South-East Asia, Indonesia's ethnic Chinese business people benefit most from partnerships with the state, relying on connections in the bureaucracy, army or government.[58] Senior ethnic Chinese business people also are major donors to the various government-sponsored charities and campaign funds at election time.[59]

Some instances of ethnic Chinese entrepreneurs operating in partnership with governments are:

- *Liem Sioe Liong's Indocement and the Indonesian Government.* Liem built his first cement plant in 1975 and seven more over the next decade. Together, they constitute the largest cement producing complex in Asia and involve an estimated total investment in excess of US$1 billion. In 1985, the Indonesian Government bought 35 per cent of Indocement's equity.[60]

56 Several individuals remarked on Riady's association with the US President, but also see *South China Morning Post International Weekly*, 'Lippo style means fast profit', 8 October 1994. Riady's son James facilitated the connection.

57 See Lippo Group of Companies, *Lippoworld*, November 1994.

58 Mackie, J.A.C., 'The Ethnic Chinese Economy in Southeast Asia', paper presented to the International Conference on Southeast Asian Chinese Culture, Economy and Society, Singapore, 21-23 January 1994.

59 Suryadinata, L., 'Chinese Economic Elites in Indonesia: A preliminary Study', in J.W. Cushman and Wang Gungwu, *Changing Identities of the Southeast Asian Chinese since World War II*, Hong Kong University Press, 1988, p. 269.

60 Kunio, Y., *The Rise of Ersatz Capitalism in South-East Asia*, Oxford University Press, Singapore, 1988, p. 48.

- *Food importer Dasuki Angkosubroto's relationship with Indonesia's food imports regulator.* Indonesia's Gow Swie Kie (Dasuki Angkosubroto) imports rice and other agricultural products. His businesses have had close relationships with the BULOG (the National Logistics Board which controls food imports).[61]
- *Sino-Thai banks and Thai governments.* Today, most large banks operating in Thailand are ethnic Chinese-controlled. This has been facilitated by government restrictions on the entry and operation of foreign banks.[62]
- *Lucio Tan and former President Marcos.* Lucio Tan of the Philippines had a meteoric rise in the business world, initially under the patronage of former President Marcos. In the early 1960s, he was an obscure employee at a cigarette factory. He then started his own small cigarette company. This was followed with a takeover of a small bank which, with the aid of special loans from the Philippines Central Bank (under the auspices of Marcos) he was able to build into a major bank.[63]

The many instances of ethnic Chinese business people in South-East Asia doing well from rent-seeking behaviour should not be taken to imply that they all are rent seekers or 'ersatz capitalists'. One study differentiates Asian conglomerates as either 'structurers', those groups which seek to create market niches for themselves by soliciting government favours, and 'builders', those groups which seek to build on superior skills and create value in established business units. Builders generate much of their return from carefully managed core businesses; whereas, structurers tend to have diversified portfolios supported by government sponsored largesse.[64] It is unlikely however, that ethnic Chinese firms can be so neatly divided into these two camps. In many South-East Asian countries, entrepreneurs have little choice but to form close relationships with political elites as there may be no other way to secure major business opportunities. For many, resources spent cultivating bureaucrats and politicians are simply another cost of production.

Traditional Chinese business structures and practices are declining in their importance, but nonetheless they remain important. As Chinese enterprises grow, they tend to lose many of their traditional Chinese characteristics, but not all. The next chapter explores many aspects of the behaviour of Asia's ethnic Chinese-controlled conglomerates that can be attributed to some aspects of the cultural background of their controllers.

....

61 Suryadinata, L., p. 274.

62 Kunio, Y., p. 49.

63 Kunio, Y., p. 72.

64 See Chu, T.C. and T. MacMurray.

Chapter 8

THE CONGLOMERATES

CONGLOMERATION OF ETHNIC CHINESE BUSINESS

The Raison d'être for Conglomeration

Markets often remain separate because of information constraints: producers of goods in surplus in one market may be unaware that the goods are in great demand in another. Conglomerates can integrate such markets to earn arbitrage profits because they operate across economies, identify market niches and draw together markets as they go. Many conglomerates also are highly diversified. This allows them to provide internally many business services, allowing them to keep costs low. It also diversifies risk.

The geographical dispersion of ethnic Chinese business people, coupled with a strong preference for internalising the cost of business services, has meant that many, if not most, of the region's diversified, international conglomerates are ethnic Chinese-owned and controlled.

Most ethnic Chinese-owned businesses are family owned. As such firms grow, they tend to gradually shed their traditional characteristics, but almost all retain some vestiges. One such characteristic is the desire to maintain and protect the family's interest in a company, no matter what size that company becomes. This desire is reflected in the behaviour of some of the family-controlled conglomerates.

The Development of the Conglomerates

Usually ethnic Chinese family businesses expand by acquiring an ever-increasing number of companies rather than by expanding existing companies. The overall business group may be large, but its individual component companies may be relatively small. This tends to mean that ethnic Chinese feature strongly in lists of the wealthiest families or entrepreneurs but are under-represented in lists of the biggest companies.

The economies of South-East Asia have large, diversified conglomerates controlled by ethnic Chinese. Indonesia's Salim Group is perhaps the best example of such a conglomerate. Among the 400 or so companies in the Salim Group is the KFC franchise for Indonesia, the largest cement producer in South-East Asia, the world's largest producer of noodles, Indonesia's biggest miller of flour, Indonesia's largest private bank, a television station and a motor vehicle assembler.

Features of the Conglomerates

A study of the top 200 ethnic Chinese-controlled businesses in Indonesia identified six common characteristics. A summary of these characteristics, which have a more general application to ethnic Chinese conglomerates across South-East Asia are:[1]

- Almost all the conglomerates are 'family firms' owned by the members of a single family.
- Most of the top conglomerates are not primarily centred in one sector; they usually have very diverse holdings.
- They usually have links with foreign capital, either joint-ventures with foreign companies or loans from foreign banks.
- Nearly all of the large conglomerates either own or are closely associated with one or more private banks, mostly local merchant-banking institutions.
- Many of the conglomerates have off-shore investments, particularly in Singapore and Hong Kong.
- Although most of the enterprises are family firms, they are dominated by 'new' entrepreneurs who are not from the old-established ethnic Chinese families and often have come from relatively humble beginnings.

A typical ethnic Chinese conglomerate has two main structural components: financial and non-financial. The financial arm normally consists of institutions such as banks, insurance and finance companies.[2] Many ethnic Chinese groups establish a financial arm to provide ready access to a reliable source of funds.[3] Many also do all their mergers and acquisitions work in-house, and often through their own banks.[4] Thus a diversified conglomerate is often able to avoid going to outsiders for legal, financial, accounting, marketing, and other services. This gives them a comparative advantage over competitors who are not as diversified who will either have to purchase their services from outside at higher prices, or (more likely) forego them.

Most large ethnic Chinese-owned or controlled concerns also have a company registered in Hong Kong, even if it is inactive. Such companies are usually vehicles for investing in Hong Kong or more importantly, in China, should opportunities arise. They may also act as the international funds gathering arm for their parent conglomerates, tapping international credit markets from Hong Kong.

....

1 See Mackie, J.A.C., 'Changing Economic Roles and Ethnic Identities of the Southeast Asian Chinese: A Comparison of Indonesia and Thailand' in J.W. Cushman and Wang Gungwu *Changing Identities of the Southeast Asian Chinese since World War II*, Hong Kong University Press, 1988.

2 Some very large ethnic Chinese-controlled conglomerates, however, do not have a finance arm component. Examples are Thailand's Saha Pathana Group and the Charoen Pokphand Group, the Formosa Plastics Group of Taiwan, the Pao and Cheung Kong Groups in Hong Kong and the Genting Group in Malaysia.

3 See Ch'ng, D., *The Overseas Chinese Entrepreneurs in East Asia: Background, Business Practices and International Networks*, CEDA Monograph M100, 1993, p. 14.

4 See Sender, H., 'Inside the overseas Chinese network', *Institutional Investor*, August 1991, p. 32.

A growing trend is for modern ethnic Chinese conglomerates across the region to form local joint ventures with foreign partners. The conglomerate gains technology transfer, marketing expertise, and often, the benefits of association with a recognised international brand, and the foreign partner gains a foothold in the local market. Also, some conglomerates use such partnerships to access Western markets. Companies controlled by Indonesia's Mochtar Riady, for example, use joint ventures to enter the foreign partner's domestic market.

Increasingly, ethnic Chinese conglomerates are structured with one holding company owned largely or wholly by the family, which owns majority shares in the key companies of the group. Those members of the group either partly or fully listed are obliged to issue annual reports. It is possible to get a piece-by-piece account of the group's fortunes by examining each annual report, but achieving an overall picture is usually not possible, particularly in the absence of a publicly available annual report for the holding company.

Only in recent years have individual companies attached to conglomerates listed on stock exchanges in the region. This is occurring because capital raising on equity markets is relatively cheap and easy. The political imperative to spread the ownership of large conglomerates also has increased in some countries.

Families and Conglomerates

Families and the Structures of Conglomerates

Often the rationale for a conglomerate structure may be found in the structure of its controlling family. It is unusual for siblings of the second generation of ethnic Chinese entrepreneurial families to work in the one firm. Typically, each offspring will have a firm or division to manage, but will also be a director of most or all of the other firms in the group. As has been mentioned, the Indonesian Sinar Mas Group has, for example, recently been re-organised to make it more streamlined and modern, and with a son or daughter of founder, Eka Tjipta Widjaja, at the head of each division.

An additional, complicating factor is that some prominent, first generation ethnic Chinese entrepreneurs were polygamous, resulting in some very large and complex families. For example, the Sino-Thai founder of the Central Group has fourteen sons and twelve daughters, who have in turn produced at least forty grandchildren.[5] In the absence of complex cross-shareholdings, the only thing holding together complex families such as these is the founding patriarch. When he dies family tensions may appear and the family's business may split apart as various sons or daughters attempt to go their separate ways.

5 See Suehiro, A., 'Family business reassessed: Corporate structure and late-starting industrialization in Thailand', *The Developing Economies*, December 1994, p. 403.

The Impact of Family Structures on Bangkok Corporate Life

Much of the increased complexity of company structures in Thailand emerged during the 1980s, when family businesses passed to the second (and in some cases, third or fourth) generation. Over the past twenty years, ownership and control within Sino-Thai family business structures had diversified to a large extent, reflecting generational change, depth and complexity. Diversification was heightened by inter-family marriage, both between ethnic Chinese families and across ethnic Chinese and ethnic Thai boundaries. Some of the connections among some top Sino-Thai families in Bangkok are:

- A third generation member of the Wang-lee family (owners of the Nakornthon Bank) married a Lamsam son (the Lamsam family owns the Thai Farmers Bank) and two fifth generation Wang-lee sons also married Lamsam daughters.[6]
- A daughter of Pothipong Lamsam, chairman of the Board of Trade, married Vachara Panachet, the vice-president of the company MMC Sittipol.[7]
- The Srifeungfung family is closely related to the Phanitchiva family with at least two marriages between the two families.[8] The Srifuengfung family is also closely connected to the Tejaphaibul family. Boonsong Srifuengfung is a director of the Tejaphaibul's Bangkok Metropolitan Bank.
- In September 1994, Virachai, the son of Suchai Virameteekul, the chairman of the M Thai Group (chemicals, a bank in Shantou and property in China) married Thipaporn, the youngest daughter of Dhanin Chearavanont, the CEO of Charoen Pokphand. Suchai and Dhanin are said to have close business links and are significant contributors to the Thai-Chinese Chamber of Commerce.[9]
- Bangkok Bank's Chartsiri Sophonpanich and a daughter of Nukul Prachaubmoh, former governor of the Bank of Thailand, are married.[10]
- Damri Darakananda, the founder of the Saha Union Group is the brother-in-law of the founder of the Saha Group, Thiam Chokwatana.[11]

---

6 See Chantavanich, S.

7 See *Bangkok Post*, 'Of marriages and mergers', Insider Column, 20 September 1994

8 See Chantavanich, S., 'From Gonsi to Business Corporatism: Socio-Cultural and Political Conditions of Ethnic Chinese Big Business Families' Success', a paper presented to the Fifth International Conference on Thai Studies, School of Oriental and African Studies, London, 1993.

9 See *Bangkok Post*, 'Of marriages and mergers', Insider Column, 20 September 1994.

10 See *Bangkok Post*, 'Of marriages and mergers', Insider Column, 20 September 1994.

11 See Ch'ng, D., pp. 76- 77.

Families and Interlinkages Between Conglomerates

There is a tendency among the top ethnic Chinese business families in the region to form connections through marriage. The practice may be natural rather than strategic, but it ensures stability and the continued concentration of assets among the region's business elite. The practice is particularly common in Thailand and Indonesia.

Chapter 3 details how many Sino-Indonesian conglomerates are related by marriage. In the Philippines, the prominent Sino-business Sycip and Yuchenco families are related by marriage.[12] Ong Tjoe Kim, the owner of the Singaporean Metro Department Store is related by marriage to the family which controls Indonesia's Matahari Department Store chain.

A byproduct of these unions is that they allow senior ethnic Chinese business people to expand their business interests. Their preference for keeping their businesses closed to outsiders means that businesses do not have to grow too large before there are insufficient family members to oversee them. Marriages with members of other business families expand the number of extended family members able to take an interest in the business. They also may bring competing business families into the fold.

Modern Enterprises With Traditional Characteristics

As mentioned, despite modernising, many founders of large businesses still are the decision makers. Singapore's Hong Leong Group, for example, has professional managers but decision making is still centralised, resting with the Kwek family. 'Every Monday the staff reports for work wondering what deals may have been sealed over the weekend.'[13] The founder of Taiwan's Formosa Plastics, Y.C. Wang, still controls the firm although it now employs more than 30 000 people. Wang directs the company through fewer than ten professional managers who are not family members. These executives, in turn, work with an administrative group of about 200 other managers. This administrative group channels information into a series of daily reports for Wang.[14] Robert Kuok is involved in the day-to-day running of his Kerry Group and other business interests, although he is a director of only one of the private and public companies he controls, South China Morning Post Holdings.

12 See Ch'ng, D., p. 48.

13 See Sender, H., p. 42.

14 See Kao, J., 'The worldwide web of Chinese business', *Harvard Business Review*, March-April 1993, p. 27.

MODERN ENTERPRISES - TRADITIONAL PRACTICES: HENRY SY

Henry Sy has emerged as one of the Philippines' biggest retailers.[15] He was born in Fujian Province and entered the retail sector in the 1950s, starting a chain of shoe stores, ShoeMart. In 1958, he built his first department store and in 1985, opened his first shopping mall. His retailing interests have concentrated at the middle and lower-middle class end of the market, which means high volume and low margins, compared with operators at the higher end. One of the keys to Sy's success has been his development of a diverse range of reliable suppliers of goods to his stores by providing them with finance from his family-controlled Banco de Oro and business development advice. Sy recently took significant minority stakes in property owner Ayala Corporation, China Banking Corporation and Far East Bank and Trust Corporation. Also, Sy's group of companies has interests in smaller retailers apart from the department store and shopping mall interests, banks and a 50 per cent share in a cement plant which dovetails with plans to build more shopping centres.

Despite the size of Sy's group, it still retains several aspects of a small family-run business. It relies principally on internally generated financing and has a skeletal management headed by Sy's two daughters and four sons. One of the daughters, Teresita Sy is understood to be Henry Sy's apparent successor as controller of the group. She works from a 'no-frills' office located in a working class area of Manila which allows her to be close to the mass market the Sy Group serves.

SOME ASPECTS OF CONGLOMERATES' BEHAVIOUR

As ethnic Chinese family-controlled companies grow, they change the way they do business. This may mean resorting to the stock exchange to raise capital, streamlining management and so on. However, one overwhelming concern throughout is to protect the controlling family's interest. The methods some of the larger ethnic Chinese family-controlled companies use to protect their controlling interests are sophisticated and modern, but the motivations are still traditional.[16]

---

15 See *Far Eastern Economic Review*, 'Strength in numbers', 21 July 1994.

16 See Allen, N., *Allied Group Limited, Allied Properties (HK) Limited, Crusader Holdings Limited, Paragon Holdings Limited, Wai Yick Limited: Investigation under S.143 (1)(c) of the Companies Ordinance, Chapter 32 of the Laws of Hong Kong*, Abridged Version, Vol. 1, Office of the Financial Secretary, Hong Kong, 1993, for a detailed exposition of a case of international share deals and loans underpinned by ethnic Chinese networks and connections.

It is important to note that the following aspects of corporate behaviour tend to arise out of the conglomerates being family controlled, rather than because the controllers are ethnically Chinese. The environments in which the conglomerates operate are also important influences on some of their practices.

Structures

Many successful ethnic Chinese families in the region have modernised their business interests along similar lines. Typically, their companies are formed into a squat pyramid format, with a private holding company at the apex, a second tier holding the most prized assets which are usually privately held, and a third tier comprising the group's publicly-listed companies. Such a structure makes it easier for the families to implement the maxim: 'what is profitable is 100 per cent mine; what is not is mostly not mine.'[17] Should there be a desire to do so, it also makes it easier to raise funds at the bottom of the pyramid from shareholders in the group's public companies, then pass these up the pyramid.

The Sino-Thai conglomerate, Charoen Pokphand (CP), is an exception to the pyramid structure. Its structure is relatively flat. There is no holding company, just a group of four public companies in Thailand, and several others elsewhere in the region. They are all linked to a myriad of private companies through cross-shareholdings. Such a structure allows profits to be moved from one unit to another.[18]

Shares and Shareholders

Ethnic Chinese businesses increasingly see the stock market as a source of ready funds that can assist in improving debt to equity ratios. Two methods of listing are an initial public offer or a 'backdoor' listing. In a backdoor listing, the cost of or constraining regulations for listing encourage some companies to take over a small company already listed and then inject their own assets into it.[19]

Once initial public offerings are made or a backdoor listing has been achieved, the preferred way to raise additional funds is through rights issues. Funds are sought only from existing shareholders who must either commit more funds to the company or see their equity diluted. Minority shareholders may be frequently offered such issues and if they want to maintain their relative stake in the firm, they must constantly contribute more cash.[20] Rights issues are one further way in which the family maintains control of a company.

The CP Group, for example, usually raises capital through rights rather than ordinary share or debenture issues, thereby ensuring that the equity and control of the founding Chearavanont family is not diluted.[21] Many Sino-Indonesian-

17 See Sender, H., p. 31.

18 See Sender, H., p. 41.

19 This was recently done by the Sino-Indonesian controlled Barito Pacific Timber which took over the Malaysian-Chinese controlled Construction and Supplies House Bhd (CASH) which was listed on the KLSE and then injected hundreds of millions of dollars of its assets into CASH. See *The Bulletin*, 'Backdoor bonanza', 14 June 1994 for further information on 'backdoor' listings.

20 See Sender, H., p. 31.

21 See Sender, H., p. 41.

controlled conglomerates have announced rights issues within the last two years.[22] Examples are the Sinar Mas-controlled Bank Internasional Indonesia which raised Rp210.9 billion (approximately A$145.4 million) from one rights issue; Lippobank which raised Rp142.8 billion (A$98.5 million) from a 1993 rights issue; the Gadjah Tunggal Group-controlled Bank Dagang Nasional Indonesia (BDNI) which raised Rp643.5 billion (A$443.8 million); and PT Astra International which has raised Rp670.9 billion (A$ 462.7 million). The Dharmala Group has floated nine of its subsidiaries; so far four have announced rights issues, raising a combined Rp2.4 trillion (approximately A$1.7 billion).[23]

The revenue from rights issues often goes towards expanding a group's operations or acquiring assets from outside it, but also towards acquiring assets already held within a group.[24] Sometimes rights issues may be used to acquire formerly private assets the controlling family no longer wants to retain.

Information Leakage

Many of Asia's conglomerates encompass a finance arm. This is particularly common among Indonesian conglomerates.[25] However, seeking loans from banks linked to a conglomerate may sometimes be risky as it usually requires revealing to the bank commercial-in-confidence information, such as business plans. If the bank belongs to a wider conglomerate that information may be passed to related companies. A borrower might, for example, approach a bank for funding for a new, high return retail venture, presenting a business plan to support the loan application. The potential borrower's plans might then be passed from the bank to its parent conglomerate's retail arm which then moves in on the opportunity, squeezing the budding entrepreneur out. As far as the group's controllers are concerned, the bank's loss of custom would be more than offset by gains elsewhere and the bank's minority shareholders (if it is listed) could be left out of pocket.

Another, related problem may arise where a bank belongs to a conglomerate which encompasses a property development arm. In this situation, the bank may foreclose early on loans when attractive pieces of real estate are offered as collateral, so that the property development arm can swoop in and pick up a bargain. One Jakarta-based interviewee related the story of how a company obtained financing from one of Indonesia's more prominent banks for a residential project near Jakarta. As the project got underway, it became apparent that it would be successful, prompting the bank to foreclose on half the loan. This enabled a property development company associated with the bank to take over half the venture.

---

22 A major Sino-Indonesian conglomerate which has not to date announced rights issues for any of its listed companies is the Salim Group.

23 See *Republika*, 'Peraup dana publik terbesar (The biggest holders of public funds)', 10 August 1994.

24 In Indonesia, two Sino-Indonesian controlled companies which have used rights issues for internal acquisitions are PT Dharmala Sakti Sejahtera and Ometraco Finance. The *pribumi*-controlled Bakrie Brothers also participated in this practice.

25 For example, the Ciputra Group, Jakarta's largest property developer also controls Jaya Bank, the Lippo Group controls Lippobank, the Salim Group controls Bank Central Asia (BCA) and the Sinar Mas Group controls Bank International Indonesia (BII).

In-House Lending

Another common feature of the conglomerates in the region is intra-group or in-house lending. Commonly, the bank or finance company will act as the banker for the other members of the conglomerate. Family-controlled conglomerates eager to preserve the family's control over the group perhaps are most prone to this, as it means not having to surrender any control to outsiders. The danger is that loans to group members may not be made on prudent or commercial grounds. Furthermore, if the fates of the borrowers are not independent, the bank's loan portfolio is inherently more risky. A disaster befalling one borrower is more likely to hit other borrowers if they are associated companies, so rather than having one bad debtor, the bank ends up with many.

Bank failures are likely to become more frequent in South-East Asia, as financial sectors are deregulated more, exposing banks and any imprudent practices to greater competition.

Governments in the region are legislating to restrict the capacity of banks for intra-group lending. In Thailand, for example, no more than 25 per cent of a bank's capital base can be lent to any single client, and in Indonesia, no bank will have more than the equivalent of 20 per cent of its capital base lent to any single client, by 1997. Rules such as these, however, may be circumvented as banks linked to conglomerates may recycle loans through one another - essentially their own loans but which take on the appearance on paper of having come from a bank outside the conglomerate.

COLLEAGUES AND NOT COMPETITORS AT THE TOP

A growing phenomenon among many prominent ethnic Chinese-controlled companies, particularly in South-East Asia, is the degree to which they move together in their quest to jointly dominate markets. This occurs at an international level, emphasising that senior ethnic Chinese business people often treat the region as a single, borderless market.[26] Examples of this phenomenon include:

- The Salim Group's 1994 purchase of a stake in Malaysia's Kuantan Flour Mills which complements Robert Kuok's large Malaysian flour milling interests. Liem Sioe Liong and Robert Kuok are partners in many ventures across Asia.
- The previously mentioned winning consortium to develop a huge tract of land adjacent to Manila's Makati business district. The consortium is headed by the Metro Pacific Corporation which is ultimately controlled by Indonesia's Liem Sioe Liong. Other members include companies controlled by Malaysian Chinese Robert Kuok, and Filipino Chinese Andrew Gotianum, Henry Sy, George Ty and Lucio Tan.[27]

....

26 Apparent business coordination among the region's largest ethnic Chinese entrepreneurs can cut across dialects and other traditional links. This tends to occur out of necessity rather than by design. Dealing only within one's dialect group is constraining, particularly at the top echelons of business.

27 See *Asian Wall Street Journal*, 'Metro Pacific Group pays $1.6 billion for Manila site', 9 January 1995.

- Indonesia's Prajogo Pangestu's planned reverse takeover of the Malaysian CASH timber company will allow Prajogo to share control of much of the Malaysian timber industry with the Rimbunan Hijau Group, controlled by Datuk Tiong Hiew King.

The growing international linkages between the region's most senior ethnic Chinese business people provide a useful mechanism for hedging risks, generating higher than normal returns through oligopolistic behaviour and sharing information.

Carving up the Region's Poultry Market

In the poultry sector, several ethnic Chinese interests are moving to establish highly vertically integrated, cross-border dominance.[28] In Indonesia, Thailand, China, Singapore and Malaysia, three Chinese-controlled companies dominate the poultry industry, from manufacturing chicken feed, to breeding and operating chicken fast food franchises.

The Chareon Pokphand (CP) Group is the key player in commercial poultry production, chicken feed production and marketing in Thailand and China, where it has some KFC franchises. In 1994, it acquired equity in PT Surya Hidup Satwa, a chicken and shrimp health products producer. CP also separately owns a chicken breeding and feed company, PT Chareon Pokphand Indonesia, in Indonesia. CP also has reportedly shown interest in possibly acquiring all or part of Australia's Goodman Fielder's Steggles poultry division.

The Sino-Indonesian Salim Group has poultry breeding and processing interests in Indonesia's Riau Archipelago, and controls the KFC franchise for Singapore through its control of the UIC Group. In Indonesia, Salim controls KFC through its majority shareholding in the Galeal Group, which also owns a supermarket chain.

In Malaysia, the major poultry producer Leong Hup Holdings Bhd recently acquired a large stake in the fast food company KFC Holdings (Malaysia).

28 See Sato, Y., 'The Salim Group in Indonesia: The development and behaviour of the largest conglomerate in Southeast Asia', *The Developing Economies*, 31(4), 1993; *The Australian* 'Goodman: No Pokpang [sic] plans', 26 August 1994; *Asian Wall Street Journal*, 'Leong Hup Holdings Bhd', 25 October 1994; *Asian Wall Street Journal*, 'Pokphand plans expansion move in Indonesia', 29 November 1994.

CASE STUDY - THE SALIM GROUP

Liem Sioe Liong (Soedono Salim) is second only to the Sultan of Brunei as South-East Asia's wealthiest individual with estimated net assets of at least US$3 billion.[29] The Salim Group has more than 400 affiliated companies, which employ at least 135 000 people.[30] In 1993, group sales were estimated to be approximately US$9 billion, and accounted for approximately 5 per cent of Indonesia's GDP.[31] The group increasingly is expanding offshore. About 35 per cent of the group's revenue now comes from overseas.[32]

The Early Years

Liem was born in 1916 in Niuzhai village near Haikou township, Fuqing, in China's Fujian Province.[33] In 1938, Liem left China for Indonesia, where, together with his brother Liem Sioe Hie, he joined an uncle's peanut-oil business in Kudus, central Java.

During the struggle for Independence (1945-49), Liem supplied the fledgling Indonesian army's Diponegoro division in central Java with food, medicines and military supplies. The then quartermaster of the division was Soeharto, now President of Indonesia. Soeharto held the position throughout most of the 1950s and Liem established himself as a reliable supplier.

In 1952, Liem moved to Jakarta from where he established relations with ethnic Chinese businessmen in Singapore and Hong Kong which helped establish his import-export business. He set up a soap factory and became the supplier of soap to the Indonesian Armed Forces. During the early Jakarta period, he moved into textiles and banking (PT Bank Windu Kencana and Bank Central Asia).

....

29 See Appendix 7 for case studies on other conglomerates. Apart from specific references, information on the Salim Group has been sourced from: *Corporate International's Company Handbook*, Hong Kong, various issues; *Far East Economic Review*, various issues; Sato, Y., 'The Salim Group in Indonesia: The Development and Behaviour of the Largest Conglomerate in Southeast Asia', *The Developing Economies*, 1993; Schwarz, A., *A Nation in Waiting*, Allen and Unwin, 1994, pp. 98-132; *South China Morning Post*, various issues; Suryadinata, L., 'Chinese Economic Elites in Indonesia: A preliminary Study', in J.W. Cushman and Wang Gungwu, *Changing Identities of the Southeast Asian Chinese since World War II*, Hong Kong University Press, 1988; Redding, G.S., *The Spirit of Chinese Capitalism*, Walter de Gruyter and Co., Berlin, 1990; *Australian Business Monthly*, 'Chinese on the rebound', March 1993; First Pacific Company Limited, *Annual Report 1993*, Hong Kong, 1994; First Pacific Company Limited, *Interim Report 1994*, Hong Kong, 1994; Pusat Data Business Indonesia, *Conglomeration Indonesia*, 2nd ed., Jakarta, 1994; Cazenove & Co, *First Pacific* (research report), Hong Kong, 28 November 1994.

30 Around 400 affiliated companies is a sizeable number but it is comparable with other multi-national companies. Australia's BHP, for instance, has majority interests in 389 companies, (including holding and non-active companies). News Corporation Ltd owns 688 companies (including holding companies) outright plus another 10 in which it has a majority interest. (See BHP, *BHP Report to Shareholders 1994: Financial Statements*, Melbourne, 1994; and News Corporations Ltd, *The News Corporation Ltd: Financial Report 1994*, Adelaide, 1994.)

31 In an interview, Anthony Salim thought the Group sales figure might be about right but could not be sure. (See *The Asian Wall Street Journal*, 'Salim group steels itself for life after Suharto', 25-26 February 1994.)

32 See *The Asian Wall Street Journal*, 'Salim group steels itself for life after Suharto', 25-26 February 1994.

33 See Sato, Y.

In 1957, President Sukarno ordered the military to take over all Dutch-owned companies as part of his campaign for Irian Jaya. The military had no access to credit nor management experience. Liem supplied both. By the time Soeharto became President in 1966, Liem was already established as a successful businessman.

On the Road to Expansion

In 1968, Liem's company, PT Mega, along with a company owned by Probosutedjo, PT Mercu Buana, were jointly designated by ministerial decree as the exclusive importers of cloves. The Government set the import price and selling price for cloves, but both companies were guaranteed a five per cent commission. Liem's part in the clove import monopoly reportedly netted his companies annual revenues of around US$340 000 between 1968 and 1970 and US$1.2 million between 1971 and 1980.[34]

In 1969, Liem and Liem Oen Kian (Djuhar Sutanto), established PT Bogasari Flour Mill which was permitted a virtual monopoly over the domestic milling of flour from wheat imported by Indonesia's National Logistics Board (*Badan Urusan Logistik Nasional*, BULOG). One recent survey found that the milling charge paid to PT Bogasari was almost three times the world price.[35] The Salim Group's control of flour milling in Indonesia has allowed it to become the world's biggest producer of instant noodles. PT Bogasari is the world's largest single commercial buyer of wheat.[36]

The profits from PT Bogasari Flour Mill and PT Mega assisted Liem in providing the capital to start Indocement in 1973. An important external source of funds was Bangkok Bank (the assistance reportedly being personally granted by Chin Sophonpanich) and from the Chien Tai Cement Company of Taiwan. Fifteen per cent of the equity for one kiln came from the Ongko Group.[37] Since its inception, Indocement has had a close relationship with the Indonesian Government. In June 1985, directly after the Group's six affiliated cement companies were incorporated into PT Indocement Tunggal Prakarsa, the Government purchased 120 000 shares in the new company for Rp364.3 billion (US$330 million). In 1989, three social foundations chaired by President Soeharto purchased Rp60 billion worth of PT Indocement's convertible bonds. The Government owns 26 per cent of Indocement.[38] Also in 1989, another ministerial decree made possible the listing of PT Indocement on the Jakarta Stock Exchange even though according to reports, it had not made the required profits in the previous two years.[39]

The Government also sets the wholesale price of cement in Indonesia. Subsequently, a large cement shortage emerged in Indonesia in 1994. The retail

34 See Sato, Y.

35 See Sato, Y.

36 See *Far Eastern Economic Review*, 'Feeding time', 30 December 1993.

37 See Sato, Y.

38 See *Far Eastern Economic Review*, 'Hard times ahead', 3 November 1994.

39 See Sato, Y.

price is not fixed, so very high profits can accrue to cement retailers. Most of Indocement's output is retailed by PT Semen Tiga Roda Prasetya, a company associated with the Salim Group.

In 1989, the Government took over Salim's 40 per cent share in the loss-making PT Cold Rolling Mill Indonesia Utama. The company now is a fully-owned unit within PT Krakatau Steel.[40]

The group's growth has been exceptional. Its total capital grew at an annual average of 46 per cent between 1970 and 1985. By 1985, it was 300 times its level in 1970.[41]

Today, the Salim Group's Bank Central Asia is the largest private bank in Indonesia. BCA was originally a knitting company based in Semarang until Liem acquired it in 1957 and restructured it into a bank. It did not experience any significant capital growth for many years. In 1973, it was a one-branch bank unable to trade in foreign exchange. However, in 1975, Mochtar Riady was appointed president, having been enticed with a 17.5 per cent shareholding. Riady immediately set about increasing BCA's net worth, largely injecting the profits from other group members to increase the Bank's capital base. The branch network expanded; new clients were solicited and cultivated, initially by asking the buyers of cement from the group's cement interests to transfer the amounts of their purchases as cash advanced payments to the BCA; the loan portfolio was expanded by lending at rates lower than other private banks; and permission to trade in foreign exchange was successfully sought.[42] BCA now has more branches across Indonesia than any other bank. It is also thought to be a significant lender to other companies in the Salim Group.

The close partnership between the Salim Group and leading *pribumi* business people is further underscored as the President's eldest daughter and eldest son each, according to reports, own 17 per cent of the available shares in BCA.[43]

One study divides the expansion of the Salim Group into four phases. First there was the entry into manufacturing phase (1968-74); followed by the development of banking (1975-78); then the cement business expansion phase (1977-81); and finally a period of conglomerate diversification into unrelated businesses (1981-85).[44] The Government has assisted significantly each of these phases.

The Salim Group often seeks to establish a dominant position in markets in which it operates.[45] Thus the group tends to enter markets in which it can dominate, for example, where there is potential for monopolies or oligopolies.

---

40 See *The Asian Wall Street Journal*, 'Salim group steels itself for life after Suharto', 25-26 February 1994.

41 See Sato, Y.

42 See Sato, Y.

43 Bambang Trihatmodjo, Soeharto's second eldest son, is also an equity partner in the Salim Group's Batam industrial estate. (See *The Asian Wall Street Journal*, 'Salim group steels itself for life after Suharto', 25-26 February 1994.)

44 See Sato, Y.

45 See Sato, Y.

Maturation - Current Developments

Currently, the Salim Group's Indonesian-based interests, grouped under the holding company Salim Economic Development Corporation, are consolidating and looking for new opportunities offshore. While the group has grown substantially under the Soeharto Government's policy of import substitution, there has been a qualitative change in the group's rate of expansion since the Indonesian Government began to pursue more export-oriented policies. Liem has re-oriented the group away from potentially loss-making heavy industry, particularly cement and steel, towards exports, particularly agribusiness and chemicals, and created a regional orientation using his extensive business connections. The Salim Group's export orientation involves supplying Indonesian raw materials to its growing regional manufacturing bases in Singapore, the Philippines, Vietnam, Australia, China and to its own Bulam complex in the Riau Islands.

The group also appears to be attempting to reduce its gearing. In 1994, for example, it raised US$500 million by selling bonds that will later become shares of PT Indofood Sukses Makmur.[46] The group is looking for new fields. In July 1994, it announced that it had the rights to operate Indonesia's fifth commercial television broadcaster, PT Indosiar Visual Mandiri.

The Group's Expansion Offshore

The Salim Group now has interests in Singapore, the Philippines, Vietnam, Australia, the former Soviet Union, Germany, and China. Each is fed by raw materials supplied from domestic Indonesian companies within the Salim Group.[47]

First Pacific

In the early 1980s, the Salim Group acquired the Hong Kong-based Shanghai Land. It transformed this into the First Pacific Group, which is controlled by Salim's First Pacific Company Ltd, registered in Bermuda. The First Pacific Group now has operations in 25 countries. Whilst the Salim Group controls First Pacific, it does so at arm's length, with First Pacific describing Salim's stake as largely 'passive'. First Pacific Company (FPC) is controlled by First Pacific Investments (FPI). FPI is registered in Liberia. This company is wholly owned by the Liem investors group. Through FPI, Liem Sioe Liong and Anthony Salim hold 18.8 per cent of FPC and with the other members of the group, a total of 47 per cent.[48] It acquired the 19-branch United Savings Bank in California. Eighty-five per cent of First Pacific's share in the Bank was recently sold to the Liem family. It also acquired Smart Communications in the Philippines, and majority equity (but under Dutch law, not control) of Dutch-based company, Hagemeyer

....

46 See *Asian Wall Street Journal*, 'Salim official denies group is providing funding for Bapindo', 19 May 1994.

47 See Sato, Y.

48 The other 'Liem investors' shareholdings in FPC through FPI are: Djuhar Sutanto (14.1 per cent), Sudwikatmono (4.7 per cent), Ibrahim Risjad (4.7 per cent), and Tedy Djuhar (4.7 per cent).

NV. Hagemeyer's turnover is approximately US$2 billion a year, and it operates in 21 countries. First Pacific has also set up the First Pacific Bank, a medium-sized bank with US$1.2 billion in assets in 1993 and 24 branches in Hong Kong. It controls First Pacific Davies which has expanded rapidly in recent years, and manages a total of 9.6 million square meters of real estate in Hong Kong, China, the Philippines, Thailand and Jakarta.[49] It also operates a security company, Guardforce, and recently it acquired control of the Thai trading company Berli Jucker Co. Ltd, and Metro Drugs in the Philippines.[50] It has opened an office in Indonesia and is now the distributor there for Microsoft. First Pacific also controls Darya Varia Laboratoria, an Indonesian pharmaceutical company.

First Pacific's interest in Berli Jucker Public Co. Ltd is shared with some 600 other shareholders. The company produces glass containers, snacks, cosmetics, and soap and was founded by a Swiss entrepreneur who settled in Thailand during the reign of King Rama V. During 1993, the company's turnover was US$298.8 million.[51] First Pacific's involvement in the Philippines is through its Philippines' flagship, Metro Pacific Corp., which also is involved in property development.[52] First Pacific's interests in China have largely been restricted to banking offices and property management, although recently it opened a potato processing factory in Liaoning Province. It has signed an MOU with Fujian Province to investigate the potential for cooperation in telephony.

First Pacific's Pacific Telelink recently entered into a joint venture with Britain's Vodafone and has captured 22 per cent of Hong Kong's mobile phone market. The group intends to launch a paging service in Indonesia and is investigating communications opportunities in China.[53] In 1993, First Pacific sold 34 per cent of its First Pacific Bank to two enterprises linked to China's Foreign Trade Ministry. The tie-up will help the bank expand into China as well as pick up more business in Hong Kong.[54]

First Pacific also has interests in Australia. Since 1991 it has owned outright the computer distributor Tech Pacific Pty Ltd. First Pacific Davies also has established a foothold in the Australian property services market with a Sydney office.[55]

By turnover, the First Pacific Group is now Hong Kong's sixth largest company. In 1993, it had a turnover of US$3.08 billion.[56] In 1994, the share of total operating profits for each of the group's four main lines of business were: marketing and distribution 45 per cent; telecommunications 15 per cent; integrated property

---

49 5.8 million square metres of real estate is managed in Hong Kong, 1.3 million square metres in China, 1.2 million square metres in the Philippines, 1.1 million square metres in Thailand, and 0.33 million square meters in Jakarta.

50 See Sato, Y.

51 See *Business in Thailand*, ' "Nok Kaew": No soap operas please!!', June 1994.

52 See *Far Eastern Economic Review*, 'Do I hear 50 billion', 1 September 1994.

53 See *Asiaweek*, 'Hard choice: A China push raises questions in Jakarta', 4 May 1994.

54 See *Asiaweek*, 'Hard choice: A China push raises questions in Jakarta', 4 May 1994.

55 First Pacific's interests in Australia are covered in more detail in Chapter 13. The Salim Group, through Bogasari, has also been a long-term, important buyer of Australian wheat.

56 See *Asiaweek*, 'Hard choice: A China push raises questions in Jakarta', 4 May 1994.

services 30 per cent; and banking 10 per cent. In 1993, 74.4 per cent of group operating profits were sourced from Asia, 17.3 per cent from Europe and 8.3 per cent from North America.[57]

Kabila Mandiri Persada (KMP)

The KMP Group is another Salim-controlled group based outside Indonesia. This group whose holding company is Kabila Mandiri Persada (KMP) Pte Ltd, was set up in Singapore in 1983. In 1990, KMP acquired the holding company of the UIC Group, United Industrial Corporation Ltd (UIC), which encompassed 31 subsidiaries and 15 allied companies, from Oei Hong Leong, son of Sino-Indonesian entrepreneur, Eka Tjipta Widjaja. Among the interests of these companies was animal feed, plastic containers, poultry and meat processing, coastal shipping and franchises for KFC and Shakey's Pizza.[58] One of UIC's prime assets is a 56 per cent controlling interest in Singapore Land, one of the biggest property owners in Singapore with assets in 1993 of US$2.2 billion.[59] UIC acquired control of Singapore Land in 1990 after a hostile takeover bid. To reduce the debt which rose with the acquisition, UIC has since sold its 470 room Le Meridien Phuket Hotel in Thailand, properties in Japan, a fleet of 77 tractors and the (loss-making) UIC Electronics.[60]

In another move, KMP announced in June 1994 that it was entering into a joint venture with the Australian subsidiary of the Bunge Group and the Sin Ban Group of Malaysia to construct and operate a S$30 million abattoir in Singapore. KMP and Bunge will each hold a 37 per cent share in the abattoir (Farmers Abattoir) and Sim Ban will hold the remaining 26 per cent. The abattoir is expected to be completed at the end of 1995. KMP owns a pig farm in Palau Bulan in the Riau Archipelago and KMP and Bunge are planning further 50-50 pig farming joint-ventures in Palau Bulan. KMP also has acquired a 40 per cent share in the pig farms operated by the Sin Ban Group.[61]

In 1994, the Salim Group moved onto the Kuala Lumpur Stock Exchange with an initial purchase of a 20 per cent stake for the equivalent of A$17.1 million in the Malaysian company, Kuantan Flour Mills.[62]

China

The Salim Group is planning to invest US$1 billion in China's Fujian Province over five years. The first stage involves US$540 million worth of investment which was announced in December 1992.[63] It also announced that Salim, with a consortium of other companies, would develop the Yuan Hong Industrial Park at Fuqing, Fujian Province, involving commercial, industrial and residential

....

57 Personal communication with First Pacific.

58 See Sato, Y.

59 See *Asiaweek*, 'Hard choice: A China push raises questions in Jakarta', 4 May 1994.

60 See *Singapore Business Times*, 'UIC, SingLand need to segment market to silence critics and reassure investors', 20 June 1994.

61 *Jakarta Post*, 'Salim, two foreign partners get piggish in Singapore', 17 June 1994.

62 See *Australian Financial Review* , 'Indonesian group in winning deal', 30 November 1994.

63 See *Australian Business Monthly*, 'Chinese on the rebound' March 1993.

developments on a 5 000 hectare site. The first phase of the project will cost almost US$200 million.

In 1994, a joint venture was announced between the Salim Group, Japan's Mazda Motor Corporation and Toem Corporation and China's Fuzhou Solid Motors Corporation to build a US$100 million commercial vehicle production plant at the Yuan Hong Industrial Park.[64]

This type of investment in China has caused some controversy in Indonesia, especially as it has been concurrent with a planned float of the Salim Group's Indofoods, giving rise to concerns that capital was being moved from Indonesia to China.[65]

Salim and Land

The Salim Group is a significant regional holder of land. It is reportedly the single largest land holder on the land-scarce, Indonesian island of Java, holding approximately 7 000 hectares near Jakarta. It controls the land for the 500 hectare site for the Batam Industrial Park and the 4 000 hectare site for the Bintan Industrial Estate, both in Indonesia's Riau Archipelago. It is also Singapore's biggest controller of land through Singapore Land which it controls through its controlling stake in UIC. Furthermore, it controls the 5 000 hectare site in Fuzhou, Fujian Province on which the Yuan Hong Industrial Park is being built, and also has land holdings in southern Vietnam.

Also, as mentioned, in early 1995, a consortium headed by the Salim-controlled Metro Pacific Corporation, won the right to develop land adjacent to Manila's Makati business district, bidding an unprecedented US$1.6 billion.

The Salim-Singapore Link

The link between Singapore's government sector and the Salim Group in Singapore's externalisation push is strengthening; the emerging relationship covers at least eight separate, international projects. The Salim Group is involved in three major industrial parks with Singaporean Government-linked companies.

The Batam Industrial Park on Batam Island in Indonesia's Riau Archipelago is a joint venture between the Salim Group, Singapore Government-linked Jurong Environmental Engineering Pte Ltd (JEE) and government-linked Singapore Technologies. Work on the park began in February 1990. Today, the park houses around 40 manufacturers.[66]

64 See *Business Review Southeast Asia*, 'Joint ventures', 14 December 1994.

65 See *Asiaweek*, 'Hard choice: A China push raises questions in Jakarta', 4 May 1994.

66 See Economic Development Board, *Singapore Unlimited: Economic Development Board Yearbook 1992-93*, Singapore, 1993.

The Bintan Industrial Park, also in Indonesia's Riau Archipelago, is a joint venture between the Salim Group, Singapore Government-linked Jurong Environmental Engineering Pte Ltd and government-linked Singapore Technologies Industrial Corporation (STIC).

The Yuan Hong Industrial Park is being managed by Singapore Pacific Management Services Pte Ltd, a joint venture between the Salim Group-controlled companies UIC, Singapore Land, and Hagemeyer Pacific Corporation Ltd, and United Overseas Land (UOL), STIC, and JEE.[67] The consortium will plan and manage the 5 000 hectare Yuan Hong Industrial Park near Fuzhou, Fujian Province. The Park will seek to attract light and medium industries from Taiwan, Hong Kong, Singapore and Japan, as well as multinational corporations. UIC, Singapore Land and UOL will each take 10 per cent shares, STIC and JEE each will have 15 per cent shares and Hagemeyer Pacific will have a 40 per cent share.[68] All up, Salim-linked companies will have 60 per cent equity in the venture.

In July 1993, Singaporean CWT Distribution and Salim-owned Hagemeyer Pacific (BVI) Corporation entered into a 50-50 joint venture, CWT Pacific Ltd, to manage two ports in China. One is Xia Long, a private port south-east of Fuqing City in Fujian. The other, Song Xia will serve tenants of the Yuan Hong Industrial Park.[69]

Singapore and Salim are in partnership in yet another project. Salim-controlled KMP Group and Singapore Land are partners in the Singapore-Suzhou Township Development Pte Ltd consortium. Singapore is now investigating the feasibility of setting up an industrial park in southern Vietnam. One of the sites being examined is land controlled by Salim. Salim and JEE also are jointly involved in office developments in Ho Chi Minh City.

In 1994, the Salim Group announced plans to build a US$40 million, 250-room, four-star hotel in Manado, northern Sulawesi in Indonesia with the Singapore Government-linked companies, Straits Steamship Land and Singapore Airlines. The hotel is to be completed in 1997 and managed by a subsidiary of Singapore Airlines.[70] Also, Straits Steamship Land and Salim's KMP are developing jointly a tourist resort featuring a hotel, apartments, a golf course and other facilities on Indonesia's Bintan Island.[71]

---

67 UOL is controlled by Singapore's United Overseas Bank (UOB). Hagemayer Pacific Corporation has no links to NV Hagemayer and is fully owned by Salim.

68 Based on information provided by the Research Department of the Singapore Chinese Chamber of Commerce and Industry.

69 Based on information supplied by the Research Department of the Singapore Chinese Chamber of Commerce and Industry.

70 See *Business Review Southeast Asia*, 16 November 1994, p. 6.

71 See *Australian Financial Review*, 'Keppel Corp. invests $548m in Jakarta', 20 July 1994.

The Group's Structure

The 'Liem Investors'

Whilst Liem Sioe Liong has been the helmsman for the Salim Group, building it to become the largest group in Indonesia, he has not done it on his own. A small group of investors known as the Liem Investors has provided some of the capital.[72] The Liem Investors is an ongoing consortium consisting of Liem and his long-term associate Djuhar Sutanto (Liem Oen Kian), their two sons Anthony Salim and Tedy Djuhar and two long-standing *pribumi* associates, Sudwikatmono, and Ibrahim Risjad (from Aceh).[73] This group has financed a number of government-assisted industrial projects, in steel, cement, sugar and rice, with the two elder Liems putting up the larger part of the capital.

Djuhar Sutanto, like Liem, was born in Fuqing and emigrated to Kudus in Central Java. Both are Fuzhou Hokkien. Sudwikatmono is a cousin of President Soeharto. Ibrahim Risjad worked in the late 1950s with Liem's younger brother and Djuhar Sutanto in distribution and trade. They also were heavily involved in the day-to-day running of the various companies, leaving Liem Sioe Liong to oversee the group as a whole.

The remaining three investors are Liem's third son, Anthony Salim (Liem Fung Seng), Djuhar Sutanto's eldest son and a younger cousin (Tedy Djuhar and Henry Pribadi respectively). All three were born in Central Java and are second generation ethnic Chinese.

Currently, the Liem Investors group is slowly disbanding, as each member increasingly focuses on his own, separate business operations. At the end of 1990, another investor in the Salim Group, Mochtar Riady resigned from the board of the BCA, reduced his shareholdings and concentrated on building up his own Lippo Group. During 1991, the Salim Group's agribusiness and cooking oils joint ventures with the Sinar Mas Group began to unwind as well. The Salim Group exchanged part of its share in the cooking oil joint ventures with Sinar Mas, for Sinar Mas' share in UIC. Concurrently, the Salim Group was restructured.

Current Group Structure

In the past, the group had no overall holding company to permit centralised ownership or management. Fast and efficient entry into new markets was best accomplished by joining with a partner already prominent in those markets. This led to the group often relying on joint ownership-joint management.[74]

Today, Liem's family plays a more prominent role in the group than in the past. Anthony Salim, Liem's youngest son and probable successor, is taking an increasing role in the group's strategic planning and management. He went to high school in Singapore (where his immediate family now lives) and was educated further in London. Consequently, he has excellent English language skills and therefore often does the negotiating with Western interests on the

72 See Sato, Y.

73 Liem Sioe Liong and Liem Oen Kian are not related.

74 See Sato, Y.

group's behalf. He now heads the group's Indonesian holding company, PT Salim Economic Development Corporation. Liem Sioe Hie, elder brother of Liem Sioe Liong, is thought to be prominent in the group's financial management side. Sudwikatmono has remained as president-director of Indocement.[75]

In 1990, the Salim Group was restructured. A Salim Group Board of Directors was set up to control all the group's interests. The Board consists of Liem (chairman of the Salim Group), Andree Halim (vice-chairman of the Salim Group and Liem's second son), Anthony Salim (group president and CEO) and several non-family directors.[76]

Under the board of directors come eleven divisions, each of which has a steering committee to determine basic policy and a division management committee to supervise day-to-day operations. A division is composed of a number of sub-divisions under which sit the individual companies. Ten divisions are concerned largely with overseeing the group's Indonesian interests and an international division oversees the group's growing overseas interests.

There are three main holding companies for the group: the Salim Economic Development Corporation which is the main umbrella for all Salim's Indonesia-based operations; KMP Pte Ltd which holds the Singapore-based companies; and First Pacific Company Ltd which although managed on a day-to-day basis quite separately from the rest of the Group's interests could be considered to hold most of Salim's other operations. These in turn contain other holding companies. Thus the Salim Group now has a branched pyramid structure for the first time, with the board of directors (Liem, his sons and professional managers) at the apex and the more than 400 companies at its base.[77]

Since the restructuring, Liem's various companies are still owned by his family and its partners. His senior staff are largely ethnic Chinese, but middle management and below is split between ethnic Chinese and *pribumi* Indonesians.

A summary of the Salim Group's current structure is set out in Figure 8.1.

Relationships With Other Ethnic Chinese Entrepreneurs

In his business dealings, Liem has maintained close relationships with other leading ethnic Chinese business figures and groups within Indonesia and throughout the region. They are often used to manage parts of his business empire. Mochtar Riady (Li Mo Tie) managed Bank Central Asia from 1975 until 1990 in addition to building his own growing regional financial empire; Eka Tjipta Widjaja (Oei Ek Tjhong) managed until the early 1990s, his own and Liem's interests in palm and other vegetable oils as well as his own extensive Sinar Mas Group; Ciputra (Chia Ching Hwa) is closely linked to Liem's real estate interests as well as managing his own Ciputra Group; Prajogo Pangestu (Pang Jun Pen) has overseen Liem's timber and plywood interests as well as his own Barito Group and recently acquired Astra Group; Malaysian Robert Kuok

[75] See *The Asian Wall Street Journal*, 'Salim group steels itself for life after Suharto', 25-26 February 1994.

[76] See Sato, Y.

[77] See Sato, Y., for a further description of the Salim Group's new structure.

Overview of the Salim Group: Structure and Key Companies

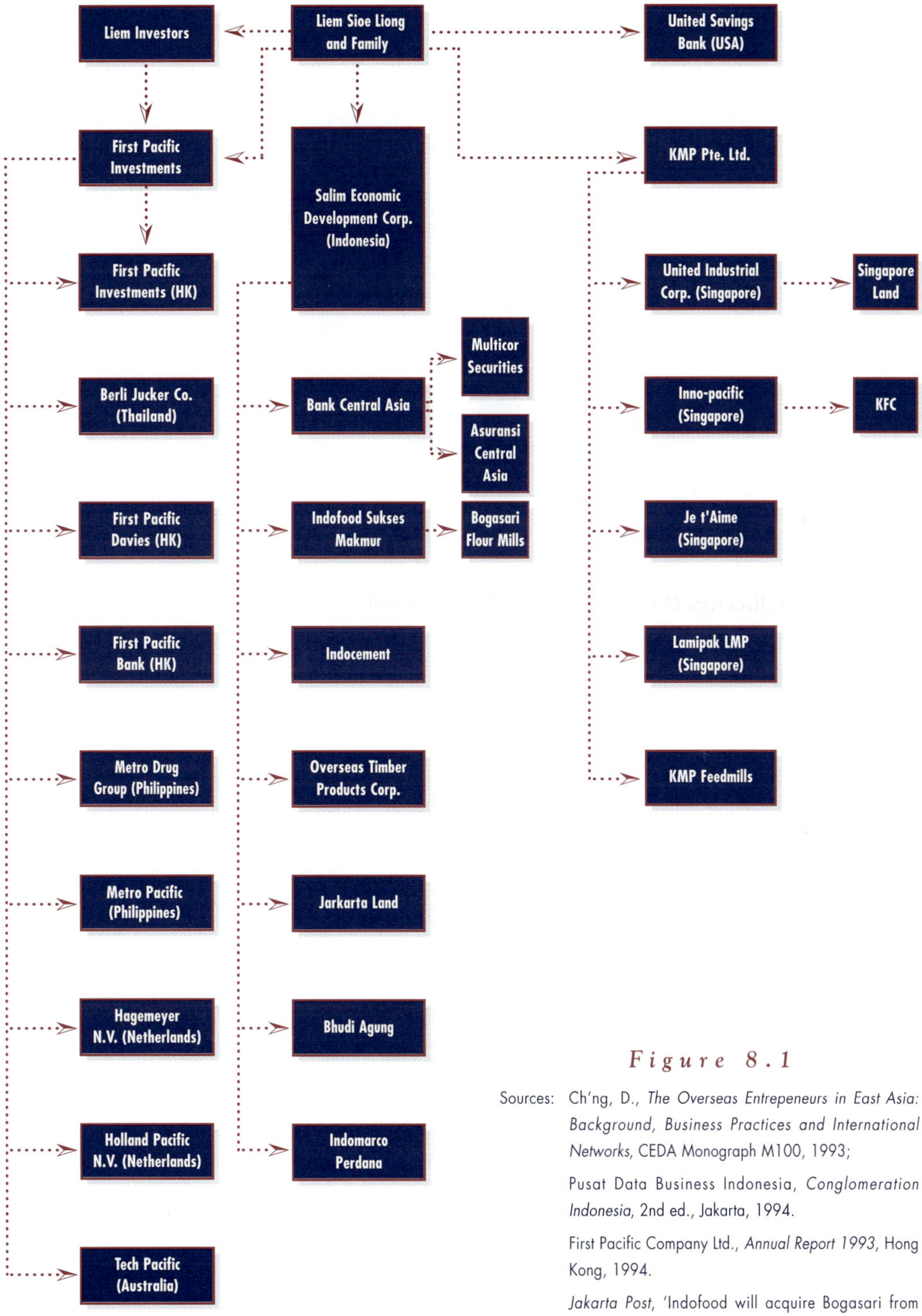

Figure 8.1

Sources: Ch'ng, D., *The Overseas Entrepeneurs in East Asia: Background, Business Practices and International Networks*, CEDA Monograph M100, 1993;

Pusat Data Business Indonesia, *Conglomeration Indonesia*, 2nd ed., Jakarta, 1994.

First Pacific Company Ltd., *Annual Report 1993*, Hong Kong, 1994.

Jakarta Post, 'Indofood will acquire Bogasari from Indocement', 19 February 1995.

provided the management expertise for Salim's flour and sugar mills; and the Taiwanese Koo family provided expertise in cement.

Securing the Future

Anthony Salim recently said in an interview that the Salim Group would remain strong in a post-Soeharto Indonesia if it was judged to be 'useful' and 'required' for the country. He thought both of these criteria would be satisfied.[78]

The group has become so big in key industries such as cement and food, that its performance has a significant impact on Indonesia's economy. The listing of some of the group's core companies also has given many other Indonesian companies and individuals a stake in the performance of the group.

As 35 per cent of the group's revenues are now sourced from overseas, any downturn in the group's performance and prospects in Indonesia should not affect a large part of the group's returns.

Another risk management strategy has been the switch away from heavy manufacturing industry reliant on protection, toward more export-oriented sectors. Such a move is preparing the conglomerate for freer international trade.

Summary of the Main Companies of the Salim Group

In Indonesia:

Indocement: publicly-listed Indocement is the largest cement producer in South-East Asia and possibly in the world. The Indonesian Government is a minority shareholder in this company. Indocement has been a substantial beneficiary of Indonesia's rapid development since the 1980s.

Indofoods: publicly-listed Indofoods is the world's largest producer of noodles and has 85 per cent of the Indonesian market. This company also has a substantial market share in milk, snack foods and baby foods.

Bogasari Flour Mills: the largest flour miller in Indonesia has well over half the domestic market; this company acts as an in-house miller and supplier of flour for Indofoods. Malaysian tycoon Robert Kuok is a substantial minority shareholder in Bogasari.

Indosteel: this is a major producer and importer of steel products. The group, however, substantially reduced its steel interests in the early 1990s, selling its holding in PT Cold Rolling Mill Indonesia Utama to state-owned Krakatau Steel, thereby withdrawing entirely from the cold-rolled steel business.

Bank Central Asia (BCA): BCA is the largest private sector bank in Indonesia. With more than 300 branches and 13 000 employees, only the four main state commercial banks are larger.

Jakarta Land: this is the Liem family's property development arm.

....

78 See *The Asian Wall Street Journal*, 'Salim group steels itself for life after Suharto', 25-26 February 1994.

In Hong Kong:

First Pacific Company: publicly-listed with a market capitalisation of more than US$1 billion, First Pacific is controlled by Salim and other associated investors. The Salim Group and Liem nonetheless are relatively passive investors in the company which is run entirely by professionally-trained managers. It is a regional conglomerate in its own right with publicly-listed companies in the Philippines, Thailand and the Netherlands, and activities throughout Asia and the Pacific.

FPB Bank Holdings: publicly-listed with a market capitalisation of US$250 million in mid 1994, this company operates the First Pacific Bank in Hong Kong. The bank has 25 branches in Hong Kong, four representative offices elsewhere in Asia and an office in Shenzhen. Three arms of the Chinese Government (MOFTEC, CITIC and China National Metals and Minerals Import and Export Company) together own 34 per cent of the bank's shares.

In the Philippines:

The First Pacific Group controls the investment bank, First Pacific Capital Corporation, Metro Drug Corporation and Smart Information Technologies.

In Singapore:

KMP Pte Ltd: a group of at least 23 companies involved in finance, property, shipping, chemicals, manufacturing, feedmills and food processing

United Industrial Corporation (UIC): a listed group holding substantial Singapore-based assets worth in excess of US$1 billion. KMP is the controlling shareholder.

In the Netherlands:

Hagemeyer NV: a publicly-listed company engaged in vehicle assembly and international trading in which First Pacific has over 50 per cent equity.

Chapter 9

CONNECTIONS AND INVESTMENT ACROSS BORDERS

Migration often follows chains, bringing together relatives and friends in the new destination, but it frequently also has a scattering effect. Most Chinese have relatives and friends who departed to other destinations around the world.[1]

The ethnic Chinese business community is distributed across Asia. Consequent connections are useful for business introductions and advice on the local market. One survey of over 150 ethnic Chinese entrepreneurs spread across a range of different countries found that more than half the domestic business partnerships were with other ethnic Chinese, as were 39 per cent of the international working relationships.[2]

A model for South-East Asian ethnic Chinese business expansion offshore could well be as follows:[3]

Step 1: Domestic expansion

Step 2: Establishment of a representative office in Hong Kong

Step 3: Investment in China

Step 4: Investment in other ASEAN countries.

Malaysia's Hong Leong Group, Indonesia's Lippo Group and the Salim Group, and Thailand's Charoen Pokphand all have expanded in this way. The establishment of an office in Hong Kong is often important for tapping into international capital markets to fund further expansion. Expansion into China frequently uses old family and dialect ties and newly forged political connections, and expansion into the rest of ASEAN can be on the basis of joint ventures with local ethnic Chinese business people with whom connections may exist already.

1 See Ip, D. and C. Lever-Tracy, 'Trailblazing into China: Networks and Linkages of Smaller Diaspora Firms', unpublished paper, 1993.

2 See Kao, J., 'The worldwide web of Chinese business', *Harvard Business Review*, March-April 1993, p. 32.

3 See Ch'ng, D., *The Overseas Chinese Entrepreneurs in East Asia: Background, Business Practices and International Networks*, CEDA Monograph M100, 1993, p. 25.

The Lippo Group - Expansion Beyond Indonesia

The Lippo Group, controlled by Sino-Indonesian Mochtar Riady, is an aggressive offshore investor.[4] Initially, Riady concentrated on building up the group's operations in Indonesia. Lippobank and Lippoland are now two of Indonesia's best known companies.

Riady's next move was to establish a presence in Hong Kong. Much of the funding for the group's subsequent expansion came from bond investors in Hong Kong, rather than from the group's Indonesian based activities. In Hong Kong, Lippo's banking activities are through its Hong Kong Chinese Bank. Lippo Asia, an investment banking arm which is investigating infrastructure projects in China, also is managed from Hong Kong.

The group's current focus is expansion into China, where the group intends to establish a branch network. In south-eastern China, Lippo works through its joint venture bank, China Mercantile Bank, which is 40 per cent owned by Lippo and 60 per cent owned by state-owned enterprises. China Mercantile Bank has a branch in Shenzhen where 70 per cent of its business is in trade finance. Other China projects include development of a 1.3 million square metre commercial and residential estate in Putian (Fujian Province), which is Riady's birthplace; partnership in a major power project, also in Putian; partnership with Singapore's Jurong Cement Limited, Pico Far East (HK) and SingKong Investment Holdings to form a joint venture with the Cement Plant Company of Beijing; and involvement in a similar consortium in a joint venture with the Shanghai Ma Lu Industrial Corporation to develop an industrial park in Shanghai.

There are longer term plans to expand into other parts of Asia. In Thailand, Lippo operates a small merchant banking operation. Also Lippo intends to activate its securities arm in Manila. In Taiwan, the group is looking at taking equity in a securities company, and in the longer term, the group is looking at Singaporean and Malaysian markets. Lippo is also represented in Vietnam.

International Chinese Associations

A more formal and non-traditional way for ethnic Chinese to maintain their connections across borders is through the meetings of the many international ethnic Chinese associations. The most prominent of these are the international dialect associations, mentioned in Chapter 2. The worldwide Teochiu Alliance

---

4 This section is based on *Asia Today*, 'Lippo leads equity stake in major China projects', May 1994; *Asian Wall Street Journal*, 'Lippo and Hong Kong arm seek projects in urban development', 20 September 1994; and information provided by the Research Department of the Singapore Chinese Chamber of Commerce and Industry.

Association, formed in 1981, covers approximately 150 Teochiu organisations and meets every two years. The most recent conference was in 1993 in the United States. Previous meetings were held in Hong Kong, Macau, Canada, France, the Philippines and Thailand.

Apart from providing venues to renew old acquaintances, the meetings give the offshore Chinese who may have lost touch with their roots and with China the opportunity to 'freshen up' dialects and other aspects of 'Chineseness'.

Non-Chinese international organisations in the region also serve inadvertently as venues for ethnic Chinese entrepreneurs to stay in touch. The ASEAN Business Forum which was established in 1991 now has 167 members; many are firms controlled by ethnic Chinese. Examples from across ASEAN include MBf Finance Bhd, Shinawatra Group, Singapore Technologies Industrial Corporation, Siam Motors Co Ltd, the Hour Glass Ltd, PT Bukaka Teknok Utama, Bank Nusa and the Matahari Group.

The World Chinese Entrepreneurs Convention

The World Chinese Entrepreneurs Convention is the world's biggest networking event for ethnic Chinese business people. It is held every two years; attracts over 1 000 participants; and is open to ethnic Chinese regardless of dialect or ancestral origins. The first such convention was held in Singapore in 1991; the second was held in 1993 in Hong Kong; and the third is to be held during November 1995 in Bangkok.

The past two conventions attracted some of the world's most successful ethnic Chinese entrepreneurs, including Li Ka-shing, Mochtar Riady, and Henry Fok. Singapore's Senior Minister Lee Kuan Yew addressed both conventions.

The conventions are run over three days and feature numerous guest speakers, evening functions and other networking events. The proceedings of the conventions are usually in Mandarin or English, with simultaneous interpretation.

Delegations of ethnic Chinese entrepreneurs to the Singapore Convention were sent from as far afield as the United States, Chile, France, Greece, Guam, Italy, Japan, Mauritius, Lesotho and Switzerland, as well as the expected Asian countries. Australia was well represented at the 1993 Hong Kong Convention. The Victorian Chinese Chamber of Commerce and Victoria's Chinese Professional and Businessmen's Association sent a joint delegation of twenty-four members.

The Victorian Chinese Chamber of Commerce and the Chinese Chamber of Commerce of South Australia have put in a joint bid to host the Fifth World Chinese Entrepreneurs Convention in 1997 in Melbourne and Adelaide.

INTERNATIONAL LINKAGES OF ASIA'S ETHNIC CHINESE COMMUNITIES

The shared history of many of the Chinese across Asia means that linkages among the various Chinese communities are inevitable. Links are through family, dialect or ancestral region. Another form of international linkage now occurring is among 'third country' ethnic Chinese, those who migrated from China to South-East Asia and then subsequently fled to a third country because of local political and social upheavals. Thus today there are sizeable Indonesian Chinese, Burmese Chinese and Vietnamese Chinese diasporas, for example. Members of these diasporas often retain close links with Indonesia, Myanmar, Vietnam, and China, and now feature among the most prominent foreign investors in these places.

Regional Investment from the Ethnic Chinese States

The ethnic Chinese-dominated economies of Hong Kong, Taiwan and Singapore are significant net exporters of capital to the region. A significant proportion of this investment undoubtedly flows via ethnic Chinese connections and networks. The significance of international network-type investment can be understated because funds will often be sent to friends and relatives residing in the host country who invest it on behalf of their foreign relatives. Such investment is often recorded as domestic investment. Occasionally, this method may have other benefits if the foreign investor wishes to invest in sectors prohibited to foreigners.[5]

Table 9.1

Ethnic Chinese States' Investment in Selected Asian Countries

(According to Rank as Foreign Investor[6])

	CAMBODIA	INDONESIA	PHILIPPINES	THAILAND	VIETNAM
Taiwan	8th	3rd	8th	8th	1st
Hong Kong	3rd	2nd	5th	2nd	2nd
Singapore	2nd	7th	7th	4th	5th

5 This is the case with the large flows of capital into the Philippines from Taiwanese Chinese for investing in land, a sector which is closed to foreigners.

6 Data for Cambodia relates to numbers of foreign invested project approvals given since 1989; for Indonesia, it relates to cumulative foreign investment between 1967 and 1994; for the Philippines, it relates to foreign investment between 1989 and 1994; for Thailand it relates to foreign investment between 1989 and 1993; and for Vietnam it relates to the existing stock of foreign investment. Information was derived from Department of Foreign Affairs and Trade, *Country Economic Briefs*.

INTERNATIONAL LINKAGES BETWEEN CHINESE COMMUNITIES

Brunei

Most of Brunei's ethnic Chinese population are Hokkien and have their ancestral origins in Jinmen. Until recently however, Brunei's ethnic Chinese were prohibited from visiting the PRC. In 1993, the Sultan of Brunei travelled to China, which led to the re-establishment of ties between the two countries and the removal of travel restrictions. A Bruneian business mission, including representatives of the Chinese Chamber of Commerce, subsequently visited China in April 1994.

Small numbers of ethnic Chinese have left Brunei and settled elsewhere, probably seeking tertiary education. Some ethnic Chinese from Brunei have permanent resident status in Australia.

Cambodia

Like Thailand's ethnic Chinese community, most of Cambodia's is Teochiu. Since 1989, the largest foreign investors in Cambodia by numbers of project approvals have been Thailand, Singapore and Hong Kong, respectively.[7] Each of these sources has significant Teochiu communities who may invest using dialect links.

Many Sino-Thai business people also established businesses in Cambodia, as did Singaporeans. The expansion and redevelopment of Phnom Penh's Cambodiana Hotel, the construction of a complex comprising 199 serviced apartments, the setting up of a tourist agency, the opening of an office equipment sales and service centre and the development of a nightclub and entertainment complex either were completed or are planned by Singaporean companies.

The Chinese Embassy in Phnom Penh plays an important role in facilitating business links between the ethnic Chinese community and China. It has been instrumental in setting up trade fairs in Phnom Penh in which Chinese-made products ranging from farm machinery to Chinese herbal medicines were displayed and sold. Since 1992, many semi-official mainland Chinese business delegations have visited Cambodia and a considerable number of enterprises from China have established local offices.

Indonesia

From 1967 to 1994, Hong Kong was the second highest cumulative investor in Indonesia with total investment of US$13.5 billion. Taiwan was the third highest with US$8.8 billion and Singapore was the seventh highest, investing US$6.2 billion.[8]

A large proportion of the Sino-Indonesian community can be considered *peranakan*, so overall, the community is relatively isolated from ethnic Chinese

7 Taiwan was the seventh largest.

8 See Department of Foreign Affairs and Trade, *Country Economic Briefs*.

elsewhere. This makes it difficult for community members to expand beyond Indonesia using ethnic Chinese links. Such expansion usually has been the preserve of *totok* businessmen, and some have been significant investors in China.

Regional economic growth has reoriented Indonesia's Chinese business people towards China. The Indonesian Government has had little choice but to let this happen: it is an inevitable consequence of Indonesia's economic expansion. As in other places in South-East Asia, Indonesia is realising that the connections of its ethnic Chinese community with other countries are commercially valuable. Similarly, as other countries in the region grow wealthier and their citizens, some of whom are ethnic Chinese, travel to Indonesia for either business or pleasure, Indonesia can gain from the resultant commerce. In response, the Government of Indonesia announced in August 1994 that it was softening the restrictions on the use of Chinese language.[9]

Indonesian Chinese in the Region

The departure of many Sino-Indonesians from Indonesia during the 1950s and 1960s now represents a potential asset for Indonesia. Now, an Indonesian Chinese diaspora is spread across a variety of countries which can help transform Indonesia's economy.

Today, Hong Kong has a significant Indonesian Chinese population. Many also went to Singapore where there are now several prominent Indonesian Chinese entrepreneurs. One of these is Ong Tjoe Kim, the founder of the Singaporean Metro Department Store. Ong spent his early years in business in Jakarta and Surabaya before leaving for Singapore in 1957.[10] He is married to the daughter of the family which owns Indonesia's Matahari Department Store chain. Ong has invested in Indonesia opening a high profile Metro store in Jakarta.[11] Another was Goh Tjoei Kok who left Indonesia for Singapore in 1954 to set up the Tat Lee Company, which specialised in rubber trading, and later, the Tat Lee Bank.[12] Yet another was S.C. Huang, who left Indonesia for Singapore where he established his first hotel in 1958. He opened several other hotels around the world including one in Perth.[13]

9 This is further discussed in Chapter 3.

10 See Chan, K.B. and C. Chiang, *Stepping Out: The Making of Chinese Entrepreneurs*, Prentice Hall, Singapore, 1994, p. 38.

11 See *Australian Financial Review*, 'Kmart in fast run at Indonesia', 30 November 1994.

12 See Chan, K.B. and C. Chiang, p. 38. Goh died in October 1994. (See *Asian Wall Street Journal*, 'Tat Lee Bank Shares surge in heavy trading', 26 October 1994.)

13 He migrated there from Singapore in the mid 1980s and died in Perth in 1994. (See *Straits Times Weekly Edition*, 'Hotelier S.C. Huang dies in Perth', 3 December 1994.)

The Hong Kong Indonesian Chinese

During the late 1950s, the Indonesian Government attempted to curb the commercial power of Indonesia's Chinese; this led to a mass exodus of Sino-Indonesians.[14] The wealthier Chinese left for Singapore, some went to Holland (where they could use their Dutch language skills) but many fled to China and Hong Kong. Macau also has a significant Indonesian Chinese community, some of whom went straight from Indonesia to Macau.

Today, there is a significant Indonesian Chinese minority living in Hong Kong. A few came directly, others passed through Singapore, but most came after first attempting to settle in China, especially in Xiamen and Fuqing. They started leaving Indonesia for China in significant numbers in the early 1950s, but it was not until the troubles of 1959-61 that they started leaving *en masse*. At this time, Beijing dispatched 'rescue' ships to Indonesia to collect dispossessed Indonesian Chinese. Many who passed through China faced difficulties during the Cultural Revolution (1966-76) when their 'Chineseness' was questioned. Between 1972 and 1975, more than 50 000 left, mostly going to Hong Kong. They now constitute around two per cent of Hong Kong's population. Many of these Indonesian Chinese had little or no assets and some became farmers in the outlying areas of the New Territories. Most of the Indonesian Chinese in Hong Kong are still towards the bottom of the economic rung. They have become isolated, particularly as very few are Cantonese - the dominant Chinese group in Hong Kong - and have formed something of a sub-culture. Some are *peranakan* and speak regional Javanese dialects, poor Hokkien or Dutch. Many feel neither Chinese nor Indonesian and are thus doubly isolated. Their existence is manifested by a number of Indonesian restaurants in Hong Kong, some of which also retail Indonesian products. Hong Kong's Indonesian Chinese remain a resource that is still to be fully tapped to promote trade and investment between Indonesia and China and Hong Kong.

Laos

Thailand is the largest foreign investor into Laos and accounts for 40 per cent of the licensed foreign investment since 1988. Perhaps a factor contributing to this phenomenon is that most Sino-Thais and Sino-Laos are Teochiu. There also is some inwards investment from Sino-Laotians living abroad, mostly from the United States, Canada, France and Australia. This investment is concentrated in

14 This section draws on Godley, M.R. and C.A. Coppel, 'The Indonesian Chinese in Hong Kong: A Preliminary Report on a Minority Community in Transition', *Issues and Studies: A Journal of Chinese Studies and International Affairs*, Vol. 26, No. 7, July 1990.

the tourism, hotel, construction, textile and garment and wood processing sectors. There also is trading and investment activity between Laos and the Sino-Laotian communities in Sydney and Melbourne.

Malaysia

In recent years, as Malaysia has looked for foreign investment opportunities, it has realised that the connections of Malaysia's Chinese might prove useful. Many Chinese see the recent liberalisation of the use of English as a signal of impending 'cultural liberalisation' in Malaysia. This has encouraged them to bring their capital back to Malaysia.

Successive Malaysian governments permitted Chinese schools to operate and this has allowed Malaysia's Chinese to retain their Chinese language and cultural skills, so that connections with the Chinese outside Malaysia have not grown cold.[15] Malaysia is now reaping the benefits of this. The NEP ensures that very few major firms in Malaysia are solely Chinese - most have *bumiputera* equity, directors and employees. As these firms trade and invest abroad using ethnic Chinese networks, *bumiputera* business people also benefit.

The preservation of the culture of Malaysia's Chinese will serve Malaysia well in the growing economic relationship between Malaysia and China.

Malaysia's Chinese may also prove significant investors in other countries. Malaysia's multiracial society may have made them more adaptable, flexible and accommodating than Chinese from more homogeneous cultures. Hence they may be more comfortable than say, Hong Kong Chinese when doing business in places such as Australia. Malaysia's tertiary education policies with racially-based quotas have led thousands of mostly Chinese Malaysians to seek tertiary education abroad, particularly in the United States, Europe and Australia.[16] This has increased the internationalisation of their outlook.[17]

Malaysia's Chinese have links to other Chinese apart from those in Australia and China. Penang's mostly Hokkien Chinese have dialect and other links to the Chinese in Manila, lower Myanmar and Taiwan, all areas where most local Chinese also are ancestrally Hokkien. The Penang Chinese Chamber of Commerce has exchanged delegations with the Manila Chinese Chamber of Commerce. Delegations between Taiwan and Penang are rarely organised because the level of business interaction between the two is so high that delegations are no longer required. Now, there is so much Taiwanese investment in Penang, particularly in electronics and computer companies, that Singapore might lose its edge in this area.

---

15 Successive governments have not clamped down on Chinese schools but they have not provided them with government assistance either. The MCA has just launched a plan to raise M$6 million to fund Chinese schools, and the DAP has long supported government assistance for 'mother tongue education' - whether it is Chinese or Tamil or something else.

16 The current official quotas stand at 55 per cent *bumiputeras*, 35 per cent Chinese, and 10 per cent Indians and those of mixed race.

17 There are many Malaysian Chinese who were educated in Australia and consequently have a close, personal knowledge of its business environment and opportunities. This is further examined in Chapter 13.

The dialect links between the Chinese in Penang and Medan, in north Sumatra, have led to a flourishing trade in vegetables and seafood. This trade is conducted mostly in Hokkien.

Penang also has a Teochiu community. Like the Teochiu elsewhere in Malaysia, often they trade in agricultural goods with Thailand (where the Chinese are primarily Teochiu.) Another aspect of this Teochiu cross-border trade is that many antique and curio shops in Georgetown are owned by Teochiu families and as a result, they have a disproportionate number of Thai artefacts on their shelves.

Thousands of Malaysian Chinese who were Chinese educated and unable to find places in Malaysia's tertiary education institutions went to Taiwan to study. As a consequence, they are now crucial for Malaysia/Taiwan links. In the past, they often lost out to English educated Chinese, but now their Chinese language skills and connections to Taiwan are greatly valued. They dominate several of Malaysia's industrial parks which have a strong Taiwanese investment presence. A Taiwan University Alumni Association in Penang caters for the graduates of Taiwan universities. Some Taiwanese Chinese also have emigrated to Penang, resulting in a Taiwanese association being formed there.

Other links between Malaysia and Taiwan derive from the small group of Kuomintang who settled in Malaysia. Initially, they formed an identifiable group in the MCA but lost influence in the late 1950s. A former president of the Malaysian Chinese Association and later, the Gerakan Party, Dr Lim Chong Eu, was a former Kuomintang leader.[18] Similarly, Tun Sir Colonel Henry H.S. Lee, founder of Malaysia's Development and Commercial Bank Bhd, co-founder of the Singapore-based Overseas Union Bank (OUB), and Malaysia's first Finance Minister was a Kuomintang leader.[19]

Myanmar

Singapore is the largest investor in Myanmar with some US$260 million in commitments, followed by Thailand (US$211 million), the United States (US$203 million) and Japan (US$101 million).[20] Since April 1992, investors from Thailand, Malaysia, Singapore, Hong Kong and Macau have invested in at least eleven hotel projects in Myanmar. [21]

Being largely Hokkien or Cantonese, Yangon's ethnic Chinese tend to have links to other Hokkien and Cantonese communities around the world. Despite Myanmar's geographic proximity to Thailand, there are few obvious dialect links between the ethnic Chinese communities of Yangon and Bangkok (where the Teochiu dominate). Instead, Yangon's Hokkien tend to have strong links to Singapore and to Penang (both of which have large Hokkien communities) and the Cantonese have strong links to Hong Kong (which is dominated by the

18 See Gomez, E. T., *Money Politics in the Barisan Nasional*, Forum, Kuala Lumpur, 1991, p. 32.

19 See Gomez, E. T., *Money Politics in the Barisan Nasional*, p. 31.

20 See Department of Foreign Affairs and Trade, *Country Economic Briefs*.

21 See *Nikkei Weekly*, 'NIEs target India, Myanmar, Vietnam', 21 February 1994.

Cantonese.) Also, despite Myanmar's relative isolation, some members of the Yangon ethnic Chinese community attend the annual meetings of the various international dialect associations. This may have the effect of renewing their international links and replenishing their 'Chineseness'.

The Burmese Chinese Diaspora

Between 1963 and 1969, pursuant to the Ne Win regime's 'Burmese Way to Socialism', much of the economy was nationalised. Many families lost their assets without due compensation and consequently left the country. Generally, the Hokkien went to Singapore and the Cantonese went to Hong Kong and San Francisco.

Since December 1988, when more liberal foreign investment laws were enacted, most foreign investment in Myanmar has been of ethnic Chinese origin. The two most important factors contributing to this are: most Western governments have not actively promoted business links with Myanmar; and the large number of Sino-Burmese who fled Burma during the 1960s now can use their connections to invest there.

Singapore's prominence as an investor in Myanmar is almost certainly due to the large number of Sino-Burmese business people now living in Singapore. Many either invest in Myanmar themselves or assist other Singaporeans to do so.

Among the larger individual investors into Myanmar is S.P. Tao, who came to Singapore from Burma. Tao is part of a consortium to build a US$30 million hotel in Yangon.[22] Another Burmese-born investor is Peter Lee who also resides in Singapore.[23] Lee's PL International Pte Ltd has formed a US$6.4 million joint venture called Myanmar Seafoods Ltd, based in Yangon and managed by Lee's Yangon-based brother. The joint venture exports prawns and fish from Myanmar to Japan and Europe and includes a cold storage facility and an ice plant.[24] The family of Aw Boon Haw, who founded the Tiger Balm empire, still has some investments in Myanmar. Aw and his family left Burma for Singapore in 1926.[25]

In 1994, Robert Kuok's Hong Kong-based Kerry Financial Services Ltd established the Myanmar Fund. The fund is seeking to raise US$50-100 million to invest in Myanmar's tourism and agribusiness sectors, infrastructure development and light engineering.[26] The development of a container terminal port in Yangon and direct investment in Mandalay Beer also are being

---

22 Information provided by the SCCCI. Tao controls the Shing Kwan Group of Companies which has total net assets of around US$200 million and is an equity holder in Singapore-Suzhou Township Development Pte Ltd. (See Singapore-Suzhou Township Development Pte Ltd., *Singapore-Suzhou Township*, promotional brochure.)

23 Many of the ethnic Chinese who have left Myanmar tend to use their Chinese names outside of Myanmar but their Burmese names when visiting or investing in Myanmar.

24 Information provided by SCCCI.

25 See Chan, K.B. and C. Chiang, *Stepping Out: The Making of Chinese Entrepreneurs*, Prentice Hall, Singapore, 1994, p. 316. The Aw family are Hakkas.

26 See *Bangkok Post*, 'Country fund looks to attract experienced investors in Burma', 20 September 1994. The Fund has been listed on the Dublin Stock Exchange which was chosen for its ease of listing and competitive cost.

considered. The Kuok Group is planning several hotels in Myanmar, a US$63 million Shangri-La Hotel and a Traders Hotel, both of which are to be in Yangon and completed in 1997, and possibly a Shangri-La Hotel in Mandalay, and it is expected that the Myanmar Fund will also invest in these.

To achieve its aims, the fund uses the connections of its director, Halpin Ho, a Sino-Burmese who left Burma for Bangkok in 1962.[27] Ho has retained his Burmese citizenship and as a consequence is able to own land in Myanmar. It is on this that the Kuok Group's Shangri-la and Traders Hotels will be built. The fund also is expected to invest US$20 million in a business complex that the Ho family is planning in Myanmar.[28]

Because of the turbulent politics of Myanmar and the region, many of its ethnic Chinese population have lived in various countries in their lifetimes. This has led them to develop strong connections across borders which do not simply follow dialect lines. Their businesses today reflect this. Several interviewees in Yangon described their turbulent family histories.

One described how his father was born in China and was educated as an engineer in the United States. The father then went to Burma to work as an engineer, but fled to India during the war, returning in 1948 to become an agent and distributor. In 1959, the family, who are Cantonese, went to Hong Kong to live. From there, they developed business interests in Hong Kong, Taiwan, Malaysia, Thailand, South Korea and Guam. Although an American passport holder, and still based in Hong Kong, the son now spends much time in Myanmar, developing an import-export business.

Another ethnic Chinese businessman who also divides his time between Myanmar and Hong Kong described how, during the 1960s, he fled from Burma to China to escape the Ne Win regime's nationalisation policies. In China, he became embroiled in Mao's Cultural Revolution and was labelled a 'capitalist roader'. He was sent to work on state farms in the country. Ultimately, he was able to leave China for Hong Kong and now has a business with operations in Yangon, Hong Kong, Kuala Lumpur, Bangkok, China and Taiwan.

Myanmar is increasingly a focus for business delegations from abroad, many of which seek to link up with the local ethnic Chinese business community. A large number of delegations come from China each year, and in August 1994, a sizeable delegation of Singaporean business people visited Myanmar. A trade and investment mission was organised by the Singapore Chinese Chamber of Commerce and Industry (SCCCI) and the Singapore Trade Development Board. It was headed by Kwek Leng Joo, the current president of the SCCCI and senior

27 Robert Kuok, a Fuzhou Hokkien, has some affinity with Myanmar. In 1961, Kuok visited Burma in search of trading opportunities. He met up with senior members of Rangoon's Chinese business community, many members of whom are Fuzhou. Subsequently, and in the light of Kuok's later success, the Yangon Fuzhous regard Kuok as something of a patriarch.

28 Ho is also the director of the Hong Kong-based Irrawaddy Advisors Ltd that helps investors put together ventures in Myanmar. The company is a joint venture between Kuok's Kerry Financial Services and Ho's Group. (See *Bangkok Post*, 'Country fund looks to attract experienced investors in Burma', 20 September 1994; and *Burma Alert*, No. 10, Vol. 5, October 1994.)

Singaporean businessman. It included 34 officials and business people; of these, 28 were ethnic Chinese, including Sino-Burmese now residing in Singapore.[29]

With foreign investment opening up and the development of a more vibrant private sector, 13 new commercial banks have been awarded licences to operate in Myanmar. As these banks are not currently permitted to deal in foreign exchange their trade financing role is very limited. Two banks, the Mayflower Bank and the Myanmar Oriental Bank are widely understood to have financial backing from ethnic Chinese interests in Singapore and Malaysia and are using local ethnic Chinese to advance this investment.[30] These two banks have been at the forefront of financial markets innovation in Myanmar, with the Myanmar Oriental Bank introducing in 1994 a credit card for Myanmar kyat-denominated transactions, the first of its type in Myanmar.[31]

Not all the investment traffic is one way. Most of the wealthy ethnic Chinese families in Yangon tend to have investments outside Myanmar. Among those interviewed, there was broad agreement that the best investment was property, and for the Hokkien, the strongly favoured destination was Singapore. This is probably due to a combination of factors. Singapore has liberal foreign investment laws, is politically stable and many of the Yangon-based Hokkien have relatives and other associates now based in Singapore to manage the property for them.

Many of the wealthier ethnic Chinese families also have sons or daughters in the United States. They usually went there to study and have remained. Many of these now are involved in the professions and undoubtedly form a reserve network which could be activated for future business if necessary.

The Philippines

During 1989 to 1994, Hong Kong was recorded as the Philippines' fifth largest foreign investor with cumulative investment of US$131.6 million. Singapore was the seventh with investments of US$42.7 million, and Taiwan was the eighth with US$36.4 million in investments.[32]

The Chinese in the Philippines have very strong links with nearby Taiwan and China's Fujian Province, possibly more so than do the Chinese of other South-East Asian countries. Most of the Filipino Chinese are ancestrally Hokkien - the dialect of Taiwan and Fujian.

---

29 See *Singapore Trade and Investment Mission to Myanmar, 22-26 August 1994*, Singapore, 1994, (mission handbook.)

30 Strictly, foreign equity in the new banks is prohibited but like most other rules in Myanmar at present, this rule has been interpreted with a degree of flexibility.

31 Until then, what little use that had been made of credit cards in Myanmar, was for US dollar transactions, largely by foreigners. Very few enterprises accept credit cards in any event, and almost all transactions must be made in cash.

32 See Department of Foreign Affairs and Trade, *Country Economic Briefs*. Foreign investment figures can be highly unreliable. The figure for Taiwan seems least accurate given that the vast majority of Philippines' Chinese are Hokkien - the same dialect as that for Taiwan, the close proximity of the two economies and the extensive family and other ties many Taiwanese have with Sino-Filipinos. It is quite likely that much of the capital coming into the Philippines from Taiwan is invested through locally based friends and relatives and is thus recorded as domestic investment.

An important factor in maintaining these links has been to preserve the Chineseness or perhaps more accurately, the 'Hokkienness,' of the Filipino-Chinese. The relatively small number of Chinese schools that exist in the Philippines have Hokkien as their language of instruction, rather than Mandarin. Also, wealthier Filipino Chinese travel to and holiday in Taiwan. This has been important in maintaining links with China and with Hokkien speakers.

The low rates of growth in the Philippines since 1980 limited the expansion of the interests of major ethnic Chinese entrepreneurs. Not surprisingly, but to the concern of the Philippines' Government, many larger entrepreneurs have invested heavily in Taiwan, Fujian and Hong Kong.[33]

Singapore

The Singapore Government strongly encourages Singaporean companies to invest in China and other fast-growing East Asian economies. Singapore's investment in China has been rapid and has focused on those areas in which business and living conditions are relatively developed and comfortable. (See Chapter 11 for more detail.)

In January 1994, President Ong Teng Cheong in his maiden speech to Parliament outlined the Government's strategies for the 'next stage of nation building'; these emphasised 'regionalisation'. Senior Minister Lee Kuan Yew later told Parliament that Singaporeans should aim to become like the Swiss and benefit from a range of high yielding assets held overseas. Prime Minister Goh added that Singaporeans should concentrate on investing in China, Vietnam and India, with Myanmar, Pakistan and Cambodia being other possibilities.

This push began in earnest in 1992. The Government's regionalisation strategy encourages local companies to take advantage of their ethnic links with China. Singapore's Economic Development Board has been instrumental in the strategy, assisting Singapore companies, particularly by looking after the government-to-government aspects of investment. The EDB is an example of how traditional Chinese business structures have been replaced by more formal, government-sponsored structures, a process described in Chapter 3.

---

33 Mackie, J.A.C., 'The Ethnic Chinese Economy in Southeast Asia', paper presented to the International Conference on Southeast Asian Chinese Culture, Economy and Society, Singapore, 21-23 January 1994.

Singapore's Economic Development Board

The Government's main mechanism to encourage the development of Singapore's 'external wing' is the Economic Development Board (EDB). The EDB was created in 1961 and its primary role was to attract foreign capital to Singapore. This role now has shifted significantly to promoting Singaporean investment abroad. To this end, it now has sixteen offices around the world.

The EDB does not advise Singaporean companies where to invest but assists in negotiating with foreign governments and government authorities. If Singaporean companies intend investing in China, for example, the EDB can assist with negotiations with the relevant provincial government or with the government in Beijing, but dealings with local governments are left to the companies themselves. Advice on where to invest is left to private consultants. The EDB will only provide assistance of this nature if it is convinced that positive benefits will flow to other Singaporean firms.

Another important role of the EDB is to act as a catalyst for consortia. Singapore-based companies are able to approach the EDB for assistance in locating suitable partners for projects. The EDB then attempts to locate such partners, either from within Singapore or from overseas. Occasionally, the EDB identifies opportunities and then alerts suitable companies to exploit them, but this is very much a secondary function.

The EDB does not charge for its services. It believes charges might lead to a loss of independence and encourage it to attempt to maximise revenue rather to than pursue those tasks which would lead to the greatest benefit for Singaporean companies.

Taiwan

The largest single investor in Taiwan in recent years has been Japan. Between 1989 and 1993, Japan invested US$2 741 million. The next largest investor was the United States with US$2 029.8 million, followed by Hong Kong with US$995.1 million.[34]

Taiwanese firms started to make substantial direct investment in South-East Asia in 1987. One of the most distinctive features of that investment has been its concentration on small- and medium-sized enterprises.[35] Total investments in

34 See Department of Foreign Affairs and Trade, *Country Economic Briefs*.

35 See Chen, T.J., 'FDI by small- and medium-sized enterprises from Taiwan', *CIER Newsletter*, November 1994.

South-East Asia and Indochina are now at least US$21.5 billion. Taiwanese investments in the top five destinations in South-east Asia and Indochina are:[36]

- Malaysia: US$7 billion (electronics, keyboards, polyester, textiles, steel, machinery)
- Thailand: US$6 billion (electronics, food processing, textiles, as small- and medium-sized businesses are most favoured)
- Indonesia: US$6 billion (pulp and paper, machinery, textiles)
- Vietnam: US$1.9 billion (textiles, agriculture/fisheries, cement, motor cycle assembly, electronics, shoes, MSG production)
- Philippines: US$600 million.

The Taiwan Government's concern at the size of Taiwan's investment in China has led to a 'Go South' policy whereby firms are encouraged to invest in South-East Asia rather than China. State-owned and KMT-owned enterprises have led the way by investing heavily in Indonesia and Vietnam.[37] This should lead to greater southwards investment by the private sector, as Taiwanese small- and medium-sized firms prefer to invest overseas where other Taiwanese firms have already invested. This enables them to use the experience and know how of the existing firms. To date, government exhortations have not involved taxation incentives. However, barriers to external investment in ASEAN and Vietnam are fewer, and the Philippines' Subic Bay redevelopment is supported. The government also encourages Taiwanese banks to set up branches in South-East Asia to promote loans to Taiwan companies intending to operate there.

Taiwan is the single largest source of foreign investment for Vietnam. Vietnam's low labour costs attract labour intensive industries, such as textiles and clothing manufacture. Malaysia's Penang State, with its excellent infrastructure, is one of the favoured destinations for Taiwanese investment in hi-tech industries. Hokkien is the main language spoken in both Penang and Taiwan and this facilitates the investment flow. Taiwan's medium-sized firms are big investors in Indonesia. Already, approximately 600 Taiwanese firms are in the Philippines. They are involved principally in manufacturing but are beginning to diversify into the tourism sector. Taiwan's Government recently provided a US$23.4 million soft loan to the Philippines for the Subic Bay development. Stage 1 of the development was completed in April 1995. So far, 140 Taiwanese companies have registered to set up factories in Subic Bay and around 40 have paid deposits and have agreed to put up their factories within a year. Commitments from these 40 companies range from US$500 000 to US$5 million and cover footwear, textiles and electronics.[38]

Taiwan has been a significant direct investor in Indonesia, particularly in the pulp and paper, non-metal mineral products, and textiles sectors. Generally,

---

36 Personal communication with the Taiwan Ministry of Economic Affairs.

37 This is analogous to the way in which Singapore state-linked companies have led the way for investment in China and Indochina.

38 Personal communication with the Philippines' Special Trade Representative in Taiwan, Manuel Tayas.

Taiwan's large firms have not been particularly active in Indonesia; they tend to be squeezed out by the big Sino-Indonesian controlled conglomerates which dominate Indonesia's economy. Those larger firms which are involved tend to devote their resources to improving production efficiency, particularly by bringing in expatriate production technicians from Taiwan and sending Indonesian workers to Taiwan for training. The larger firms tend to produce primarily for the Indonesian market. Taiwan's small- and medium-sized firms have been active investors, however. These are export oriented and attracted by the availability of low-cost labour. According to one survey,

> *FDI by small Taiwanese firms is often initiated by local ethnic Chinese Indonesians or local raw material suppliers; FDI by large Taiwanese firms is carried out in cooperation with local ethnic Chinese Indonesians or local sales agents.*[39]

A survey of 33 Taiwanese firms investing in Thailand found that in each case, the initial idea for investment originated either in the parent companies (not surprisingly) or from ethnic Chinese entrepreneurs in Thailand. The larger firms investing in Thailand preferred local partners to provide an additional source of capital; whereas, the smaller firms preferred local partners as a useful source for making connections and identifying market opportunities.[40]

Thailand

Between 1989 and 1993, after Japan, Hong Kong was the second largest foreign investor into Thailand, investing a cumulative US$1 691.7 million. Singapore was the fourth highest, investing US$1 092 million, and Taiwan was the eighth highest with US$72.8 million.[41]

The Teochiu dominate Thailand's business sector and a significant proportion of the investment coming from Hong Kong, Singapore and Taiwan probably comes from their Teochiu business communities assisted by Teochiu based in Thailand.

Although the Sino-Thais have become highly assimilated into Thai society they have retained contact with Chinese language and culture to ensure that they are not cut-off from ethnic Chinese elsewhere in Asia nor from the Chinese in China.

Up to the beginning of the 1950s, the Chinese business community in Thailand continued to send their young sons and daughters abroad to China and particularly Shantou (Swatow), Hong Kong, and Singapore, where they could learn Mandarin and English. Those generations strengthened the regional network of personal relationships first built by their parents.[42] This practice has

39 See Ku, Y.H., 'Taiwan's FDI in Indonesia', *CIER Newsletter*, November 1994.

40 See Chen, H.M. and D.N. Liu, 'Taiwan's FDI in Thailand', *CIER Newsletter*, November 1994.

41 See Department of Foreign Affairs and Trade, *Country Economic Brief.*

42 See Suehiro, A., 'Family business reassessed: Corporate structure and late-starting industrialization in Thailand', *The Developing Economies*, December 1994, p. 404.

allowed them to remain well-connected to ethnic Chinese networks across Asia and to become significant investors in China.[43]

Although most of the ethnic Chinese in Laos and Cambodia are also Teochiu, there appears to be little evidence of any family, business or other connections between them and the Teochius of Bangkok. The Teochiu network-based investment in Laos, Cambodia and Vietnam probably originates from the Teochiu in northern Thailand.

The Yunnanese Chinese in northern Thailand have close links with the Yunnanese in Myanmar and Yunnan. In the past, much of the border trade between Myanmar and Thailand was conducted via Yunnanese networks, particularly trade in Thai-manufactured consumer goods. It is commonly believed in Thailand that the illegal trade in gemstones and opium and its derivatives between Thailand, Myanmar and Yunnan occurs through Yunnanese networks.

Vietnam

The largest foreign investor in Vietnam is Taiwan, having invested US$1 854 million to date. Second highest is Hong Kong with US$1 623 million, and fifth highest is Singapore with US$620 million. Total approved foreign investment in Vietnam is US$9 420 million to date.[44] Thus, the three ethnic Chinese-dominated economies account for 43.5 per cent of total investment to date. Malaysia, which has a sizeable ethnic Chinese population, is the sixth largest foreign investor with US$578 million.

According to a survey by Vietnam's State Committee for Cooperation and Investment, Vietnam approved some US$7 billion for 793 direct investment projects between 1988, when a liberalised foreign investment law was adopted, and November 1993. Taiwanese companies accounted for US$1.5 billion or 21 per cent of the total direct investment and were involved in 110 projects. ASEAN-based companies invested, or planned to invest, in 136 projects worth a total of US$816 million. Singapore firms were involved in 50 investment projects in Vietnam, of which 11 were related to the hotel or tourism trades.[45]

Singapore is likely to improve its position as a foreign investor given a series of recent government-to-government measures designed to facilitate investment. In 1992, both signed a guarantee to provide safeguards to Singapore investments against nationalisation by the Vietnamese Government. The two countries also granted each other Most Favoured Nation Status, and a Singapore-Vietnam Business Council, with an office in Hanoi, was established.[46] Furthermore, during Singapore Prime Minister Goh Chok Tong's 1994 visit to Vietnam, a double taxation agreement between the two countries was signed.[47]

....

43 It is difficult to establish how much investment in mainland China has originated from Thailand, as the Thai Government does not keep reliable figures on levels of investment in mainland China.

44 See Department of Foreign Affairs and Trade, *Country Economic Brief.*

45 See *Nikkei Weekly*, 'NIEs target India, Myanmar, Vietnam', 21 February 1994.

46 See Carnegie, G. and D. Sharpe, *Singapore*, Asia Australia Briefing Paper, Vol. 2, No. 10, 1993, The Asia-Australia Institute, University of New South Wales, 1993.

47 See *Far Eastern Economic Review*, 'Business Briefing', 17 March 1994.

The links of the ethnic Chinese in Vietnam with other ethnic Chinese now come from two sources: family, dialect and other ties that are long standing and which predate the mass exodus in 1978-79; and ties with the overseas Vietnamese who have left Vietnam since 1975, many of whom are ethnic Chinese.

Thus before 1975, Vietnam's ethnic Chinese community had trade and business ties with the ethnic Chinese in Taiwan, Hong Kong, Singapore, Thailand, and Cambodia. The 1978-79 exodus expanded these contacts to include groups in North America, Australia and Europe.[48]

The Vietnamese Chinese Diaspora

The Vietnamese diaspora (both ethnic Vietnamese and Chinese) will become a significant economic force in future as it begins to develop and trade on its worldwide networks. To underline these links, one survey found that at the end of 1987, the ethnic Chinese of Ho Chi Minh City had relatives in at least twenty other countries.[49]

Paradoxically, this diaspora is now being called upon by the Vietnamese Government to participate in Vietnam's economic development. One of the major sources for renovating the private sector has been capital supplied from overseas Vietnamese. Also, there is other foreign ethnic Chinese investment in Vietnam. The first foreign private company to go into Vietnam in a joint venture with a local company was owned by Sino-Indonesian interests, and of the 140 foreign representative offices in Ho Chi Minh City at the end of 1989, more than 100 were from ethnic Chinese-owned or ethnic Chinese-related enterprises.[50]

THE INTERNET - A NEW WAY TO NETWORK

Ethnic Chinese networking is being strengthened rather than diminished by technological advances. Improvements in transport infrastructure such as improved air links are drawing communities together. The Internet is also beginning to be used as a networking device.

Like other groups of individuals sharing mutual interests, the members of dialect and other ethnic Chinese groups are using the Internet to communicate across the world with each other. An example of a recently formed Internet discussion group is the 'Hakka Global Network', which currently has a membership of 70. It has a 'Hakka Chinese Homepage' in which Hakka Chinese and other interested users can discuss various aspects of Hakka culture. Among the items discussed are the history of the migration of the Hakka people, their distribution around the world and notable Hakka politicians and business people.

48 See Tran Khanh, *The Ethnic Chinese and Economic Development in Vietnam*, Institute of Southeast Asian Studies, Singapore, 1993, p. 97.

49 See Tran Khanh, p. 97.

50 See Tran Khanh, p. 98.

Chapter 10

THE ROLE OF FOREIGN-CHINESE IN THE TRANSFORMATION OF CHINA

... China is complex and what you might call the 'turbulence' of business life there makes it very different from business in the West ... In many ways though, it's a mistake to see China as one country in a business sense. It's really a collection of quite autonomous markets, each very different ... Also, doing business in China is more about relationships than the style of business here, which is based more on logic and the law.[1]

OVERVIEW OF FOREIGN INVESTMENT IN CHINA

Foreign investment in China is booming. The largest source for investment is the Chinese diaspora. In 1994 alone, China attracted US$33.8 billion in new foreign investment.[2] According to official figures, Hong Kong and Macau accounted for around 70 per cent of this, and Taiwan another 8 per cent. By comparison, investment from the United States for the period accounted for 7 per cent of the total, and from Japan, just 4 per cent.[3] Much of the foreign investment in China comes from ethnic Chinese sources.

As elsewhere in the region, foreign-Chinese investors in China have a range of mechanisms at their disposal to help facilitate their investments and to maximise their profits.[4] At times, one of these may be their Chineseness: their culture, language and ancestral links. In south-eastern China, such factors may open doors, because most foreign-Chinese have their ancestral origins there. However, as the focus of foreign-Chinese investment shifts further north, to Shanghai, Jiangsu, Shandong, Tianjin and Beijing, clan, dialect and other historical links are less useful to them. Consequently, it is likely that foreign-Chinese investment as a proportion of total foreign investment declines as the investment moves further away the from the South-East.

To date, foreign-Chinese have been important as foreign investors in China for several reasons. The proximity to China of the ethnic Chinese dominated and capital-surplus economies of Hong Kong and Taiwan, and the linguistic abilities, cultural empathy, and in some areas, particularly in the South-East, family and clan links, all contributed to the early prominence of foreign-Chinese investors in China.

1 From an address to Lion Nathan Ltd's 1994 Annual General Meeting by CEO Douglas Myers.

2 See Department of Foreign Affairs and Trade, *Country Economic Brief: China*, May 1995.

3 Both these figures need to be regarded with caution. Hong Kong is undoubtedly a big investor, although some investment attributed to it is channelled via Hong Kong from elsewhere, including Taiwan. Establishing how much investment follows this route is not possible.

The Role of Connections in China

China's markets are developing; the institutional rules of the game are still embryonic and not always enforced; and the distribution of information about business opportunities is asymmetrical. Connections are important for doing business anywhere, but in a business environment such as China's, they are especially important.

Those who are best at forming connections, or those who already have them, are at an advantage. Family, language and cultural ties, mean that many foreign-Chinese are well placed to access business opportunities in China.

However, as China's administrative, legal and institutional infrastructure develop and the 'rules of the game' become apparent to all, the advantage foreign-Chinese entrepreneurs have probably will lessen.[5] As Singapore's Senior Minister Lee Kuan Yew noted at the Second World Chinese Entrepreneurs Convention, Westerners operating within China's weak legal framework feel vulnerable but foreign-Chinese, provided they have the right connections, can protect themselves. '*Guanxi* capability will be of value for the next twenty years at least, until China develops a system based on the rule of law, with sufficient transparency and certainty to satisfy foreign investors', said Lee.[6]

Foreign-Chinese investors do not always have family- or clan-oriented links; most foreign-Chinese investment in China does not occur along clan or family lines, nor is it targeted at investors' ancestral areas of origin. Instead, many prominent foreign-Chinese entrepreneurs, particularly from Hong Kong, have good connections with senior officials in larger cities (Shanghai, Tianjin and Beijing). These are particularly important for larger investment projects, which involve infrastructure and real estate development.

The quality of local infrastructure is the most important factor governing the distribution of investment in China. For this reason, Guangdong and comparatively recently, Shanghai and its surrounding districts, are favoured.

FOREIGN INVESTMENT IN CHINA SINCE 1979

As China opens to foreign investment, the ethnic Chinese are developing as an international force in commerce. Economic reform has provided foreign-Chinese with profitable outlets for surplus capital, a means of industrial restructuring and a basis for further industrial growth. Their investment has been a vital factor in

---

4 To avoid confusion in terminology, the term 'foreign Chinese' is used in this chapter to refer to ethnic Chinese from South-East Asia, Hong Kong, Taiwan and other ethnic Chinese not residing in the PRC.

5 It follows that not all ethnic Chinese investment into China is directly productive. Much of it will prove profitable but only because it is associated with trade quotas and licences, restricted allocation of land use rights, the granting of residency rights (with, for example, the associated privileged access to private housing markets for speculative purposes), and the allocation of bank credit. (See The World Bank, *China: Foreign Trade Reform*, Washington DC, 1994, p. 244.)

6 From the text of the address given by Lee Kuan Yew to the Second World Chinese Entrepreneurs Convention, held in Hong Kong in November 1993, and reproduced in: The Chinese General Chamber of Commerce of Hong Kong, *The 2nd World Chinese Entrepreneurs Convention: Commemorative Album*, 1994, p. 85.

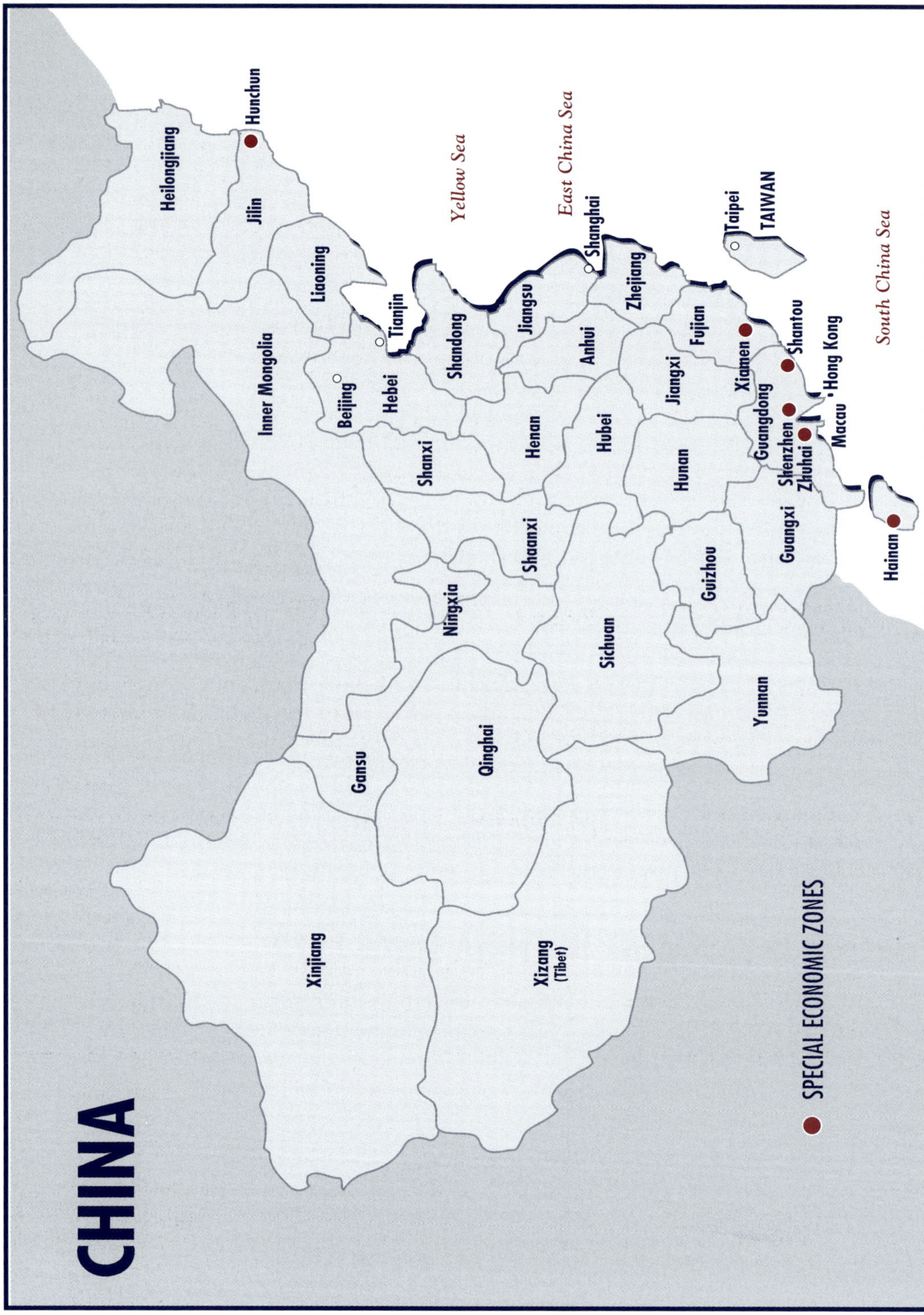
CHINA
Heilongjiang
Hunchun
Jilin
Liaoning
Inner Mongolia
Beijing
Tianjin
Hebei
Shanxi
Shandong
Yellow Sea
Jiangsu
Shanghai
East China Sea
Zhejiang
Anhui
Henan
Hubei
Shaanxi
Ningxia
Gansu
Qinghai
Sichuan
Xinjiang
Xizang
(Tibet)
Fujian
Jiangxi
Hunan
Guizhou
Yunnan
Guangxi
Guangdong
Xiamen
Shantou
Shenzhen
Zhuhai
Macau
Hong Kong
Hainan
Taipei
TAIWAN
South China Sea
SPECIAL ECONOMIC ZONES

Figure 10.1

revitalising south-eastern China, turning it into a dynamic, export-oriented economy. Foreign Chinese also play an important role in distributing goods produced in China on world markets, particularly through Hong Kong marketing channels.

While foreign-Chinese investors have some advantages investing in China, they too can face difficulties.[7] Some entrepreneurs withdrew abruptly from large projects when faced with bureaucratic obstacles, or when Chinese authorities sought to impose tighter restrictions and controls, particularly on ownership and rates of return.[8]

The results of foreign investment in China since 1985 have been stunning. By 1994, the amount of cumulative realised foreign capital surpassed US$100 billion.[9] This was spread across more than 167 500 foreign invested enterprises (FIEs), including wholly-owned companies, joint ventures and cooperative enterprises. With the contributions of local partners and re-invested profits, the total capitalisation of the FIEs was US$245.6 billion, 62.8 per cent (US$150.2 billion) of which was attributed to foreign investors. The acceleration of foreign investment in China is underscored by the fact that two-thirds of it (US$38 billion) had been invested in the preceding two years.[10]

With rising land and labour costs in the South-East, particularly in Guangdong, foreign investors increasingly seek opportunities further afield, particularly along China's east coast (Jiangsu, Zhejiang, Shanghai and Shandong) and in the north-eastern provinces (Liaoning, Tianjin and Beijing). South-eastern China's rapid economic growth has created the need for substantial upgrading of infrastructure to overcome bottlenecks in the electricity supply system and transport and port facilities.

FOREIGN-CHINESE INVESTMENT IN CHINA

Much of the foreign investment in China is attributed to foreign-Chinese. They have 'out-invested' the United States, Japan and the European Union combined, by a factor of more than five to one, contributing well over 80 per cent of both the number of projects and investment since 1979. Between 1985 and 1993, foreign-Chinese investment grew from less than 50 per cent of the total to more than 80 per cent.[11]

7 There have been some instances of foreign-Chinese business people being detained by the authorities in China, with officials apparently claiming jurisdiction over the business people on the basis of their ethnicity rather than their citizenship.

8 Robert Kuok, for example, withdrew from a plan to redevelop a shopping centre in Beijing because of a dispute with the local partner, and Gordon Wu has abandoned plans for two additional power projects in China because of a dispute over rates of return. (See Waldron, S., 'Indonesian Chinese Investment in Indonesia: Magnitude, Motivations and Meaning', *Australia-Asia Papers No. 73*, Centre of the Study of Australia Asia Relations, Griffith University, March 1995.)

9 See Department of Foreign Affairs and Trade, *Country Economic Brief: China*, May 1995.

10 See MOFTEC, *International Trade News*, Beijing, 1994, p. 1.

11 Chan, M. and Zhu, W., 'The Hong Kong-Taiwan-South Korea factor in China's exports and its impact', China Business Centre, Hong Kong Polytechnic, *Working Paper No. 33*, 1994.

Table 10.1

Sources of Foreign Capital in China

(Cumulative 1979-93)

SOURCE COUNTRY	NUMBER OF ENTERPRISES	PER CENT	FOREIGN INVESTMENT (US$ billions)	PER CENT
Hong Kong	106 769	63.7	47.5	69.1
Taiwan	20 612	12.3	6.4	9.3
Macau	4 188	2.5	1.9	2.8
Singapore	3 037	1.8	1.5	2.2
Thailand	1 361	0.8	0.8	1.2
Sub-Total	136 042	81.2	58.1	84.6
United States	11 554	6.9	3.7	5.4
Japan	7 096	4.2	3.3	4.8
Other	14 314	8.6	4.4	6.4
Total	167 500	100.0	68.7	100.0

Source: State Commercial Bureau, *FDI in China: Analyses of Trends & Future Directions, 1993*; MOFTEC, *International Trade News*, 16 May 1994.

Table 10.1 shows the recorded origins of foreign investment in China.[12] Taiwanese investment in China is, however, substantially under-reported in official data. Investment from this source is likely to be at least 20 per cent of the total rather than the 9.3 per cent of official figures.[13]

Among the two largest foreign-Chinese investors, in terms of capital invested and the number of companies they control there, are two from South-East Asia. One is the Sino-Thai agribusiness group, Charoen Pokphand (detailed in Appendix 7), which has more than seventy operational investments in China, including its core agribusiness activities and Shanghai real estate development. The other is the Sino-Indonesian Oei family, which controls Indonesia's Sinar Mas Group. It manages and controls more than eighty companies in China, particularly in Fujian, Zhejiang, and Shanxi.[14] In both these cases, investments in

12 The data, however, need to be interpreted with caution. Some of the investment has originated in China, but reinvested through Hong Kong and back into China in order to take advantage of tax and other privileges accorded to 'foreign' investment. Hong Kong is also likely to be over-represented as a source of investment. Many Taiwanese companies route their investment in China through Hong Kong on account of past Taiwan Government restrictions and to disguise the destination of their investment. Many South-East Asian Chinese entrepreneurs also invest in China through Hong Kong. Some of the larger regional conglomerates from Singapore, Malaysia, Indonesia and Thailand have established a second headquarters there. These branch offices serve several purposes. They allow companies to tap the Hong Kong capital market more easily for expansion funds. In this respect a number of prominent South-East Asian conglomerates have already floated their regional interests on the Hong Kong Stock Exchange. Raising money in this way protects them from accusations of 'capital flight' in their home countries. Listing in Hong Kong also allows these groups to diversify the political and country risk they face. Finally, as Hong Kong is the most important gateway to China, in terms of access and expertise, it is the obvious base from which to launch investments in China.

13 Personal communication with the Chung Hua Institute of Economic Research, Taipei.

14 These investments are detailed in a case study on China Strategic Holdings in Chapter 11.

China were made through publicly-listed companies in Hong Kong. Other South-East Asian Chinese-controlled groups investing in China through Hong Kong vehicles are the Sino-Indonesian Salim and Riady families and the Dharmala Group; the Malaysian Kuok, Hong Leong and Berjaya groups; the Sino-Thai Bangkok Land Group; and the Singaporean Far East Group.[15]

Tables 10.2(a) and (b) show the distribution of foreign investment in China. Table 10.3 shows the distribution by region. While the South-East has received the bulk of foreign investment to date, the Yangtze Delta and the Bohai Gulf region, particularly Shandong Province and Tianjin recently have attracted substantial investment.

In major industrial centres like Shanghai, Western multinationals enjoy some advantage in joining with large state industries, although Chinese from Hong Kong and Taiwan remain the largest investors.[16]

The Overseas Hainanese and Investment in Hainan Province

Another new focus for foreign-Chinese interest in China is Hainan, an island of around seven million people off the coast of Guangdong. More than two million Chinese living in over fifty countries outside China are of Hainanese origin. There are also approximately one million overseas Hainanese and their dependents who have returned to Hainan.[17] The declaration of Hainan as a separate province and Special Economic Zone in 1988 has re-energised overseas Hainanese communities around the world. Various Hainanese associations in Malaysia have formed clan holding companies to invest in Hainan using dialect and family links.

Hainan is now China's largest SEZ - 65 times the size of the other four SEZs put together in terms of land size, and four times their size in terms of population. The regulatory rules in Hainan are also more generous than those in the other SEZs.

The provincial government intends to turn Hainan into an international resort destination. Generous tax and other incentives are provided, including several casino licences for joint ventures. In the past, infrastructure was poor and there were few international-standard hotels. Now, many large projects are underway or completed. By 1992, the provincial government approved 89 foreign and domestic tourism related projects worth a total of US$1.5 billion.[18] Many of these were, or will be, undertaken by overseas Hainanese investors.

---

15 Many of these have invested in property development. Shanghai, for example, has 165 million square feet of property under construction, which is likely to lead to a severe glut of commercial and residential property. (See *Far Eastern Economic Review*, 'Where to put your money: How the experts see it', 20 April 1995.)

16 Summary of World Broadcasts, Far East Weekly Series, BBC, London, 26 October 1994.

17 See Feng, C. and D. Goodman, 'China's Hainan Province: Economic development and investment environment', Unpublished paper, University of Technology, Sydney, 1994.

18 See *Far Eastern Economic Review*, 'Life is a beach?', 5 August 1993.

Table 10.2(a)

Foreign Investment in China

Number of operating enterprises and capital invested in the top ten recipient provinces, end of 1993[19]

PROVINCE	NUMBER OF ENTERPRISES	PER CENT	FOREIGN CAPITAL INVESTED (US$ billions)	PER CENT
Guangdong	44 705	26.7	58.6	39.0
Fujian	11 990	7.2	11.2	7.5
Jiangsu	18 082	10.8	10.0	6.7
Shanghai	8 056	4.8	9.3	6.2
Shandong	12 561	7.5	8.0	5.3
Hainan	7 390	4.4	7.8	5.2
Liaoning	7 365	4.3	5.4	3.6
Beijing	6 516	3.9	5.2	3.5
Zhejiang	8 085	4.8	4.4	2.9
Guangxi	4 368	2.6	4.0	2.7
Ten Largest Recipients	129 118	77.1	123.9	82.6
Total for China	167 507	100.0	150.2	100.0

Source: State Commercial Bureau, *FDI in China: Analyses of Trends and Future Directions*, 1993; MOFTEC, International Trade News, 16 May 1994; State Statistical Bureau, *China Statistical Yearbook 1994*, Beijing, 1995, p. 531.

Table 10.2(b)

Foreign Investment by Sector, 1979-92

SECTOR	NUMBER OF ENTERPRISES	PER CENT	FOREIGN INVESTMENT (US$ billions)	PER CENT
Manufacturing	68 638	81.4	44.9	65.4
Public Utilities, Infrastructure and Real Estate	6 908	8.2	16.5	24.0
Restaurants, and Retail Trade	2 436	2.9	1.8	2.7
Agriculture	2 168	2.6	1.4	2.0
Construction	1 571	1.9	1.4	1.5
Telecoms	1 182	1.4	1.2	1.8
Other	1 468	1.7	1.9	2.7
Total	84 371	100.0	68.7	100.0

Source: State Commercial Bureau, *FDI in China, Analyses of Trends and Future Directions*, 1993.

....

19 Foreign capital investment includes direct foreign investment plus accumulated profits.

Table 10.3

Destination of Foreign Direct Investment in China by Region (1993)[20]

	NUMBER OF ENTERPRISES	PER CENT	FOREIGN CAPITAL (US$ billions)	PER CENT
South-East				
Guangdong	44 705	26.7	58.6	39.0
Fujian	11 990	7.2	11.2	7.5
Hainan	7 390	4.4	7.8	5.2
Guangxi	4 368	2.6	4.0	2.7
Total South-East	64 453	40.9	81.8	54.5
Yangtze Delta				
Jiangsu	18 082	10.8	10.0	6.7
Shanghai	8 056	4.8	9.3	6.2
Zhejiang	8 085	4.8	4.4	2.9
Total Yangtze Delta	34 223	20.4	23.7	15.8
Bohai Gulf				
Shandong	12 561	7.5	8.0	5.3
Liaoning	7 365	4.3	5.2	3.5
Beijing	6 516	3.9	5.4	3.6
Tianjin	6 004	3.6	3.0	2.0
Hebei	3 798	2.3	3.1	2.0
Total Bohai Gulf	36 244	21.6	24.5	16.3
Three Coastal Regions	138 920	82.9	130.0	86.6
Total for China	167 507	100.0	150.2	100.0

Source: State Commercial Bureau 1993; MOFTEC, *International Trade News*, 16 May 1994; State Statistical Bureau, *China Statistical Yearbook 1994*, Beijing, 1995, p. 531.

20 While final data for all provinces at the end of 1993 is not yet available, the figures for Guangdong, Fujian and Jiangsu are US$58.6 billion, US$16.2 billion and US$7.3 billion. (See Guangdong Province, *Statistical Yearbook*, 1994; Fujian Province, *Statistical Yearbook*, 1994; *Jiangsu Tongjinianjian* 1994.)

The Northwards Shift of Foreign-Chinese Investment - The Case of Jiangsu Province

Only of late has Jiangsu Province attracted significant foreign investment. There were around 2 000 FIEs at the end of 1992 but more than 24 000 by the end of 1994.[21] Reflecting their more recent development, most of the FIEs are much smaller than those in the South-East. Those in the South-East typically employ around 150 workers but those in Jiangsu, average around 100 workers. More than half the foreign investment in the province is invested in the Suzhou region. Over 70 per cent of Suzhou's share has been invested in the city's rural counties, Kunshan, Wuxian and Zhangjiagang. The bulk of the rest of the foreign-invested sector is concentrated along the Suzhou-Nanjing railway line, although Nanjing itself has received just ten per cent of the province's foreign investment. Jiangsu's share of foreign investment therefore is concentrated in the southern part of the province, south of the Yangtze River.[22]

Hong Kong, Macau and Taiwanese sources have contributed well over 70 per cent of realised investments in Jiangsu to date, although US, Japanese and European sources represent a larger proportion in terms of agreements approved.[23] It remains to be seen how many of these approvals will eventuate. The relative skill of foreign-Chinese investors to turn approvals into realised investments partly accounts for their predominance.

With relatively cheap land and labour, Jiangsu is an attractive destination for foreign-Chinese investors seeking a production base in the Yangtze Delta region.[24] It has a significant collective sector, essentially town and village enterprises, and a relatively small and decentralised state sector.[25] It is close to Shanghai and is historically relatively wealthy.

Foreign-Chinese investment in Jiangsu has re-oriented the province's production towards exports. Despite its position as a leading industrial province, production in the past was essentially oriented to the domestic market. Jiangsu contributed as little as five per cent share of China's exports. In the last two years, this has changed dramatically. By the end of 1994, Jiangsu had emerged as China's third largest exporting province, behind Guangdong and Shanghai, having overtaken Fujian.[26] Much of this is due to the foreign sector. The share of FIEs in export volumes grew from 3-6 per cent in 1992, to 13 per cent in 1993, and to 40 per cent in 1994.[27]

....

21 Commission of Foreign Economic Relations and Trade, Jiangsu Province.

22 Commission of Foreign Economic Relations and Trade, Jiangsu Province; *Jiangsu Tongjinianjian* 1994, p. 225; pp. 321-23.

23 Commission of Foreign Economic Relations and Trade, Jiangsu Province.

24 An example of the advantages of dealing with a decentralised administration is provided by Suzhou. The city has established a 'one chop' bureau for foreign investment applications headed by the mayor. This is in contrast to Shanghai where applications have been known to require as many as 60 separate 'chops'. (See *South China Morning Post*, 2 February 1995.)

25 Most of the state sector is under the control of city governments rather than the central or provincial government. In 1993, the collective sector contributed 58 per cent of the Province's industrial output compared with the state sector's 34 per cent. (See *A Statistical Survey of China*, 1994, p. 75.)

26 See *South China Morning Post*, 16 January 1995, p. B3.

27 Commission of Foreign Economic Relations and Trade, Jiangsu Province.

WHY HAVE THE ETHNIC CHINESE DOMINATED FOREIGN INVESTMENT IN CHINA?

As mentioned, the dominance of ethnic Chinese in foreign investment in China can in part be attributed to their historical and cultural links and linguistic advantages. The problems that non-Chinese investors face include language barriers, the incompatibility of Western and Japanese management styles with Chinese practices, the distinctive bureaucratic organisation of the Chinese workplace, difficulties in China associated with firing workers and eliminating inefficient work practices, poor quality control, low labour productivity, differences in negotiating practices, the long time-frames needed to negotiate contracts, and particularly, difficulties associated with the lack of a fully established legal framework.

Foreign-Chinese investors in China are not immune to labour management and quality control problems. Some Taiwanese investors operating in China have faced significant labour management problems. However, foreign-Chinese are more culturally and linguistically empathetic than most other foreign investors, and it is likely that such problems do not occur as frequently as for other foreign investors.

The difficulties that some Japanese and South Korean companies have faced in China focused on problems with management style, hiring and firing Chinese workers and quality control. Japanese companies also faced a wave of strikes in Guangdong Province in 1993.[28] Similarly, US corporations have faced difficulties. US executives reportedly needed personal bodyguards in Shenyang in Liaoning Province after a dispute at the General Motors joint-venture, Jinbei Automotive, following staff cuts and the removal of a well-connected local official from the company's board of directors. Microsoft still faces a possible ban on its products, a result of a dispute over technical standards for its Chinese character software, which was developed in co-operation with a Taiwanese company. Also, Goldman Sachs saw its agreement to participate in a large power project in Shandong, which took 18 months to negotiate and involved an investment of US$180 million, vetoed by Beijing.[29]

To the extent that foreign-Chinese investors have been able to minimise, though not altogether avoid, these difficulties, they have done so by concentrating their investment away from older, more-established industrial areas. Most of their investments are in smaller cities, townships and villages where it is possible to deal with a much lower level of government. They make small initial investments, within the level of decision making of local officials. The result is that some of the regulatory intervention and central and provincial government scrutiny that larger investments attract is avoided. As foreign-Chinese investors move into the

---

28 See Japan External Trade Office, *JETRO China Newsletter*, 1993 (103), pp. 13-21, 104:2-8; *Far Eastern Economic Review*, 9 September 1993, p. 46-49; Economist Intelligence Unit, *Business China*, 3 May 1993, pp. 1-2. Some of the problems Japanese companies have experienced in China may be in part due to residual animosity in China against the Japanese arising from Japanese occupation of some parts of China earlier this century.

29 See *Far Eastern Economic Review*, 24 February 1994, p. 14; 14 April 1994, p. 69, 75.

more established industrial areas, and partner large state-owned enterprises, they too will face problems.

New foreign investments projects that are within the ambit of local government can go as high as US$10 million, although for a long time, the general limit was US$1 million. Evidence from surveys of foreign-invested firms in Guangdong, Fujian and Jiangsu (for all the results of the surveys see the annex to this chapter) suggest that foreign-Chinese investors prefer to initially make a small investment and then expand their commitment, as there are fewer barriers to the expansion of an existing investment than to a large initial investment. A variety of other methods of remaining under the purview of local government also have evolved, such as dividing larger investments into a number of smaller projects, which can be consolidated into a single enterprise later. The efforts of foreign-Chinese investors to keep their initial investments relatively small has meant that many such investments have grown rapidly, including some growing to employ as many as 10 000 workers within a few years.

Large numbers of small to medium-sized labour intensive industries generate much needed employment for a generally underemployed rural workforce. These improve local government finances without the dependent relationship that can result from a few or one large-scale investment. Subsequently, many towns and villages appear to avoid involvement with multinational companies, even when they have the authority to approve larger projects.

Western and Japanese companies and those foreign-Chinese seeking big projects often make their initial contacts at ministry or provincial government level. There are cash shortages and other problems at every level of government in China, but often more so at these higher levels. Profitable alliances may result from ventures struck at this level, but foreign investors risk being steered towards particularly sick state enterprises.

Town and village governments have available greenfield industrial sites and are not as strapped for funds as their more senior counterparts. Thus they often can offer more attractive tax and land packages to small investors. The ability to deal directly with local governments is vital to foreign-Chinese investment success in China.

Networks are essential to foreign-Chinese success in China. They allow access to the right officials at the township or village level. Local officials also can introduce investors to officials in other townships. Benefits flow both ways through the networks. On the other side, established foreign-Chinese business people can introduce new potential investors to the township, and assist the governments of townships with investments and bank credit in Hong Kong and beyond.

THE ROLE OF FOREIGN-CHINESE IN CHINA'S INTERNATIONAL TRADE

While China as a whole experienced a trade deficit of US$12.2 billion, Guangdong and Fujian Provinces registered an international trade surplus of almost US$10 billion in 1993.[30] By 1994, however, China recorded a trade surplus of US$5.3 billion due largely to a 31.9 per cent surge in exports on the previous year.[31]

The contribution of foreign-invested enterprises in Guangdong and Fujian to the South-East's exports rose from 35 per cent in 1990 to 50 per cent by 1993. When the value of local processing industries and the compensation trade are included, the foreign sector's contribution to exports from Guangdong was 62 per cent by the end of 1993.[32]

China's capacity to import capital items such as plant and machinery depends substantially on the increasing volumes of exports from the South-East. Without this contribution, China's rapid economic growth and much of its economic reform program would be subject to more severe balance of payments constraints. Given that half the South-East's export volumes came from foreign-invested companies - and in the South-East, foreign investment is almost exclusively a foreign-Chinese domain - and that 85 per cent of the South-East's exports pass through Hong Kong marketing channels, foreign-Chinese entrepreneurs have played a critical role in China's international trade, and hence its development.

Hong Kong now handles 35 per cent of China's international trade: 43 per cent of exports and 25 per cent of imports. Hong Kong also provides the main channel through which Taiwanese trade and investment flows.

The transformation of the economies of China's south-eastern provinces and economic restructuring in Hong Kong occurred concurrently. Manufacturing has been relocated from Hong Kong to Guangdong, and Hong Kong's economy has become more services-oriented. The number of import-export houses in Hong Kong also has increased rapidly from around 14 000 in the early 1980s to more than 89 000 by 1992.[33] Correspondingly, China's state-controlled foreign-trade

....

30 These figures need to be interpreted with some caution, however, given the tendency for goods produced in the inner provinces for export to be transhipped through the coastal provinces.

31 See Department of Foreign Affairs and Trade, *Country Economic Brief: China*, May 1995.

32 See Guangdong Province, *Statistical Yearbook*, 1994, pp. 304-5. Processing industries are those domestic firms, whose business consists of processing raw materials for foreign-owned companies, overwhelmingly from Hong Kong, delivered to them and collected on completion. Hong Kong estimates suggest that there are about 55,000 such firms in Guangdong alone (See Overholt, W., *The Rise of China: How Economic Reform is Creating a new Superpower*, Norton, 1993, pp. 189-91). Processing industries are far more numerous than those involved in compensation trade (whereby firms pay for inputs by supplying a proportion of their output) as is the value of their production. Both together, however, involve the delivery of a substantial proportion of Guangdong's domestic export production to ethnic Chinese entrepreneurs in Hong Kong and Taiwan, who thereafter market them domestically and internationally. The extent of these kinds of operations in Fujian is harder to quantify as the production of statistical information by the provincial government is much less sophisticated, but they are likely to be quite extensive in Jinjiang county in southern Fujian, which covers the cities of Quanzhou, Jinjiang and Shishi.

33 Baldinger, P., 'The birth of Greater China', *The China Business Review*, May-June 1992; *South China Morning Post*, 2 July 1994, p. B4.

corporations which monopolised China's foreign trade until the reform era, have declined in importance, particularly in the South-East. In 1985, after six years of reform, including the establishment of three Special Economic Zones, foreign-trade corporations still controlled more than 85 per cent of Guangdong's foreign trade. By 1993, this had fallen to 35 per cent, despite the volume of trade increasing more than four-fold during the period.[34]

THE TRANSFORMATION OF THE SOUTH-EAST

The relative backwardness of the South-East prior to the economic reform era was not always so great. The self-sufficiency strategy of the Maoist period effectively closed China to foreign trade. The 'Stalinist' emphasis on the development of heavy industry meant that the South-East was not able to fully exploit its comparative advantage in light industry and sub-tropical agriculture. Also, Fujian was starved of productive investment as it was considered the front line for any possible confrontation with Taiwan. The result was that living standards in the South-East rose by barely half the recorded increase elsewhere during the period 1958-78.[35]

Economic reform did not reverse this stagnation until 1985. Despite the four SEZs at Shenzhen, Zhuhai, Shantou and Xiamen, little improvement occurred, apart from improvements in agricultural production resulting from the ending of the rural commune system and the deregulating of farm produce markets. The SEZs, far from acting as magnets for foreign capital seeking an export production platform, were kept going by domestic investment. They also registered an overall trade deficit.[36]

The big change for the South-East came in 1985, when the whole of the Pearl River Delta and the triangle delineated by Xiamen, Quanzhou and Zhangzhou in southern Fujian opened to foreign capital. Foreign-Chinese investors subsequently dominated investment flows into the region, contributing at least 85 per cent, approximately US$32 billion of total foreign direct investment of US$38.8 billion during the period, 1979-92.[37]

---

34 This may also be attributable to the fact that many more entities in China are now allowed to conduct their own international trade without having to go through the large state-controlled foreign trade corporations.

35 See Maruya, T., (ed.), *Guangdong: "Open Door" Economic Development Strategy*, Institute of Developing Economies, Tokyo, 1992, pp. 18-21.

36 Linge, G. and D. Forbes, *China's New Spatial Economy*, OUP, 1990, pp. 14-26. Possible reasons why the SEZs met with little success before 1985 are that they were relatively new, were set up by central government decree, were administered bureaucratically and concentrated on providing physical infrastructure, such as factory space and housing. Administered by non-locals and Mandarin speakers, particularly in Xiamen, they provided few opportunities for Chinese business networks to operate.

37 Guangdong Province, *Statistical Yearbook* 1993:346; Fujian Province, *Statistical Yearbook,* 1993, pp. 346-49; Tracy, N., 'The making of a new little dragon: The Overseas Chinese and the transformation of Guangdong', *Working Paper No. 36*, 1994.

Why the Sudden Investment Rush?

The speed of the transformation can be attributed to several factors. By the mid 1980s, rising production costs in Hong Kong and Taiwan meant that their more labour intensive manufactures were losing their competitive edge on world markets. Past export success also meant Hong Kong and Taiwan manufacturers had accessible reserves of funds available for new investment. The opening of the Pearl River Delta and southern Fujian provided outlets for both. Labour intensive industries were moved out of Hong Kong and Taiwan to sources of abundant cheaper labour and land.

Initial reforms produced rapidly growing township and village enterprises. The result was rising living standards in both rural and urban areas in the early 1980s. By the mid 1980s, however, the momentum of this type of simple development began to decline.[38] The entry of large numbers of small-scale foreign-Chinese entrepreneurs gave new impetus to township and village enterprises, providing them with joint-venture partnerships, sub-contracting and new export markets. For their part, foreign-Chinese investors provided upgraded machinery and expertise in management, design, quality and marketing.

More than a third of the South-East's industrial output now comes from the non-state, non-town and village enterprise sector, of which FIEs account for more than three-quarters.[39] This contrasts significantly with the rest of China. (See Table 10.4.) The ownership structure of industry in the South-East therefore is quite distinct from that of the rest of China.[40] In 1993, the South-East was responsible for more than 40 per cent of the combined output of the non-state and foreign-owned sectors for the whole of China.[41]

38 Lardy, N., 'Chinese foreign trade', *The China Quarterly*, 131, 1992.

39 *A Statistical Survey of China*, 1994, pp. 75-76; Guangdong Province, *Statistical Yearbook*, 1994, p. 92.

40 The only possible exception to this is the city of Shanghai where the largely non-state sector contributed 27.8 per cent of total industrial output in 1993. Shanghai still has, however, a dominant state sector, which was responsible for 59 per cent of industrial output in 1993. (See *A Statistical Survey of China*, 1994, pp. 75-76.)

41 *A Statistical Survey of China*, 1994, p. 76.

Table 10.6

Guangdong - Distribution of Foreign Investment

(At 31 December 1993)

	NUMBER OF FIEs	PER CENT	FOREIGN CAPITAL (US$ millions)	PER CENT
Guangzhou	5 498	12.3	10 191	17.4
Foshan	3 119	7.0	4 843	8.3
Total	8 617	19.3	15 034	25.7
Shenzhen	9 096	20.3	10 457	17.8
Huizhou	2 031	4.5	3 694	6.3
Dongguan	3 462	7.8	6 258	10.7
Total	14 589	32.6	20 409	34.8
Zhuhai	3 207	7.2	3 005	5.1
Zhongshan	1 178	2.6	1 672	2.9
Jiangmen	2 083	4.7	2 458	4.2
Total	6 468	14.5	7 135	12.2
Shantou	3 083	6.9	3 119	5.3
Chaozhou	822	1.8	862	1.5
Jieyong	1 629	3.6	1 409	2.4
Shanwei	737	1.7	786	1.3
Total	6 271	14.0	6 176	10.5
Shaoguan	495	1.1	519	0.9
Heyuan	811	1.8	1 250	2.1
Meizhou	999	2.2	569	1.0
Quigyuan	667	1.5	798	1.4
Total	2 972	6.6	3 136	5.4
Yangjiang	315	0.7	471	0.8
Zhanjiang	1 241	2.8	1 630	2.8
Maoming	1 155	2.6	899	1.5
Zhaoqing	2 202	4.9	2 156	3.7
Total	4 913	11.0	5 156	8.8
Projects Under Provincial Government	875	2.0	1 522	2.6
Total	44 705	100.0	58 568	100.0

Source: Guangdong Province, *Statistical Yearbook*, 1994, p. 327.

Fujian Province

Fujian Province is much less developed than Guangdong. While it was the second most successful province after Guangdong in attracting a total of 12 000 FIEs and around US$16 billion in investment by the end of 1993, this was just a third of the investment that Guangdong attracted.

Table 10.7

Fujian: Direct Foreign Investment[46]

(1979-93)

	NUMBER OF FIEs	PER CENT	CAPITAL (FDI) (US$ millions)	PER CENT
Fuzhou	2 967	23.2	2 041	30.0
Xiamen	2 238	17.5	2 344	34.4
Quanzhou	3 931	30.7	1 181	17.3
Zhangzhou	1 128	8.8	478	7.0
Putian	742	5.8	407	6.0
South-East (total)	8 039	62.8	4 410	64.7
Samming	465	3.6	61	0.9
Namping	538	4.2	152	2.2
Ningde	412	3.2	77	1.1
Longyan	387	3.0	73	1.1
Total	12 808	100.0	6 814	100.0

Source: Fujian Province, *Statistical Yearbook*, 1994, pp. 318-320, 305.

....

46 Capital represents FDI only and does not include re-invested profits. The capital for Quanzhou and Zhangzhou as a result appears considerably understated.

Table 10.8

Fujian: Sources of Foreign Investment

NUMBER OF FIEs	PER CENT	CAPITAL (FDI) (US$ millions)	PER CENT	
Hong Kong	7 686	64.1	10 632	65.7
Macau	244	2.0	404	2.5
Indonesia	64	0.5	100	0.6
Malaysia	76	0.6	121	0.7
Philippines	244	2.0	391	2.4
Singapore	384	3.2	751	4.6
Thailand	23	0.2	23	0.1
Taiwan	2 754	23.0	2 663	16.5
Sub-Total	11 475	95.6	15 085	93.3
Japan	228	1.9	232	1.4
USA/Canada	238	2.0	506	3.1
EU	53	0.4	281	1.7
Australia	28	0.2	65	0.4
Others	2	0.0	1	0.0
Total	11 990	100.0	16 170	100.0

Source: Fujian Province, *Statistical Yearbook*, 1994, pp. 310-11.

Foreign-Chinese investment is, however, more prominent in Fujian than in Guangdong. It accounts for around 95 per cent of the total number of investments and capital.[47] In the main area of activity, the Xiamen-Quanzhou-Zhangzhou triangle (an area of around 4 000 square kilometres), the Taiwanese are as important as the Hong Kong Chinese are in the Pearl River Delta. Close dialect and family links exist between many people from Taiwan and those in this area. In Fuzhou by contrast, it is ethnic Chinese entrepreneurs from South-East Asia, who are the most active.

In 1992 in Fujian, FIEs accounted for 24 per cent of industrial output by value; held 21 per cent of capital stock; and were responsible for 42 per cent of international trade.[48] In both the southern triangle and the capital Fuzhou, FIEs were responsible for over half of industrial production and more than 80 per cent of exported manufactured goods. In Xiamen, they contributed almost 70 per cent of industrial output by 1993.[49]

[47] Xiamen Foreign Investment Executive Committee, 1994; Fujian Province, *Statistical Yearbook*, 1993, p. 346.

[48] Fujian Province, *Statistical Yearbook*, 1993, p. 359.

[49] Xiamen Foreign Investment Executive Committee, 1994; Summary of World Broadcasts, Far East Weekly Economic Series, BBC, London/330, 27 April 1994 WG/3.

Foreign-Chinese investors have been particularly important in injecting funds into Fujian's state enterprises. Quanzhou has entirely abolished its state sector. Its 41 state-owned companies were sold in 1992 to a joint-venture between Hong Kong-based Oei Hong Leong (a son of Sino-Indonesian entrepreneur Eka Tjipta Widjaja who was born in Quanzhou), and the city government. Management rights and majority equity were ceded to Oei.[50] The enterprises manufacture a range of products including pharmaceuticals, dairy products, beer, televisions, textiles and clothing, and machinery. They employ more than 20 000 workers.[51]

In Fuzhou, more than half the city's state enterprises were in joint-ventures with foreign investors by early 1994.[52] Control of the city's most profitable state enterprise, Fuzhou Brewing, was sold to Singapore interests, with a view to trebling production. In both Fuzhou and Xiamen, Singapore government instrumentalities are reforming and developing public utilities and facilities.[53]

Unlike in Guangdong, however, foreign capital is not spread throughout Fujian Province. It is heavily concentrated within the Xiamen-Quanzhou-Zhangzhou triangle, where almost two-thirds of all FIEs in the province are found.[54] (See Table 10.7.) Surprisingly, the largest concentration by number of enterprises is not in either Xiamen SEZ or Fuzhou, but in the area around the coastal city of Quanzhou, including the smaller cities of Jinjiang and Shishi. This is because the Quanzhou region was an important source of migration in the nineteenth and early twentieth centuries, and many foreign-Chinese now have ancestral and other links to the region.

Although a source of migration in the past, Fuzhou was not a major source. Thus today, it lacks the thousands of small- and medium-sized foreign-invested firms that have been set up in the Pearl River Delta, eastern Guangdong and southern Fujian. It has little more than 20 per cent of Fujian's FIEs. Fuzhou, and the nearby Mawei Economic and Technological Development Zone, however, have been relatively successful in attracting many of the larger foreign-Chinese entrepreneurs. Robert Kuok, Liem Sioe Liong and Pipat Tantipipatpong, three of South-East Asia's more successful entrepreneurs who are ancestrally from the Fuzhou region have made substantial investments there. Other prominent foreign Sino-business people who have invested in the area include Hong Kong's Li Ka-shing and Indonesia's Mochtar Riady, both of whom have major infrastructure projects underway, and Oei Hong Leong.[55]

The pattern of foreign investment in China's South-East shows that the three most important regions owe their predominant positions to their ability to link up with foreign-Chinese investors. Investment in the Pearl River Delta is overwhelmingly from the Cantonese community and comes predominantly from

50 Oei Hong Leong's investments in China are the focus of a case study in Chapter 11.

51 Corporate International, *Corporate International's Company Handbook*, Hong Kong, May 1993, pp. 58-59.

52 Summary of World Broadcasts, Far East Weekly Economic Series, BBC, London/0330, 27 April 1994 WG/3.

53 *Straits Times Weekly Edition* 24 January 1993, p. 19; Xiamen Foreign Investment Executive Committee, 1994.

54 In part, this is likely to be due to particular concessions provided to FIEs in this area.

55 Economist Intelligence Unit, *Business China*, 3 May 1993, pp. 4-5.

Hong Kong. In Guangdong's eastern region, significant investment comes from Singaporean, Thai and Hong Kong Teochiu Chinese, who have their ancestral origins there. Likewise, south-eastern Fujian is the ancestral home of the Hokkien, the largest ancestral dialect group in Taiwan and South-East Asia. However, foreign-Chinese investment is more widespread than this. The Taiwanese have a strong presence in Guangdong, where they account for approximately 20 per cent of FIEs and associated capital.

China Reaching Out to the Diaspora

Hundreds, if not thousands, of business delegations now leave China each year. Many contact local ethnic Chinese communities across Asia and Australia and local Chinese chambers of commerce, in their quest for investment for their home areas in China. Many delegations originate from specific parts of China and frequently attempt to make contact with their former compatriots now living abroad. A business delegation from Fuzhou in Fujian Province visited the timber and logging city of Sibu in Malaysia's Sarawak in 1994, for example. Sibu has a high concentration of Chinese who are ancestrally from Fuzhou.

All countries in the region, including Australia, receive business delegations from China. Some chambers in the region reported that they receive 'hundreds' of business delegations from China each year. Such a massive influx of people from China to the rest of Asia is undoubtedly an important factor in re-energising the region's Chinese communities and further integrating the economies of the region.

CHANGING INVESTMENT PATTERNS: NEW DESTINATIONS FOR FOREIGN-CHINESE INVESTMENT IN CHINA

Township and village enterprises, (which with urban collectives constitute the collective sector), and the non-state and foreign sectors, now account for around half of China's industrial output.[56] Away from the South-East, in those areas where the collective sector is most prominent, particularly in Jiangsu, Zhejiang and Shandong, the economy is relatively dynamic.[57] It is to these provinces that foreign investment, particularly foreign-Chinese investment, is increasingly drawn. By the end of 1993, these three provinces had the largest numbers of FIEs after Guangdong and Fujian, and in each case the pace of foreign investment accelerated sharply after 1992. The three provinces also accounted for 46 per cent of the total output of China's collective sector in 1993.[58]

56 *A Statistical Survey of China*, 1994, p. 75.

57 Korean firms are increasingly important investors in Shandong Province.

58 *A Statistical Survey of China*, 1994, p. 76.

One recent study on the changing patterns of Taiwanese investment in China confirms these trends but also suggests other shifts are underway.[59] The report suggests that new Taiwanese investment now has moved sharply away from the South-East towards two new areas. The first is the Upper Yangtze Delta region incorporating Jiangsu and Zhejiang but also the relatively impoverished Anhui Province, which adjoins Jiangsu. The second area consists of the three provinces of the inner South-East which are adjacent to Guangdong - Guangxi, Hunan and Jiangxi. Table 10.9 shows the distribution of new Taiwanese investment between 1989 and 1992. While in 1989-90, the South-East took more than 60 per cent of new projects and more than 70 per cent of the capital invested, in 1991-92 those same proportions were shared by the two new regions, with the Upper Yangtze Delta the most prominent.[60]

However, as mentioned earlier, it is likely that actual Taiwanese investment makes up 20 per cent of total foreign investment in Guangdong. On this basis, there would be about 8 000 Taiwanese foreign-invested enterprises in Guangdong.[61] Local officials in the South-East, however, have commented that inflows of Taiwanese investment seemed lower during 1993 and 1994. This was particularly the case in southern Fujian, where the Taiwanese had been the most prominent investors until 1992.[62]

59 CERD Consultants, Hong Kong, 1994.

60 There are some qualifications to these figures, however. They only include projects, which have been processed through official Taiwanese channels, and have therefore been approved directly by the Government or by the Taiwan Investment Approval Committee.

61 This is many more than official Taiwanese data indicates.

62 Personal communication with the Xiamen Foreign Investment Executive Committee.

Table 10.9

Changing Patterns of Taiwanese Investment in China

(US$m)

	1989-90 NUMBER OF FIEs	1989-90 CAPITAL	1991-92 NUMBER OF FIEs	1991-92 CAPITAL
South-East				
Guangdong	349	367.3	170	165.1
Fujian	615	639.2	165	80.2
Hainan	79	30.7	334	217.6
Sub-Total	1 043	1 037.2	669	462.9
Inner South-East				
Guangxi	30	8.7	416	348.7
Hunan	11	2.6	796	928.4
Jiangxi	17	9.8	700	516.1
Sub-Total	58	21.1	1 912	1 793.2
Shanghai	4	1.6	358	282.0
Yangtze Delta				
Jiangsu	40	17.4	1 595	1 528.9
Zhejiang	80	40.1	527	348.0
Anhui	22	4.8	1 046	1 230.9
Sub-Total	142	62.3	3 168	3 107.8
North-East				
Beijing	48	29.2	363	161.1
Tianjin	28	18.6	249	109.5
Liaoning	1	1.8	279	180.5
Hebei	22	19.0	238	132.2
Shandong	58	33.4	168	108.6
Other	67	180.2	300	169.8
Sub-Total	224	282.2	1 597	861.7
China Total	1 663	1 601.2	8 460	6 954.9

Source: CERD Consultants, Hong Kong, 1994; Chan, M. and W. Zhu , 'Past, Present and Future Trends in the Taiwan-China Relationship', China Business Centre, 1994.

EMPLOYMENT CONSEQUENCES OF FOREIGN-CHINESE INVESTMENT

The most obvious impact of foreign-Chinese investment in China is the enormous increase in the industrial capacity of these investors. Just as the Pearl River Delta was being opened to foreign capital in 1985, Hong Kong's manufacturing sector employed 950 000 people, the highest figure on record. As a result of many manufacturing industries, particularly the more labour intensive, moving into China, this figure had fallen to just under 500 000 in 1994. However, at the same time, Hong Kong industry employed approximately four million workers in Guangdong alone. The move into Guangdong has allowed Hong Kong entrepreneurs to increase their manufacturing capacity at least four-fold in the last ten years. Apart from employment due to direct investment, there is employment generated in the 55 000 or so small local firms in Guangdong that owe their existence to subcontracting work from Hong Kong companies.[63]

By the end of 1993, foreign-Chinese-owned enterprises and joint ventures employed around 5.5 million workers in Guangdong and 1.5 million in Fujian.[64] As these south-eastern provinces contain around half the foreign-Chinese investment in China, it is possible that approximately 14 million people in China were being employed by foreign-Chinese investors by the end of 1993.[65] This number could well have increased to around 18-20 million by the end of 1994.[66]

Going into China: Chen Hsong

For many years Chen Hsong has been the largest producer of plastic injection moulding machines in Hong Kong. Founded in 1958, it made steady progress in the territory and expanded to Taiwan in 1980. In 1990, it established its own foundry to produce the ductile iron castings needed for its moulding machines. The combined output of its Hong Kong and Taiwan facilities is in excess of 3 500 machines annually. As a result of it entering into three joint ventures in China, the group has added the capacity to produce a further 7 500 machines each year, thus trebling its output and making it the largest producer of injection moulding machinery in the world. Recently it established production facilities in India.[67]

---

63 Overholt, W., *The Rise of China: How Economic Reform is Creating a New Superpower*, Norton, 1993, pp. 189-91.

64 Guangdong Province, *Statistical Yearbook*, 1994, p. 327; Fujian Province, *Statistical Yearbook*, 1993, p. 357; 1994, p. 307.

65 Another estimated puts the figure at 15 million in early 1994. See Zhang, C., 'A memorandum on the workers' situation in foreign capital enterprises', *Chinese Industrial and Commercial News*, 24 June 1994, p. 6.

66 Summary of World Broadcasts, Far East Weekly Economic Series, BBC, London/0346, 17 August, 1994 WG/8; *Sunday Morning Post*, 3 July 1994, p. M4; *South China Morning Post International Weekly*, 3-4 December 1994, p. B1.

67 Corporate International, *Corporate International's Company Handbook*, June 1994, pp. 38-39.

Going into China: VTech Holdings

VTech Holdings originally produced computer games. However, as a result of the opportunities presented by the opening of China, particularly the availability of new sources of land and labour close to Hong Kong, it diversified into personal computers, telecommunications and computerised toys. Subsequent further diversification reduced its dependence on the saturated personal computer market as it moved into notebook and powerbook computers under the brand name *Laser*. The firm currently employs more than 10 000 people in Guangdong Province and is listed on both the Hong Kong and London Stock Exchanges.[68]

68 *Corporate International's Company Handbook*, p. 634.

Annex

Surveys of Foreign-Invested Firms in Guangdong, Fujian and Jiangsu

To analyse the importance of foreign-Chinese in developing China's economy, 200 foreign-invested firms were surveyed in each of Guangdong, Fujian and Jiangsu Provinces (600 in total). The surveys provide a suggestive, though not comprehensive, view of the role of foreign-Chinese investors in China.

In Guangdong, firms selected for interview were in Nanhai county and Panyu. Nanhai county is part of the administrative district of Foshan, and has attracted foreign capital since the opening of the Pearl River Delta in 1985. It is an important centre for town and village activities, and has a per capita savings ratio among the highest in China.

Panyu is the administrative district of the provincial capital of Guangzhou. Until recently, its economy was dominated by 'compensation trade', whereby firms pay for imported technology and machinery by delivering a percentage of their output, usually to a Hong Kong firm, until the debt is settled.

In Fujian, the Xiamen Special Economic Zone (SEZ) was selected. SEZs are the longest established destinations for foreign investment in China, and collectively, are still significant destinations for foreign capital. Quanzhou in Fujian was chosen largely because of the number of foreign-Chinese with ancestral links to the city.[69]

In Jiangsu, firms were surveyed in Suzhou and Nanjing. Jiangsu is China's leading province in terms of industrial output (Guangdong is the leading province in terms of total output). Also, relatively few foreign-Chinese have ancestral links to the province (allowing a contrast with Guangdong and Fujian in which most foreign-Chinese have their ancestral origins).[70]

Within Jiangsu, Suzhou was chosen because it receives most of the Province's foreign investment as well as being the provincial centre for industrial production.[71] For many investors, the attraction of Suzhou is its proximity to Shanghai and its relatively lower land and labour costs.

Nanjing was chosen as a contrast to Suzhou and to establish the extent of foreign investment away from the immediate coastal zone in the Lower Yangtze Valley. Although it is the provincial capital, it does not have all the advantages of Suzhou; it is around four hours by road from Shanghai and while transport links are improving, they are still poor. Unlike Suzhou, however, it is located on the Yangtze River giving it access to the sea. Past links with the Kuomintang may also mean that it has attracted investment from Taiwan.

69 Quanzhou was referred to as 'Zaitan' by Marco Polo, and in the thirteenth century was considered the largest port in the world.

70 In the aftermath of the communist takeover in 1949, a number of prominent industrialists did leave the Province for Hong Kong, however.

71 As measured by value of output. (See *Jiangsu Tongjinianjian* 1994, pp. 294-96; 321-23.)

Timing of Investment

An important determinant of the timing of initial foreign investment in China, was the time at which the province or city was 'opened' to foreign investors. The surveys of foreign-invested firms in Nanhai, Panyu, Quanzhou and Xiamen found that initial investment was recent, with most made after 1987. The recent acceleration of foreign investment is illustrated by the significant numbers of firms surveyed which date from 1991. The exception is Xiamen, which became an SEZ in 1979, where half the investments initially were made between 1988 and 1990.

Table 10.10

Date of Establishment of Venture in China

(Per Cent)

	GUANGDONG		FUJIAN	
	NANHAI	PANYU	QUANZHOU	XIAMEN
1991-93	58	70	60	29
1988-90	31	26	36	49
Before 1988	11	4	4	22
Total	100	100	100	100
Number of Firms	100	106	95	97

In Jiangsu, most of the foreign-invested firms surveyed in both Suzhou and Nanjing had been formed since 1991; 86 per cent in Nanjing and 88 per cent in Suzhou. In Nanjing, 57 per cent had been formed since 1992. By contrast, only three had operated before 1988. The pattern of investment is therefore quite unlike that in Xiamen and Nanhai, where most companies surveyed were established before 1992, but somewhat similar to that found in Panyu and Quanzhou.

In Nanhai, Panyu, Quanzhou and Xiamen, foreign investment was overwhelmingly from foreign-Chinese, who accounted for 98-99 per cent of the investors in all areas. (See Table 10.11.) Rare exceptions included four Japanese and two Korean investors.[72]

....

72 These results imply a greater predominance of foreign-Chinese investment than suggested by official statistics. This may reflect the nature of the localities in which the surveys were undertaken. The surveys do, however, discern between ethnicity and nationality, which official figures do not. The eleven North American Chinese investors would, for example show up in official figures simply as 'North American'.

Table 10.11

Ethnicity of Foreign Investors

(Per Cent)[73]

FOREIGN CHINESE FROM:	GUANGDONG NANHAI	GUANGDONG PANYU	FUJIAN QUANZHOU	FUJIAN XIAMEN
Hong Kong & Macau	71	72	72	35
Taiwan	24	21	19	47
South-East Asia	1	1	5	12
US/Canada	2	4	1	4
Other	-	-	1	1
Total Foreign Chinese	98	98	99	99
Non-Chinese	2	2	1	1
Total	100	100	100	100
Number of Firms	107	112	97	106

Responses indicate the strength of Hong Kong Chinese investment, more than 70 per cent in Nanhai, Panyu and Quanzhou, and over a third in Xiamen. Taiwanese are present as substantial minorities in all areas, constituting almost half the investors in Xiamen. In addition, there were twenty South-East Asian Chinese, eight from the Philippines, seven from Singapore, three from Malaysia and two from Indonesia.

Foreign-Chinese investors also made up the vast majority of foreign investors in both Nanjing and Suzhou. However, in both cities, non-Chinese investors were more important than in Nanhai, Panyu, Quanzhou and Xiamen. In Jiangsu, there were twenty non-Chinese investors (nine per cent of the sample) - 11 per cent in Nanjing and six per cent in Suzhou.[74] These were fairly equally divided between American, Japanese and European owned companies. Investors from Hong Kong and Macau were the most prominent, making up 61 per cent of investors in Nanjing and 56 per cent in Suzhou. Taiwanese were the second largest group with around 20 per cent of investments in each city. American-Chinese were the next largest group, with ten investments in Nanjing and seven in Suzhou, more than seven per cent of the total. The only other significant group were seven Singapore investors in Suzhou.[75]

....

73 In some cases foreign investors from more than one group were in partnership. In such cases each has been recorded separately.

74 These figures allow for the fact that there were 232 foreign investors in the 200 companies surveyed in Jiangsu.

75 The Singaporean interest in Suzhou is likely to be related to the Singapore Government-led consortium to build Singapore-Suzhou Township, on the outskirts of Suzhou. (The township is further discussed in Chapter 11.)

Size of Investment

Tables 10.12 and 10.13 show the relatively small size of most ventures surveyed in Nanhai, Panyu, Quanzhou and Xiamen. Over 80 per cent involved a total investment by all partners (including local partners) of under US$5 million. Investments of under US$1 million were in the majority in Nanhai and Quanzhou, and accounted for 44 per cent in Panyu and 34 per cent in Xiamen.[76] Data on number of workers employed yield a similar picture. Nearly half the FIEs surveyed in Nanhai, Panyu, and Xiamen and two-thirds in Quanzhou consisted of small factories that employed fewer than 200 workers. These operations contrast with the large state manufacturing enterprises that dominate China's industrial sector.

The size of investments in both Suzhou and Nanjing followed that of Nanhai, Panyu and Quanzhou, with around half of all investments being US$1 million or less. At the other end of the scale, however, nine per cent of the firms surveyed in Nanjing and ten per cent in Suzhou, represented investments of US$10 million or more. This was more than for Nanhai, Panyu and Quanzhou but similar to Xiamen.

Fifty-six per cent of firms surveyed in Nanjing and 45 per cent in Suzhou employed fewer than 100 workers, and in both cities more than 70 per cent employed fewer than 200. At the other end of the scale, ten per cent in Nanjing and eight per cent in Suzhou employed more than 500 workers. Although most of the firms surveyed in Jiangsu were formed only within the previous two years, growth patterns appear to be emerging already, given the declining proportion of firms employing fewer than 50 or 100 workers.

Table 10.12

Total Investment in the Venture

(Per Cent)

	GUANGDONG		FUJIAN	
	NANHAI	PANYU	QUANZHOU	XIAMEN
Hong Kong & Macau	71	72	72	35
Under US$1 million	52	44	62	34
US$1-4.9 million	33	41	27	49
US$5-9.9 million	11	12	6	6
US$10 million or more	3	3	5	11
Total	100	100	100	100
Number of Firms	100	105	97	100

76 These figures accord with official data which similarly indicate small average investments.

Table 10.13

Number of Workers Currently Employed

(Per Cent)

	GUANGDONG		FUJIAN	
ENTERPRISES EMPLOYING:	NANHAI	PANYU	QUANZHOU	XIAMEN
Under 200	46	49	67	47
200-999	41	42	31	42
1000 or More	13	9	2	10
Total	100	100	100	100
Number of Firms	100	105	97	100

A reasonable assumption would be that the small scale of operations reflects the small size of the investors. Table 10.14 indicates that a substantial minority of investors are small, with total assets of under US$5 million; however, most firms can be classified as medium or large, including 35 publicly-listed companies, and another 26 described as transnational corporations. The size of investing companies cannot therefore fully explain the prevalence of small-sized foreign investments in China.

Table 10.14

Size of the Foreign Investor

(Capitalisation US$m)

	GUANGDONG		FUJIAN	
	NANHAI	PANYU	QUANZHOU	XIAMEN
Small (under US$5 million)	25	51	46	34
Medium or Large	75	49	54	66
Total	100	100	100	100
Number of Firms	99	99	59	56

Evidence suggests that the smallness of many operations, in the areas surveyed, is a product of policy, not of constrained resources. Table 10.15 shows that large, as well as, small investors choose this strategy. In each of Nanhai, Panyu, Quanzhou and Xiamen, over 70 per cent of larger investors were in projects capitalised at under US$5 million.

Table 10.15

Size of investment by Size of Investors

(Nanhai, Panyu, Quanzhou and Xiamen in US$m)

AMOUNT INVESTED:	SMALL INVESTORS (per cent)	LARGE INVESTORS (per cent)	TOTAL (per cent)
Under US$1 million	62	37	47
US$1-4.9 million	36	40	39
US$5 million or More	2	23	14
Total	100	100	100
Number of Firms	120	188	308

This seems a matter of policy rather than of limited resources or commitment because over half of the larger investors (a majority in three of the four areas) also had one or more other ventures in China, often in the same location.

Survey evidence from Suzhou and Nanjing is similar to that from Nanhai, Panyu, Quanzhou and Xiamen.

Role in Trade

The surveys undertaken in Guangdong and Fujian demonstrate the role foreign-invested firms play in promoting exports. Table 10.16 shows that less than ten per cent of surveyed firms in Nanhai, Panyu and Xiamen and 13 per cent in Quanzhou do not export at all; whereas, substantial majorities of firms in each locality export most or all of their output.

Most FIEs in Jiangsu also were export-oriented. Nanjing, unlike the other regions surveyed, showed 54 per cent of companies, exporting less than half their product, and more than 20 per cent not exporting at all. This reflects strong domestic demand and suggests that in Nanjing at least, FIEs were beginning to make inroads into the domestic market, competing with state enterprises. The firms surveyed in Suzhou, by contrast, were as oriented to export markets as those surveyed in the South-East, with 65 per cent exporting more than half their output. Among the Suzhou firms, a significant minority were selling onto the domestic market, with some 25 per cent exporting less than a quarter of their production.

Table 10.16

Proportion of Product Exported

(Per Cent)

	GUANGDONG		FUJIAN	
	NANHAI	PANYU	QUANZHOU	XIAMEN
All	26	52	45	35
Most	35	35	26	39
Less than Half	30	12	17	17
None	9	2	13	8
Total	100	100	100	100
Number of Firms	100	104	87	99

Foreign-invested firms contribute directly to exports by selling abroad the goods they produce. In turn, other firms in China supply these firms with raw materials, plant and equipment. As Tables 10.17 and 10.18 show, substantial though varying proportions of the firms surveyed in Guangdong and Fujian also use at least some domestically-produced raw materials, machinery, equipment and spare parts.

Table 10.17

Foreign-Invested Firms Sourcing Raw Materials and Spare Parts Within China

(Per Cent)

	GUANGDONG		FUJIAN	
	NANHAI	PANYU	QUANZHOU	XIAMEN
Raw Materials	60	30	59	58
Spare Parts	50	37	56	43

Table 10.18

Sources of Machinery and Equipment

(Per Cent)[77]

	GUANGDONG		FUJIAN	
	NANHAI	PANYU	QUANZHOU	XIAMEN
China	49	23	31	24
Imported	79	93	87	82
Number of Firms	100	105	84	97

The contribution of foreign investors to China's exports is not restricted to providing marketing channels or capital, but also involves introducing new technology and organising production. As Table 10.18 shows, large majorities of firms surveyed in Nanhai, Panyu, Quanzhou and Xiamen, ranging from 79 per cent to 93 per cent, imported at least some of their machinery and equipment. Between one-third and two-thirds also use expatriate managers, most often from Hong Kong or Taiwan. Many foreign investors also play a part in designing the product: over half of those in Nanhai and Panyu, over a quarter in Quanzhou and nearly two-fifths in Xiamen.

Local Dialect Skills and Connections

Table 10.19 shows that 58 per cent of the foreign investors in those firms surveyed in Nanhai and 71 per cent in Panyu spoke Cantonese: 38 per cent and 47 per cent were of local origin; and 28 per cent and 32 per cent still had relatives in the locality. In Fujian, especially away from the SEZ, local connections determine investment location even more. Ninety-nine percent in Quanzhou and 80 per cent in Xiamen were Hokkien speakers: 88 per cent and 62 per cent were of local origin; and 86 per cent and 49 per cent still had relatives in the area. While localities varied substantially in the extent to which foreign investors had local connections, there was no substantial or consistent variation, within localities, between small and larger investors.

[77] Many use both local and imported machinery, hence the percentages add up to more than 100 per cent.

Table 10.19

Local Connections of Investors

(Per Cent)

	GUANGDONG		FUJIAN	
	NANHAI	PANYU	QUANZHOU	XIAMEN
Speak Local Dialect	58	71	99	80
Local Origin	38	47	88	62
Local Kin	28	32	86	49
Number	99	105	92	91

Table 10.20

Local Connections of Investors from Hong Kong and Taiwan

(Per Cent)

GUANGDONG	NANHAI		PANYU	
	HONG KONG	TAIWAN	HONG KONG	TAIWAN
Speak Local Dialect	70	11	88	11
Local Origin	50	-	53	17
Local Kin	37	5	41	6
Number	66	19	75	18

FUJIAN	QUANZHOU		XIAMEN	
	HONG KONG	TAIWAN	HONG KONG	TAIWAN
Speak Local Dialect	100	100	54	98
Local Origin	95	63	54	72
Local Kin	95	56	54	44
Number	64	16	24	43

The Taiwanese are substantial minority investors in Guangdong: 24 per cent in Nanhai and 21 per cent in Panyu. Table 10.20 shows that very few of these are Cantonese speakers or of local origin. Although there is a small Cantonese community in Taiwan, investment in Guangdong from Taiwan is coming from many non-Cantonese Taiwan investors. Four Taiwanese investors in the Nanhai survey and seven in Panyu had a partner from Hong Kong.

Table 10.20 also shows that among the Hong Kong investors in firms surveyed in Nanhai, 30 per cent did not speak the main dialect of Hong Kong, Cantonese, and in Panyu, the figure was 22 per cent. These proportions appear high, even though there are non-Cantonese minorities in Hong Kong. Some of these investors could be Taiwanese or South-East Asians operating in China from a Hong Kong base.

Of those in the Fujian surveys who said they were Taiwanese, 100 per cent in Quanzhou and 98 per cent in Xiamen spoke Hokkien, and substantial majorities in both places were of local origin, with many still having relatives in the area. It is likely that these investors were largely native Taiwanese, descendants of the Fujianese who settled in Taiwan before 1949.[78] Of the 21 South-East Asian investors in Fujian, 90 per cent spoke Hokkien, two-thirds were of local origin and 72 per cent still had local relatives. Three of the four American Chinese there also speak the local dialect.

Of the Hong Kong investors in those firms surveyed in Fujian, 72 per cent of respondents in Quanzhou and 35 per cent in Xiamen, had strong local connections. In Quanzhou all of them were native speakers and almost all were of local origin, and in Xiamen over half were native speakers and over half were of local origin. A high proportion of Hong Kong investors in these areas were not Cantonese but Hokkien; this suggests they were either Hokkien speakers from Hong Kong (as was mentioned in Chapter 4, approximately two per cent of Hong Kong's residents are Hokkien), or South-East Asian Chinese operating from a base in Hong Kong.

As expected, among the foreign-Chinese investors in the firms surveyed in Jiangsu, local connections were not as important as those in Guangdong and Fujian. In both Suzhou and Nanjing, fewer than half the Chinese investors spoke the local dialect or had a local family connection. This was particularly the case in Suzhou where just six per cent of the foreign-Chinese investors spoke the local Wu dialect, and ten percent had relatives in the region. In Nanjing, 32 per cent of the surveyed foreign-Chinese investors spoke the local dialect, and 22 per cent had relatives in the area. The relatively high number of investors with local connections in Nanjing may be explained by the city's past links with the Kuomintang.

[78] As discussed in Chapter 4, most of the mainlanders, who took refuge in Taiwan after 1949, came from other parts of China.

Role of Local Partners

Substantial majorities of foreign-Chinese who had invested in ventures surveyed in Nanhai, Panyu and Quanzhou and two-fifths in Xiamen had entered into partnerships with local Chinese. (See Table 10.21.)

In Suzhou and Nanjing, despite the much lower importance of local connections, the vast majority of investments among the companies surveyed involved partnerships with local Chinese. In fact, of the six cities in which firms were surveyed, Suzhou had the lowest number of wholly-owned foreign-invested companies. This was surprising as the city authorities claim to encourage such arrangements. Thus, it seems, where foreign-Chinese investors lack pre-existing local connections, they prefer to have a local partner who establishes local connections.

Table 10.21

Venture Type

(Per Cent)

	GUANGDONG NANHAI	GUANGDONG PANYU	FUJIAN QUANZHOU	FUJIAN XIAMEN
Wholly Foreign-Owned	16	38	38	61
Joint Venture or Cooperative	84	62	62	39
Total	100	100	100	100
Number	100	105	97	99

Among those foreign-investing firms surveyed, the most common choice for a local partner was a township or village enterprise (owned by a local government), or a local government body itself. In Nanhai, Panyu and Quanzhou, such bodies constituted over 70 per cent of local partners. In Xiamen, with its SEZ status, many of the local partners were private. Both larger and small investors sought the same kind of partners: 73 per cent of the local partners of small investors and 65 per cent of the local partners of larger investors were at township and village level.

Firms surveyed in Jiangsu were more likely to partner the state sector than those surveyed in the South-East. However, control of the state sector in Jiangsu has been decentralised. Most of the sector now is controlled by city governments and it was with these that most partnerships were made. In Suzhou, not one partnership with either the central or provincial governments was encountered. In Nanjing, around six per cent of the investments involved the central government or one of its instrumentalities, and a further seven per cent involved the provincial government, the largest proportion of the six cities surveyed. In Nanjing, 29 per cent of the partnerships involved the city government and a further 14 per cent involved county or township governments; 16 per cent of partnerships were solely with local private companies. In Suzhou, 31 per cent of the partnerships involved city government, 40 per cent town and village enterprises, and a further 13 per cent county or township governments.

A major difference between Jiangsu and the South-East was the greater number of investments in which the foreign investor held less than a controlling interest. In Nanhai, Panyu, Quanzhou and Xiamen, foreign-Chinese investors held a controlling interest in 80 per cent of the companies surveyed, but in Jiangsu this was true for around 50 per cent (54 per cent in Suzhou and 48 per cent in Nanjing.) Two reasons for this involve the greater distance from the investor's home base necessitating greater managerial inputs from the local partner and the bargaining power of potential local partners, particularly those in the state sector.

Table 10.22

Chinese Partner of Joint Ventures and Cooperatives

(per cent)

	GUANGDONG		FUJIAN	
	NANHAI	PANYU	QUANZHOU	XIAMEN
Central or Provincial Government	2	2	4	13
District or City Government	21	17	13	18
Township or Village Enterprise/ Collectively-Owned Enterprise	76	78	71	18
Private	1	3	13	50
Total	100	100	100	100
Number	84	62	24	38

Partnerships with higher levels of government were avoided by firms surveyed in Nanhai, Panyu, Quanzhou and Xiamen, regardless of their size or sources of investment. Table 10.22 shows that partnerships with central or provincial government-owned enterprises or bodies were few in Xiamen and negligible elsewhere. Furthermore, fewer than a third of partnerships in Xiamen, and much fewer elsewhere, were with city levels of government or higher. Of all respondents in Nanhai, Panyu, Quanzhou and Xiamen, only 13 per cent were in partnership with a state organisation of the level of city or above.

Xiamen, an SEZ under central government control, has supposedly fostered an open environment for foreign investors. Nevertheless, nearly two-fifths of respondents complained about excessive regulations and the perceived inefficiency of the Xiamen Government. In Nanhai, Panyu and Quanzhou, however, such complaints were rare.[79] On the other hand, the level of the local partner did not affect access to credit within China. In every locality, those with Chinese partners were more likely to obtain loans from banks in China than were the wholly foreign-owned ventures. Overall, 48 per cent of those with China

79 Their concerns were the usual worries of business, including competition, difficulties in getting access to capital, problems with recruiting good workers, followed by problems with infrastructure and with getting good managers.

partners and 42 per cent with township and village partners, but only 28 per cent of the wholly foreign owned, obtained such credit.

Table 10.23

Sources of Additional Capital

(Per Cent)

	GUANGDONG		FUJIAN	
	NANHAI	PANYU	QUANZHOU	XIAMEN
Banks in China	51	33	40	30
Banks Overseas	7	10	5	15
Other	4	3	4	9
None	44	59	56	51
Total	100	100	100	100
Number	98	104	91	96

Bank loans within China were by far the largest source of additional capital, cited by proportions of respondents ranging from 30 per cent in Xiamen to 51 per cent in Nanhai. Loans from overseas banks were much rarer. This probably reflects the suppression of interest rates in China: this makes loans sourced from banks there comparatively cheap. Also, banks outside China may perceive that doing business in China is particularly risky. Chinese banks may also be more accessible for smaller investors: 44 per cent of larger investors had borrowed from banks in China, as had 38 per cent of small investors; only 14 per cent of larger investors sourced their funds from banks outside China. Only three per cent of smaller investors used outside sources.

With most investments undertaken jointly with rural industry, the pattern of investment in Suzhou is similar to that found in Nanhai, Panyu and Quanzhou. However, it does differ considerably from that found in Xiamen, largely as a result of Suzhou's small number of wholly-owned investments. Foreign investment in Nanjing differs from that in the other five cities, as partnerships with the state sector account for over 40 per cent of the total. There is also a much lower level of involvement with rural industry. However, the Suzhou area has attracted around half Jiangsu's foreign investment while Nanjing is relatively unimportant for foreign investors. This situation is unlikely to change in the short to medium term, because Suzhou is close to Shanghai but not under its control. Developments in Suzhou are therefore of more significance and tend to confirm the implications drawn from examining FDI in the South-East. Foreign-Chinese investors prefer to seek partners and invest at the local level where high level permission is not required.

Spillover Effects Elsewhere in China

The development of the South-East has led to growing inequalities between its wage levels and standards of living and those of other areas. Nevertheless, pre-reform China also had substantial inequalities, particularly between rural and urban residents. The South-East was a disadvantaged area, and some of those groups that are now benefiting were previously among the most disadvantaged. The ultimate impact of foreign investment in the south-eastern provinces will depend on how and to what extent its effects extend to other parts of China. The surveys cannot capture the movement of investment up the coast or inland, but nonetheless suggest some repercussions in other parts of China.

Table 10.24

Proportion of Ventures Obtaining Supplies from Other Provinces in China

(Per Cent)

	GUANGDONG		FUJIAN	
	NANHAI	PANYU	QUANZHOU	XIAMEN
Raw Materials	13	20	40	31
Machinery	11	8	21	20
Spare Parts	7	6	23	29
Total	100	100	100	100
Number	100	105	84	91

Table 10.25

Proportion of Companies Selling Products in Other Provinces in China

(Per Cent)

	GUANGDONG		FUJIAN	
	NANHAI	PANYU	QUANZHOU	XIAMEN
Proportion	51	27	39	48
Number	100	104	98	100

Table 10.24 shows that some of the ventures surveyed in Guangdong and a large minority in Fujian purchase raw materials, machinery and spare parts from other parts of China. Their products also supply other provinces (Table 10.25).

The greatest and most dramatic impact, however, has been the movement of more than ten million migrant workers from the relatively poor interior provinces to the South-East to work in these foreign-invested ventures. Local labour has been insufficient to meet the demand. Furthermore, the greater experience of local workers gives them access to higher level jobs and their membership of villages and townships often allows them to benefit from the profits. Consequently, these people frequently are unwilling to take production line factory jobs. The surveyed firms had a great dependence on migrant workers from many other provinces of China. The proportion of firms using such workers ranged from 77 per cent in Quanzhou and 80 per cent in Nanhai to 84 per cent in Xiamen and 85 per cent in Panyu. They constituted most of the workforce in 57 per cent of ventures in Nanhai, 54 per cent in Panyu, 43 per cent in Quanzhou and 41 per cent in Xiamen.

Table 10.26

Employment of Internal Migrant Workers by Surveyed Firms

RANK	PROVINCE OR REGION OF ORIGIN	NUMBER OF EMPLOYING FIRMS
1	Sichuan	199
2	Hunan	165
3	Guangxi	79
4	Northwest	71
5	Jiangxi	65
6	Anhui	59
7	Hubei	47
8	Henan	40
9	Shaanxi	27
10	Shandong	10
11	Fujian	6
12	Northeast	5
13	Zhejiang	5

In a society which was previously highly segmented, with fixed residence and little horizontal movement, workers from diverse and widely distant parts of China are now being thrown together. What the impact will be on them, and on their home areas, if and when they return, is yet to be seen.

Foreign capital has only become significant in Jiangsu since 1992. Consequently, land and local labour have not become as scarce as they are in Guangdong. Nor has the rapid growth of the foreign-invested sector yet drawn large numbers of workers from the nearby provinces into its factories. Among surveyed firms, very few employed migrant labour from other provinces. No factory in Nanjing had a majority of migrant workers and only three per cent did so in Suzhou.

Employment Growth

While 53 per cent of firms surveyed in Nanhai, Panyu, Quanzhou and Xiamen started with fewer than 100 workers, only 32 per cent had fewer than that number at the time of the survey. While six per cent started with more than 500 workers, 16 per cent had at least that many when surveyed. Of the 34 ventures that employed more than 1 000 workers when surveyed, three started with fewer than 50 workers, three with 50 to 99, three with 100 to 199 and nine with 200 to 499.[80]

Table 10.27

Workers Currently Employed by Starting Date of Venture

(Firms Surveyed in Nanhai, Panyu, Quanzhou and Xiamen)

YEAR STARTED	FEWER THAN 200 WORKERS (per cent of firms)	500 OR MORE WORKERS (per cent of firms)	NUMBER OF FIRMS
1993	70	4	84
1992	61	19	80
1991	44	12	49
1986-90	40	24	164
1985 or Before	24	29	17

Table 10.27 suggests a strong relationship between numbers of workers employed and the age of a venture. The more recently established the foreign-invested venture, the smaller its workforce. High but variable proportions of surveyed ventures had plans to expand further in future: 46 per cent in Nanhai, 75 per cent in Panyu, 79 per cent in Quanzhou and 81 per cent in Xiamen.

The position of ethnic Chinese as the leading foreign investors in Jiangsu confirms their ability to expand their operations beyond their ancestral provinces. Their mode of operation, based on extending personalised networks, can be effective even when they do not have long established links to build upon. There are now at least 10 000 foreign-Chinese-owned companies operating in Jiangsu. A new manufacturing base is being established rapidly, further adding to their industrial and international trading capacity, and despite their very recent establishment, these companies show clear growth patterns. A significant number of companies have increased their workforces substantially and the number of small enterprises employing fewer than 50 workers has declined.

80 These figures do not, however, take account of the different duration available for growth in a sample within which many had only been established for a year or two.

Chapter 11

SOUTH-EAST ASIAN CHINESE INVESTMENT IN CHINA

The distance and the associated costs mean that most investment in China from South-East Asia comes from conglomerates, rather than from small and medium-sized firms. Most of these large companies establish a base in Hong Kong to manage their expansion into China. Hong Kong also is used to tap international capital markets. Thus, whilst the decision to invest might be made by South-East Asian Chinese, much of the funds invested may not derive from South-East Asia.

INVESTMENT IN CHINA FROM SELECTED SOUTH-EAST ASIAN COUNTRIES

Sino-Indonesian Investment in China

Very few Sino-Indonesians speak Mandarin. It is Indonesia's *totok* community that primarily has links to ethnic Chinese outside Indonesia and with China. Several Sino-Indonesian firms have invested significantly in China, raising funds in Hong Kong. Much of this investment is comparatively recent, particularly as Indonesia only re-established relations with China in 1990. Sino-Indonesian investment in China is a politically contentious issue in Indonesia and often goes either unreported or under-reported in the Indonesian media.

The significant Sino-Indonesian investors in China appear in Table 11.1.

Mochtar Riady is one of the biggest Sino-Indonesian investors in China. His Tati Group, a Lippo subsidiary, is reported to be planning to invest US$10 billion in China during the coming years. The destination for much of this will be near Putian, Riady's father's birthplace in Fujian Province, where Lippo's industrial and residential zone, Tati City, is underway and a 2 400 MW power plant has been constructed. Meizhou Island, near the planned Tati City, also is being developed into a residential and tourist zone. Funding for this is not likely to be sourced from Indonesia but from Hong Kong and China.[1] To date, Lippo has invested about US$1 billion in China. Lippo also is developing apartments, office complexes and hotels in Zuhai and Fujian worth US$500 million in cooperation with China Travel Services. Chung Po Investment Company was set up by the two joint venture partners to execute the projects.[2] Lippo also controls at least a 40 per cent share in Chinese Mercantile Bank.[3]

1 *Economic and Business Review Indonesia*, 'Indonesian-Chinese see prospects in "old country"' 13 August 1994.

2 'Indonesian-Chinese see prospects in "old country"'.

3 'Indonesian-Chinese see prospects in "old country"'.

Table 11.1

Significant Indonesian Investors in China[4]

INVESTOR	INVESTING IN	LOCATION
Mochtar Riady	- Industrial Park - Property - Banking - Cement Factory	- Fujian - Fujian - Meizhou - Beijing
Eka Tjipta Widjaja	- Pulp and Paper - Banking	- Guangdong - Ningbo
Liem Sioe Liong	- Cement Factory - Housing - Shoe Industry, Silk - Infrastructure - Bonded Zone	- Wuhan - Tianjin - Fujian - Fujian - Wuhan
Suhargo Gondokusumo	- Housing	- Fujian
Burhan Uray	- Agribusiness - Timber	

Liem Sioe Liong's Salim Group also is investing in China. Salim's China Pacific Group has invested in shoe, cooking oil, hotel and property interests. Liem also signed a contract with the Fujian Government to set up a company called Fujian Auto Industries. The company plans to produce at least 30 000 Suzuki Futura cars annually.[5] Liem also invests through a ten per cent share in a scheme that groups more than 30 Fujian descendants living overseas, known as the Fujian Clan.[6]

Sino-Philippines Investment in China

The bulk of Sino-Philippine investment is in small enterprises, largely in Fujian Province. Many of the more prosperous Chinese Filipinos have been prevailed upon by local government leaders in their 'home' villages in China to contribute to development there, something which also would serve to honour their ancestors.

As Chapter 3 described, the Ramos Administration is concerned at investment in China by the Philippines' Chinese. Consequently, he advised six of the Philippines' most successful ethnic Chinese businessmen to form a consortium to undertake infrastructure development in the Philippines.

4 *Economic and Business Review Indonesia*, 'China or Indonesia? The pros and the cons', 13 August 1994.

5 'Indonesian-Chinese see prospects in "old country"'.

6 'Indonesian-Chinese see prospects in "old country"'.

Sino-Lao Links to China

There is a relatively large Chinese Embassy in Vientiane. Border agreements between the two countries have been signed and high level visits are comparatively commonplace. The Chinese Embassy in Vientiane has sponsored at least three business delegations from China, with the participants mostly coming from Yunnan. There are now over twenty mainland Chinese companies represented in Vientiane. Trade between China and Laos is increasing rapidly, although from a low base. In 1993, two-way trade was worth an estimated US$40 million, with the balance strongly in China's favour. Unofficial border trade between Laos and China is estimated at US$10 million a year.

Malaysian Chinese Investment in China

For many years after Independence, Malaysia and China had an uneasy relationship. Malaysia did not permit its citizens to visit China; this constrained trade.

The relationship improved in 1985 when Malaysian Prime Minister Mahathir visited China. A bilateral trade agreement was concluded in 1988, and travel restrictions were lifted on Malaysians wishing to visit China. Dr Mahathir's high profile visit to China in mid 1993 signalled a maturing of the relationship. Dr Mahathir led a 283-strong delegation, including 143 business people, approximately 70 per cent of whom were Malaysian Chinese. Among those accompanying the Prime Minister were the Foreign Minister, the Minister for Primary Industries, the Minister for Transport, the Minister for Tourism, and the Chief Ministers of Penang, Pahang and Sarawak. Dr Mahathir met with Li Peng, Qiao Shi (Chairman of the National People's Congress), Jiang Zemin, Chinese business people, and provincial governors. Dr Mahathir returned from the trip saying that it was his best ever overseas trip. Outcomes of the visit included the signing of some thirty agreements and joint ventures. China and Malaysia also agreed to have at least twelve weekly direct flights between Kuala Lumpur to Beijing from 1995.

Deputy Prime Minister and Finance Minister Anwar Ibrahim led another business delegation to China in 1994 which promoted further trade and investment between the two countries.

Official figures on the level of Malaysian investment are difficult to obtain. However, a number of larger Malaysian companies, both Chinese and *bumiputera* controlled, either have invested in or are looking to invest in China. Both the Malaysian-Chinese controlled Berjaya and Genting Groups have invested in China. Malaysian investment interest has centred on the provinces of south-eastern China, particularly Guangdong and Fujian, where most Malaysian Chinese have their ancestral origins.

Malaysia's Hainanese have become significant investors in Hainan. The community has been energised since Hainan was declared a separate province from Guangdong and declared a Special Economic Zone in 1988. The Kuala Lumpur Hainanese formed a holding company for direct investment into Hainan and Penang's Hainanese organised business delegations to Hainan. The economic transformation of their ancestral province has revitalised Malaysia's Hainanese.

Importantly, Malaysian Airline System (MAS) has introduced direct flights between Penang and Hainan.

Most of Penang's majority Chinese community are Hokkien and approximately 80 per cent have their origins in the Fujian port city, Xiamen. There has been significant investment in Xiamen from Penang and this has been facilitated in part by two direct flights per week between the two cities. Penang and Xiamen also recently entered into a 'twinning' arrangement. The Penang Chinese Chamber of Commerce organises an annual trade mission to Xiamen and the annual Guangdong Trade Fair.

Each year Malaysia receives trade and business delegations from China. Many delegations go beyond Kuala Lumpur to make contact with their respective dialect groups. For example, the Penang Chinese Chamber of Commerce receives about thirty delegations a year from China, and increasingly delegations travel from China's Fuzhou district to Malaysia's Sibu and Kuching, where there are sizeable Fuzhou populations.

Like the Singaporeans, Malaysian Chinese prefer to invest in and trade with those parts of China that are relatively developed.

Sino-Burmese Links to China

One of the first acts of the State Law and Order Restoration Council (SLORC) was to sign a border trade agreement with the vice-governor of China's Yunnan Province. Twenty-three items still are prohibited from being privately traded across the border. They include rice, tea, oil, gems, arms and narcotics.[7] Since 1989, the border trade, (including items prohibited from trade) has been worth in excess of US$1 billion annually. This trade has been assisted by joint Myanmar-China efforts to improve roads in the border areas.[8]

Mainland Chinese, especially those living in Yunnan Province, also are becoming significant investors in Myanmar, particularly in Mandalay and Lashio. Local Chinese buy property on behalf of the mainland Chinese.

Although Taiwan has a majority Hokkien population, there are almost no links between the Yangon-based Hokkien and Hokkien-dominated Taiwan. There is little direct investment from Taiwan in Myanmar and little trade between the two. Myanmar has not recognised Taiwan and actively discourages any dealings with Taiwan.

---

7 Chinese beer is a prohibited import, but is openly available all over upper Myanmar, usually from restaurants owned by ethnic Chinese.

8 See Mya Maung, 'On the road to Mandalay', *Asian Survey*, May 1994.

Singapore's Investment in China

Singapore increasingly is investing in China. In 1993, for example, around half of the offshore investment projects that Singapore's Economic Development Board assisted in were in China.[9] However, despite 77 per cent of its population being Chinese, Singapore's ancestral family ties and other links to China are fast diminishing. For Singaporean Chinese, their ethnic Chinese origins might still be a useful 'door opener' in China but not their ancestral provincial origins. This is largely as a result of the growing Westernisation of Singapore and the Singapore Government's Speak Mandarin campaign which tends to displace regional dialect skills.

Table 11.2

Recent Singaporean Joint Ventures in China

(Distribution by Province[10])

PROVINCE	NUMBER OF JOINT VENTURES	PROPORTION OF TOTAL (per cent)
Jiangsu/Shanghai	120	30.4
Hebei/Beijing	58	14.7
Guangdong	56	14.2
Fujian	39	9.9
Shandong	37	9.4
Sichuan	24	6.1
Zheijiang	10	2.5
Yunnan	8	2.0
Liaoning	8	2.0
Guangxi	6	1.5
Anhui	5	1.3
Henan	5	1.3
Hainan	4	1.0
Hubei	4	1.0
Heilongjiang	2	0.5
Jiangxi	2	0.5
Guizhou	2	0.5
Shanxi	2	0.5
Shaanxi	1	0.3
Jilin	1	0.3
Hunan	1	0.3

9 See *The Economist*, 'Singapore: Giant Leaps', 2 April 1994. Singapore also receives many business delegations from China each year. In 1993, for example, at least 140 such delegations were received.

10 This table has been compiled from non-published information prepared by the Research Department of the Singapore Chinese Chamber of Commerce and Industry. The Chamber compiled the information from public announcements. Thus, numbers are likely to be underestimated and biased in favour of large companies and publicly-listed ones. Nonetheless, the data demonstrate the relative importance of the various provinces insofar as Singaporean investment in China is concerned.

For many Singaporeans who are used to the comforts of modern Singapore and its highly structured business environment, doing business outside the major urban areas in China is difficult, regardless of ancestral origins.[11] These days, the links with China that matter for investment purposes tend to be politically rather than clan based, a result of the groundwork laid by senior Singaporean ministers in China. These factors are borne out in the distribution of Singapore's investments in China.

As Table 11.2 shows, despite 80 per cent of Singapore's Chinese having ancestral origins in either Guangdong or Fujian Provinces, only 24.1 per cent of recently announced projects are in either province. Very few Singaporeans have ancestral origins in Jiangsu or Hebei Provinces and yet 45.1 per cent of recent projects are there. Thus, Singapore might well be a 'gateway to China' for Western investors, but the means of access will usually not be traditional Chinese networks.

The Singapore Government has undertaken a series of measures to make operating in China easier for Singaporeans. It is attempting to export 'soft infrastructure' to China so that Singaporean investors in China will find familiar legal, financial and administrative arrangements there. The government-linked Development Bank of Singapore (DBS) established a representative office in Beijing in March 1993 which it hopes to upgrade to a branch. DBS Securities also has been accredited as a foreign securities agent and international underwriter for 'B' shares on the Shanghai Stock Exchange and is planning for the same status on the Shenzhen Stock Exchange.[12] Singapore Airlines also is increasing the number of direct flight destinations it has in China.

Furthermore, Singapore's biggest undertaking abroad, the Singapore-Suzhou Industrial Township, which will feature a residential and industrial park, will be constructed employing Singaporean-style public administration and other 'soft infrastructure'. The Singapore taxi company NTUC Comfort also will operate in Suzhou. Thus, when Singaporeans go to invest in Suzhou, they will be able to fly to Shanghai on Singapore Airlines, get a Singapore NTUC taxi out to the township and do business in a Singaporean business environment. Clearly, this is a long way from using clans to invest in China.

---

11 One group of Singaporeans is thriving in the China trade business, graduates from the now closed, Chinese-languauge Nanyang University, who in the past were on the outer in English-speaking Singapore. Their language proficiency is increasingly attracting a premium as Singapore seeks closer economic relations with China.

12 Information provided by the Research Department of the Singapore Chinese Chamber of Commerce and Industry.

The Singapore-Suzhou Industrial Township

Singapore plans to build an industrial park at Suzhou, near Shanghai. The Singapore-Suzhou Industrial Township will accommodate 600 000 residents and provide 360 000 jobs. The Singapore Government will provide S$2.5 million seeding money annually, and a consortium of nineteen Singaporean companies will spend an additional S$318 million.[13]

The Township will take 10-15 years to complete and will be the biggest foreign venture that Singapore has undertaken. The 70 square kilometre site will be held under a fifty-year lease. Once the Township is developed fully, it is expected to attract US$20 billion in investment. Land preparation and infrastructure development for the first two square kilometres should cost around US$100 million.[14]

The Mayor of Suzhou is relatively young and a Harvard graduate. Several interviewees in Singapore cited this as an important factor in Singapore's decision to set up near Suzhou: the mutual empathy between the mayor and the Singaporeans helped facilitate the process.

Sino-Thai Investment in China

Sino-Thais are among some of the biggest foreign investors in China. The Sino-Thai Charoen Pokphand (CP) Group is possibly the largest foreign investor in China to date. It operates around 30 animal-feed mills across China; produces five million day-old chicks a week; and is China's second biggest motorcycle dealer. It also is investing in a US$1 billion real estate development in Pudong, Shanghai's main economic zone.[15] In 1992, CP derived revenues of US$500 million from China.[16] Bangkok Bank, the Pornpat Group, and companies controlled by the Srifeungfung family also are present in China.

Thailand's Government strongly promotes investment links with China. In a move which will capitalise on the significant Yunnanese Chinese community in Thailand, especially in the northern provinces, it recently established a consulate and commercial office in Kunming, the provincial capital of Yunnan. Furthermore, former Prime Minister Chuan Leekpai led a large, official Thai business delegation to China in 1993.

13 See *The Economist*, 'Singapore: Giant Leaps', 2 April 1994.

14 See Singapore-Suzhou Township Development Pte Ltd, *Singapore-Suzhou Township*, (promotional brochure).

15 See *Business Review Weekly*, 'China without boundaries', 25 July 1994.

16 *Time*, 'The secret weapon', 10 May 1994.

There is some Sino-Thai investment in Shantou, the ancestral home of most of Thailand's ethnic Chinese. To capitalise on the investment and trade flow between Bangkok and Shantou, Bangkok Bank has opened an office in Shantou. One Sino-Thai group recently was awarded the right to construct and operate a pulp and paper project near Shantou, representing a commitment of as much as US$1 billion.[17]

Case Study: China Strategic Holdings

China Strategic Holdings (CSH)[18] provides a good example of how connections in China can be used successfully to expand business. The company has invested using the connections of the chairman and birthplace connections of his father. The strength of the connections has become a marketing tool for the company's shares on various stock markets around the world.

China Strategic Holdings

(CSH, based in Hong Kong)

Major Shareholders: Sanion Enterprises (35.7 per cent). Oei Hong Leong owns 70 per cent of Sanion. Cheung Kong (headed by Li Ka-shing) is also a shareholder.

Chairman: Oei Hong Leong.

Executive Director: Sukmawati Widjaja (sister of Oei Hong Leong).

Market Capitalisation, 1994: US$256 million.

Main CSH Companies: China Strategic Holdings; China Tyre Holdings; China Industrial Management Holdings (CIML); Hangzhou Zhongce Rubber; Double Happiness Tire Industries.

Main activities: A holding company for investment and management in China of varied manufacturing and processing operations.

Main areas of activity: Hong Kong, China, Singapore.

The chairman of CSH is Oei Hong Leong, son of Eka Tjipta Widjaja, the Sino-Indonesian founder of Indonesia's Sinar Mas conglomerate. Oei was sent to China for his education, but was sent to the countryside during the Cultural Revolution. After leaving China, he went to Singapore where he transformed

....

17 See *Australian Business Monthly*, 'Chinese on the rebound', March 1993.

18 *Asiaweek*, 24 August 1994; *China Trade Report*, May 1993, p. 12; *Dun's Asia Pacific Key Business Enterprises*, 1993/4; *Corporate International's Company Handbook*, Hong Kong (various issues); *Far Eastern Economic Review*, various issues; *Forbes Magazine*, 18 July 1994; *South China Morning Post*, various issues; *South China Morning Post International Weekly*, various issues, including 'Oei laments 'slow' mainland payments', 29 October 1994; *Straits Times Weekly*, 6 March 1993; *Asia Today*, 'Sinar Mas: Building a global empire in agribusiness, finance', May 1994; *Asian Wall Street Journal*, 'Oei's China Strategic hits some snags on mainland', 24 November 1994, and 'China Strategic Holdings Ltd', 28 November 1994.

United Industrial Corporation (UIC) into a prominent and diversified group. In 1991, Oei's stake in UIC was sold to Indonesia's Salim Group and Oei left for Hong Kong where he acquired control of Ruby Holdings which was later renamed China Strategic Holdings. CSH now is a significant investor in China.

The Widjaja family in Indonesia has a stake in CSH, as does Li Ka-shing. Oei also acquired a stake in Singapore's Singapore Causeway Investment.

In China, Oei concentrated on investing in state-owned enterprises using extensive contacts he built up among top officials, some of which were made in the countryside during the Cultural Revolution. CSH now controls more than eighty companies in China, representing an outlay of approximately US$400 million. Some of CSH's stakes in enterprises have been floated on stock exchanges in New York and Singapore (majority voting rights are usually retained). Like many other direct investors in China, Oei acquires assets cheaply, reorganises and then floats them in a public offering. In Ningbo (Zhejiang Province) he took control of a pulp and paper mill in 1992 for US$25 million and will invest US$1 billion in it by 1996, which will make it China's largest paper factory. He bought a 51 per cent stake in the Hangzhou Zhongce Rubber Factory, already Zhejiang's biggest foreign currency earner and subsequently granted the company a US$9 million interest free loan to finance expansion and new equipment. Oei raised more capital by floating China Tire Holdings, the holding company for his two China tyre joint-ventures, Hangzhou Rubber and Double Happiness, on the New York Stock Exchange in 1993. China Tire Holdings is the second largest producer of motor-vehicle tyres and the third largest of motor-cycle tyres in China.

In 1993, Oei's China Industrial Management Holdings (CIML) took a 60 per cent stake in 41 of the 42 state enterprises in Quanzhou (Fujian).[19] These interests include pharmaceuticals, dairy products, televisions, textiles, garments and machinery and a brewery; in total these employ 20 000 workers. CIML will contribute substantial investment funds and assume management of the enterprises. Also, Oei has set up a joint venture to take control of 14 state-owned salt companies in Shanxi, where he was sent during the Cultural Revolution.

In August 1994, China Strategic Holdings announced one of its most ambitious projects to date: a partnership with US-based Customs Coal to lead a consortium to build an 800 kilometre coal slurry pipeline linking Shanxi with coastal Shandong Province. China is already the world's leading coal producer but its major coalfields are distant from the booming coastal provinces where energy needs and shortages are acute. Transport infrastructure is unable to economically get coal to the areas of greatest need and some coastal provinces, notably Guangdong, find it cheaper to import coal from abroad. When it is completed in 1997, the pipeline will carry 15 million tonnes of coal slurry a year to ports in Shandong Province. The total investment is projected at US$889 million.

CSH's expansion in China has been rapid. Because of this rapidity and the shortage of experienced managers with Chinese language abilities who will agree to live and work in China, it has recruited from Chinese communities around the world, including from Australia.

[19] Quanzhou is Oei's father's birthplace.

Chapter 12

THE NETWORKS AND WESTERN BUSINESS AT HOME AND ABROAD

LINKING UP WITH OUTSIDERS AT HOME

Across much of Asia, prominent ethnic Chinese business people in wholesale and retail trades control a web of distribution networks. Many business people from outside Asia have been able to link up with ethnic Chinese entrepreneurs to access these networks. Local ethnic Chinese entrepreneurs often use such links with Western and Japanese partners to access cheaply new technology and foreign capital.

Whilst, in many instances an alliance with ethnic Chinese entrepreneurs can supply good commercial know how for outsiders seeking to do business in Asia and access to ethnic Chinese networks, linkages with local, indigenous entrepreneurs may also be useful. The ethnic Chinese can supply the commercial connections but indigenous Indonesians, Malaysians, and so on, often can supply superior connections to the local bureaucracy and political elite, so that foreign companies going into South-East Asia may find it an advantage to have both local ethnic Chinese and indigenous business people as partners.

Ethnic Chinese Entrepreneurs' Links with the Japanese

Post WWII Linkages

Since World War II, Japanese manufacturers have linked up with ethnic Chinese entrepreneurs in South-East Asia, seemingly on the premise that the Japanese have the industrial know how, while the region's ethnic Chinese business people, through their transnational links, have the distribution capability. The linking up of Japanese car makers with ethnic Chinese entrepreneurs to distribute Japanese made cars, motor-cycles and trucks and their components across South-East Asia has been particularly systematic. At one time or another:

- Malaysian entrepreneur Loh Boon Siew was the distributor for Honda motorcycles in Malaysia. His Kah Motor Company was also the Malaysian distributor for Honda passenger motor vehicles.[1]

....

1 See Ch'ng, D., *The Overseas Chinese Entrepreneurs in East Asia: Background, Business Practices and International Networks*, CEDA Monograph M100, 1993.

- Sino-Thai Thaworn Phornprapha's Siam Motors was the distributor of Nissan passenger cars and trucks.[2]
- The Sino-Indonesian Astra Group was the Indonesian distributor for Toyota, Honda (motorcycles) and Daihatsu vehicles.[3]
- The Indonesian Krama Yudha Group was the sole agent for Mitsubishi vehicles in Indonesia.[4]
- The Sino-Indonesian Imora Group was the sole Indonesian agent for Honda passenger cars.[5]
- The Sino-Indonesian Salim Group was the distributor for Mazda passenger cars, Suzuki motorcycles and four wheeled vehicles (commercial vehicles and passenger cars), and Nissan passenger cars.[6]

Two other examples of Japanese manufacturers using South-East Asian ethnic Chinese distribution networks for non-automotive products are:

- Sino-Thai Mongkul Kanjanapas' Thong Sia Company has held the franchise for the distribution of Japan's Seiko watches in South-East Asia since the 1950s.
- A Salim Group controlled company, PT Citra Caraka, is the sole agent and distributor in Indonesia for Japan's NEC Computers.

Increasingly, Japanese manufacturers have linked up with ethnic Chinese entrepreneurs to produce goods outside Japan. Around 90 per cent of the private sector joint ventures Japanese interests now have in South-East Asia are with local ethnic Chinese.[7] In the past, such joint ventures allowed Japanese manufacturers to avoid South-East Asia's high tariff barriers by manufacturing locally, but increasingly, Japanese manufacturers seek to avoid relatively high labour costs in Japan, with Japanese capital and technology transfer being the attraction for the ethnic Chinese. Examples of such joint ventures include:[8]

- Textile ventures in Thailand between the Sino-Thai Bodhiratanangkura family and Japan's Shikishima Spinning and Nomura Trading during the 1950s and 1960s.
- Retail ventures in Thailand between the Sino-Thai Saha Group and the Japanese retailers Isetan and Yaohan.

2 See Ch'ng, D.

3 See Ch'ng, D.; and Sato, Y., 'The Salim Group in Indonesia: The development and behaviour of the largest conglomerate in Southeast Asia', in *The Developing Economies*, December 1993.

4 See Sato, Y.

5 See Sato, Y.

6 See Sato, Y.

7 See Business Review Southeast Asia, *Southeast Asia Business Omnibook*, Options Publishing, 1995, p. 493.

8 See Ch'ng, D.; *Far Eastern Economic Review*, 'Lodes of land', 22 November 1990; and *Asian Wall Street Journal*, 'Lippo Industries to set up circuit-board plant', 10 October 1994.

- Thailand's Union Yoshida Industries, a zip fastener manufacturing venture between the Sino-Thai entrepreneurs Thiam Chokwatana and Damri Darakananda, and Japan's Yoshida Kogyo.
- A household electrical appliances venture in Taiwan between Taiwan's Tatung Group and a Japanese partner.
- Chemicals and glass ventures in Thailand between the Sino-Thai Srifeungfung family and Japan's Asahai Group.
- Glass ventures in Indonesia between the Sino-Indonesian Roda Mas Group and Japanese interests.
- A printed circuit boards venture in Indonesia between the Sino-Indonesian PT Lippo Industries and Japan's Mitsubishi Corporation and Kyosha Co.

The process of linking up with ethnic Chinese in the region is receiving renewed institutional backing in Japan. The Osaka Foreign Trade Association plans conferences with Chinese groups in Hong Kong, Taiwan and Singapore. The association includes approximately 300 companies, including Matsushita Electric Industrial Co., Sanyo Electric Co., Toyota Motor Corporation and Mitsui and Co.[9] The association met with the Hong Kong General Chinese Chamber of Commerce during October 1994, and a similar meeting is planned with the Singapore Chinese Chamber of Commerce and Industry for 1995. The plan is to forge close links to Chinese chambers in East Asia, and provide a more formal framework for Japanese companies to link up with ethnic Chinese business.

Linkages Between the West and Ethnic Chinese Networks

Increasingly, Western firms recognise the benefits of establishing joint ventures with ethnic Chinese entrepreneurs in Asia to either develop their business interests in South-East Asia or to access the China market.

A recent example is an agreement between the large US retail chain Walmart Stores Ltd and Thailand's Charoen Pokphand (CP) Group to open a chain of discount stores in China.[10] The two also have a joint venture, Wal-Mart Ek Chor Hong Kong Co., for stores in Hong Kong.[11] CP is an ideal partner for Walmart, as it is well connected in China and is already one of the largest single foreign investors there. It also has some retail experience, being the franchisee for 7-Eleven convenience stores in Thailand. In another pairing with an ethnic Chinese business group, Walmart engaged Pacific Region Export Ltd, a subsidiary of the Sino-Indonesian Salim Group, to act as a purchasing agent for Walmart Stores in Asia.[12]

9 *The Nikkei Weekly*, 'Osaka groups seek overseas Chinese ties', 30 May 1994.

10 See *Far Eastern Economic Review*, 'Business briefing', 28 July 1994; and *Asian Wall Street Journal*, 'C.P. Pokphand Co.', 17 October 1994.

11 To date, three such stores have been opened, trading as the Value Club chain.

12 See Salim Group, *An Overview of the Salim Group*, Jakarta, 1993, p. 36.

Other Western firms to link up with CP include the Dutch Heineken Company (to operate a brewery in China), and the Dutch Makro Holding NV (to invest jointly in two China-based consumer goods manufacturers).[13]

Western firms have also linked up with ethnic Chinese interests in their expansion to South-East Asia. In November 1994, the giant US K Mart Corporation signed a letter of intent with Indonesia's PT Multipolar Corporation, a subsidiary of the Sino-Indonesian Lippo Group. Multipolar will operate K Mart stores under licence in Indonesia. This is not the first time a Western firm has used Multipolar as a distributor across Indonesia. In the past, IBM and Multipolar teamed up to sell IBM's computer applications to Indonesia's emerging banking sector.[14] In a similar fashion, the US-owned Southern Pacific Hotels Corporation (SPHC) has signed an agreement with Sino-Indonesian company PT Jan Darmadi Corporation to establish up to twenty new hotels across Indonesia. Most of the hotels will be in the budget category through SPHC's Travel Court chain.[15] Increasingly, Australian companies are linking up with ethnic Chinese business people in Asia. This is analysed in Chapter 13.

THE EXPANSION OF ETHNIC CHINESE BUSINESS BEYOND ASIA

Ethnic Chinese business people are often able to triumph where others fail. Connections and networks are used to do business in markets where institutions such as legal frameworks and property rights are underdeveloped. Outsiders not used to doing business in such unstructured environments usually find themselves at a competitive disadvantage. Similarly, many ethnic Chinese entrepreneurs face difficulties in adjusting to markets which are highly structured, such as those in the West.

To date, attempts by ethnic Chinese business people to expand their interests outside Asia have met with mixed success. Real estate remains the main and safest target for investment.[16] It is relatively secure and simple to administer.[17] Investments in other areas have led to some high profile failures.

Recent Acquisitions in the West

Currently, the major drawcard for ethnic Chinese international investment is China. Those ethnic Chinese entrepreneurs seeking to invest outside Asia tend to be those with poor or no connections in China; those seeking to diversify away

13 See *The Economist*, 'A bruiser from Bangkok', 26 November 1994; and *Business Review Southeast Asia*, 'CP Group', 16 November 1994.

14 See *Australian Financial Review*, 'Kmart in fast run at Indonesia', 30 November 1994.

15 See *The Australian*, 'SPHC plans 20 hotels in Indonesia', 15 November 1994.

16 In early 1995, for example, Singaporean Kwek Leng Beng's CDL Hotels International and a Saudi partner acquired a controlling stake in New York's Plaza Hotel, which was formerly controlled by US property investor Donald Trump. (See *Straits Times Weekly Edition*, 'CDL and Saudi prince reach agreement to take over Plaza Hotel', 15 April 1995.)

17 Chapter 13 details the real estate acquisitions in Australia made by ethnic Chinese investors in recent years.

from China; or those used to operating in highly structured business environments such as Singapore and increasingly, Malaysia. There is little investment of significance in the West from ethnic Chinese investors outside these groups.

A desire to diversify away from China has created some considerable investment in the West, particularly from the Hong Kong Chinese in Canada. The investment is facilitated by Hong Kong Chinese now living in Canada. In 1991, an estimated 35 000 to 40 000 Hong Kong Chinese residing in Hong Kong were actually Canadian citizens.[18] Perhaps the largest single Hong Kong Chinese investor in Canada is Li Ka-shing's Hutchison Whampoa Group. Li's son, Victor Li, has Canadian citizenship. In 1987, Li began a five-year acquisition plan for a major Canadian oil company, Husky Oil. In 1991, Li Ka-shing's total Canadian investment was an estimated US$800 million.[19] The group also owns Felixtowe, Britain's largest container terminal, bought in 1991, and the communications division of British Aerospace.

Another senior Hong Kong entrepreneur, Sir Run Run Shaw, is now the largest shareholder in the US retailer R.H. Macey and Co.[20]

Dickson Concepts, an emerging Hong Kong company attracted considerable interest when it acquired ST Du Pont of France in 1987 and Harvey Nichols, one of Britain's oldest department stores, in 1991. In Thailand, GSS Electronics, an electronic components maker, acquired Array Technology based in Silicon Valley in the United States, in 1990. By securing a marketing base in the United States, the company's sales have grown rapidly. In December 1992, Christiani & Nielsen (Thailand) announced it would buy out its parent company Christiani & Nielsen A/S. The acquisition by an Asian subsidiary of its European parent was seen as symbolic at the time.[21] Table 12.1 summarises these acquisitions.

Another important acquisition in the West was the controlling interest in the Dutch distribution company Hagemeyer NV by Hong Kong-based First Pacific, which is controlled by the Sino-Indonesian Salim Group. Hagemeyer has a US$2 billion annual turnover and operates in 21 countries.

Ethnic Chinese interests are making a small inroad into the Japanese market. In March 1992, the Li Ka-shing, Robert Kuok and Japanese Yaohan Groups announced plans to construct a shopping centre, condominiums and a theme park on a 700 000 square metre site in Sapporo on Japan's northern Hokkaido Island. Phase one of the project, due for completion in 1995, will cost around US$910 million.[22]

---

18 Ai, L.C., 'When many are fleeing Hong Kong, others are finding it's profitable to go back', *The Wall Street Journal*, 24 January 1992, in Kotkin, J., *Tribes*, Random House, New York, 1993, p. 183.

19 See Sender, H., 'Inside the overseas Chinese network', *Institutional Investor*, August 1991, p. 34.

20 See Sender, H., 'Inside the overseas Chinese network', p. 34.

21 See Yamaguchi, M., 'The Emerging Chinese Business Sphere', Nomura Asian Perspectives, Nomura Research Institute, July 1993.

22 See Yamaguchi, M. The Japanese chairman of Yaohan is based in Hong Kong.

Table 12.1

Some Recent Major Mergers and Acquisitions in the West Using Ethnic Chinese Capital from Asia

ETHNIC CHINESE COMPANY	YEAR ANNOUNCED	TARGETED COMPANIES	COUNTRY	MAIN BUSINESS	CONSIDERATION (US$M)
Hong Kong					
Hutchison Whampoa	1991	Felixtowe	UK	Port	125
	1991	Microtell	UK	Telecomm-unications	n.a.
	1991	Husky Oil	Canada	Mining	n.a.
Semitech-Global	1991	Sansui Electric	Japan	Electronics	n.a
Dickson Concept	1991	Harvey Nichols	UK	Retail	93
Thailand					
GSS Electronics	1992	Array Technology	United States	Electronics	30
Christiani & Nielsen	1992	Christiani & Nielsen A/S	Denmark	Construction	80

Source: based on a table in Yamaguchi, M., 'The Emerging Chinese Business Sphere', *Nomura Asian Perspectives,* Nomura Research Institute, July 1993, p. 5.

Problems in Diversifying Away from Asia

Generally, ethnic Chinese entrepreneurs investing in the more mature economies of the West can expect lower rates of return than they are used to at home. In recent years, however, some ethnic Chinese entrepreneurial forays to the West have gone awry.

The Hong Kong-based New World Development's US$538 million takeover of Ramada Inns in 1989 at the peak of the US property market is widely regarded as a flop, as is Thailand's Unicord Company US$285 million buy-out of US tuna packager Bumble Bee Seafoods. In both instances the ethnic Chinese buyer 'overpaid and underestimated the difficulty of the American market.'[23] The Ramada Inns (since renamed the Renaissance Hotels and Resorts) made a loss each year until they broke even at the end of 1994.[24] Unicord sold Bumble Bee Seafoods to a group of US investors for US$155 million in March 1995.[25]

In 1989, Singapore's large food and beverage manufacturer, Yeo Hiap Seng Ltd, acquired, for US$52 million, a controlling stake in the Chun King Corporation of the United States and Canada, a manufacturer and distributor of pre-prepared

23 *Business Week*, 'The Chinese Dealmakers of Southeast Asia', 11 November 1991.

24 See *Far Eastern Economic Review*, 'Outward bound', 21 July 1994.

25 See *Far Eastern Economic Review*, 'Business briefing', 2 March 1995.

Chinese food. Chun King lost US$170,000 in 1990, US$4.1 million in 1991 and recorded losses in each subsequent year that Yeo Hiap Seng was the controlling shareholder. In 1994, the decision was made to sell Chun King and a S$31 million write-off was made for the company.[26] Yeo Hiap Seng's stake in Chun King was sold eventually, but only after unexpectedly protracted negotiations which led to higher than expected losses for the group. Cumulative losses from the acquisition contributed to the turmoil, referred to in Chapter 7, among members of the controlling Yeo family.

Generally, ethnic Chinese-controlled firms investing in the West face unfamiliar business environments. In the West, market information tends to be distributed more evenly than in the developing markets in Asia, and fewer market niches can be accessed through connections and networks. In such an environment, the way ethnic Chinese business people have traditionally done business provides them with little comparative advantage and may often be a hindrance.[27]

Just as Westerners are often well-advised to seek local partners in much of Asia to help them get around the vagaries of 'know who' business, ethnic Chinese business people similarly can benefit by seeking local partners for their investments in the West.

26 See *Asian Wall Street Journal*, 'Team at the top enhances Yeo Hiap Seng', 30 September 1994.

27 Acknowledgment of this has induced at least one Hong Kong-based securities group to invest in particular stocks on Asian bourses because they were unlikely to invest in the West and more likely to restrict their investments to the Asian region. (See Marco Polo Pacific Dynasty Fund, Hong Kong, prospectus summary.)

Chapter 13

AUSTRALIA AND THE NETWORKS

Many of Asia's ethnic Chinese business people are familiar with Australia from visits for vacations, medical treatment, and most importantly, education. Mochtar Riady's son James, who is now the CEO of the family's Lippobank was educated at the University of Melbourne.[1] Tedy Djuhar, the son of 'Liem Investor' Djuhar Sutanto, was educated at the University of New England.[2] Chote Sophonpanich, the third son of Chin Sophonpanich and until recently, a senior vice-president of Bangkok Bank, graduated in economics from the University of Sydney.[3] Malaysian Low Yow Chuan was educated in Australia at a secondary and tertiary level. His Low Yat Group is now a major property investor in Australia.[4] Geelong Grammar is the alma mater for many prominent South-East Asian Chinese, including two of Robert Kuok's sons.

Malaysian and Bruneian Chinese Alumni Links with Australia

Malaysia and Australia have particularly strong links, a result of thousands of Malaysian students attending Australian tertiary institutions. Malaysian Chinese constitute the majority of Malaysian students in Australia - around 10 000 per annum at present - and a significant proportion of the Australian alumni. Similarly, they make up a large proportion of the estimated 100 000 Malaysians who hold Australian permanent resident status. These people cross cultures. They are Malaysian; they are ethnically Chinese; and they are familiar with Australia, a useful attribute for doing business in Australia or with Australians. Many of the members of the Kuala Lumpur-based Malaysia-Australia Business Council (MABC) were educated in Australia, including the Council's vice chairman, Bill Chin.

Since many of Brunei's Chinese do not have citizenship status they cannot attend Universiti Brunei Darussalam. Consequently, many Bruneian ethnic Chinese leave Brunei to continue their tertiary studies and comprise the majority of

1 The links the Riady family has with Australia are apparent in the naming of some Hong Kong companies associated with it. Many have been named after Queensland towns, for example, Kingaroy Ltd, Emerald Ltd, Nerang Ltd, Ipswich Ltd, Hughendon Ltd, Longreach Ltd, and Rockhampton Ltd. (See Allen, N., *Allied Group Limited, Allied Properties (HK) Limited, Crusader Holdings Limited, Paragon Holdings Limited, Wai Yick Limited: Investigation under S.143 (1)(c) of the Companies Ordinance, Chapter 32 of the Laws of Hong Kong*, Abridged Version, Vol. 1, Office of the Financial Secretary, Hong Kong, 1993.)

2 See Ch'ng, D., *The Overseas Chinese Entrepreneurs in East Asia: Background, Business Practices and International Networks*, CEDA Monograph M100, 1993; *Asiaweek*, 'Hard choice: A China push raises questions in Jakarta', 4 May 1994; and Pusat Data Business Indonesia, *Conglomeration Indonesia*, 2nd edition, Jakarta, 1995.

3 See Ch'ng, D.

4 *Australian Financial Review*, 'Low Yow Chuan comes back to Sydney business', 29 April 1994.

private students coming from Brunei to Australia to study. Like the Malaysian Chinese, many of these Bruneian students and former students are culturally empathetic with Australia.

INVESTMENT IN REAL ESTATE

To a large extent, ethnic Chinese business people currently tend to import rather than create wealth in Australia. In the last three years, hundreds of millions of dollars worth of direct foreign investment has come into Australia from ethnic Chinese business people in Asia, mostly from Singapore, Malaysia, Hong Kong, Taiwan, and Indonesia.[5] Many ethnic Chinese business people favour investment in real estate, preferably in a stable political environment such as Singapore and increasingly, Australia. (See the Annex at the end of this chapter for a list of some recent acquisitions.)

Among the biggest recent property investors in Australia have been Malaysian and Singaporean Chinese and much of their investment is 'network investment'. Many have been assisted by sons, daughters and other relatives who are located in Australia, often for tertiary education, who have been able to look for the real estate purchases. One example is the Ho Brothers. One brother Ho Whye Chung lives in Singapore, and the other brother, Ho Whye Tong, lives in Australia permitting him to search for attractively priced property. Through this partnership, the brothers acquired Brisbane's MLC complex in December 1992 for A$55 million and Queensland's Palm Cove Travelodge resort in April 1993 for A$22 million.[6]

As Japanese investors pull out, and incur massive losses, having bought at the height of the property boom, ethnic Chinese investors from Asia have been buying into Australian real estate at relatively low prices. Unlike many of the ethnic Chinese investors, the Japanese do not have the extensive family and other connections to Australia in which sound investment advice relating to local economic conditions can be internalised.

The use of family and other networks to facilitate the investment is suggested by the pattern of acquisitions around Australia. Many significant purchases by Malaysian investors are in Melbourne where there is a sizeable Malaysian Chinese community. Much of the investment from Taiwan is in Brisbane real estate where there is a significant Taiwanese community, and Indonesians appear to favour Perth property where there is a sizeable Sino-Indonesian community.

5 China also has made some significant investments. For example, CITIC Shenzhen Company acquired the Chateau Melbourne Hotel in early 1994 for approximately A$12 million. (See *Australian Financial Review*, 'Chinese buy the Chateau Melbourne', 13 April 1994.)

6 See *The Australian*, 'Singapore investor in $41m splurge', 7 April 1994.

OTHER INVESTMENT

Apart from real estate other types of investments are beginning to attract some interest. Such investment comes largely from Singaporean business people, possibly because they are at ease with the relatively highly structured corporate environment in Australia.

Two notable recent examples were Jack Chia's takeover of the Players Biscuits Group and Ong Beng Seng's acquisition of music store chain Brashs.

The Takeover of Players Biscuits

In 1994, Singaporean-based entrepreneur Jack Chia, through his Jack Chia-MPH Ltd, gained control of Australian biscuit company, the Players Group Ltd, after a protracted takeover battle.[7] Chia's stake represents an investment of approximately A$20 million. Chia intends expanding Players' export sales to Japan, Korea and possibly China. The takeover was achieved when Players' founder sold his stake citing that Players needed someone like Chia to promote the company's products throughout Asia. In Australia, Jack Chia-MPH Ltd also controls the Melbourne-based Dollar Sweets confectionary manufacturer and Long Homes Ltd.

The Acquisition of Brashs

Singaporean Ong Beng Seng emerged, in 1994, as the owner of Australia's Brash Holdings, whose main asset is the Brashs record and hi-fi chain. Ong paid A$40 million for the chain which has an annual turnover of approximately A$500 million.[8] Typical of decision-making in many ethnic Chinese firms, Ong's decision to buy Brashs 'left bystanders stunned by its speed.'[9] He has since brought Singaporean staff into the head office, off-loaded whitegoods lines and introduced more of a customer service culture. Ong is building a regional conglomerate based on lifestyle industries. In Australia, he also owns hotels and the Australian licence to distribute Hyundai vehicles.

7 See *Australian Financial Review*, 'Chia bid a typical stunt: Player', 4 May 1994; *The Australian*, 'Players, Lane unveil merger to block Chia, 11 July 1994; *The Australian*, 'Chia withdraws conditions on bid', 20 July 1994; *Australian Financial Review*, 'Chia takes the biscuit after Player sells out', 31 August 1994; and *The Australian*, Chia-MPH finally takes the biscuit', 18 October 1994.

8 See *Australian Financial Review*, 'Singapore developer emerges as preferred buyer for Brash', 23 June 1994.

9 See *The Straits Times*, 'Ong Beng Seng's Brash swoop stuns observers, angers lobbyists', 24 June 1994.

Australia's investment climate has also attracted the Sino-Indonesian Gemala Group. In 1988, it acquired Century Batteries, a battery manufacturer in Brisbane which now is the second largest battery producer in Australia.[10] The *peranakan* Wanandi family control the Gemala Group. Since many Indonesian *peranakan* Chinese cannot speak or read Chinese and are relatively cut-off from ethnic Chinese networks, they find it easier to expand to the West than to China.

Sino-Indonesian interests also acquired the Australian computer firm Imagineering Technology Ltd, which was subsequently renamed Tech Pacific Australia Pty Ltd. It is now Australasia's largest independent distributor of microcomputer software, hardware and related equipment. The firm was acquired by the First Pacific Group, which is Hong Kong-based but controlled by Indonesia's Liem Sioe Liong.[11]

As part of a wider regional trend, many ethnic Chinese controlled companies are tending to list on more than one stock exchange. Subsequently, the Australian Stock Exchange (ASX) has seen several 'backdoor' listings by ethnic Chinese companies, perhaps as part of a strategy to diversify political risk and to draw on multiple sources of capital. Ten Asian listings are on the ASX: several of these are subsidiaries of mainland China enterprises; and others are controlled by ethnic Chinese, mainly from Hong Kong and Singapore.[12] Singaporean-based Huangpu Holdings controlled by the Hong Kong-based trading group Man Po Group achieved a 'backdoor' listing on the ASX by taking a A$3.8 million majority shareholding in the former real estate company Collings, in 1994. Man Po Holdings, as Collings is now known, will expand into property development and export-import.[13] On the other hand, Hong Kong-based developer Wah Tung International achieved a direct listing in April 1995. Listings by Asian companies can be difficult given the stringent disclosure rules of the ASX, and because Australian regulators may be unfamiliar with the legal and business environments in which many Asian companies have been operating.[14]

Ethnic Chinese firms from the region also invest in Australia to service the needs of Australia's growing Chinese community. Sing Tao Newspapers, based in Hong Kong, set up the Chinese language *Sing Tao Jih Pao* daily newspaper in Sydney.[15] Lippo Finance Australia set up in Sydney in 1990. It is a subsidiary of the Sino-Indonesian Lippo Group. A factor in its establishment was an assumption that there would be large capital inflows to Australia from Sino-Indonesians and the

....

10 *Economic and Business Review Indonesia*, 'The Gemala Group: Bad debt? Not true, says Sofjan Wanandi', 13 August 1994.

11 See Salim Group, *An Overview of the Salim Group*, Jakarta, 1993. First Pacific originally bought into Imagineering in 1989 believing the company was a solid investment. However, after its initial foray, it found that it had to keep committing more funds to the company to protect the initial investment until it finally took the company over in 1991. (Personal communication with First Pacific; and *Australian Financial Review*, 'First Pacific takes over Imagineering', 21 June 1991.)

12 See *The Australian*, 'The Asia scepticism', 27 April 1995.

13 *Australian Financial Review*, 'Collings leaves door ajar to take Asia-Pacific tack', 3 August 1994; and 'Huangpu takes the helm at Collings', 8 November 1994.

14 See *The Australian*, 'Asia listings must leap hurdles on hard road to market', 27 April 1995.

15 *Sing Tao Jih Pao* has a circulation of 25,000-28,000. (See *Margaret Gee's Australian Media Guide, November 1994-March 1995*, 47th edition, Melbourne 1994, p. 202.)

company could play a facilitating role in this. Another Sino-Indonesian bank, Bank Internasional Indonesia, a member of the Sinar Mas Group, opened a representative office in Sydney in April 1995. The office is likely to specialise in trade financing and later may seek merchant banking status.[16]

Lippo Finance Australia

Lippo Finance Australia (LFA) is one of the first South-East Asian Chinese-controlled conglomerates to set up a fully operational office in Australia. The company is a fully owned subsidiary of the Jakarta-based Lippobank, controlled by Mochtar Riady.

LFA is based in Sydney and specialises in providing trade finance. Most of the company's customers are local Chinese involved in food export and import with Asia. Most ethnic Chinese involved in international food trade are Teochiu, and so too are most of LFA's customers. Indeed, LFA's current managing director is Teochiu.

Apart from trade financing, LFA provides mortgage financing and other financial services, assists Australian firms in finding joint venture partners in Asia (particularly in Indonesia) and also scouts for Australian partners on behalf of the clients of Lippobank.

LFA also assisted in the formation of Asia Property Australia, a subsidiary of the Lippo Group (Hong Kong). This new company will engage in medium-sized residential property development, a complementary service to the mortgage financing provided by LFA.

Ethnic Chinese business people interviewed in Asia identified several constraints and perceived constraints on investing in Australia. The taxation system was regularly cited. They perceived that Australia had a relatively high level of taxation compared with markets elsewhere, and it was a complex system, making compliance costly. Australia's fringe benefits tax (FBT) was the most frequently cited problem. The FBT, as it applies to business entertaining, was seen as unnecessarily penalising one of the main ways in which Asian business people do business, over a meal and outside the office.

Predictably, Australia's relatively high labour costs (wages plus on-costs) were also cited as a factor. For this reason, Australia was seen more as a place for property rather than manufacturing investment.

Another problem identified by some interviewees was the rule prohibiting any shareholder from holding more than ten per cent of a bank's equity. This is a strong disincentive for many Asian, family-controlled banks considering setting

[16] See *Australian Financial Review*, 'Indonesian bank for Australia', 28 April 1995; and *The Australian*, 'Indonesian bank plants Sydney seed', 28 April 1995.

up a fully-integrated bank in Australia. For these banks, business goodwill is attached to the business expertise and acumen of the controlling family. Once the family loses control, as would be the case for a bank established in Australia, the value of such a bank would be lower than otherwise.

AUSTRALIAN COMPANIES LINKING UP WITH THE NETWORKS TO INVEST AND TRADE ABROAD

Linking Up with Ethnic Chinese in the Region

Many major Australian companies have recognised the benefits of forming partnerships with well-connected ethnic Chinese entrepreneurs to gain access to third markets.

The Australian company Wesfarmers Ltd, for example, recently signed a memorandum of understanding with Medical Research International Ltd, a subsidiary of the Hong Kong-based China Strategic Holdings (CSH) which is controlled by Oei Hong Leong. The two companies plan to jointly investigate coal mining ventures in China. At the time of the announcement, Wesfarmers' corporate affairs director said that his company would supply the 'know how' and Oei would supply the 'know who'.[17]

Another example of an Australian company linking up with ethnic Chinese interests to invest in a third market is the Australian subsidiary of the British/ Dutch Bunge Group. In June 1994, Bunge entered into a joint venture with the Sino-Indonesian controlled Salim Group through its Singapore-registered company KMP Pte Ltd, and with the Sin Ban Group of Malaysia, to construct and operate a S$30 million abattoir in Singapore. KMP and Bunge will each hold a 37 per cent share in the abattoir and Sin Ban will hold the remaining 26 per cent. The abattoir should be completed at the end of 1995. KMP owns a pig farm in Indonesia's Riau Archipelago, where KMP and Bunge plan more pig farming joint-ventures.[18]

The Adelaide-based pharmaceuticals company Faulding, recently formed an alliance with some ethnic Chinese business people to open doors in China. The company was keen to invest in China, but first went to Hong Kong to look for business people with good connections on the mainland. Introductions were made through some Hong Kong Chinese who were distant relatives of some officials in the Foshan municipal government. (Foshan is in China's Guangdong Province.) The Hong Kong business people negotiated with the Foshan municipal government on behalf of Faulding to buy a 90 per cent stake in Foshan Horizon Pharmaceutical Company Ltd, a large state-owned pharmaceuticals company with an annual turnover of approximately A$23 million. Faulding's stake represents an initial investment of up to A$40 million. Faulding plans to

---

17 See *Australian Financial Review*, 'Wesfarmers finds a 'know-who' joint venture partner', 23 November 1994.

18 *Jakarta Post*, 'Salim, two foreign partners get piggish in Singapore', 17 June 1994. It was also announced that KMP had acquired a 40 per cent share in the pig farms operated by the Sin Ban Group.

use its stake to produce pharmaceuticals for the Chinese market and possibly later to produce Chinese medicines to market to ethnic Chinese consumers in South-East Asia. For their part in arranging the deal, the Hong Kong business people were given a parcel of Faulding shares.[19]

Australia's Fosters Brewing Group has entered into an agreement with the Hong Kong-based Wheelock Pacific Group, controlled by Peter Woo, to investigate the feasibility of brewing joint ventures in China. Wheelock brings its connections and China experience to the partnership and Fosters brings its brewing and marketing know how. In January 1995, the first China joint venture was announced with the purchase (reportedly for US$6.4 million) of control of a Tianjin brewery. The joint venture, the Tianjin Fosters Brewery Company, plans to upgrade and expand the existing site. Fosters already has China-based brewery interests in Shanghai and Guangdong.[20]

Other Australian firms have linked up with ethnic Chinese interests to invest in their domestic market. Australia's Lend Lease Corporation has signed agreements with Indonesia's Sino-controlled Sinar Mas conglomerate to do business in Indonesia with several of Sinar Mas' arms.[21] The agreement enables the partners to establish six joint ventures - three in financial services and three in property management. In most of the ventures, Lend Lease and Sinar Mas reportedly will have a 50-50 shareholding. Initially, the joint ventures will target pension funds management, wholesale and retail funds management and property services in Indonesia. Property development, payroll services, property funds and life insurance will be explored later.

Australia's AMP Society has also sought to enter the Indonesian market via a joint venture with Sino-Indonesian interests. Together with the Sino-Indonesian controlled Panin Bank, it formed PT AMP Panin Life. AMP provides the funds management and marketing expertise, and Panin provides an existing financial services network to support the life insurance joint venture.[22] Panin Bank also has a joint venture with another Australian company, the Australia and New Zealand Banking Group (ANZ). The Jakarta-based venture, PT ANZ Panin Bank, specialises in trade and investment financing.[23]

Another Australian-ethnic Chinese business linkage has arisen with Thai Distribution Centre Ltd in Thailand. In 1994, Australia's Davids Holdings Group (through its Davids Asia Pte Ltd), the Central Group, controlled by the Sino-Thai Chirathivat family, and another Sino-Thai controlled group, Robinson Department Store PCL, jointly acquired 80 per cent of this firm. Thai Distribution Centre Ltd will establish a national grocery distribution operation in

19 For the broad details of the acquisition, see Faulding, *Annual Report, 1994*, Adelaide, 1994, p. 12. Other details are from personal communications with Faulding.

20 See *Asian Wall Street Journal*, 'Briefs: Foster's Brewing Group', 11 January 1995.

21 See *Asia Today*, 'Sinar Mas: Building a global empire in agribusiness, finance', May 1994; and *Australian Financial Review*, 'Lend Lease off to China via Indonesia', 21 March 1994. Contrary to some media reports, the agreements between Sinar Mas and Lend Lease do not encompass the two jointly going into China, only for joint ventures in Indonesia.

22 See *Australian Financial Review*, 'AMP boss leaves top Jakarta job', 18 August 1994.

23 See ANZ Panin Bank, 'Banking services in Indonesia', promotional brochure.

Thailand.[24] Once again, the arrangement is one where all parties contribute some otherwise lacking attribute. The two Sino-Thai partners have connections and local market knowledge and Davids Holdings has additional wholesale expertise.

Linking Up with Ethnic Chinese at Home to Enter Asia

As set out in Chapter 5, Australia has a significant ethnic Chinese community, but unlike many other countries, Australia's Chinese are drawn from across Asia, including China. Not all Australian Chinese are well connected overseas but some are, and these connections form a potentially valuable national asset.

Not only are non-Chinese Australian businesses linking up with ethnic Chinese entrepreneurs in Asia, but increasingly with Australian Chinese to go offshore together to do business. Usually the non-Chinese Australian side brings financing and technology to the relationship and the Australian Chinese side, contacts, language abilities and general knowledge of the in-country business environment.

Ways to link up with ethnic Chinese entrepreneurs in Australia include making connections through the Chinese chambers of commerce and similar organisations. These chambers and associations are examined in detail in Appendix 5 and a list of them, their addresses and contact persons appears in Appendix 4.

The East Meets West functions, which so far have been held in Sydney and Melbourne and organised by Kean Lau of the Jasper Group, the Australian Chamber of Manufacturers and various ethnic chambers of commerce, are another method of forming contacts between Australian Chinese and non-Chinese business people. The inaugural East Meets West function was held in Melbourne in April 1994 in a large Chinese restaurant and was attended by around 300 business people. Such a large turnout demonstrated the high degree of interest that both Australian Chinese and non-Chinese firms have in making closer contacts with one another.

In a similar vein, Austrade established a pilot Export Development Through Ethnic Communities program in Sydney in 1993. The program entails activities such as business matching, networking, and cross-cultural business information seminars. The program has been run in conjunction with other government agencies, industry organisations, and bilateral chambers of commerce. A number of communities are included such as the Chinese, Middle Eastern, Indian, Turkish, Polish, Indonesian and Vietnamese. However, most clients are ethnic Chinese. The program encourages ethnic manufacturers and producers to export their goods and services and matches ethnic traders with small- to medium-sized manufacturers and producers, especially those with exportable goods and services but without the resources to export on their own.

Austrade plans to extend the program nationwide. This might also include designating ethnic program coordinators in each Austrade State Office and increasing the range of Austrade information available in other languages.

....

24 See *Australian Financial Review*, 'Davids on verge of Thai food venture', 21 November 1994.

The benefits from Austrade's ethnic business matching activities are tangible. One former Chinese student now living in Australia whose father managed a power station in China, attended one of the seminars for the Chinese community. After the seminar, he was introduced to an Australian manufacturer of electrical components; this introduction led to the sale of US$380 000 worth of switchgear to the power station. Another seminar participant, an ethnic Chinese whose relatives own a retail chain in Indonesia, has since been appointed the sole agent for Indonesia by an Australian chemicals manufacturer.

Various state and federal agencies also are facilitating linkages between ethnic and mainstream business communities in Australia. The Office of Multicultural Affairs (OMA) in the Department of the Prime Minister and Cabinet is running its Productive Diversity program to make employers aware of the benefits of a multiethnic workforce. In 1995, OMA in conjunction with AusIndustry and Austrade is conducting a series of workshops in state capitals across Australia, bringing together ethnic chambers of commerce, other business organisations, state government agencies and representatives from ethnic communities. The workshops are focusing on concrete outcomes, particularly on networking between ethnic and mainstream business organisations, leading to mutually beneficial cooperation in overseas business ventures.

The Office of Trade and Investment of the Victorian Department of Business and Employment has on an informal basis, been keeping lists of Melbourne-based Chinese consultants. It makes these available to non-Chinese Australian businesses eager to do business in China and other Asian markets. This has resulted in some viable pairings, an example of which is discussed below. The office also has several Australian Chinese staff who facilitate linkages with their first hand knowledge of regional markets and cultures and their language skills.

Many consulting businesses attempting to facilitate trade and investment in China are owned and operated by Australian Chinese born in China. Many achieved permanent residency status after China's Tiananmen incident. These consultants have as their main connections in China relatives and former classmates who are now in middle-ranking positions. Most seek to make money from charging commissions on the business they bring in and also from looking after mainland Chinese delegations when they come to Australia.

The following are recent examples of mainstream Australian companies linking up with Australian Chinese to do business abroad.

The Moran Health Care Group

The Moran Health Care Group is one of the biggest private operators of hospitals, nursing homes, retirement villages and medical centres in Australia, having an annual turnover of at least A$125 million and assets of at least A$300 million. It is owned and managed by its founder Doug Moran, and his family. The group increasingly is specialising in boutique hospitals which attract patients from Asia looking for world-class health care.

The Moran Health Care Group signed an agreement with State Projects, a division of the NSW Government's Public Works Department which has considerable expertise in building public hospitals and educational facilities.

With their expertise, the Moran Health Care Group and State Projects plan major developments in areas of need in Asia.

The Moran Health Care Group formed an alliance with Denis Wong, a Sydney-based Chinese businessman, who is developing a tourism-based complex in Beijing. Wong facilitated meetings between the Moran Group and Chinese health officials and negotiated on behalf of the Moran Group. The group now plans to build a 1 500-bed hospital near Wong's proposed complex. A member of Wong's family relocated to Beijing to be closer to the proposed business.

The Moran Group considers that the proposed hospital will be important to demonstrate to the Chinese Government the capabilities of the Moran Group when it, combined in future with State Projects, seeks further joint ventures in China. Part of the benefits offered by the Moran Group to the Chinese authorities will be technology and skills transfer. As the hospital proceeds, the Moran Group intends that Chinese nationals will be trained in the group's Australian hospitals before working in Moran's Beijing hospital. The hospital will be equipped with substantial and sophisticated equipment, representing outlays for the Moran Group of tens of millions of dollars. Moran's long record of substantial charitable works in Australia should testify further to the group's bonafides as far as the Chinese are concerned.

Apart from the mutual benefits clearly evident in Moran's proposed Beijing hospital, another reason why the group has been able to form an effective partnership with ethnic Chinese interests is perhaps the group's similarity to a traditional ethnic Chinese business. The group is family owned and managed, decision making is centralised, business is occasionally progressed on the basis of connections and friendships as well as the underlying economic fundamentals, and expansion is usually funded out of retained earnings rather than through public offerings. Shared characteristics such as these may make it easier for non-Chinese companies to link up successfully with Chinese ones.

Parsons Galloway Foundation Pty Ltd

Parsons Galloway Foundation is a wholly Australian-owned consulting group, which undertakes regional management and marketing work in technology and service industries. The firm also provides trade and investment advice for international Chinese companies and supports business delegations from China.

Some of the directors of the company are of Chinese origin, but the principals are non-Chinese. Two directors live and work in Melbourne's Chinatown to better develop their *guanxi* (contacts) with the local Chinese community.

The firm operates by developing long-term connections, such as from university days and contact with Chinese students from abroad, and then letting opportunities arise. The principals seek out opportunities to expand their connections, such as lecturing at the Beijing Foreign Affairs College in late 1995.

Like the Moran Group, the structure of the Parsons Galloway Foundation replicates the ethnic Chinese firms with which it does business. It has very low overheads, and contracts work out rather than taking on employees, thus keeping variable costs to a minimum. This allows the firm to 'travel lightly' and be more flexible.

The Parsons Galloway Foundation currently acts as business advisers to the Melbourne-based international headquarters of Guangzhou Television, south-eastern China's leading television and radio broadcaster. The firm prepares international marketing and business plans for private and public Australian organisations, and presents a broad range of product, service and business opportunities to overseas Chinese markets.

Hip Hang Trading

Hip Hang Trading is a partnership between Duncan Grady and two Chinese-born partners, William Chen (based in Australia) and Geoff Huang (based in China).[25] The company was formed in 1992 and specialises in exporting to China Australian-made building products such as hot water systems, bathroom ware and spa pools.

After a difficult first year, Hip Hang's first order came from a close family friend of Huang - a container load of bathroom products for a new hotel. Today, the company employs 14 staff in China, has showrooms in Guangzhou and Beijing and exports eight container loads of building products to China each month. The family contacts of the two Chinese-born partners have proved important ingredients for the firm's success to date.

S.E.A. Food International

In five years, Malaysian-born Ray Teh's Australian-based seafood export business has grown from a turnover of A$250 000 to around A$11 million.[26] The business started in the mid 1980s as a Brisbane fresh fish shop. With his ethnic Chinese background, Teh identified market niches in Australia which he quickly moved to fill. The Vietnamese population near the fish shop was not interested in buying fillets of barramundi and coral trout, but wanted whole, less expensive fish. Teh filled his shop with whole, ungutted mackerel and within a few weeks, sales increased from 20-30 kilos to 2-3 tonnes. Next, tanks were installed so that live crayfish and crabs could be sold. Soon, wholesale orders began to pour in from Asian restaurants.

Following this initial success, Teh branched out into seafood exports. With his knowledge of South-East Asian seafood preferences, Teh has sold varieties of fish to Singapore and Malaysia that are popular there but not in Australia.[27] He capitalises on the Chinese New Year period when seafood is in particular demand. Similarly, spanner crabs which are not for popular eating but abound in Australian waters, are frozen and sold to Taiwan. The marketing of the crabs has been sensitive to their destinations. They have been renamed 'Dragon crabs' and sold in red and yellow packaging (fortuitous colours for many Chinese).

25 Personal communication with the Office of Multicultural Affairs, Department of the Prime Minister and Cabinet.

26 Personal communication with the Office of Multicultural Affairs, Department of the Prime Minister and Cabinet.

27 This is a case of an ethnic Chinese business person using the specialised knowledge that comes from having lived in various locations and integrating the otherwise divergent markets, as described in Chapter 6. Seafood not preferred in one market is sent to one where it is, earning arbitrage profits.

In 1992, Teh moved into exporting live crayfish, king crabs and abalone after he purchased a live crayfish factory in Tasmania. Previously a domestic operation, the factory now exports about 70 per cent of its total product.

Teh's success can be attributed to an ability to identify niche markets and then to develop them; an ability to buy cheaply in a low demand market to sell for more in high demand markets; and an understanding of the culture and cuisine of the customer.

CASE STUDY: THE ROAD TO CHINA - LINKING UP WITH AUSTRALIA'S CHINESE

Since the decision to allow some 40 000 Chinese students to stay in Australia and apply for permanent resident status, many of the former Chinese students have formed companies to use their contacts in China and Hong Kong.

One such company, Pacifique Sino, has linked up with a non-Chinese Australian firm, Townsend Chemicals, so Townsend Chemicals can export to China and Hong Kong. The pairing of the two firms presents a useful case study as to how mainstream Australian companies can benefit from linking up with firms formed by former Chinese students now living in Australia.[28]

Townsend Chemicals

Townsend Chemicals is a fully Australian-owned company based in Dandenong, Victoria. It was formed in 1975. Initially, Townsend Chemicals produced plasticisers for PVC. It now produces polyester polyols, thermoplastic polyurethanes and urethane adducts. The firm is flexible in its production, tailoring chemicals to suit client needs. Currently, the company has 30 full-time staff at its Dandenong plant and does all R&D on site.

Townsend Chemical's Export Strategy

The four main chemical products manufactured by Townsend Chemicals are all in great demand in Asia. Asia is becoming the world's largest producer of footwear, and Townsend's urethane adducts are used in producing polyurethane adhesives that attach a shoe's sole to its upper. The market for urethane adducts in Australia is about 100 tonnes annually and shrinking as protection for textiles, clothing and footwear is scaled back. On the other hand, Townsend Chemicals estimates that the Asian market is about 6 000 tonnes and growing. It estimates that the pairs of shoes produced annually in China are at least 3.1 billion; 0.4 billion in India; 0.35 billion in Indonesia; and 0.32 billion in Thailand. Consequently, the company's marketing and export strategy principally targets China, Hong Kong, Taiwan, Malaysia, Singapore, Japan, Thailand, Indonesia, South Korea and India, as well as Brazil, South Africa, Europe and the United Kingdom.

....

28 Information for this case study has come from interviews with Tony Wilson, marketing manger, Townsend Chemicals and Joseph Zheng, director, Pacifique Sino.

In 1980, Townsend Chemicals first sold urethane adducts to adhesive companies in South Korea. A good relationship was established with buyers there. Next, the company sold urethane adducts to adhesive firms in Japan, even though Japan manufactures these chemicals. That Townsend Chemicals sold its products in Japan where they faced a high degree of local competition, was a selling point in the firm's sales pitch to prospective buyers in other Asian countries.

The Taiwanese market was approached next as it has 63 adhesive manufacturers, all potential customers for Townsend Chemicals' products. Notwithstanding this, Townsend Chemicals' marketing manager visited Taiwan every year for eight years before achieving a significant order. Six companies were approached directly on the first visit, with additional companies approached on successive visits. The company now has a considerable presence among the 63 adhesive manufacturers.

As labour costs in both Taiwan and South Korea have risen, manufacturers in both markets have relocated to lower labour-cost economies. As the shoe manufacturers have relocated, Townsend Chemicals has been carried to new markets, particularly Indonesia and China.

Part of the trade strategy has included both the marketing manager and the managing director of the firm visiting Asia four to five times a year for extended stays, with the purpose of staying in touch with the market, renewing contacts and building up a long-term presence. Having contacts, a recognised name, and familiarity are very important for doing business in Asia. For this reason, Townsend Chemicals has found that the 'same face' needs to keep visiting year after year.

Townsend Chemicals' Focus on China

Townsend Chemicals' first foray into the giant China market began with a visit to Guangdong Province by its marketing manager. For the first three days, he used a translator supplied by Austrade but after that he was able to establish contacts unaccompanied. Townsend Chemicals has since considered establishing an office in Guangzhou but decided this could prove too costly and complex. Thought was given to appointing an agent, but the company prefers to have first hand knowledge of its market. Townsend Chemicals does not plan to set up a plant in China as this would be too costly. Also, there are concerns that once the appropriate technology was transferred to China it might fall into the hands of competitors. Consequently, Townsend Chemicals covers Guangdong itself.

Nevertheless, the rest of China is too large for Townsend Chemicals to handle by itself. The firm estimates approximately 10 000 shoe manufacturers are in China. This is too many to approach individually, so the strategy has been to approach adhesive manufacturers in China which sell their products to shoe manufacturers.

Townsend Chemicals approached an Australian-Chinese firm, Pacifique Sino, to assist in marketing its products in China (particularly in the Shanghai region), locating potential customers (there is no central registry of adhesive manufacturers) and doing marketing surveys. Being a relatively recent arrival to Australia from Shanghai, the director of Pacifique Sino has current knowledge of and connections with the Shanghai region.

In return, Pacifique Sino will earn a commission from its sales. Contact with Pacifique Sino was made through the Office of Trade and Investment at the Victorian Department of Business and Employment.

To ensure that Pacifique Sino better satisfies Townsend Chemicals' needs, Townsend Chemicals has provided the firm with training in marketing as well as ensuring it has a full understanding of Townsend Chemicals' operations, products, sales methods and story.

To date, Pacifique Sino has assisted in the setting up of a seminar for local shoe manufacturers in Shanghai which was addressed by Townsend Chemicals' managing director and marketing manager. A translator was also provided. This was organised from Melbourne by telephone and fax, emphasising the connections Pacific Sino has in Shanghai. Pacifique Sino organised for warehouse space in Hong Kong to keep some stock. Pacifique suggested this so orders from China and Hong Kong could be met quickly. The company also translated Townsend Chemicals' promotional materials into Chinese. In October 1994, Pacifique Sino arranged a stand for Townsend Chemicals at the Shanghai footwear fair. Hong Kong-based contacts were used for this as they had greater expertise than Pacifique Sino's Shanghai-based people.

Pacifique Sino has approached other adhesive companies in China. Adhesive companies are located by looking for advertisements in trade journals and Chinese telephone directories. Any link a partner in Pacifique Sino might have with the purchasing officer of an adhesive company is also used. Some, for example, are old classmates, friends or relatives.

Pacifique Sino

Like many new, small Australian-Chinese firms, Pacifique Sino's business is conducted from an office in the unit where its owner/controller lives. This keeps costs down and also allows the owner to work for extended hours. The director/controller, Joseph Zheng, is a native Shanghainese who came to Australia to study engineering. Following the completion of his studies, he set up the company. Seeding money for Pacifique Sino came from friends and relatives in Hong Kong and China, although setting up costs were kept to a minimum.

Zheng belongs to the Melbourne-based Chinese Professionals Association, through which he met a representative from the Office of Trade and Investment of the Victorian Department of Business and Employment. This contact listed Pacifique Sino with the Office of Trade and Investment and made the match with Townsend Chemicals.

Pacifique Sino is seeking involvement in four major areas: commodities trading (electrical equipment, telecommunications equipment, chemicals, clothing); consulting services (interpreting and translating, especially specialist translating in legal, chemical and engineering areas); infrastructure developments in China (the firm has connections to Beijing's Ministry of Power and is keen to assist Australian companies in bidding for contracts); and business delegations (appointments, travel and accommodation arrangements are made for business delegations from China).

Pacifique Sino has representative offices in Hong Kong, Shenzhen, Beijing, Shanghai, Zhouquan (Fujian Province) and Hangzhou (Zheijiang Province). These representatives are mostly other firms which have agreed to represent Pacifique Sino on the basis that it in turn represents them in Melbourne. Some of these offices belong to relatives and friends.

Pacifique Sino has four partners in Hong Kong and one each in Shanghai and Beijing. The partners in China are friends and relatives of the Melbourne-based partners.

When Zheng was forming Pacifique Sino he felt that because business in Australia depends heavily on legal structures, compared with China where transactions are more personalised, he needed legal assistance. Consequently a (non-Chinese) friend who is a lawyer was offered equity in Pacifique Sino to act as its legal adviser.[29] The legal adviser drew up the agency agreement presented to Townsend Chemicals, as well as assisting with Pacifique Sino's incorporation.

[29] As with many ethnic Chinese businesses, equity rather than a fee for service was offered.

RECENT SIGNIFICANT REAL ESTATE ACQUISITIONS BY ETHNIC CHINESE FROM THE REGION

The following list of some recent acquisitions of Australian real estate by ethnic Chinese investors from Asia demonstrates the scale and distribution of the investment. Much of this investment has occurred along 'network' lines - properties have been acquired by ethnic Chinese educated in Australia, or who have relatives residing in Australia for example. Many of the vendors were Japanese investors who, in many instances have incurred heavy capital losses on their sales.

There are a number of benefits arising from such investment. Real estate investment is a good confidence building measure. If an investment goes well, other types of investment may follow, such as in manufacturing and other more employment-generating activities. Familiarisation with ethnic Chinese investors in Australia may also facilitate investment in their home countries by Australian firms, possibly in partnership with the investing ethnic Chinese.

Recent acquisitions by ethnic Chinese business people from Asia include:

New South Wales

- The Cosmopolitan Centre (73 room hotel, 30 shops, 197 space car park and restaurant) in Sydney's Double Bay was sold to Singapore's Ow Chio Kiat for A$22.2 million in March 1994.[30]
- Sydney's Manly Hotel was sold to Malaysian (probably Chinese) interests for A$7.9 million in October 1994.[31]
- The Sydney's Parkroyal Parramatta was sold to Singapore's United Overseas Bank Group for A$15 million in November 1993.[32]
- The Parramatta Travelodge was sold to a Hong Kong buyer "for about" A$18 million in April 1994.[33]
- Two strata-titled floors in the tower at 51 Druitt Street in Sydney's CBD were sold to a Singaporean investor reportedly for A$5.97 million in December 1993.[34]

30 See *The Australian*, 'Singapore buyers bag two hotels', 8 March 1994, and *Australian Financial Review*, 'Singapore tycoon buys into Sydney centre', 10 March 1994.

31 Personal communication with JLW TransAct.

32 Personal communication with JLW TransAct, and see *The Australian*, 'Wee snares hotel in Kajima sell-off', 22 March 1994.

33 See *The Australian*, 'Offer for Parramatta Travelodge after a day', 8 April 1994; and *Australian Financial Review*, '$18m offer for CRI hotel', 8 April 1994.

34 *The Australian Financial Review*, 'Singaporean buys two CBD floors for $6m', 9 December 1993.

- Sydney's 280 room Century Radisson Hotel was sold to Wee Cho Law's United Overseas Bank Group of Singapore for A$42 million in March 1994.[35]
- Sydney's Furama Hotel was sold to Singaporean interests for A$37 million in February 1994.[36]
- Sydney's CBD twelve storey Grace Building was sold to Malaysia's Low Yat Group, headed by Tan Sri Low Yow Chuan, for around A$16 million in January 1994.[37] The group plans to convert the building into a retail, commercial and residential complex.
- The Pelican Beach Travelodge at Coffs Harbour was sold to Malaysian interests for A$7 million in January 1994.[38]
- The AMP building at Sydney's 32 Martin Place was sold to Singapore's United Overseas Bank Group for A$22 million.[39]
- Sydney's Paddy's Market site was sold to Robert Kuok's group "for about A$22 million" in early 1994.[40] The Kuok Group plans to construct a A$120 million retail and residential tower on the site.[41]
- Sydney's Darling Harbour Metro Inn was sold to the Singaporean Furama Group for A$36 million.[42]
- A controlling interest in Sydney's Hyatt Kingsgate Hotel and the Birkenhead Shopping Centre in Sydney's inner west were sold to Singaporean investor Kwek Leng Beng's CDL Hotels International Ltd for A$40.9 million in April 1994. The vendors were brothers Ho Whye Chung of Singapore and Ho Whye Tong of Sydney.[43]
- Sydney's Capital Centre and the Sydney Hilton Hotel were sold to Hong Kong media investor C.K. Ma for approximately A$130 million in 1993.[44]
- The Parramall Shopping Centre in Sydney's Parramatta was sold to Hong Fu (Australia) Pty Ltd, a group of Hong Kong investors led by George Chan for A$6.9 million in April 1994.[45]

35 See *The Australian*, 'Wee snares hotel in Kajima sell-off', 22 March 1994; and *The Australian*, 'Kajima unloads Radisson for $42m', 6 April 1994.

36 Personal communication with JLW TransAct.

37 The buy seems to have been an astute purchase. The Japanese Shimizu Corporation bought the building in 1990 for A$38 million, spending a further A$40 million to refurbish it. See *The Australian*, 'Low Yat pays $16 million for Grace Building', 24 January 1994.

38 The replacement cost of the hotel has been estimated to be A$24 million. See *The Australian*, 'Malaysian buys Pelican Beach for $7m', 24 January 1994.

39 See *The Australian*, 'Wee snares hotel in Kajima sell-off', 22 March 1994.

40 See *The Australian*, 'Wee snares hotel in Kajima sell-off', 22 March 1994.

41 See *Australian Financial Review*, '$120m home and retail scheme for Paddy's site', 20 April 1994.

42 The hotel cost the Japanese company Kajima A$90 million to develop. See *The Australian*, 'Wee snares hotel in Kajima sell-off', 22 March 1994.

43 See *The Australian*, 'Singapore investor in $41m splurge', 7 April 1994.

44 See *The Australian*, 'Offer for Parramatta Travelodge after a day', 8 April 1994.

45 See *The Australian*, 'Asian investors buy Parramall for $7m', 19 April 1994.

- Sydney's Erskine Park Village Shopping Centre was sold to a syndicate of Hong Kong and Singaporean investors for A$5.6 million in October 1994.[46]
- Sydney's Travelodge at Rushcutters Bay was sold to Malaysia's Low Yat Group for A$13.4 million in December 1993.[47] In October 1994, the group announced its intention to build a A$25 million residential development on the site.[48]
- Sydney's Darling Harbour Harbourside Marketplace retail centre was sold to Thomas Tiong and Kar Wai Chan for A$120 million in October 1994.[49]
- The former ABC site in Sydney's Darlinghurst was sold to Robert Kuok's Kuok Group for an estimated A$10.5 million in November 1994. Plans are to develop more than 200 residential units on the site.[50]
- Sydney Plaza tower in Sydney was sold to a Perth based consortium dominated by Australian Chinese and Singaporean interests for A$22 million in November 1994.[51]
- Plans for a A$60 million residential development in Sydney's Milson's Point and a A$414 million residential development in neighbouring Kirribilli were announced by Singapore's Dr Stanley Quek and Liang Court Holdings in 1994.[52]
- A Vaucluse mansion was sold to a Hong Kong businessman, Shu Ng, for A$1.56 million in December 1994.[53]
- Sydney's Glenview Hotel and Convention Centre was sold to Singapore's Singatronics Ltd and Accor Asia Pacific for A$15.3 million in September 1994.[54]
- Sydney's World Square project was refinanced by Malaysian Chinese interests with additional funds of A$46 million in November 1994.[55]
- Sydney's Hotel Nikko Potts Point was sold to Singapore's Hotel Plaza Ltd for A$108 million in November 1994.[56]

46 *The Australian*, 'Sydney centre fetches $5.6m for Colony Town', 18 October 1994.

47 Personal communication with JLW TransAct. Also, see *The Weekend Australian*, 'The Thakral Group gets an instant hotel chain', 26-27 March 1994.

48 *The Australian*, 'Low Yat plans six Sydney unit blocks', 1 November 1994.

49 See *Australian Financial Review*, '$120m Darling Harbour deal to yield handsome return', 6 October 1994.

50 *The Australian*, 'Kuok in second plunge', 26 November 1994.

51 See *Australian Financial Review*, 'Sydney Plaza goes to Asian group for hotel', 29 November 1994.

52 See *Australian Financial Review*, 'Singapore pair invest in Sydney', 25 November 1994.

53 See *Australian Financial Review*, 'Chocolate mansion sells', 5 December 1994.

54 *The Australian*, 'Singapore shipping giant lifts spending to $154m', 2 November 1994.

55 See *Australian Financial Review*, 'Malaysians put up $46m to help refinance Sydney's World Square', 18 November 1994.

56 *The Australian*, 'Hotel Plaza spree ends with $108m Nikko contract', 22 November 1994.

- The Wyong Plaza Shopping Centre on the NSW central coast was sold to a Singaporean investor for A$10 million in April 1994.[57]
- The Ramada Hotel in Sydney's North Ryde was sold to Singapore's Hai Sun Hup for A$39 million in May 1994.[58]
- Sydney's Parkroyal Darling Harbour was sold to Singapore's United Overseas Land for A$50 million.[59]
- Challenge Bank House in Sydney's Martin Place was sold to Singapore's Overseas Union Group for A$21.75 million in September 1993.[60]
- A fifteen-storey tower at 53 Martin Place in Sydney was sold to Singapore's Overseas Union Bank for A$36 million in December 1994.[61]

Victoria

- Melbourne's Palm Lake Hotel was sold to the Kah Motor Company, controlled by Malaysia's Loh Boon Siew, for A$7.53 million.[62]
- Melbourne's Victoria and Sheraton on Spring Street Hotels were acquired by Malaysia's United Industries in 1993 when MUI bought 53 per cent of Hong Kong's Morning Star Holdings.[63]
- Melbourne's Radisson President Hotel was sold to Hong Kong investor, Dr Li Dak Sum for A$66 million in July 1994.[64]
- A fifteen-storey building at 356 Collins Street in Melbourne was sold to a consortium of six Singaporean investors for A$9.75 million in August 1994.[65]
- Melbourne's Olderfleet CBD building was sold to Singapore's Pan Malayan Holdings for A$40 million in October 1994.[66]
- Melbourne's Radisson President Hotel was sold to Hong Kong's Roxy Property Investment Company, controlled by Dr Li Dak Sum for A$62.5 million in October 1994.[67]

....

57 See *Australian Financial Review*, 'Singapore investor pays $10m for Wyong Plaza shopping centre', 3 May 1994.

58 See *Australian Financial Review*, 'Singaporeans buy Ramada for $39m', 27 May 1994.

59 See *Australian Financial Review*, 'The Asian money trail', 29 April 1994.

60 See *Australian Financial Review*, The new mandarins', 29 April 1994.

61 See *The Australian*, 'Singapore's OUB pays $36m for base in Sydney', 21 December 1994.

62 *The Australian Financial Review*, 'Malaysians take stake in Melbourne hotels', 10 December 1993.

63 *The Australian Financial Review*, 'Malaysians take stake in Melbourne hotels', 10 December 1993.

64 See *Australian Financial Review*, 'Melbourne Radisson sold to HK investors', 1 August 1994.

65 See *Australian Financial Review*, 'Singapore syndicate buys CBD building', 4 August 1994.

66 See *Australian Financial Review*, 'Singapore buyer's $40m for Olderfleet', 21 October 1994.

67 *The Australian*, 'Radisson President sold for $65m', 27 October 1994.

- The Melbourne Banks Hotel was sold to Ong Beng Seng for A$22 million in 1993.[68]
- Melbourne's Eden on the Park was sold to Malaysia's Kah Motor Company for A$15.15 million in 1991.[69]
- Three properties in Melbourne's Southbank precinct were sold to Hong Kong's Wing On Company for approximately A$60 million in May 1994.[70]

Queensland

- Brisbane's Myer Centre was sold to Thomas Tiong and Kar Wai Chan, who apparently reside in Australia, for A$200 million in 1992.[71]
- Brisbane's Broadway on the Mall Shopping Centre was sold to Thomas Tiong and Kar Wai Chan for A$31.42 million in 1994.[72]
- The Jewel of the Reef Hotel at Palm Cove, near Cairns was sold to the Wah-Chang International Group of Singapore in 1992.[73]
- The MLC complex in Brisbane was sold to the brothers Ho Whye Chung of Singapore and Ho Whye Tong of Sydney for A$55 million in December 1992.[74]
- The Palm Cove Travelodge Resort near Cairns was sold to the brothers Ho Whye Chung of Singapore and Ho Whye Tong of Sydney for A$22 million in April 1993.[75]
- The Kenmore Shopping Village, west of Brisbane was sold to Singaporean Denis Jen's Intro International Ltd for A$22 million in 1991.[76]
- The Mermaid Waters Super Centre retail complex and two adjoining sites on Queensland's Gold Coast were sold to Singaporean Denis Jen's Intro International Ltd for A$21-22 million in April 1994.[77]
- Brisbane's Mayfair Crest Hotel was sold to Hong Kong businessman Dr Dak Sum Li's Carlton International Group for A$56.5 million in 1990.[78]

---

68 *The Australian*, 'Singapore play for Chevron on Gold Coast', 6 December 1994.

69 See *Australian Financial Review*, 'Kah group in $20m plan to re-position hotel chain', 19 July 1994.

70 *The Australian*, 'HK's Wing On wraps up $60m of Southbank', 8 June 1994.

71 See *Australian Financial Review*, '$120m Darling Harbour deal to yield handsome return', 6 October 1994.

72 See *Australian Financial Review*, '$120m Darling Harbour deal to yield handsome return', 6 October 1994.

73 *The Australian Financial Review*, 'Top spot to Asian buyer', 8 March 1994.

74 See *The Australian*, 'Singapore investor in $41m splurge', 7 April 1994.

75 See *The Australian*, 'Singapore investor in $41m splurge', 7 April 1994.

76 See *Australian Financial Review*, 'Jen's $21m swoop on Gold Coast sites', 7 April 1994.

77 See *Australian Financial Review*, 'Jen's $21m swoop on Gold Coast sites', 7 April 1994.

78 See *The Australian*, 'Li adds Parkroyal to portfolio for $63m', 30 March 1994.

- Hope Island on Queensland's Gold Coast is being subdivided by Singaporean retailer Janine Tay. It is a A$60 million subdivision.[79]
- Half of Brisbane's Woodridge Shopping Plaza was sold to Taiwanese investor Huang Kai-fong for approximately A$13 million in July 1994.[80]
- The Brisbane suburb of Camira will be developed by Singapore's Chan Brothers Group. The plans announced in October 1994 are for a A$60 million residential development.[81]
- The Gold Coast's Le Boulevard retail and commercial complex was sold to Singapore's Janine Tay for A$11 million in November 1994.[82]
- Seven shopping centres in Queensland were sold to Taiwanese entrepreneur, Fu Hsien-ta now residing in Brisbane and controlling Yu Feng's Pty Ltd, since 1992. The centres in Brisbane are: Sunnybank Plaza (A$48.0 million), Cannon Hill shopping centre (A$35.2 million), Stafford City shopping centre (A$31.1 million), Mt Gravatt Plaza (A$12.75 million), Sunny Park shopping centre (A$12.7 million), and one third interest in Woodridge Plaza (A$8.76 million). The centre on the Sunshine Coast is the Big Top Shopping Centre (A$11.6 million).[83]
- A parcel of land adjacent to the Chevron Hotel in Surfers Paradise was sold to Singapore's Ong Beng Seng for A$42.4 million in October 1994.[84]
- Brisbane's fourteen-storey Sherwood House building was sold to Chung-Yi Pty Ltd, owned by Taiwanese investors living in Australia and Taipei for A$6.3 million in December 1994.[85]

South Australia

- The Quality Hotel in North Adelaide was sold to Singapore's Cockpit Hotels Group, controlled by the Teo family for A$4 million in November 1994.[86]
- Adelaide's Glenelg Ramada Hotel was sold to Singapore's Hai Sun Hup Group for A$45 million in October 1994.[87]
- Adelaide's Terrace Inter-Continental was sold to the Hai Sun Hup Group for A$38 million in May 1995.[88]

---

79 See *Australian Financial Review*, 'Mrs Tay launches $60m dream project', 1 December 1993.

80 See *Australian Financial Review*, 'First foray by Taiwanese', 27 July 1994.

81 See *Australian Financial Review*, 'Project developers Chan can see the trees for their woods', 21 October 1994.

82 See *Australian Financial Review*, 'Tay emerges as Le Boulevard buyer', 23 November 1994.

83 See *Australian Financial Review*, 'Fu achieves goal at 7 shopping centres', 2 December 1994.

84 See *Australian Financial Review*, 'Surfers Chevron sale first in forecast property surge', 1 November 1994.

85 See *Australian Financial Review*, 'Chung-Yi buys again', 9 December 1994.

86 *The Australian*, 'Teos tipped as hotel's buyer', 9 November 1994.

87 *The Australian*, 'Singapore shipping giant lifts spending to $154m', 2 November 1994.

88 See *Australian Financial Review*, 'Hai Sun Hup in $38m swoop', 15 May 1995.

- Plans for a A$200 million redevelopment of Wirrina Cove, a resort south of Adelaide, by Malaysia's MBf were announced in June 1994.[89]

Western Australia

- Perth's Radisson City Hotel was sold to Singapore's Straits Trading Company Ltd for A$46 million in January 1994.[90]
- Perth's Parmelia Hilton was sold to Hawaiian Investments, a consortium of largely Australian and Malaysian Chinese for A$30 million in November 1993.[91]
- Perth's Noranda Square Shopping Centre was sold to Hawaiian Investments for A$13.7 million in October 1994.[92]
- Perth's eighteen-storey London House CBD office tower was sold to Hawaiian Investments for A$28.5 million in December 1994.[93]

Australian Capital Territory

- Canberra's Red Hill shops were sold to Hong Kong kung fu movie star, turned property developer Jackie Chan, recently.[94]

---

89 See *Australian Financial Review*, 'Malaysians close to buying Carpenter', 15 June 1994.

90 *The Australian*, 'Singapore buyers bag two hotels', 8 March 1994.

91 See *Australian Financial Review*, 'Hawaiian to close Parmelia deal this week', 25 November 1994.

92 *The Australian*, 'Hawaiian lays out $13.7m for Perth centre', 14 October 1994.

93 See *Australian Financial Review*, 'Lord McAlpine sells Perth office tower for $28.5m', 4 January 1995.

94 See *Australian Financial Review*, 'Big spenders behind the buying spree', 29 April 1994.

Chapter 14

LINKING UP WITH THE NETWORKS: SELECTING A PARTNER

This chapter is not about cultural aspects of doing business with the region's ethnic Chinese entrepreneurs. Rather, it seeks to draw from foregoing chapters some basic principles for linking up with the business networks. In essence, these principles go to the selection of an appropriate ethnic Chinese business partner.

THE RIGHT PARTNER

Because of the pre-eminence of East Asia's ethnic Chinese business entrepreneurs in specific markets, in entire economies, and to a degree in the regional economy, they are highly valuable as business partners. Not only can they provide preferred entree to their own domestic markets, but their ability to treat the entire region as a single market, and their pre-eminent role in the transformation of south-eastern China, make them appropriate partners for Australian companies seeking access to the region. The region's ethnic Chinese entrepreneurs are willing to link up with 'outsiders' who have something to offer them. Indeed, a number of 'outsiders', including Australians, are already involved in successful strategic partnerships of this nature.

The key is to select the right partner. Given the degree of heterogeneity in the ethnic Chinese community, or perhaps more accurately communities, of the region - for example the Hokkien or Cantonese - Australian companies will need to take care to ensure that their choice of partner is appropriate to the market or markets they seek to enter.

Dialect, country of birth or current residence, and the extent of family or other networks in the targeted markets are all issues that bear on the critical question of appropriateness.

Dialect is an important consideration. The principal dialect of Taiwan, for example, is unintelligible to speakers of the main dialect in Hong Kong. The language of business and the government sector in Taiwan and China is Mandarin; however, many Hong Kong Chinese are not fluent in Mandarin. Nor are many South-East Asian Chinese .

At the same time, while Mandarin-speaking Sino-Vietnamese, for example, might be useful as translators in Taiwan, they are unlikely to be able to 'open doors' there. Most Sino-Vietnamese are ancestrally Cantonese, and very few have any family, clan or other links to Taiwan.

Also many ethnic Chinese outside China, Hong Kong and Taiwan do not speak, read or write any Chinese dialect at all.

A Local Partner

As a general rule, and this is also largely a matter of common sense, the best choice of partner will be a local one in the targeted market. When doing business in an unfamiliar business environment, a well-connected local business partner can bring a host of advantages. Local partners have local knowledge, local commercial, and where necessary, political connections, and access to local distribution networks. As was discussed in Chapter 7, prominent ethnic Chinese-controlled companies in the region tend to move together jointly to dominate markets. In such circumstances, Australian companies may see advantage in joining forces with the established market leaders rather than compete against them.

For their part Australian companies may offer local ethnic Chinese partners access to technology, and modern management and marketing tools, among other advantages.

Australian Chinese as Partners

While a local partner may generally provide the best entree to a domestic market, non-Chinese Australians may see advantage in first seeking a partner from within Australia's own extensive and well organised ethnic Chinese business community. In the previous chapter, the case study on Townsend Chemicals demonstrated how an Australian company and an ethnic Chinese firm, both Melbourne-based, linked together to do business in China.

Apart from proximity, Australian Chinese partners offer the particular advantage of familiarity with Australian society, the business environment, and its rules and regulations. In other words, they understand the position of non-Chinese Australian business people and can 'speak the same (business) language'. They are ideally placed, therefore, to interpret the region's overseas Chinese business networks to non-Chinese Australian counterparts.

Australia's ethnic Chinese community is one of the most diverse in the world, with links to every country in the region, including China. Community organisations include Chinese chambers of commerce, mutual-help societies and various vocational, professional and informal business groupings. Many of these have an international trade and investment orientation and are therefore a good starting point in the search for an appropriate partner. Non-Chinese Australians may see advantage, where possible, in joining and become well integrated with ethnic Chinese business organisations of which an ethnic Chinese partner is a member. Among other things, these organisations may be able to help sort out difficulties that arise in the partnership.

Third Country Markets

Connections in third markets in the region may also be prospective. Austrade recommends that Australian companies seeking to enter China consider a partner in Hong Kong, where the business community speaks English, is familiar with Western business practices, and is well-connected to the market. Companies may consider exporting first to Hong Kong and letting their Hong Kong partners on-sell to the more complex China market. The same advice may be relevant to

Australian companies wanting to invest in China. As the home to several of the ethnic Chinese sub-diasporas, for example the Sino-Indonesians and the Sino-Burmese, Hong Kong may also be a good source of entrees to the Indonesia and Myanmar markets. Similarly, Taiwan, with its linguistic and cultural ties to China's Fujian Province, is a good place to link up with partners for Fujian business. Hokkien connections and Taiwan's 'Go South' investment drive might also make it a suitable place to seek partners to access the Philippines market.

The presence of large numbers of Sino-Burmese in Singapore, who lead that country's investment drive into their former homeland, and the Singapore Government's concurrent investment push into China and Vietnam, make Singapore an especially prospective source of possible partners. Moreover, the Government of Singapore has already undertaken much of the necessary legal and other groundwork necessary for investing in these markets, a significant bonus for Australian partners of Singapore firms.

This is recognised implicitly in the *strategic business linkages initiative* that both the Australian and Singapore governments are pursing with the aim of bringing businesses of the two countries together to explore jointly opportunities in third country markets in the region. China, Indonesia, India and Vietnam have been identified as offering the best prospects.

In the case of China, the choice of a Singapore Chinese partner is complicated by the fact that most of Singapore's investment in that country to date has been outside the geographical areas where the overwhelming majority of Singapore Chinese have their ancestral origins. Rather than clan origins or dialect connections, Singapore's current business links with China owe much to the political groundwork that has been laid by senior Singapore Ministers. One direct result of this is the construction now underway by Singapore of an industrial park and associated township at Suzhou, near Shanghai. The Singapore-Suzhou Industrial Township may offer particular advantages to Australian companies partnering Singaporeans in China.

Using Occupation-Dialect Links

Chapter 2 examined in some detail the traditional role of dialect in ethnic Chinese business throughout the region, including the link between dialect and certain occupations. Occupation-dialect links are declining in importance, but in some cases may still be of value for Australians seeking business opportunities in specific markets.

One area where the link continues to be important is regional trade in fresh foods, particularly fruit and vegetables, rice and seafoods, which still is significantly controlled by the Teochiu. In a similar line, the Teochiu are prominent in Australia as operators of Asian grocery shops. Against this background, an Australian company seeking to export food products to South-East Asia could link up with a Singapore Teochiu food trader, who could distribute the product throughout the region using the Teochiu-food trade link.

Chinese Chambers of Commerce

The Chinese chambers of commerce and other ethnic Chinese business organisations in the region are excellent sources of possible partners, especially local ones. Many chambers publish regular newsletters for their members featuring foreign firms looking for local partners or wishing to trade. Australian firms rarely avail themselves of this service.

Some places have more than one Chinese chamber of commerce.[1] Many countries in the region have a national Chinese chamber, and then many smaller, regionally-based Chinese chambers grouped beneath it. Malaysia, for example, has the Associated Chinese Chambers of Commerce and Industry of Malaysia as its peak Chinese chamber at the national level, but also many regional chambers such as the Kuala Lumpur and Selangor Chinese Chamber of Commerce and Industry. The Philippines, on the other hand, has many regional chambers but two peak chambers at the national level, the Federation of Filipino Chinese Chambers of Commerce and the Filipino Chinese General Chambers of Commerce. Consequently, Australian firms intending to locate potential business partners through Chinese chambers may need to approach more than one chamber. Appendix 3 provides the names and addresses of some of the more prominent Chinese chambers of commerce and similar Chinese business organisations in the region.

Chinese trade associations and guilds can be an efficient way to locate potential partners in the one industry. These associations are listed in the local telephone directory. As was mentioned in Chapter 4, Taiwan, for example, has hundreds of trade associations, many highly specific and most able to provide lists of members and their areas of specialisation.

Australian Chinese chambers of commerce and other ethnic Chinese business organisations are all linked in one way or another to the East Asian networks. Appendix 4 provides the names and addresses of some of the main Chinese business organisations in Australia. Similarly, the bilateral chambers of commerce in Australia can be useful places to look for partners. The Australia Taiwanese Chamber of Commerce and the Australia-Brunei Chamber of Commerce, discussed in Appendix 5, are just two examples.

Local Business Guides

Many high quality, English-language business guides provide details on Chinese-controlled and other businesses in the region. Some examples are:

- The *1995 Taiwan Yellow Pages* produced by the Yellow Pages Corporation. The guide details many of Taiwan's industry and trade associations which are most business people's first port of call when doing business in Taiwan, as well as many companies.[2]

---

1 This may be for historical reasons, or the various chambers represent different dialect groups, or for local political reasons.

2 Available for US$120 (including airmail postage) from PO Box 81-02, Taipei, Taiwan.

- The Yellow Pages Corporation also produces Yellow Pages guides for Shanghai, Shenzhen, Xiamen, Guangdong, Tianjin and Yunnan.[3]
- The Hong Kong General Chamber of Commerce Handbook.
- Hong Kong Trade Development Council directories.
- Indonesia's top 300 business conglomerates are detailed in *Conglomeration Indonesia* produced by Informasi Pusat Data Business Indonesia. The two-volume guide features company addresses, names, family background of directors and principal figures in the company, company history, cross shareholdings, company structure, principals and lines of business.[4]
- In Australia, there are several business guides in which companies wishing to advertise to the Chinese community are able to do so. Australian Chinese companies also advertise in these guides. Two examples are the 600 page Melbourne *Chinese Business Guide 1995* and the 336 page *Queensland Chinese Business Guide 1995*.[5]

These guides are in addition to the handbooks of members produced by most Chinese chambers and other, similar organisations in the region.

Using Ethnic Chinese Staff

Increasingly, Australian companies and government agencies employ Asian, or more specifically, ethnic Chinese staff to assist in their Asian strategies. Often such staff are employed because of their linguistic skills and general knowledge of Asia, but the contacts and business skills possessed by many such employees may be undervalued or simply not recognised. Companies and government agencies wanting to do business in the region should consider having ethnic Chinese employees not simply because of the language and cultural skills but also because of their connections and business skills.

Due Diligence Assessments

'There are going to be many casualties in China. Everywhere else, joint venture contracts are carefully spelt out and exit plans are made clear, but in China this just isn't happening. Many joint ventures in China are nothing like the text book way of doing things - Westerners seem to come to China and forget everything they were ever told about forming business partnerships'.[6]

Due diligence assessments which examine the corporate history and soundness of prospective partners are big business throughout Asia. They also can verify the claims made by prospective partners. The biggest customers of due diligence firms

3 Available for US$95 each (airmailed), also from PO Box 81-02, Taipei, Taiwan.

4 Available from the publisher at 54 i-j Kartini VII, Jakarta 10750, Indonesia.

5 The Melbourne guide is published by Chinese Business Guide Pty Ltd at 1/6 View Tech Place, Victoria, 3178; the Queensland guide is published by Trevgold Marketing Promotions at PO Box 62, Broadway, Brisbane, 4006.

6 Expatriate managing director of a large Hong Kong-based company, interviewed by the East Asia Analytical Unit in February 1995.

are American companies seeking local joint-venture partners in Asia. Assessments can be expensive but can ultimately prove wise investments. As an example, one United States firm passed up a US$300,000 assessment on a new Hong Kong-based business partner only to later lose much of its US$30 million stake in the joint venture it formed.

Currently, Australian companies are not major customers of due diligence advice. Australian firms however, are strongly advised to consider employing due diligence advice when seeking a local partner with whom they are unfamiliar. This is particularly the case in China, the Philippines, Vietnam and Thailand, where legal protection for foreign investing firms is still not fully developed.

Some sizeable Australian firms have invested in China with Hong Kong-based ethnic Chinese companies, and these ventures have failed because of poorly selected local partners. Assess the debts and commitments of state-owned enterprises in China, as well as their capacity to deliver what is promised, before entering into partnerships with them.

GOVERNMENTS AS FACILITATORS

Australian governments, both federal and state, can help to expand Australia's links to the region's ethnic Chinese networks, chiefly by promoting a greater international business role for Australia's ethnic Chinese entrepreneurs, in their own right and in collaboration with non-ethnic Chinese Australian entrepreneurs. Its very diversity is possibly the Australian Chinese business community's greatest strength, and the community as a result is well-placed to tap into a wide range of networks and markets.

Governments and the private sector have each recognised this potential in a number of intiatives aimed at forging closer cooperation between the mainstream and the various ethnic business communities in Australia. The private sector-sponsored *East Meets West* functions, Austrade's pilot *Export Development through Ethnic Communities Program*, and the *Productive Diversity* and associated programs of the Office of Multicultural Affairs, in some cases in cooperation with other agencies such as AusIndustry and Austrade, are examples.

Governments should give continuing support to initiatives of this sort, with a view to encouraging a more integrated approach to offshore business by mainstream and ethnic Chinese business organisations. The facilitating role of governments is, however, necessarily limited. Ultimately, it is up to the business organisations themselves to formalise their relations, create and maintain databases and to carry out a 'matchmaking' function between ethnic Chinese and non-ethnic Chinese, Australian entrepreneurs.

The role of the Australian Government role may be greater, on the other hand, in forging overseas 'strategic business alliances' along the lines of the Singapore-Australia *Strategic Linkages Initiative*. Depending on the success of this venture, the Government should give consideration to extending the intitiative to link up with other major regional business hubs, for example Bangkok, for third country business. Closer ties with individual Chinese chambers of commerce in the region should also be forged in order to facilitate business pairings and the formation of consortia.

Government encouragement for the Australian Chinese community's endeavours to host in Australia a forthcoming *World Chinese Entrepreneurs' Convention*, an annual event that brings together over one thousand of the most successful ethnic Chinese business people, is also recommended.

Appendix 1

INTERVIEWEES

The East Asia Analytical Unit gratefully acknowledges those individuals in the region who consented to be interviewed for this project.[1] However, the views expressed in the text cannot necessarily be attributed to the interviewees. Among those interviewed were:[2]

AUSTRALIA

Jeff Chan
President
Australia-Taiwanese Chamber of Commerce

Philip Chan
Managing Director
Lippo Finance Australia
Sydney

Stephen Chan
Office of Trade and Investment
Victorian Department of Business and Employment

Wilson Chan
Secretary
Hong Kong Business and Professional Association of Queensland

Barry Chao
President
Great Wall Business Association

Dr Alexander Chen
Director
Chinese Cultural and Education Centre Sydney

Henry Chi
Chinese Culture Centre

David Ching
President
Chinese Professional and Business Association

David Ch'ng
Faculty of Business
Swinburne University of Technology

Dr Charles Coppel
Associate Professor
Melbourne University

Danny Doon
President
Chinese Restaurateurs Association

Dennis Duong
President
Australia Chinese Teo-Chew Association Sydney

Fred Fenech OAM
Senior Export Counsellor
Australian Trade Commission

1 All interviews outside Australia were conducted by the East Asia Analytical Unit and interviews within Australia were shared between the unit and consultant to the unit, Professor Pookong Kee. Additional interviews were undertaken in the PRC by consultant Noel Tracy as part of survey work undertaken on behalf of the unit. Additionally, a seminar was held in Canberra during December 1994 to discuss preliminary findings of the study. Attendees at this seminar included: Bernard Trevanion (Australian Confederation of Commerce and Industry), Scott Waldron (Griffith University), Dr On Kit Tam (ADFA), Ky Cao (Finance International Pty Ltd), David Ch'ng (Swinburne University of Technology), Professor Pookong Kee (Victorian University of Technology), Noel Tracy (Flinders University of South Australia), Fred Fenech (Austrade), and representatives from the Office of Multicultural Affairs, the Office of National Assessments, the China Desk of the Department of Foreign Affairs and Trade, and the East Asia Analytical Unit.

2 Surnames are in uppercase where there are more than two parts to an individual's name.

T.B. Feng
Secretary
Australia-China Business and Trade Association

King FONG OAM
Vice-President
Sydney Chinatown Chamber of Commerce

Chau FUNG
President
Sun Chua Luen Professional Chef Association

Hov Shao HAN
Secretary
Australia Mainland Chinese Association

Robert Ho
Sydney Chamber of Commerce

Alfred Huang
President
Chinese Chamber of Commerce of South Australia

Thomas Hung
President
Oriental Travel Agencies Consortium

Sylvia Huynh
NSW Indo-China Chinese Association

Peter James
Export Development Manager
PolyPacific Pty Ltd
Victoria

Professor Wolfgang Kasper
Department of Economics and Management (ADFA)
University of New South Wales

Professor KEE Pookong
Director
Centre for Asia-Pacific Studies
Victoria University

Bernard Khut
Deputy Vice-President
Chinese Chamber of Commerce
South Australia

Jack Ko
President
Hong Kong Club

Dr Moni LAI Storz
Department Sociology and Anthropology
Caulfield Campus Monash University

Lawrence Lau
President
Australian Chinese Community Association of New South Wales

Albert Lee
Former President
Chinese Professional and Business Association

Wellington Lee OBE, OAM
Foundation President
Chinese Chamber of Commerce
Victoria

Constance Lever-Tracy
Senior Lecturer in Sociology
Flinders University of South Australia

Ms Lim
Administrator
Chinese Restaurateurs Association

Dr Andrew Lim
President
Australian Chinese Medical Association

LIM Chuen Ren
Vice-President Chinese Chamber of Commerce
Victoria

Dee Yan LIN
Secretary
Australia Chinese Teo-Chew Association
Sydney

William Lin
Taiwanese Association of Australia
Melbourne Branch

Eddie Liu
Secretary
Chinese Club of Queensland

Frank Liu
President
Chinese Community Society of Victoria

Peter Liu
President
Chinese Club of Queensland

Vincent Liu
National Chen-Chi University Alumni Association of Melbourne

Dr Alexius Loo
President
Chinatown Business Association

Dick Low
President
Ning Yung Society

Emeritus Professor Jamie Mackie
Australian National University

Doug Moran
Chairman of the Moran Group of Companies
Sydney

Alistair J. Nicholas
Managing Director
Far East Research and Communications Pty Ltd
Sydney

Kevin Pai
Mandarin Association of Melbourne

Elizabeth Parsons, Jeremy Simpson
Directors
Parsons Galloway Foundation Pty Ltd
Melbourne

Tina Schmidt
Secretary, Taiwanese Australian Business Association
Queensland

Peter Shen
Australian National University

SU Peng Yu
Office of Trade and Investment
Victorian Department of Business and Employment

Dr On Kit TAM
Department of Economics and Management (ADFA)
University of New South Wales

Noel Tracy
Lecturer in Politics
Flinders University of South Australia

Ray TRAN
Secretary
Indochina Chinese Association of NSW

Henry Tsang OAM
Deputy Lord Mayor
Sydney City Council

Tony Wilson
Marketing Manager
Townsend Chemicals Pty Ltd
Victoria

Dr Clement Wong
Convenor
Social Action and Anti-Discrimination Committee
Chinese Association of Victoria

Francis Wong
President
Australia-Brunei Chamber of Commerce

James Wong
Executive Director
Western Australian Chinese Chamber of Commerce

Zhi-Lin YANG
Vice-President
Australia-Shanghai General Chamber of Commerce

Wah YEO
Chinese Fellowship of Victoria

Katie Young
China Liaison Director
Hunt and Hunt Lawyers

Robert Yung
President
Chinese Masonic Society

Joseph Zheng
Director
Pacifique Sino Pty Ltd
Victoria

HONG KONG

Sally AW Sian OBE
Chairman
Sing Tao Ltd

Ling Chan
Analyst
Kerry Investment Management Ltd

Dr Thomas Chan
China Business Centre
Hong Kong Polytechnic University

Professor CHIU Ling-Yeong
Department of Chinese
University of Hong Kong

Simon Goddard
Associate Director
Kroll Associates (Asia) Ltd

Professor Ambrose Yeo-Chi KING
Pro-Vice Chancellor
Chinese University of Hong Kong

J.P. Lee MBE
Director
Lippo Group

Simon Lee
Director
Hong Kong Queensland Government Centre

Terence Ma
President
Australian Chinese Association of Hong Kong

Stuart McGregor
Managing Director
San Miguel Brewery Hong Kong Ltd

Robert Mills
Regional Marketing Manager
Ansett Australia

Derek Murphy
Group Vice President
First Pacific Company Ltd

Professor S. Gordon Redding
University of Hong Kong Business School

Professor WANG Gungwu
Vice-Chancellor
University of Hong Kong

The Hon. Dr Philip Wong
Honorary Treasurer
Chinese General Chamber of Commerce
Member of the Hong Kong Legislative Council

Professor WONG Siu-lun
Department of Sociology
University of Hong Kong

Ricky Yue
Director
Kerry Investment Management Ltd

INDONESIA

H. Junus Jahja
Director
Institute for Studies on Ethnic Chinese Assimilation in Indonesia
Secretary of the Advisory Board
Islamic Information Centre for Ethnic Chinese

Augusto P. Nilo
Group Managing Director
Sinar Mas Group

Dr Onghokham
University of Indonesia

Robinson Pangaribuan
Journalist/Editor
Prospek business magazine

Roosniati Salihin
Senior Executive Vice President
Panin Bank

Mr Kristoforus Sindhunatha
SH Chairman, Agency of the Communication and Comprehension of the National Unity (BAKOM-PKB)
President
PT Indulexco Consulting Group

Laksamana Sukardi
CEO
Reform Consulting;
Treasurer
Partai Demokrasi Indonesia

Dr THEE Kian Wie
Senior Research Associate
Centre for Economic and Development Studies
Indonesian Institute of Sciences

Paul Wong
Head of Sales and Trading
Niaga Securities

MALAYSIA

Tan Sri Dato' CHAN Choong Tak
Secretary-General
Gerakan Party

Bill CHIN Kok Howe
Vice Chairman
Malaysia-Australia Business Council

Dato' Joseph Chong
Managing Director
Westmont Holdings Sdn Bhd

CHUAH Guan Lee
General Manager
Kwong Wah Yit Poh Press Bhd

Stephen Duthie
Staff Correspondent
Asian Wall Street Journal

The Hon. GOIK Hock Lai
State Legislative Councillor
Political Secretary to the Chief Minister of Penang

Edmund Terence Gomez
Institute of Advanced Studies
University of Malaysia

KONG Sio Joo
Executive Secretary
Kuala Lumpur and Selangor Chinese Chamber of Commerce and Industry

Dr KUA Kia Soong
Democratic Action Party Member of Parliament

LIM Chuan Boon
Executive Secretary
The Federation of Hokkien Associations of Malaysia

LIM Guan Eng
Democratic Action Party Member of Parliament

K.T. Lim
Penang Chinese Chamber of Commerce

LIM Say Chong
President
Malaysian International Chamber of Commerce and Industry

LIM Yu Tey
Assistant Secretary for Commerce
Kuala Lumpur and Selangor Chinese Chamber of Commerce and Industry

Paul Low
Malaysian Chinese Association
Member of Parliament

MEW Jin Seng
Honorary General Secretary
Kuala Lumpur and Selangor Chinese Chamber of Commerce and Industry

NEOH Hang Been
Executive Secretary
Penang Chinese Chamber of Commerce

Dato OON Chin Seang
Penang

Raphael Pura
South-East Asia correspondent
Asian Wall Street Journal

TAN Kit Chin
Assistant Secretary for Industries
Kuala Lumpur and Selangor
Chinese Chamber of Commerce and Industry

TEH Eng Aun
Penang Chinese Chamber of Commerce

Senator Dr TOH Kin Woon
Gerakan Party Member of Parliament

WONG Yim Fatt
Penang Chinese Chamber of Commerce

MYANMAR

AUNG Myint
Myanmar Chinese Chamber of Commerce

KHIN San Yin
Manager
Automar Co Ltd

E. Khong
Myanmar Chinese Chamber of Commerce

CC Kwong
Managing Director
Automar Co. Ltd.

KYAW Lwin
Winner Enterprise Ltd;
Myanmar Chinese Chamber of Commerce

Serge PUN
Chairman
SPA International

SEIN Hlaing
Myanmar Chinese Chamber of Commerce

SENG Leong
President
Myanmar Chinese Chamber of Commerce

SOE Myint
Myanmar Chinese Chamber of Commerce

PEOPLES' REPUBLIC OF CHINA

XU Yunhong
Vice Governor of Zhejiang Province and Mayor of Ningbo

(Many individuals were also interviewed as part of the 600 foreign-invested firms surveyed in China for this study.)

PHILIPPINES

Gloria L. TAN Climaco
Chairman and Managing Partner
Sycip Gorres Velayo & Co.

SINGAPORE

Dr GOH Keng Swee
Former First Deputy Prime Minister of Singapore

Fiona Hu
formerly Director of Research, Singapore Chinese Chamber of Commerce and Industry
now Associate Director of Marlin Land Hong Kong

Vanessa LOH Li Yoon
Manager (Marketing/Commercial)
Singapore-Suzhou Township Development Pte Ltd

Peter Sung
CEO
Tuan Sing Holdings;
PAP Member of Parliament

Leo Suryadinata
Associate Professor
Department of Political Science
National University of Singapore

Dr TING Seng Kiong
Senior Manager
Jurong Environmental Engineering Pte Ltd

Professor John Wong
Director
Institute of East Asian Political Economy
National University of Singapore

Dr YAO Souchou
Research Fellow
Institute of Southeast Asian Studies

YONG Yaw Nam
Assistant Head
International Business Development Division
Economic Development Board

TAIWAN

Jim Jin-Heng CHANG
Director
Overseas Chinese Affairs Commission

Dr Tain-Jy CHEN
Research Fellow and Director
Chung-Hua Institute for Economic Research

Dr Lee-in Chen CHIU
Research Fellow
Chung-Hua Institute for Economic Research

Chin CHUNG
Associate Research Follow
Chung-Hua Institute for Economic Research

Richard C. Lin
Associate Professor
Soochow University

Manual R. Tayas
Special Trade Representative
Philippine Trade and Investment Center

Dr Chunto TSO
Director
Taiwan Institute of Economic Research

Dr Jimmy Wang
Vice-Convenor, International Affairs Committee
Chinese National Federation of Industries

Bernard T. Wu
Special Assistant to Chairman
Far Eastern Textile Ltd

Steven Wu
Director
Industrial Development and Investment Center
Ministry of Economic Affairs

THAILAND

Supang Chantavanich
Associate Professor
Institute of Asian Studies
Chulalongkorn University

Dr Nimit Nontapunthawat
Executive Vice President
Bangkok Bank

Dr Boonsong Srifeungfung
President
Thai-Chinese Chamber of Commerce

Vichai Rupkumdee
Dean
School of Social Development
National Institute of Development Administration

Preecha Watanakunakorn
Managing Director
Pornpat Engineering Co. Ltd.

Appendix 2

TRANSLITERATION OF CHINESE PLACE NAMES

The following chart provides the Pinyin and Wade-Giles expressions for China's provinces and some more important cities.

PINYIN	WADE-GILES
Anhui	Anhwei
Fujian	Fukien
Gansu	Kansu
Guangdong	Kwangtung
Hebei	Hopei
Heilongjiang	Heilungkiang
Hunan	Hunan
Jiangsu	Kiangsu
Jiangxi	Kiangsi
Jilin	Kirin
Liaoning	Liaoning
Ningxia	Ningsia
Qinghai	Tsinghai
Shaanxi	Shensi
Shandong	Shantung
Shanxi	Shansi
Sichuan	Szechwan
Xinjiang	Sinkiang
Yunnan	Yunnan
Zhejiang	Chekiang
Beijing	Peking
Guangzhou	Canton
Fuzhou	Foochow
Shantou	Swatow
Xiamen	Amoy
Nanjing	Nanking
Taishan	Toishan
Xinhui	Sun Wei
Jinmen	Quemoy
Tianjin	Tientsin

Source: See Tan, T.T.W., Your Chinese Roots: The Overseas Chinese Story, Times Books International, Singapore, 1986, pp. 250-51.

Appendix 3

CHINESE CHAMBERS OF COMMERCE IN EAST ASIA

Following is a list of key Chinese chambers and similar Chinese business organisations in East Asia.

BRUNEI

Chinese Chamber of Commerce
Chinese Chamber of Commerce Building
72 Jalan Roberts, 2-4th Floor
Bandar Seri Begawan 1902, Brunei

HONG KONG

Chinese General Chamber of Commerce
24-25 Connaught Road C./F, Hong Kong

Chinese Manufacturers Association of Hong Kong
34/F, CMA Building
64-66 Connaught Road C, Hong Kong

Hong Kong Chinese Importers and Exporters Association
7-8th Floor, Champion Building
287-91 Des Veoux Road, Hong Kong

JAPAN

Tokyo Chinese Business Asssociation
2-13-10 Akebono-machi
Tachikawa-shi, Japan

Kobe Chinese Chamber of Commerce
3-1-1 Kaigan-dori, Chuo-ku
Kobe-shi, Japan

Yokohama Association of Chinese Residents
No. 134
Yamashita-co, Naka-ku
Yokohama, Japan

MACAU

Macau Chinese Chamber of Commerce
18-20 Largo Do
Senado, Macau

MALAYSIA

The Associated Chinese Chambers of Commerce and Industry of Malaysia
Ground Floor, Chinese Assembly Hall
1 Jalan Maharajalela
505150 Kuala Lumpur, Malaysia

Kuala Lumpur and Selangor Chinese Chamber of Commerce and Industry
1st Floor, Chinese Assembly Hall
1 Jalan Maharajalela
505150 Kuala Lumpur, Malaysia

Penang Chinese Chamber of Commerce
9th Floor, Penang Chinese Town Hall Building
22 Pitt Street
10300 Penang, Malaysia

Sabah United Chinese Chamber of Commerce
Kinabalu Foundation
Floor 10B Wisma Pendidikan
PO Box 12176
88824 Kota Kinabalu
Sabah, Malaysia

MYANMAR

Myanmar Chinese Chamber of Commerce
No. 1-5, Shwedagon Pagoda Road
PO Box 707
Yangon, Myanmar

PHILIPPINES

Federation of Filipino-Chinese Chamber of Commerce and Industry Inc.
6th Floor, Federation Centre
Muelle de Binondo Street
PO Box 23
Manila, Philippines

SINGAPORE

Singapore Chinese Chamber of Commerce and Industry
47 Hill Street
Singapore

TAIWAN

Chinese National Association of Industry and Commerce
4th Floor, 7 Roosevelt Road, Section 1
Taipei, Taiwan

General Chinese Chamber of Commerce of the Republic of China
7th Floor, Rose Mansion
162 Sin Yee Road, Section 3
Taipei, Taiwan

Taiwan Chamber of Commerce
4F, 158 Sung Chiang Road
Taipei, Taiwan

Chinese National Federation of Industries
12/F, 390 Fu Hsing South Road, Section 1
Taipei, Taiwan

THAILAND

Thai-Chinese Chamber of Commerce
233 South Sathorn Road
Bangkok, Thailand

Appendix 4

CHINESE BUSINESS ORGANISATIONS IN AUSTRALIA: NAMES AND ADDRESSES

A list of most Chinese organisations in Australia is available in the Department of Immigration, Local Government and Ethnic Affairs' *Directory of Ethnic Community Organisations* published in 1992. Following, however, is an updated though not exhaustive list of some of the main Australian Chinese business organisations and relevant bilateral chambers.

Australian Capital Territory

Australia China Business Council
PO Box E14, Queen Victoria Terrace, Canberra, ACT 2600
Tel: 06 273 2311
Fax: 06 273 3286

Australia Taiwan Business Council
GPO Box 2605, Canberra, ACT 2601
Tel: 06 257 2022
Fax: 06 257 2018

New South Wales

Sydney Chinatown Chamber of Commerce
18-20 Goulburn St, Sydney, NSW 2000
Tel: 0418 257 3213
Fax: 02 281 5943

Australia China Chamber of Commerce and Industry (NSW)
GPO Box 3671, Sydney, NSW 2001
Tel: 02 451 3130
Fax: 02 451 3575

Queensland

Chinatown Business Association
Suite 4A, 31 Duncan St, Fortitude Valley, Qld 4006
Tel: 07 252 9559

Taiwanese Australia Business Association
99 Gregory Terrace, Spring Hill, Qld 4000
Tel: 07 832 2288
Fax: 07 832 0999

Australia Taiwan Business Council (Qld)
Taiwan Trade Centre, GPO Box 556, Brisbane, Qld 4001
Tel: 07 231 3566

Hong Kong Business and Professionals of Queensland:
18 Woodsiana St, Robertson, Qld 4109
Tel: 07 345 6823
Fax: 07 305 8287

Australia China Chamber of Commerce and Industry (Qld)
375 Wickham Terrace, Brisbane, Qld 4000
Tel: 07 831 1699
Fax: 07 832 3195

South Australia

Chinese Chamber of Commerce, SA
198 Greenhill Rd, Eastwood, SA 5063
Tel: 08 406 1674
Fax: 08 373 5793

Australia-Brunei Chamber of Commerce
163 Giles St, Adelaide, SA 5000
Tel: 08 232 2711
Fax: 08 232 2717

Australia China Chamber of Commerce and Industry (SA)
198 Greenhill Road, Eastwood, SA 5063
Tel: 08 373 2166
Fax: 08 371 1690

Victoria

Chinese Chamber of Commerce of Victoria
GPO Box 4218NN, Melbourne, Vic 3001
Tel: 03 890 4111
Fax: 03 898 0692

Chinese Professional and Business Association of Victoria
GPO Box 1811Q, Melbourne, Vic 3001
Tel: 03 642 0000
Fax: 03 642 0599

Australia-China Business and Trade Association
Victoria Street, Brunswick, Vic 3056
Tel: 03 381 1866
Fax: 03 367 4974

Australian Chinese Medical Association
PO Box 217, Abbotsford, Vic 3067
Tel: 03 650 4738
Fax: 03 654 5775

Australia-Shanghai General Chamber of Commerce
11 Gertrude St, Fitzroy, Vic 3065
Tel: 03 416 1205
Fax: 03 853 1316

Australia Taiwanese Chamber of Commerce
532 Riversdale Road, Camberwell, Vic 3124
Tel: (03) 8820459
Fax: (03) 8820695

Australia China Chamber of Commerce and Industry (Vic)
L. 4 343 Little Collins St, Melbourne, Vic 3000
Tel: 03 602 5664
Fax: 03 602 5619

Oriental Travel Agencies Consortium
353 Exhibition St, Melbourne, Vic 3020
Tel: 03 663 4648
Fax: 03 663 2364

Sun Chua Luen Professional Chef Association
50 Little Bourke St, Melbourne, Vic 3000
Tel: 03 639 2969

Western Australia

Western Australia Chinese Chamber of Commerce
L. 45 Bankwest Tower, St Georges Terrace, Perth, WA 6000
Tel: 09 481 8228
Fax: 09 481 8288

Australia China Chamber of Commerce and Industry (WA)
c/- St John of God Medical Centre, 175 Cambridge St, Wembley, WA 6014
Tel: 09 381 7498
Fax: 09 388 2437

Appendix 5

AUSTRALIAN CHINESE ORGANISATIONS: AN OVERVIEW

An attempt in 1992 to list as many as possible of Australia's ethnic organisations identified 80 Chinese 'ethnic' organisations in Australia.[1] Now there are more than 200 Chinese business, professional, social, cultural, and religious organisations in Australia.

Australia's growing number of increasingly diverse Chinese organisations serve a variety of functions. As discussed in Chapter 1, Chinese organisations in overseas Chinese communities historically were based on district, clan, dialect, guild and other bases. Such associations functioned as mutual help associations before trade unions had evolved and government or other organised assistance was either non-existent or minimal. In Australia, early organisations were commonly those based on people from the same district in China, for example, the See Yap Society of Melbourne and the Zhongshan Association of Sydney.[2] The members of both associations came from different parts of China's Guangdong Province. Other organisations based on the immigrants' 'old world' identity included the Chinese Masonic Society and the Kuomintang, which was involved in 'Han' Chinese nationalism and early attempts to overthrow the Manchu-Qing Dynasty in China.

Some early organisations in Australia provided mutual help in settlement. Such 'new world' mutual help organisations provided financial and social support. These organisations were particularly important as little public welfare and other assistance was available to Chinese immigrants in the nineteenth or first half of the twentieth century.

Another category of 'new world' organisations, craft and trade guilds, often corresponded with dialect or regional groupings because of occupational-dialect linkages. These were less common in Australia than among the ethnic Chinese communities of South-East Asia, as Australia's Chinese population was relatively small, and initially, relatively homogeneous.[3]

In Australia now, government services and programs for immigrants are well developed and professional bodies are abundant. Consequently, many Chinese community organisations now aim to maintain cultural links, including the

---

1 See Department of Immigration and Ethnic Affairs, *Directory of Ethnic Organisations*, AGPS, Canberra, 1992.

2 See Yap means 'Four Districts' and comprises Ning Yung, Lung Kong, Hoi Ping and Yun Ping in Guangdong's Pearl River Delta.

3 Chapter 2 contains more detail on occupational-dialect linkages and the attendant craft/dialect-based organisations.

teaching of Chinese language and social-cultural activities. State and federal governments encourage and support these activities.

In the last five years, many internationally-oriented trade, business, and professional Chinese organisations have emerged in Australia's large capital cities. Australia's growing commitment to economic and other ties with countries in the Asia-Pacific region has helped to stimulate interest in various Chinese chambers of commerce and related business and professional groups.

Importantly, many, if not most of Australia's Chinese business associations welcome non-Chinese Australians as either members or associate members. Consequently, they can be an important first step for non-Chinese Australian companies who wish to form links with the Australian Chinese community and possibly, their connections overseas. Appendix 3 contains a list of some of the main Chinese business organisations and services in Asia and Appendix 4 contains that for Australia.

ANALYSING AUSTRALIA'S CHINESE ORGANISATIONS

To better understand the role played today by Australia's Chinese organisations, thirty-one prominent ones were surveyed.[4] Included were Chinese chambers of commerce; Chinatown associations; trades, vocational and professional associations; general community organisations; birthplace, dialect and alumni associations; Chinese political associations; and more informal Chinese business groupings. The bodies surveyed ranged from those which are relatively new to three which have existed for over one hundred years. The organisations surveyed also varied considerably in size, ranging from 3 000 to fewer than 50 members.

Characteristics

Older Chinese Organisations

Among the organisations surveyed that had existed for five or more years, there was a relatively good understanding of Australian society, culture and economy. They typically have a strong commitment to preserving Chinese cultural heritage. Thus, they could be described as effectively bi-cultural in that their members are well integrated with mainstream Australian society, but they retain a strong appreciation for their Chinese backgrounds. Many of these organisations were formed and run by immigrants from Malaysia, Singapore, Hong Kong, and south-eastern China. Most of their members are well established in business or the professions. A number also appear to have good links with Australia's mainstream political parties. Two examples are the Chinese Fellowship and Chinese Community Society of Victoria.

---

4 Not all organisations were surveyed, but an attempt was made to survey a representative mix. Interviews with the chief office bearer or his or her nominee were conducted either face-to-face or over the telephone. A structured questionnaire containing over 25 questions was used to collect a range of common information about each organisation. The questionnaire also contained questions on the interviewee's perceptions of the comparative advantages of being Chinese in international business activities, and characteristics regarded as important in the business success of the Chinese.

Some of these organisations were formed and are still run by former overseas students. The Hong Kong Club in Melbourne started as a Hong Kong students' association in 1981. As many students from Hong Kong became permanent residents and immigration from Hong Kong grew, the Hong Kong Club served the wider Hong Kong community, including recent settlers with no education links with Australia. As many Hong Kong migrants returned to Hong Kong to work, a sister association, the Australian Chinese Association of Hong Kong, was formed in Hong Kong to serve the needs of returned migrants. This association also has expanded its interest and activities to include trade and investment between Hong Kong and Australia. Its members have begun to facilitate Hong Kong investment in Australia and Australian business interest in Hong Kong and south-eastern China.

A number of older organisations have a relatively high proportion of older members who came to Australia mostly from China's Guangdong Province and Hong Kong and have not learned English. They are strongly attached to their respective associations and tend to be monolingual, having little command of Mandarin or other Chinese dialects apart from their own. As a result, they are unable to converse easily with non-Chinese or with many of the recent arrivals from northern China and Taiwan, where Mandarin and Hokkien respectively (rather than Cantonese) are used. Two organisations which have a high proportion of these older, more traditional Chinese are the Ning Yung Society and the See Yup Society.

Newer Chinese Organisations

The Chinese organisations formed in the last five years have tended to re-invigorate the Chinese business community. Their members mostly have come from China and Taiwan, tend to be younger and possess up-to-date knowledge of their countries of origin. Their members also appear to have good relations with people in positions of influence and power, including senior government officials. They enthuse over business ventures oriented to the mainland or Taiwan. Two such organisations are the Australia Taiwanese Chamber of Commerce and the Australia-Shanghai General Chamber of Commerce.

Some of the members of the newer organisations, however, may not yet have good English-language skills or a great knowledge of the intricacies of Australia's business environment, such as the tax system, business culture, and social networks. They are, on the other hand, usually fluent in Mandarin and generally have command of written Chinese, which is not always the case with Chinese from Malaysia, Singapore, and Vietnam. The English language barrier has particularly restricted their interaction with the wider Australian society. These difficulties may encourage some to consider returning to their home countries.

Australia's Chinese Organisations Drawing Australia into Asia

Many Chinese organisations active in Australia are oriented to international trade and investment. If their memberships do not have direct connections abroad, they might have ancestral dialect or clan ties abroad which could be reactivated. At the very least, they will be typically empathetic with the social and business cultures of the Chinese abroad.

When asked to identify ways in which the Chinese organisations and their leaders contribute to Australia's economic links with Asia, the interviewees saw their most useful role as providing a 'bridge' between Australia and specific overseas countries or even between Australia's state and federal governments and the governments of their country of origin. Many saw themselves as well placed to offer up-to-date and reliable information on investment and market opportunities overseas, and some believed they could provide advice facilitating investment from overseas into Australia.

Within Australia's Chinese communities, many regarded their prime contribution as helping new migrants and advising business and professional migrants on the Australian business environment and the tax system. More generally, they promoted Chinese culture, including the maintenance of the Chinese language, traditional family values and work ethics.

AN OVERVIEW OF SOME OF AUSTRALIA'S MAIN CHINESE CHAMBERS OF COMMERCE

Chinese chambers of commerce can now be found in all the bigger Australian capitals including Melbourne, Sydney, Perth, Brisbane, and Adelaide. Key ethnic Chinese chambers include the Chinese Chamber of Commerce in Victoria, the Chinese Chamber of Commerce of New South Wales, the Chinese Chamber of Commerce of Western Australia, and the Chinese Chamber of Commerce of South Australia Inc.

Apart from general Chinese chambers, three other types of chambers of commerce can be found in Australia. The first includes Chinese chambers that have a China or Chinese focus but comprise a high proportion of office bearers or members who are ethnically not Chinese. Examples are various Australia-China Chambers of Commerce that aim to promote trade-motivated relations with China and the Chinese. Related chambers include those that focus on Taiwan, Singapore, Hong Kong, and Malaysia.

A more recent trend is the formation of ethnic Chinese chambers of commerce with a birthplace focus, including the Australia Taiwanese Chamber of Commerce, the Australia-China Business and Trade Association, the Great Wall Business Association in Victoria and the Australia-Brunei Chamber of Commerce in South Australia. The latest development is to establish sub-regional chambers. An example is the Australia-Shanghai General Chamber of Commerce formed in early 1994 in Melbourne.

Among ethnic Chinese entrepreneurs interviewed in Asia, particularly in Kuala Lumper and Singapore, those Australian chambers which were best known were the Western Australia Chinese Chamber of Commerce and the Chinese Chamber of Commerce of Victoria.

The Chinese Chamber of Commerce, Victoria

The Chinese Chamber of Commerce of Victoria was established in 1987 by half a dozen immigrant and Australian-born Chinese from business or professional backgrounds. The founders were the prominent community activist Wellington Lee OBE, a third-generation, Darwin-born pharmacist, who is one of the founding members of the Chinese Professional and Businessmen Association as well as the foundation chairperson of the Federation of Chinese Associations; Sam Leong, a Hong Kong-born solicitor who has subsequently returned to Hong Kong; Stephen Ng, a former Telecom financial analyst now in private accounting practice; Gordon Hong, a public relations consultant; Cyril Lee, managing director of Oceanic Food, a seafood supplier; and Steven Cheung, managing director of Makmur Enterprise, an Indonesian-born manufacturer of dim sum and other frozen food products.

In 1989, the chamber became more active and began to articulate the business interests of the Chinese. This development was facilitated by the growing national and state interest in closer economic ties with the booming Asian economies. The membership grew steadily as interest came not only from within the Chinese business and professional communities but also Anglo-Australian businesses, including large accounting firms, real estate agents, and legal firms.

The chamber organised public functions with relatively high profile speakers from government and businesses. One function in 1991 featured the then Victorian Minister for Tourism and attracted 220 participants. After this, the chamber began to be noticed by 'mainstream' business and government agencies. The chamber, for example, provided a visible Asian presence when the legal firm, Gadens Ridgeway, organised the Zhuhai Special Economic Zone Investment Forum in Melbourne. Other firms increasingly look to the chamber for representatives or involvement when they undertake activities relating to China.

Now the chamber has more than 200 members, it is well positioned to develop from being a voluntary association to a professional one, with a secretariat staffed with full-time officers to service its functions.

The chamber has promoted itself as the peak Chinese business association for dealing with federal and state governments. It now regularly hosts receptions, dinners, and other functions for visiting delegations from China, receiving an average 12-15 of these per year.

The chamber's eleven-member delegation to the Second World Chinese Entrepreneur Convention in Hong Kong in December 1993 was accorded considerable attention by the conference organiser and the Hong Kong media. With the South Australian chamber, it is bidding for the 1997 Fourth World Chinese Entrepreneurs Convention. A three-member delegation led by its president and vice-president recently visited the Thai-Chinese Chamber of Commerce and the Singapore Chinese Chamber of Commerce and Industry with financial support from the Victorian Tourism Commission.[5]

....

5 The World Chinese Entrepreneurs Convention is further discussed in Chapter 9.

The chamber originally chose the dragon as its logo because it represented its values: fairness, determination, strength and friendliness. However, in 1994, the committee decided that the chamber should assert itself in a new era when Australia was looking towards Asian markets and decided to change its logo to mark this move. It convened a public logo competition. It wanted the new logo to convey in symbolic terms the Chamber's desire to bring Chinese business people together as a community, to assist and promote their various businesses, to act as an advocate on behalf of the Chinese community, and also to support Australian companies wishing to do business with Asians both locally and internationally. The winning design featured a red and blue 'yin-yang' symbol. The blue accompanied by the Southern Cross represented Australia and the red, the Chinese.

The Chinese Chamber of Commerce of South Australia

The Chinese Chamber of Commerce of South Australia, was founded in 1989. It has around 150 members; many are active in business.

Membership is open to non-Chinese, and about 40 per cent of the membership is non-Chinese.

The chamber aims to promote trade within Australia and with South-East Asia; improve the Australian Chinese profile in Australia; and encourage Australian Chinese to participate actively in local politics.

The chamber holds business talks and seminars bi-monthly; visits annually China and South-East Asian countries; hosts dinners and receptions for visiting delegations, and holds business exhibitions in Australia and overseas. The chamber is investigating the feasibility of building a retirement village in South Australia to attract affluent ethnic Chinese from abroad.

The Western Australian Chinese Chamber of Commerce

The Western Australian Chinese Chamber of Commerce was established in 1987. It has around 450 members, is open to non-Chinese, and has no specific requirements for membership. Non-members can participate in chamber activities.

The chamber is governed by a council and is divided into eight functional sub-committees. The chamber attempts to have a wide representation on the governing council to 'feel the pulse of the community'.

The chamber is well organised, has a staffed secretariat and produces numerous detailed and high quality publications. It sent delegates to the Second World Entrepreneurs Convention in Hong Kong in 1993. Its main activities include: facilitating business networking; organising trade missions; holding 'coffee shop forums' to which guest speakers are invited; running skill enhancement programs; and holding social events.

The coffee shop forums are held monthly. Weekly networking evenings are held and a guest speaker provides the focus for Australian Chinese and non-Chinese business people to meet and make connections. Also, regular trade missions are organised by the chamber. Recent missions have visited Laos, Indonesia, Malaysia, Hong Kong and China, and Vietnam.

The Australia-Shanghai General Chamber of Commerce

The Australia-Shanghai General Chamber of Commerce was formed in April, 1994 and officially registered in November, 1994.

The chamber has 80 members, 60 individual and 20 corporate members. The chamber receives support from the Australian and Chinese Governments. It has invited Chinese and Australian government officials and senior business figures to act as its advisers.

The main aim of the chamber is to facilitate trade and investment between Australia and China, especially Shanghai, seeing itself as a bridge for the growing trade and other ties between the two countries.

The chamber aims to: provide commercial information; act as an agent and consultant in commercial affairs; recommend and guide investment projects; organise trade talks; and conduct training courses.

The chamber has links with 19 Shanghainese organisations around the world. A standing councillor of the chamber, Meng Bin-Hua, is China's business representative in Australia and also is an economic commissioner of the Shanghai Municipal People's Government.

The chamber plans to form a subsidiary to invest in China and Australia. It is planned that the company will invest A$500 000 in a leisure village on Chang Xin Island, off Shanghai's coast.

The Australia Taiwanese Chamber of Commerce

The Australia Taiwanese Chamber of Commerce was founded in 1990. All 45 members are Taiwanese business people and professionals.

The chamber assists and supports understanding of the business environments of Australia and Taiwan. Chamber members meet monthly to exchange business news.

The chamber plans to develop a computerised list of business people in Australia and Taiwan who are eager to trade with and invest in Taiwan and Australia respectively. This list would facilitate the matching of business interests.

The Australia-Brunei Chamber of Commerce

The Australia-Brunei Chamber of Commerce was formed in March 1994 to encourage business links between Australia and Brunei. It has 20 individual and 30 company members. Most members are ethnic Chinese business people but the chamber's membership is open to non-Chinese.

The chamber promotes business between Australia and Brunei by providing up-to-date information, particularly on agricultural production, fishery and forestry, to business people in the two countries. The chamber plans to set up five regional branches in Australia and perhaps a branch in Brunei.

The chamber sees its main responsibility as providing correct information to business people and directing them to the right business partners and in the right directions. If it does this successfully, the chamber will build up a strong network and strengthen its national service, which it hopes will enable it to seek funding from the Australian and Brunei Governments. The chamber is developing close relations with the Brunei-Australia Business Council in Brunei and the Australia-Brunei Business Council in Australia.

OTHER LEADING CHINESE ORGANISATIONS

Chambers of commerce are not the only organisations within Chinese communities for Chinese people involved in business and related pursuits. Other groups interested in international, domestic, or local area business activities have formed organisations. For example, the Chinese Professional and Business Association (CPBA) in Melbourne shares many of the interests of the Chinese Chamber of Commerce of Victoria. Other specialist associations are based on country or region of origin, fields of trade or professions.

Other formal organisations focus on social, cultural, welfare and religious aims. However, the interaction among individuals in these organisations often have commercial outcomes. The more active members of such community organisations tend to hold memberships in more than one organisation. The overlapping of birthplace, dialect, professional, economic and socio-cultural identities or interest offers fertile grounds for business ideas and projects to germinate.

The following sections provide details of a sample of Chinese social, professional, business and other organisations in Australia, apart from the chambers of commerce. They are grouped by their fields of activity, shared interest or background.

Business and Trade Associations

The Chinese Professional and Business Association, Victoria

The Chinese Professional Business Association was founded in 1974 by Dr Tsiang and Dr Foo (medical practitioners), Mr Chun, Mr Siu (a surgeon), and Mr Teo and Mr Ho (public accountants).

The association has 170 members, and opens its membership to non-Chinese as associate members. Most members come from Hong Kong and South-East Asian countries. To join the association, people have to be professionals, owners of businesses or have tertiary qualifications. It is a non-profit association, which aims to provide an environment for members to interact.

The association holds two informative or educative seminars every three months, both formal and informal. It also holds an annual black tie function and celebrates the Chinese New Year. The association has raised funds for various causes including a hostel for elderly Chinese and a fund to assist students from China.

Australia-China Business and Trade Association

The Australia-China Business and Trade Association was established in June 1994 and is based in Melbourne. Most of its members are students, former students, and new immigrants from China. Some of them are involved in the export-import business between China and Australia. The association aims to provide general assistance to members and provide members with advice on how to develop trade between Australia and China and between Australia and South-East Asia.

The main activities of the association include conducting seminars on: import and export procedures, Australia's taxation system and financial systems and the stock exchanges of China and Australia.

The association also holds monthly meetings to discuss relevant current issues. It receives visitors from China and organises social functions to allow for business networking.

The association claims its members have good relations with and connections in China and seeks to mediate between Australian and Chinese business people. Non-Chinese Australian business people are able to approach the association for introductions in China and advice on how to do business there.

Great Wall Business Association

The Great Wall Business Association was established in August 1993, and is based in Melbourne. The association has 28 individual members and 46 company members, mainly from China. To join the association, people need to be involved in business and be recommended by two existing members.

The association was formed by a group of mainland Chinese students and business people resident in Australia, who felt a need to assist other Chinese students to build up links with both the Australian and Chinese Governments. The main impetus for its establishment came from the difficulties experienced by mainland Chinese students in securing employment.

Most of the members are involved in small businesses such as cornershops, vegetable shops, clothes shops and import-export businesses. The association assists new Chinese migrants to settle into Australian society, and helps them establish businesses. The association claims to have good links with the Beijing, Shanghai and Guangdong Foreign Investment Commissions.

Hong Kong Business and Professionals Association of Queensland

The Hong Kong Business and Professionals Association of Queensland was established in 1992. The association has 150 individual members and ten company members. The association opens its membership to non-Chinese. Many members have come from Hong Kong but some are Australian-born Chinese.

The main purpose of the association is to assist members to settle smoothly and better understand Australian culture and society. The association seeks to enhance and disseminate understanding of both Australia's and Hong Kong's business and cultural environments. Members are assisted in developing businesses in Australia.

Taiwanese Australia Business Association (Queensland)

The Taiwanese Australia Business Association (Queensland) was established in 1993. It has 200 individual members and membership is open to non-Chinese. Its members are all involved in various types of business.

The association supports people in Australia with information on Taiwan, and assists them in finding appropriate business partners in Taiwan.

'Chinatown' Associations

Sydney Chinatown Chamber of Commerce

The Sydney Chinatown Chamber of Commerce was founded in 1988. It has 140 company members, including restaurateurs, grocers, jewellers, and general retailers.

The association's main role is to represent small businesses in negotiations with governments. It also supplies information to governments and circulates information to its members. Some of the association's members are members of the Sydney Chinatown Police and Citizens Consultative Committee.

The association facilitates, coordinates, and administers business and cultural activities in Chinatown. Each year the association conducts Chinese music concerts to entertain the public, holds Chinese painting exhibitions, runs Chinese New Year Festivals and participates in raising funds for charitable causes.

China Town Business Association (Queensland)

The China Town Business Association (Queensland) was established in 1987. Its 60 company members are from Brisbane's Chinatown. The association opens its membership to non-Chinese. The association promotes Brisbane's Chinatown and Chinese culture and claims good commercial links to Hong Kong.

Trades, Vocational and Professional Associations

Sun Chua Luen Professional Chefs Association

Chinese chefs from Hong Kong established the Sun Chua Luen Professional Chefs Association in Melbourne in 1984. It has 120 members. The association provides mutual and social support among Chinese chefs and is an extension of the Hong Kong Chefs Association. Members need three years' experience as chefs to qualify for full membership. The association meets monthly and holds an annual carnival to display the arts of Chinese cooking to the public.

The association helps restaurateurs locate suitable chefs from overseas.

Chinese Restaurateurs Association of Victoria

The Chinese Restaurateurs Association of Victoria was founded in 1984. It has more than 220 members. Full members must own a restaurant but non-Chinese restaurateurs and interested people who do not own restaurants can be associate members.

The association runs food festivals, promotes training schemes for chefs, holds Chinese cooking competitions, raises funds for Chinese community groups, educates members and represents the interests of its members. Every year it helps to organise the Chinatown Food Carnival. The association supports the Victorian Elderly Chinese Association through fund-raising activities.

Currently, the main challenge for the association is to assist its members to effectively compete against fast food chains. The association also helps to train chefs and young people to develop skills in catering and hospitality. The association also sends some of its members to China to learn more about Chinese regional cuisines and to exchange culinary expertise with Chinese chefs in China.

Oriental Travel Agencies Consortium

The Oriental Travel Agencies Consortium was founded in 1992. It has 21 company members who are owners of or partners in travel agencies.

The consortium aims to 'stabilise' the market prices of air tickets and boost the bargaining power of members with the airlines. The consortium promotes tourism and assists members to maximise profits and claims to have good business links with Hong Kong, Taiwan, Japan, Singapore, Malaysia and China.

Australian Chinese Medical Association

Chinese medical doctors formed the Australian Chinese Medical Association in 1983. Australia has many medical practitioners from Malaysia, Hong Kong, and Singapore who trained in Australian universities.

For a time, a number of these Chinese doctors were interested in forming an Australian Chinese Medical Alumni Association. However, ultimately, a 'Chinese AMA' was formed.

In Victoria, the association has more than 200 members. The association assists Chinese medical practitioners to raise awareness about mainstream medical issues and ethnic community issues. The association also helps Chinese practitioners upgrade their skills.

The association provides four scholarships a year to medical students, two at the University of Melbourne and two at Monash University. It also provides some financial assistance to those universities wanting to send surgeons to China to train Chinese doctors. The association has contacts with overseas Chinese medical associations especially those in the United States.

General Community Organisations

The Ning Yung Society

The Ning Yung Society was founded more than 110 years ago in Melbourne and is the sister organisation of the See Yup Society. It is one of the oldest Chinese community organisations in Melbourne and most of its members are well integrated into the wider Australian society. Although originally a district association, it has broadened its activities to become more a general community organisation.

The Ning Yung Society has more than 1 000 families as members, all with ancestral origins in the Ning Yung community in China. The society supports government community and welfare work and each year it assists the Melbourne City Council to organise the Chinatown New Year Festival. During the Ching Ming Festival (Tomb Sweeping Festival), the society honours its ancestors at its South Melbourne Seeyup Temple.[6]

In the past, the society's members were mostly chefs and gold fossickers and later vegetable gardeners and furniture makers. Now, most are business and professional people.

There are Ning Yung associations all over the world, the biggest of which is in the United States. There are 1 300 000 'units' (based on source families in China) of Ning Yung members worldwide.

Chinese Fellowship of Victoria

The Chinese Fellowship of Victoria was founded in 1971. It currently has 650 family members. Non-Chinese can become associate members.

The fellowship operates two Chinese schools on weekends. It promotes Chinese arts and culture, including painting, tai-chi, chi-kung and traditional Chinese dancing and is committed to preserving the cultural heritage of the Chinese and promoting traditional Chinese values.

Most of the fellowship's members are well integrated into mainstream Australian society. The fellowship seeks to play the role of a mediator between the Government and the Chinese community. It has no formal links with Chinese organisations abroad.

Chinese Club of Queensland

The Chinese Club of Queensland was formed in 1953. The club has around 500 Chinese members.

The club sees its role as strengthening ties between Australia and China. It also promotes Chinese culture and language education and raises funds for charitable works.

6 The long history of Melbourne's Chinese community is reflected by the construction some 160 years ago (or around the fifth year of Xian Feng [1831-61] of the Qing Dynasty) of the See Yup Society Temple.

It has purchased a three-storey property near Brisbane's Chinatown as its permanent office and plans to have full-time administrative staff. Funding for the club is principally derived from a number of prominent Queensland Chinese business people.

Chinese Community Society of Victoria

The Chinese Community Society of Victoria was founded more than 70 years ago to represent the various Chinese community groups in Victoria. More recently, it has campaigned for Chinese students to stay in Australia after the 1989 Tiananmen Square incident. The society includes many of Victoria's key Chinese community leaders. It claims its members have good links with Chinese communities in the United States, Canada, South-East Asia, Taiwan and other Australian States.

The society hopes to put more effort into educating the younger generations to prevent the erosion of Chinese cultural values.

Australian Chinese Community Association of New South Wales

The Australian Chinese Community Association of New South Wales was established in 1974 and has approximately 5 500 members. It is a registered charity and acts as an advocate, assists new Chinese migrants in their resettlement, and promotes mutual understanding between the Chinese and non-Chinese communities in Australia. The association receives approximately half its revenue from the Federal and State Governments. The association has some property holdings, including the building in which its central office is housed. Altogether, there are six offices in Sydney located where there are significant local Chinese populations. These are staffed mostly by volunteers.

The association recently opened a A$3.8 million, 46-bed private nursing home in the Sydney suburb of Earlwood. The nursing home caters for elderly Chinese residents; has bilingual staff; and serves Chinese meals. *Feng shui* principles were used in designing the home.

Birthplace Associations

NSW *Indo-China Chinese Association*

The Indo-China Chinese Association was established in 1981. It has 3 000 members, mostly Chinese from Indochina. It is a welfare-oriented association, promoting Chinese culture, assisting members to integrate into Australian society, and providing social support.

The association concentrates on the well being of the Chinese elderly, women and youth. It runs a Chinese school, and recently, with the assistance of the school, produced a Cantonese-language video on domestic violence and parenting education for Chinese women. Also it runs employment skills seminars and plans to open a child care centre.

The Hong Kong Club

The Hong Kong Club was first established in 1965 as the Overseas Hong Kong Students Association of Victoria. The name was changed to the Hong Kong Club in 1979 to reflect a growing professional and business membership. In 1985, the club was incorporated in Victoria under the Associations Incorporation Act 1981. The club has more than 200 families as members.

The club aims to provide opportunities for members to meet regularly, foster friendships, and exchange experiences and ideas. The club organises social functions and activities and produces a monthly newsletter.

Some members of the club still work and do business in Hong Kong. They provide up-to-date information about Hong Kong's business environment to other Australian business people interested in doing business in Hong Kong or south-eastern China. The club has a sister association in Hong Kong known as the Australian Chinese Association of Hong Kong.

Australian Mainland Chinese Association

The Australian Mainland Chinese Association was formed in 1990 and has around 3 000 members, all from China. A large proportion of them came to Australia to study.

The association assists PRC overseas students to settle in Australia. Many of its members have English language difficulties and it provides assistance in this area.

Taiwanese Association of Australia (Melbourne Branch)

The Taiwanese Association of Australia (Melbourne Branch) was first registered in April 1993. The association has 50 family members, mostly from Taiwan.

The association assists Taiwanese migrants to settle in Australia, especially students enrolled in secondary and tertiary education institutions here. The association holds frequent seminars by scholars and intellectuals from Taiwan. It also provides up-to-date information on Taiwan's business environment to Australian business people considering doing business in Taiwan.

Alumni Associations

National Cheng-Chi University Alumni Association of Melbourne

The National Cheng-Chi University Alumni Association is a classmate association of the prestigious National Cheng-Chi University of Taiwan. The university specialises in politics, economics, international relations, foreign languages and public administration. It is an important source of graduates for Taiwan's civil service, including its Ministry of Foreign Affairs. The Melbourne association was founded in November 1990 and has 50 individual members, who are former students and staff of the Cheng-Chi University.

The association supports former students and staff members who are now overseas and there are more than 100 Cheng-Chi Alumni Associations all over the world. Members include business people, professionals, civil servants and politicians. The headquarters of the National Cheng-Chi University Alumni Association is in Taiwan.

Associations Involved in Community Politics

Mandarin Association of Melbourne

The Mandarin Association of Melbourne was founded in 1976. The association has 400 families as members, mostly from Taiwan and China. The association's name in Chinese means the 'Free China Association' and it has a sister association in Taiwan known as the Taiwan-Melbourne Association.

Most of the association's members are business people and professionals. It claims to have good connections in Taiwan, China and South-East Asia. Although primarily a political organisation, some of its members are involved in exporting Australian primary goods to Taiwan and South-East Asia.

Political or Quasi-Political Organisations

Chinese Nationalist Party (KMT)

The Chinese Nationalist Party (Kuomintang) has branches in Melbourne and Sydney. It is associated with the international Kuomintang which was formed to support Dr Sun Yat Sen's campaign to overthrow China's Qing Dynasty. In Victoria, the Party claims to have over 1 000 members.

Chinese Masonic Society

The Chinese Masonic Society was established in Australia in 1897 and has more than 650 members. (The society is not related to the Freemasons.) The movement was formed around 300 years ago by a monk from China's Shao Lin Temple. Its purpose was to unite the China's majority Han Chinese population to overthrow the Qing-Manchu Government. It became a clandestine organisation and branches were formed overseas among Chinese immigrant communities. The society has retained the basic goal of maintaining the Chinese culture and loyalty to China.

Most of the society's members are business people in the service sector. It runs Mandarin classes, helps to promote the Chinese New Year Festival and raises funds for charities.

The society has sister societies all over the world, including in China, Taiwan, the United States, Canada, the Philippines, and South Africa.

Chinese Community Cultural Centre

The Chinese Community Cultural Centre is an official organisation of the Taiwanese Government. The centre was established to maintain links with Chinese overseas. The Melbourne centre was established in 1987. Another centre is in Sydney and one is planned for Perth.

The centres aim to satisfy the welfare and cultural needs of the Chinese communities and report directly to the Overseas Chinese Affairs Commission in Taipei. The centre is regarded by some as Taiwan's instrument in its rivalry against Beijing in winning the hearts of the 'overseas' Chinese.

Centre facilities are accessible to all. Members of the public can use the centre's library of Chinese books and magazines from Taiwan.

Dialect Group Associations

Australian Chinese Teo-Chew Association (Sydney)

The Australian Chinese Teo-Chew Association was founded in 1988. It has 430 members, all with ancestral origins in Shantou and its surrounding districts.

The association supports the Sydney Teochiu community and provides assistance to new arrivals. It is represented in the worldwide Teochiu Alliance Association, representatives of which meet every two years to promote international networking among Teochiu communities.[7] Many of the association's members are from Indochina.

---

7 See Chapter 9 for further information on the association.

Appendix 6

A NOTE ON *FENG SHUI* AND LUCKY NUMBERS

A number of traditional beliefs held by some ethnic Chinese people may be relevant in a business context.

FENG SHUI

One of these is *feng shui* or 'geomancy' which concerns the positioning of objects, including buildings, furniture and tombs, so that they are in harmony with the earth's natural forces. Not all ethnic Chinese adhere to the principles of *feng shui*. However, it is particularly prevalent among the Hong Kong Chinese and those who are wealthy enough may seek *feng shui* advice on building and interior design.

Feng Shui and Chinese Cemeteries

Across Asia, Chinese cemeteries are usually sited along the sides of hills. Such sitings are believed to be essential to protect the souls of the deceased from demons. Australia's growing Chinese population has now made the establishment of private Chinese cemeteries in Australia feasible.

One Adelaide funeral company is investigating the feasibility of setting up a Chinese cemetery near Adelaide. It has found an ideal site with an appropriate incline in the Adelaide Hills and there are plans to divide the cemetery into speech groups, as is the practice elsewhere. The company also sent an employee to Hong Kong to attend Chinese funerals to observe what proceedings are appropriate.

Land which has been used in the past as a burial site is considered to have very poor *feng shui* for new housing or buildings. Also housing erected opposite an existing cemetery has bad *feng shui*. A land developer seeking to sell housing to ethnic Chinese people would be well advised to avoid such sites.

In Thailand, some Sino-Thais as well as some ethnic Thais, employ *feng shui*. Among the Malaysian and Singaporean Chinese, *feng shui* is taken less seriously. However, the positioning of the doors and door knobs in Singapore's new Hyatt Hotel was changed, apparently on the advice of a *feng shui* expert, and in Malaysia, some interviewees claimed a prominent Chinese businessmen on Penang has experienced a run of family misfortunes which were attributed to poor *feng shui* in the siting of his house. Another entrepreneurial South-East Asian ethnic Chinese family also had a run of bad luck, including the loss of much of the fortune built up by the first generation. Some have attributed the blame to the poor *feng shui* of the family's ancestral tombs.

Feng shui can be big business. Evidence of this can be provided by passenger car maker Volvo which conducted an advertising campaign in Asia in early 1995 with the slogan 'Volvo. Because of the Feng Shui'.[1] *Feng shui* also was deemed important enough by the developers of a A$3.8 million nursing home for elderly Chinese in Sydney (mentioned in Appendix 5) to have *feng shui* principles incorporated into the nursing home's design to attract residents.

LUCK, LUCKY NUMBERS AND SYMBOLS

Among ethnic Chinese people engaged in small business, the role of luck can be an important factor in business. Many ethnic Chinese shopkeepers across Asia attach great importance to ensuring that the first potential customer for the day makes a purchase. Many are prepared to drop their price considerably to ensure that at least something is purchased. This is especially the case if the business has recently commenced operation.[2]

Many ethnic Chinese, again, particularly Hong Kong Chinese, believe that certain numbers are lucky or unlucky. The number 8 is considered lucky because in Cantonese it is a homonym for 'rich'. Subsequently, many Hong Kong businesses attempt to be associated with the number 8. A recent Hong Kong restaurant review featured ten of Hong Kong's top restaurants, of which nine had managed to have telephone numbers with at least one 8 in them, two had numbers with at least 88 in them, and another two had telephone numbers with 8888s. One even had the business name of 'Tables 88', located at number 88 in its street.[3] The Christmas Island Casino has followed suit. Set up largely by Sino-Indonesian interests to serve the Chinese communities of South-East Asia, it can be reached by calling the island's operator and asking for extension 8888. Alternatively, the casino can be reached by mail - its post office box number is 888.[4] Similarly, tickets for the Chinese Chamber of Commerce of Victoria's 1995 Chinese New Year Ball were deliberately priced at A$80 and A$88.

Just as 8 is a lucky number, 4 is considered unlucky. In Cantonese, 4 is a homonym for 'death' and 2 is a homonym for 'easy'. Thus 24 is particularly unlucky. The importance of beliefs held by some Chinese should not be underestimated. One property consultant interviewed for this study recounted how a Chinese couple were satisfied with every aspect of a Canberra house they were considering for purchase except its house number. Appeals to the local government for permission to change the house number failed, so the purchase fell through.

1 See for instance, full-page advertisements in the 9 January 1995 issue of the *Asian Wall Street Journal* and the 19 January 1995 issue of the *Far Eastern Economic Review*.

2 If the first customer makes a purchase then the business will be especially profitable. If the customer is allowed to go away without making a purchase this signals bad luck.

3 See Durack, T., 'Hot in Hong Kong', *Australian Gourmet Traveller*, October 1994.

4 See *Far Eastern Economic Review*, 'Christmas gamble', 8 July 1994.

Such symbolism has commercial use. For example, New South Wales Lotteries initially undertook some marketing research to establish which ethnic groups would be most appropriate for targeted advertising campaigns. Australian Chinese were found to be the most suitable group, particularly around Chinese New Year. So, since 1992, the company has issued A$2 scratch lottery games specifically for Chinese New Year. The lottery tickets are red and yellow and feature the relevant animal for the incoming New Year. Panels that are scratched off reveal winning combinations of numbers featuring auspicious symbols as well as the number 8. During the twelve weeks that the 1992 Chinese New Year 'Lucky Monkeys' game was run, revenues for the A$2 tickets increased between A$150,000 and A$200,000.[5]

The Experiences of Ansett in Hong Kong

As part of its expansion offshore, Ansett Australia set up an office in Hong Kong. In setting up its new operations to service its flights between Australia and Hong Kong, Ansett has been careful to pay due consideration to local cultural nuances and superstitions. Prior to opening its office, Ansett employed the services of a *feng shui* master so that *feng shui* principles could be incorporated into the office lay out. This was done not so much that the office's senior management had any great belief in *feng shui*, but more to make the locally engaged staff and clients feel more at ease.

The flight from Hong Kong to Sydney has the flight designation 888; yellow is avoided in the cabin interiors; and meals served on board are designed around Cantonese tastes. Cabin staff also undergo intensive cultural training, emphasising the need for greater respect to be shown to elderly Chinese, for example.

The Airline has also been cautious in translating its promotions into Chinese. The 'Spaceships are coming' campaign which Ansett ran in Australia also ran in Hong Kong, except when translated into Chinese script, 'spaceship' also means 'empty everyday'. The campaign was modified slightly to avoid this connotation. (Similarly, when Ansett first began promoting its Australian domestic flights in Singapore, the Chinese characters for Ansett could also be read as 'peaceful death'. The characters were subsequently modified to read 'peaceful speed'.)

Particular days of the year are considered by many Chinese to be particularly auspicious. The third day of the third lunar month is a fortuitous time for weddings, so most airlines out of Hong Kong have a rush of bookings from honeymooners around this time.

Despite all Ansett's cultural sensitivity, the routes it flies out of Hong Kong remain extremely price sensitive. Nonetheless, the market is also very status conscious and Hong Kong is still one place where first class seats sell.

---

5 Office of Multicultural Affairs, 'Winning new sales with ancient symbols', Productive Diversity information brochure.

Appendix 7

THE CONGLOMERATES - EIGHT CASE STUDIES

This appendix comprises case studies of ethnic Chinese companies in East Asia. They are:

- Hopewell Group (Hong Kong)
- Li Ka-shing Group (Hong Kong)
- Pao/Woo Group (Hong Kong)
- Tomei Group (Hong Kong)
- Bangkok Bank Group (Thailand)
- CP Group (Thailand)
- Robert Kuok Group (Malaysia, Hong Kong)
- Quek/Kwek Groups (Malaysia, Singapore).

WU FAMILY[1]

Main Companies:

a) Hopewell Holdings

Major Shareholders: Gordon Wu and family (37.3 per cent)
Chairman: James Man-hon Wu
Managing Director: Gordon Ying Sheung Wu
Market Capitalisation: June 1994, $3.764 billion
Main Activities: Construction, engineering and property company
Activities Mainly Located: Hong Kong, China, Macau, Thailand, Philippines, Indonesia

b) CEPA (Consolidated Electric Power Asia Ltd)

In November 1993, Hopewell's power station operations throughout Asia were listed separately as a newly formed subsidiary CEPA in Hong Kong, with separate placements with institutions in Europe, Asia and the United States.

Major Shareholders: Hopewell (46 per cent to rise to 63 per cent in two years)
Chairman: Gordon Ying Sheung Wu
Managing Director: Stewart W.G. Elliot
Market Capitalisation: $1.880 billion

....

1 See *Far Eastern Economic Review; Forbes Magazine*, 18 July 1994; *South China Morning Post; Asian Wall Street Journal*; Yamaguchi, M., 'The Emerging Chinese Business Sphere', *Nomura Asian Perspectives*, July 1993, Vol 11, No. 2; *Corporate International's Company Handbook*, Hong Kong, June 1994.

Gordon Wu initially built his international interests on the basis of ambitious infrastructure projects in south-eastern China, where he was a pioneer. However, the extension of his activities around the region to the Philippines, Thailand, India, Pakistan and Indonesia has reduced his dependency on China and strengthened his bargaining power. In most of the countries where Wu invests, he is careful to first make good political connections.

He first became involved in China in the mid-1980s, at a time when few dared to commit significant funds there. He has won considerable credibility by devoting large sums to power plants and highways, and has a record of successful and profitable completion, using foreign capital flowing into the region.

China's need for power is escalating. In 1993, the Government announced it would boost investment in power development by 50 per cent in that year and encourage foreign investment in power projects with the aim of providing electricity for 95 per cent of rural residents by 2000. China is already the fourth largest generator of power in the world but its per capita consumption is still only in 80th position.

Hopewell completed a first major power station in Guangdong in 1987 (Shajiao B), and a second (Shajiao C) is under construction. Wu's power stations provided about 35 per cent of Guangdong's electricity at the end of 1994.

When CEPA was formed at the end of 1993, the company aimed to finance at least ten and up to twenty more power stations in China, in a dozen provinces including Guangxi and Inner Mongolia, over the next six to seven years, at a cost of over $8 billion.

Wu negotiated very favourable terms with Guangdong, which insulated him against risks of future foreign exchange losses (half the electricity tariff was to be paid in foreign currency) and guaranteed his profits. Towards the end of 1993, however, a central government policy change prohibited any further such agreements and sought to cap power profits at around 12 per cent. Wu made a rapid change of direction, abandoning, at least for the current time, his 'China first' strategy. His attention has since turned to Indonesia where there are fewer currency uncertainties, and where returns of 20 per cent or higher on power developments are permissible.

After a series of meetings with Indonesian officials in December 1993, Gordon Wu won rapid approval for CEPA to construct power plants at Paiton in Indonesia. In September 1994, CEPA signed a contract with Indonesia to build a US$2 billion coal-fired power station in Java. The plant is to be operational by 1998, with an expected return of 20 per cent. CEPA agreed to list it on the JSE, floating about 25 per cent of it.

In China, Hopewell is also working on a triangle of major highways linking the cities of the Pearl River and Hong Kong. The first stage of a six lane, 123 kilometre super highway, from Guangzhou to Shenzhen was opened to traffic in July 1994. It was completed in 26 months, at a cost of US$1.2 billion, a particularly impressive achievement given delays with land acquisition and the fact that Wu had not built a highway before. Traffic demand on the tollway, which cuts the travelling time from five to two hours, was predicted to build up to 35 000 a day after ten years. This figure now seems likely to be approached within the first year and decade projections are set at 100 000. Later stages will connect Guangzhou and Zhuhai, near Macau, and then a third leg, with a 4.6 kilometre bridge across the Pearl River, will complete the triangle.

Profits will be generated via tolls, but will come mostly from the property rights granted beside the route. Hopewell has a 30 year lease on land at the ten interchanges where feeder routes join the highway, and will take 40 per cent of profits from the major commercial and shopping complexes being developed on these sites, with a total floor space on completion in 1996 of ten million square feet. It is expected that each will become the nucleus of a new town.

In mid 1993, Hopewell began constructing a mass transit system in Bangkok, a US$3-$4 billion project involving road, rail and property development; the first leg is scheduled for completion in 1996. Bangkok Bank is acting as the financial adviser for the project which will be listed on the Stock Exchange of Thailand.

In early 1994, he won a contract to build and operate a power plant in Luzon, the Philippines. Shares for this are also planned to be floated locally.

Wu moved beyond the region when he signed a deal worth US$7.7 billion in October 1994 for CEPA to construct eight coal-powered units in Pakistan and develop the necessary coal fields.

Gordon Wu's own large infrastructure projects on a number of occasions have led him to seek collaboration and joint financing with Li Ka-shing's Cheung Kong and Walter Kwok's Sun Hung Kai Properties, as well as with Japanese and Western interests.

LI FAMILY[2]

Main Companies:

a) Cheung Kong

Major Shareholders: Li Ka-shing (34.9 per cent)
Chairman: Li Ka-shing
Deputy Chairmen: George Magnus, Victor Li
Market Capitalisation: $10.283 billion
Main Activities: Hong Kong's largest private property developer; investments
Activities Mainly Located: Hong Kong, China
Main companies: Green Island Cement, Hutchison Whampoa

b) Hutchison Whampoa

Major Shareholders: Cheung Kong Holdings (43 per cent)
Chairman: Li Ka-shing
Managing Director: Canning Fok

2 *Corporate International's Company Handbook*, Hong Kong, June 1994; *Far Eastern Economic Review*; *Forbes Magazine*, 18 July 1994; *Fortune International*, 28 June 1993; *Jetro China Newsletter*, 102, January-February 1993; Lippo Ltd, Hong Kong, *Annual Report*; Masaaki Yamaguchi, 'The Emerging Chinese Business Sphere', *Nomura Asian Perspectives*, July 1993, Vol 11 No.2; *South China Morning Post*; *Time*, 10 May 1993.

Market Capitalisation: $14.722 billion
Main Activities: One of Hong Kong's largest conglomerates. Property development, cargo handling, container terminals, trading, retailing, oil and gas, telecommunications, electricity utilities
Activities Mainly Located: Hong Kong, China, UK, Canada
Main Companies: Cavendish, Fortress Stores, HIT, HK Paging, HK Cellular, Husky Oil (Canada), Millicom Cellular (UK), Pacific Century Group, Park'n Shop, Watson's

c) Hongkong Electric

Major Shareholders: Hutchison Whampoa (34.6 per cent)
Chairman: George Magnus
Managing Director: Ewan Yee Lup-Yuen
Market Capitalisation: $5.897 billion
Main Activities: Electric power utility supplying Hong Kong Island
Activities Mainly Located: Hong Kong

Li Ka-shing's purchase of a major share in the British-owned Hong Kong-based company, Hutchison, in 1979 was a milestone in replacing British with ethnic Chinese interests in Hong Kong. The Li companies grew during the 1970s and 1980s through activities in Hong Kong, involving timely land deals and property development, container terminal operation (HIT is the world's largest private container terminal operator) and development of a number of retail chains with a total of nearly 400 outlets. More recently, the companies have moved successfully into pagers and cellular phones (Hong Kong Paging and Hong Kong Cellular).

Li Ka-shing spent much of the 1980s diversifying away from Asia. He bought Husky Oil (a major oil refiner) in Canada and 75 per cent of the port of Felixstowe in Britain. In Vancouver, with its 350 000 Chinese population, he joined a consortium in 1988 to build a 200 hectare business and housing complex on the Expo site. A significant loss making venture was a foray into European telecommunications with the purchase of Millicom Cellular.

Generally, Li's push away from Asia was not as profitable as had been hoped and in the 1990s, he refocused on China. The switch led to internal disagreements and the departure of Hutchison's managing director, Simon Murray, in September 1993. Murray has since been replaced by Canning Fok, marking a return to greater family control.

The Group's investments in China, although late in starting, are diverse and substantial. By mid 1993, commitments included construction and operation of a container terminal in Shanghai (enabling goods to arrive directly instead of being shipped from Hong Kong); property development with reclamation work in Shenzhen; redevelopment of two 20,000 container berths at Zuchai Port at Shantou in Guangdong Province; port and other development on Hainan Island; redevelopment of Fuzhou's CBD and a 35 per cent stake in stage two of Hopewell's super highway, at a total cost of US$2.3 billion. Li also is involved in Hopewell's Guangdong power plant and in developing shopping centres in Shanghai and Beijing, a zinc refinery in Zhuzhou, power plants in Hebei, container handling in Zhuhai and further container port ventures at Yantian and Zhuhai.

Li Ka-shing entrusted his satellite television division, Star TV, covering the whole of South-East Asia, to his younger son Richard who built it up and then sold it to Rupert Murdoch. Richard Li's Pacific Century Group now controls the Singapore-listed Seapower Asian Investments, whose main asset, along with property holdings, is Top Glory Insurance, which has since aggressively expanded.[3] It hired many sales agents from its Australian-based rival, National Mutual, and expanded its workforce from 300 to 1 500, aimed to reach 2 000 by March 1995, and to double that by 1999. Two China-backed insurers are to inject US$13 million into the parent company as it is expected that a change of rules will open the market for selling insurance in China.

Other East Asian activities have also been initiated. Park'n Shop outlets have been opened in Taiwan; Li companies are involved in substantial redevelopment in Kuala Lumpur; and plans have been announced to have a part in the construction of a shopping centre, condominiums and a theme park in Hokkaido in Japan.

Apart from Gordon Wu, Li has joint ventures and business links to other ethnic Chinese entrepreneurs in the region, including Mochtar Riady, through his Lippo Group; Oei Hong Leong, the Hong Kong-based controller of China Strategic Holdings; Robert Kuok; Cheng Yu-tung of New World Developments; and Lee Shau-kee of Henderson Land. Li enjoys good relations with the Chinese Government. Furthermore, he has developed close ties with the business-oriented members of the families of Chinese leaders. He has worked closely with Hong Kong-based companies such as China Venturetech, Citic Pacific and Shougang Hongkong which are controlled by the Chinese Government.

PAO/WOO FAMILY[4]

Main Companies:

a) Wheelock & Company

Major Shareholders: Pao Family Trustees (48.6 per cent)
Chairman: Peter Woo Kwong-ching
Deputy Chairman: H. Sohmen
Market Capitalisation: 1994, $4.618 billion
Main Activities: One of Hong Kong's largest conglomerates. Recently changed name from World International. Long-term property, hotel and infrastructure investments held through Wharf; trading under Wheelock Marden (unlisted), retail with Lane Crawford, property development through Hong Kong Realty and Trust Company which controls Realty Development Corporation; management of China investment by foreign companies through Wheelock Pacific
Activities Mainly Located: Hong Kong, China, Singapore, USA

3 Control was bought from the Sino-Indonesian Soeryadjaya family.

4 See *The Australian; Corporate International's Company Handbook*, Hong Kong, June 1994; *Far Eastern Economic Review; Forbes Magazine*, 18 July 1994; Masaaki Yamaguchi, 'The Emerging Chinese Business Sphere', *Nomura Asian Perspectives*, July 1993, Vol 11 No.2; *South China Morning Post*, various issues.

b) Wharf Holdings

Major Shareholders: Wheelock and Co. (50 per cent)
Honorary Chairman: Peter Woo Kwong-ching
Chairman: Gonzaga Li
Deputy Chairman: Stephen T.H. Ng
Market Capitalisation: June 1994, $9.269 billion
Main Activities: One of largest investment companies in Hong Kong. Large property holdings, hotels, ferry, tramways. Stakes in container terminal operator, cross harbour tunnel, telecommunications (cable TV)
Activities Mainly Located: Hong Kong, China, Singapore, United States
Main companies: Wharf Communications Investments (Communications); Wharf Cable; New T&T HK; WOL Communications; Wharf Hong Kong (Property, Infrastructure, Terminals and Transport); Wharf China (Property and Infrastructure); Wharf Beijing; Wharf Shanghai; Wharf Dalian; Wharf Wuhan; Wharf Sichuan; Wharf International (Hotels; Property and Investments); O millioni Hotels (O millioni North America and O millioni Asia Pacific); Marco Polo Developments; Wharf Hotel Investments; Harbour Centre Developments; Beauforte Investors; Allied Investors

The founder of this group was Y.K. Pao, a native of Ningbo, Zhejiang Province. He came to Hong Kong after World War II, acquired an aging ship and set up the Worldwide Shipping Company. This company now owns the world's largest merchant fleet. He then diversified, buying hotel, property and other companies. Wharf purchased O millioni (Omni) Hotels, a four-star American chain in 1988 to build up its hotel network and to expand into an international chain using the O millioni name. O millioni Hotels comprises two divisions, O millioni North America and O millioni Asia Pacific, formerly known as Marco Polo International. The two divisions represent some 44 luxury hotels in the United States, three in Hong Kong and one in Singapore, with a total of 17 650 guest rooms.

In 1991, Y.K. Pao died and control of the family's business interests passed to his son-in-law, Peter Woo. With this came a change in the previous conservative management style and a shift in focus from shipping to property, infrastructure and telecommunications. There are plans to increase the hotels, by 1998, to sixty in North America and to twenty in Asia, with Bangkok, Jakarta and Kuala Lumpur seen as key cities for expansion. T&T Hong Kong aims to reach all Hong Kong households by 1996, when its cable TV network is completed.

Woo recently stepped down as chairman of Wharf, leaving the more routine administration of its ongoing activities in the hands of an established professional team. Instead he is responsible for new developments in China, through the recently renamed Wheelock & Co.[5] The new developments centre on Ningbo, Y.K. Pao's ancestral home, and Wuhan, the capital of Hubei, a potential inland transport hub and key node in emerging Shanghai-Hong Kong transport links.

....

[5] In early 1995, it was announced that Woo would also be stepping down from Wheelock in 1996. (See *Asian Wall Street Journal*, 'Growth is aim of new Wheelock board', 17 March 1995.)

In Ningbo, plans have been announced to spend US$15-20 million to upgrade the port for containers. In Wuhan, fifteen letters of intent have been signed for investment in a container port, railway modernisation, industrial park development and a power plant project. Wheelock & Co. also invested in a cable TV network there. Elsewhere, it has a US$5.6 million cable TV joint venture in Chengdu, Sichuan, and has declared plans or taken stakes in railways, expressways and residential development in Guangdong.

Unlike many Hong Kong entrepreneurs who stress their Chinese credentials as they focus on China, Woo also presents himself as a bridge and manager for Western investment in China. Wheelock, once a Jardine company, is a name well known in the West and half of its senior staff are non-Chinese. This appeal to the West is beginning to produce results. A joint venture has been signed with the Virgin Group, to bring their megastores to the region, first to Hong Kong in 1995 and then to China and Taiwan. Also, as mentioned in Chapter 13, a partnership has been signed with Australia's Fosters Brewing Group, which is planning large scale beer production in China.

TOMEI[6]

Major Shareholders: Semi-Tech Global (12.2 per cent), Lau Wing Hung (12.6 per cent)
Chairman: Johnny Lau Wing Hung
Vice Chairman: Lee Yat Wing
Market Capitalisation: $108 million (1994)
Main Activities: Consumer electronics with emphasis on audio products, venture capitalism
Activities Mainly Located: Hong Kong, China, Malaysia, Indonesia

Tomei was founded in 1974 by Japanese educated and trained Johnny Lau, initially to distribute Japanese capacitors and other electronic components. Lau was an early producer of inexpensive sound equipment and one of the first to move his production to China, first subcontracting in 1980 and then establishing a factory in Zhongshan, in the Pearl River Delta in 1981.

Thenceforth Tomei experienced rapid growth. It listed on the Hong Kong stock exchange in 1988 and became the world's largest producer of policaricon capacitors and the third largest producer of personal cassette players. In 1991, it had five per cent of the world market for earphones; made 60 per cent of all CD players produced in China and Hong Kong; and accounted for ten per cent of all Hong Kong electronic exports, supplying Sony, Philips, RCA and others.

By 1993, Tomei had twelve plants in Guangdong (subcontractors or joint ventures), generally in the villages, employing more than 26 000 people, and a further 350 people in the head office in Hong Kong. Lau develops contacts and expertise allowing for great flexibility, and claims to be able to bring a production

6 See *Corporate International's Company Handbook*, Hong Kong, June 1994; *Far Eastern Economic Review*, 19 September 1991; *South China Morning Post*; and *Time*, 10 April 1993.

line on stream in three months. His company also has a manufacturing facility in Malaysia and a sub-assembly joint venture with the Dharmala Group in Indonesia, a minority shareholder in Tomei.

Since 1990, Tomei has diversified, taking small stakes in Hong Kong electronics firms and nursing them to a point where they can be listed. Lau promotes his company as a conduit for component manufacturers struggling with high labour costs in Japan, South Korea and Taiwan, so they can expand their business to Indonesia and China.

Lau's most important partner in Hong Kong is James Henry Ting. A Ting company, Semi-Tech Global (capitalised at $590 million in 1994) is the second major shareholder in Tomei, which in turn holds Semi-Tech shares. Ting's companies are controlled by Semi-Tech Microelectronics, which he set up in Canada in the early 1980s. Semi-Tech gained control of Singer Sewing Machine Inc. of the US and Singer Europe in 1989. Singer, as a Semi-Tech subsidiary, formed a joint-venture with the Industrial and Commercial Bank of China in 1993 to bring hire-purchase agreements to China for the company's products - it has six stores in Shanghai and one in Guangzhou. Semi-Tech Global also owns Sansui Electric of Japan and G.M. Pfaff in Germany, and is active in Hong Kong, China, Japan, the United States, Europe and Latin America.

SOPHONPANICH FAMILY[7]

Founder: Chin Sophonpanich 1910-1988, born Thailand, educated in China
Origin: Shantou, Guangdong
Other family: Chatri Sophonpanich (son of Chin), President of Bangkok Bank
Robin Chan (son of Chin), Hong Kong-based, Chairman of Commercial Bank of Hong Kong
Chatsiri Sophonpanich (son of Chatri), Executive Vice-President Bangkok Bank
Charn Sophonpanich (son of Chin), Director Bangkok Bank
Chai Sophonpanich (son of Chin), Managing Director of Bangkok Insurance Co.
Choedchu Sophonpanich (son of Chin), Heads Bangkok First Investment and Trust
Chodchoy Sophonpanich (daughter of Chin), Managing Director of Diners Club, environmental activist

....

7 *Corporate International's Company Handbook*, Hong Kong, June 1994; *Dun's Asia Pacific Key Business Enterprises*, 1993/4; *Far Eastern Economic Review*; *Forbes Magazine*, 18 July 1994; *Fortune*, 28 June 1993; *International Business Week*, 12 July 1994; Limlingan, V.S., 1986, *The Overseas Chinese in ASEAN: Business Strategies and Management Practices*, Vita Development Corporation, Manila, 1986, pp.116-119; *Far Eastern Economic Review*, 'A Matter of Might and Men', 28 July 1983; Akira Suehiro, 'Bangkok Bank: Management Reforms of a Thai Commercial Bank', *East Asian Cultural Studies*, Vol 28, 1989, pp.108, 116; Masaaki Yamaguchi, 'The Emerging Chinese Business Sphere', *Nomura Asian Perspectives*, July 1993, Vol 11, No.2; Suehiro, A., 'Family business reassessed: Corporate structure and late-starting industrialization in Thailand', *The Developing Economies*, December 1994, p. 393; Chantavanich, S., 'From Gonsi to Business Corporatism: Socio-Cultural and Political Conditions of Ethnic Chinese Big Business Families' Success', a paper presented to the Fifth International Conference on Thai Studies, School of Oriental and African Studies, London, 1993; Kraar, L., 'The wealth and power of the Overseas Chinese', *Fortune*, March 1971; *Asian Wall Street Journal*, 'Bangkok Bank passes torch to co-founder's grandson', 30 September 1994; and *The Irrawaddy*, 'City Realty plans hotel in Burma with Thai Cont', 15 December 1994.

Main Companies.

a) Bangkok Bank

Thailand's largest financial and trading conglomerate
Main Shareholders: 'The bank believes that members of the Sophonpanich family make up the largest group of shareholders. Due to the large number of individual family and related shareholders and the often indirect nature of the holdings, the bank is not able to state or give a reliable estimate of the aggregate family shareholdings' (Bangkok Bank Prospectus, 1994)
Executive Chairman: Chatri Sophonpanich
President: Chatsiri Sophonpanich
Bangkok Bank Companies: Some 160 associated firms by 1983, including Bangkok Insurance Co. and Bangkok First Investment and Trust
Market Capitalisation: 1993, US$4.76 billion
Main Activities: Banking and financial services, commodity trading
Activities Mainly Located: Thailand, Hong Kong, Taiwan, China, South-East Asia, Japan, United States, Germany

b) Asia Financial (Hong Kong)

Main Shareholders: Robin Chan (27.3 per cent), Tokai Bank (10 per cent), Bangkok Bank
Chairman: Robin Chan
Executive Director: Ki-Chit Lau
Market Capitalisation: US$268 million (1994)
Asia Financial Companies: Asia Financial was formed in 1990 by merger of Asia Insurance and Commercial Bank. Also in the Group, Bangkok Mercantile
Main Activities: Banking, insurance, commodity trading
Activities Mainly Located: Hong Kong, Taiwan, Macau, San Francisco, China

Bangkok Bank is the the largest bank in South-East Asia. In 1993, it was ranked among the top 500 companies in the world, with nearly 24 000 employees. It has an international network of branches in Hong Kong, Macau, Singapore, Taipei, Kuala Lumpur, Jakarta, Tokyo, Osaka, New York, Los Angeles, Hamburg and London with a recently re-opened branch in Ho Chi Minh City and three new ones in Beijing, Shanghai and Shantou, the ancestral home for many Thai Chinese. In addition, the Bank and the members of the Sophonpanich family who control it, have holdings in a multitude of other companies, at home and abroad, mainly engaged in various financial services or in commodity trading.

Chin Sophonpanich, then a rice trader of moderate resources, founded Bangkok Bank with some partners in 1944. Bangkok Bank began by providing loans to budding Chinese entrepreneurs, many of whom had unsophisticated or non-existent book-keeping, and were usually unable to secure a loan from established Western banks. Thus like so many other ethnic Chinese enterprises, Bangkok Bank began by identifying and filling a market niche. As Bangkok Bank's clients grew, so did the Bank. It opened its second branch, in 1954, in Hong Kong (the first Thai bank to do so) and thereafter enjoyed rapid growth and developed a regional and international network. This was assisted by Chin's extensive and close personal contacts amongst leading ethnic Chinese entrepreneurs such as Robert Kuok, Robin Loh (of the Robin Group and Robina of Singapore and Hong Kong), Liem Sioe Liong of Indonesia and the heads of the Harapan and

Frank Tao groups. Some contacts were developed from 1958 to 1963 when Chin left Bangkok for Hong Kong as a result of political conflicts with Thailand's leaders. This group became known as 'the Bangkok Bank Group' many of whom are still investors in Bangkok Bank through a holding company.[8] Later Chin became more closely associated with the Thai Government. During the early 1970s, the Deputy Prime Minister General Praphas Charusathiara was chairman of the Bank while Chin Sophonpanich was president. The Thai Government held a ten per cent interest. Bangkok Bank also pioneered retail banking in Thailand.

Deposits grew by 27 per cent a year between 1962 and 1972 and then somewhat more slowly, by 21 per cent a year, between 1977 and 1984. By 1981, the bank employed over 16 700 people and had 248 domestic branches and 15 branches or agencies overseas. The family was estimated to have holdings in 130 companies in Thailand, 20 in Hong Kong, and ten elsewhere.

While Bangkok Bank remains large and profitable, other Thai banks are encroaching on its dominant position. In 1973, its nearest rival, the Thai Farmers Bank, controlled by the Sino-Thai Lamsam family, had a capitalisation only 36 per cent as big as that of Bangkok Bank; by 1993, it was 55 per cent. One of the principle reasons for this is that as Chin's son Chatri acquired management control, management became more professionalised and, increasingly, loans were granted less because of the borrowers' relationship with the Sophonpanich family and more because of the underlying financial soundness of the borrowers and their plans. Chatri, who became a Christian, was less connected to the ethnic Chinese networks than his father. Similarly, the new president, Chatsiri, Chatri's son, is also western educated, having an MBA and a Masters degree in engineering. Because of the personalised lending in Chin's time, Bangkok Bank became a big lender to Sino-Indonesian entrepreneurs, but was ultimately affected by many bad loans in Indonesia and has subsequently retreated considerably from that market. The Sino-Indonesian Dharmala Group is reportedly still a major client, however.

Formerly, Bangkok Bank owned substantial interests in three banks in Hong Kong but now has only one. It sold the Hong Kong Chinese Bank to the Lippo Group for US$40 million in 1983. By 1993, the Lippo Group, using it as their starting base in Hong Kong, built their assets to US$1 billion by an aggressive diversification and branch expansion policy.

A branch of the family is settled in Hong Kong. Robin Chan, Chin's oldest son by his first wife, is head of Asia Financial incorporating Asia Insurance and the Commercial Bank. Bangkok Bank injected substantial sums into the Commercial Bank in its early days which still retains the reputation for having a mostly Teochiu client base. Asia Insurance currently operates three branches in the territory as well as one in Macau, a representative office in Taiwan, a broking business in San Francisco and a joint venture in Guangdong with the provincial government's Guangdong Enterprises. In 1993, Commercial Bank opened its first

8 Under Thai law, as much as 25 per cent of a domestic bank's equity may be foreigner-held.

representative office in Shenyang, Liaoning, and upgraded its Shenzhen office to a branch. The group's Bangkok Mercantile company is possibly the largest importer of rice to Hong Kong.

In June 1994 a project was announced for a partnership between Taiwan Tuntex (75 per cent), Mitsui and the Bangkok Bank to construct a petrochemical plant in Thailand. Bangkok Bank is also affiliated with City Realty Co. Ltd, a major Bangkok land developer. Chali Sophonpanich is managing director, and its projects include a large four-five star hotel to be build in Yangon in Myanmar.

CHEARAVANONT FAMILY[9]

Founders: Brothers Chia Ek Chor and Chia Seow Whooey
Head: Dhanin Chearavanont (youngest son of Ek Chor)
Other Family Directors of CP Companies: Jaran Chearavanont (former group chairman); Sumeth Chearavanont; Montri Chearavanont; Julin Unaphum (son in-law of Jaran); Vallop Chearavanont; Tanin Chearavanont; Cherdchai Chearavanont, Pongthep Chearavanont

Main Companies:

Major CP groups include: Charoen Pokphand Group, (20,000 employees); Charoen Pokphand Feedmill Co.; CP Intertrade; Orient Telecom and Tech (Hong Kong, formerly called Chia Tai); Telecom Asia (Hong Kong, 25 per cent owned by Orient Telecom); CP Pokphand (Hong Kong); Charoen Pokphand (Indonesia); CP Prima (Indonesia)

Main Activities: A broad ranging conglomerate. Agribusiness (animal feedmills, food processing); brewing; manufacturing (motorcycles, machinery); telecommunications; property development; retail and petrol station chains; petrochemicals, etc
Location of main activities: Thailand, Hong Kong, China, Taiwan, Indonesia, Portugal, Turkey

The Charoen Pokphand (CP) Group (or *Zheng Da* among the Teochiu in Thailand) was founded some seventy years ago by two Chinese brothers, Chia Ek Chor and Chia Seow Whooey who arrived in Thailand in 1919 as penniless immigrants from the Shantou/Chaozhou region of Guangdong. Chia Ek Chor had four sons, and the youngest of these, Dhanin (then aged 25), took control of

....

9 See *Corporate International's Company Handbook*, Hong Kong, June 1994; *Dun's Asia Pacific Key Business Enterprises*, 1993/4; *Far Eastern Economic Review*; *Forbes Magazine*, 18 July 1994; *Fortune International*, 28 June 1993; *International Business Week*, 12 July 1994; Limlingan, V.S., *The Overseas Chinese in ASEAN: Business Strategies and Management Practices*, Vita Development Corporation, Manila, 1986, p119; *South China Morning Post*, various issues; Masaaki Yamaguchi, 'The Emerging Chinese Business Sphere', *Nomura Asian Perspectives*, Vol 11/2 July 1993; Ch'ng and K. Ross, 'Growth strategies of the Charoen Pokphand Group, Thailand', *Swinburne University of Technology Faculty of Working Papers*, Serial No. 102, 1993; Chantavanich, S., 'From Gonsi to Business Corporatism: Socio-Cultural and Political Conditions of Ethnic Chinese Big Business Families' Success', a paper presented to the Fifth International Conference on Thai Studies, School of Oriental and African Studies, London, 1993; *The Economist*, 'A bruiser from Bangkok', 26 November 1994.

the group in 1964. Chia Seow Whooey had nine sons. The family business has been kept together after the death of the founders, with each branch controlling 50 per cent. The children of Ek Chor are all active in the business; the other branch are still shareholders and directors but they are less involved. CP started out in the farm-seed business and moved into animal feeds and then into chicken farming and processing with initial technical support coming from the US poultry giant, Arbor Acres. Today, it is possibly the largest single foreign investor in China.

Although Group interests extend to petrochemicals, motorcycle and automotive parts, real estate and telecommunications, 60-70 per cent of Group revenue is derived from agribusiness. During the 1980s, CP became Asia's biggest exporter of processed and frozen chickens, mainly to Japan, China and Brazil.

In Thailand and China, it developed a network of contract farms and built its own slaughterhouses and processing plants. CP's success is largely due to its innovative contract farming which originated in 1970. Under agreements in which farmers are contracted to CP to raise poultry and other stock, CP provides technical advice on vaccination, cleaning sheds, and beak trimming; financial advice on borrowing and guarantees for building sheds, other equipment and working capital; day-old chicks, feeds and medicines at agreed intervals, prices and quantities; and guarantees to buy back the poultry, once fully grown, to be processed. The scheme operates as a type of futures market for chickens. CP guarantees to purchase given quantities of fully-grown chickens ahead of time. By introducing contract farming to poultry, pig, prawn and duck farming, CP lowered its risks and necessary outlays on capital assets by minimising its investments in land, buildings, equipment and labour.

In 1988, CP sold 26 million day-old chicks in China, rising to 114 million in 1992, by which stage CP was supplying their feed from 30 China-based feedmills. The key has been intensive marketing and distribution, with sales agents, and local government officials paid on commission. The Shanghai poultry breeder Shanghai Dajiang (50 per cent owned by CP Pokphand) controlled 15 to 20 per cent of China's 100 000 tonnes of annual chicken exports in 1993; it was partly floated on the Shanghai Stock Exchange in 1993, raising some US$42 million. This capital will be used to expand Shanghai Dajiang's broiler farms and feedmills, and to set up a fast food chain in Shanghai and the neighbouring provinces of Jiangsu and Zhejiang.

CP set up its first venture, Conti Chia Tai, in Shenzhen in 1981 and was an early entrant into China. It now has operations in 26 of China's 30 provinces. It is well connected to the Chinese Government - Dhanin Chearavanont is one of a number of senior ethnic Chinese businessmen in the region consulted by the Chinese Government on business and political affairs - and with local officials. Most of CP's China ventures are on a 50/50 basis with, for example, a provincial grain bureau or a city or county government. Shanghai's municipal government is a partner in each of the CP's ten ventures in the city. Local officials are sometimes taken aboard as well paid employees. The group's total assets in China were estimated at US$1.3 billion in 1993.

Its China investments are mainly conducted through its Hong Kong subsidiary, CP Pokphand. Its market capitalisation in 1994 was US$694 million, and it had

36 very varied businesses in China in 1993. These activities included developing a poultry production, processing and distribution network and other agribusiness, motorcycle and machinery factories, real estate and property development (a shopping centre, housing, amusement park and holiday resorts), investment in the government satellite program, fast food (through Kentucky Fried Chicken franchises), brewing (in alliance with Heineken) and petrol station chains. There are also plans for oil refineries, petrochemicals and department stores.

CP Pokphand (HK) manages and owns shares in four joint ventures in China through Ek Chor China (a Bermuda-registered company). Two make motorcycles, supplying 15 per cent of the domestic market; one makes carburettors; and the other makes approximately one third of the air-conditioner compressors used in China's domestic vehicle production. In 1993, Ek Chor China was the first Sino-foreign joint venture listed on the New York Stock Exchange.

Following its success in China, CP has set up agribusiness ventures in Indonesia (with a 49 per cent share in Charoen Pokphand Prima and 25 per cent in Charoen Pokphand Indonesia), Turkey (where it operates five feedmills), Malaysia and Portugal and is a major investor in Taiwan, where recently it sold its Taiwan Sizzler restaurant franchises for almost US$10 million. It also has a successful chain of 7-Eleven franchise stores in Bangkok and elsewhere in Thailand.

By the early 1990s, the Group consisted of almost 280 member firms, very few of which are listed (see Table A7.1). Despite this, its current shareholding composition is relatively simple and can be divided into three groups. They are: the Chearavanont family headed by the Chia brothers, Chia Ek Cheow and Chia Shiau Hui; investment companies held exclusively by the Chearavanont family; and the Group's more significant member firms. With the exception of Arbor Acres (Thailand) Co., a joint venture with a US firm, approximately 80 per cent of the stock of almost every member of the CP Group is held either directly or indirectly by the Chearavanont family.

In recent years, CP has diversified into telecommunications. CP's Hong Kong company, Orient Telecom and Technology, and the US Nynex Corporation are partners in Telecom Asia, which was floated on the Stock Exchange of Thailand. It has a current capitalisation in excess of US$9 billion. In 1990, the joint venture was awarded the monopoly right to operate a two million line phone network for 25 years in Bangkok, being the first private sector company to be awarded the right to provide local services. Also, Orient Telecom and Technology has various property interests in Bangkok, Hong Kong and China. Telecom Asia is pursuing concessions to develop and operate telephones for ten million people in several major Chinese cities. Discussions with Hebei province may result in supplying 200 000 telephone lines and associated infrastructure.

Table A7.1

The Listed Members of the CP Group

	STOCK EXCHANGE	MARKET CAPITALISATION (Nov 1994, US$m)	NET 1993 PROFIT (US$m)	CP STAKE (per cent)
Ek Chor China Motorcycle	New York	360	20	72
CP Pokphand	Hong Kong, London	622	44	56
Hong Kong Fortune	Hong Kong	107	0	64
Orient Telecom & Technology	Hong Kong	896	12	51
CP Indonesia	Jakarta	234	13	71
CP Prima	Jakarta	198	6	92
CP Enterprise	Taipei	132	2	30
Shanghai Dajiang	Shanghai	141	17	44
CP Feedmill	Bangkok	839	48	39
CP Northeastern	Bangkok	60	3	59
Bangkok Produce Merchandising	Bangkok	49	3	37
Bangkok Agri-Industrial Products	Bangkok	118	4	73
Telecom Asia	Bangkok	9 030	23	29
Siam Makro	Bangkok	875	6	15

Source: *The Economst*, 'A bruiser from Bangkok', 26 November 1994.

The structure of multiple inter-related companies, transnational ownership linkages, and a tendency to conduct many activities through private companies, often mask CP's influence. For example, in 1993 a deadly fire at a Bangkok toy factory raised a public outcry against the neglect of safety requirements by the Taiwanese owners. Ultimately it was revealed that CP had shareholdings in the factory, together with Taiwanese interests, and the Hong Kong firm, Kader International, and that a member of the Chearavanont family had managed the factory.

In July 1993, CP formed a joint venture, Petro Asia (Thailand) Co., with China's state-owned China Petrochemical Corporation and the Petroleum Authority of Thailand. The new company will invest in trading and distributing petroleum products in Thailand, Indochina and China, and is considering building an oil refinery in Guangdong.

ROBERT KUOK[10]

Family Head: Robert Kuok (Kuok Hock Nien)

Other Family: Philip Kuok (brother); Kuok Khoon Chen (son); Kuok Khoon Ean (son); Chye Kuok (cousin)

Main Companies

In Malaysia:

Kuok Brothers

Some Kuok Brothers Companies: Perlis Plantations (sugar, tin and iron ore); Federal Flour Mills
Main Activities: Plantations; commodity trading and processing (palm oil, rubber, rice and flour milling, sugar refining); wood processing (veneer and plywood manufacture); iron and tin
Location of Main Activities: Worldwide

In Singapore:

Kuok (Singapore) Ltd

Chairman: O.K. Kuok
Kuok Company: Kuok Oils and Grains
Main Activities: General trading, holding and property

In Hong Kong:

a) Kerry Group

Private holding company

b) Shangri-La, Asia

Major Shareholders: Kuok Family
Chairman: Pho Ba-quan
Executive director: Kuok Chong Heng
Market Capitalisation: 1994, US$1.4 billion
Main Activities: Newly listed holding company for Kuok family owned hotels in Hong Kong and China

c) TVE Holdings

Major Shareholders: Shaw Holdings (35 per cent); Kerry group (31 per cent)
Chairman: Sir Run Run Shaw
Managing Director: Kuok Khoon Ho

....

[11] *China Business Review,* issues 3, 10 and 11 of 1992; *Corporate International's Company Handbook*, Hong Kong (various issues); *Dun's Asia Pacific Key Business Enterprises*, 1993/4; *Far Eastern Economic Review*, various issues; *Forbes Magazine*, 18 July 1994; *Fortune International*, 28 June 1993; Lim Mah-hui, 'The Ownership and Control of Large Corporations in Malaysia: The Role of Chinese Businessmen', in Lim L. and P. Gosling, *The Chinese in Southeast Asia*, Vol I, Maruzen Asia, Singapore, 1983; *South China Morning Post*, various issues; Verchere, I., The Changing World of Robert Kuok', *Insight*, August 1978.; Masaaki Yamaguchi, 'The Emerging Chinese Business Sphere', *Nomura Asian Perspectives*, July 1993, Vol 11, No.2.

Market Capitalisation (June 1994): US$183 million
Main Activities: Entertainment, leisure, retailing, travel and movie production, property
Location of Main Activities: Hong Kong

d) Television Broadcasts Ltd

Major Shareholders: Shaw Holdings (31 per cent), Kerry Group (32 per cent)
Chairman: Sir Run Run Shaw
Managing Director: Kuok Khoon Ho, Chye Kuok
Market Capitalisation (June 1994): US$1.55 billion
Main Activities: Television broadcasting. Mandarin language programming for overseas markets
Location of Main Activities: Regional

e) South China Morning Post

Major Shareholders: Kerry Media (35 per cent)
Chairman: Kenneth Edward Cowley
Chief Executive: Lindley John Holloway
Market Capitalisation: US$900 million
Main Activities: Daily Newspaper, bookshops, magazine
Location of Main Activities: Hong Kong

Robert Kuok's interests epitomise the kind of diversified, transnational ethnic Chinese conglomerate that has grown out of commodity trading, and that is now moving rapidly into new territory in China and the region, and into new fields such as global communications. Although ten Kuok companies are listed, many more are not, making it difficult to gauge the size and the performance of the Group overall.

The family business, at first a grocery shop then moved into commodities trading, was founded in what was then Malaya by Robert Kuok's father, an immigrant from Fujian who established friendly relations with the Sultan of Johore. Robert Kuok was born in Malaya in 1923. He founded his first company Kuok Pte Ltd., general merchants, in Singapore after the war and formed Kuok Bros, rice, sugar and flour merchants in Malaya. His brother, a member of the Communist Party of Malaya was killed by British troops during the Emergency and the family subsequently spent some years in London.

When he returned at the end of the 1950s, he founded Malaya's first sugar refinery and developed a worldwide network for trading and processing commodities. He bought sugar from Cuba and sold it to Indonesia, establishing a close relationship with Liem Sioe Liong, and becoming a partner in Liem's Integrated Sugar Mill and Plantations in Indonesia. He imported raw sugar from Thailand; refined it in Malaya; and sold it to China via his Hong Kong-based commodity brokerage. In the 1960s, he also had agencies for supplying China with cameras, refrigerators and dyeing materials. He created Perlis Plantations in Malaysia where he harvested his first crop of sugar cane in 1973, and he acquired interests in sugar mills in Thailand. He became known as the 'sugar king' with 1.5 million of the world's 16 million tons a year international sugar trade passing through his hands.

He was similarly engaged in world trading and transnational division of labour with rice (bought from Thailand, sold in Malaysia and Singapore) and wheat (bought from the United States and Australia and processed in his mills in Malaya or in Liem's in Indonesia). He established Malayan Veneer in the 1960s to manufacture veneer and plywood, 95 per cent of which was exported to Asia, the United States, and Europe via Kuok Bros (Singapore). From commodity trading and processing, he diversified into shipping and thence into insurance, shipyards and engineering, palm oil and rubber, bridges, pylons, oil rigs, railways and hotels.

By the late 1970s, the Kuoks were one of the wealthiest families in Malaysia and with their series of interlocking companies, they were one of a small number of systematically linked dominant groups amongst the top 100 firms. They also had corporate roots in Singapore and Hong Kong. As early as 1983, Kuok-controlled Kerry Industrial joined a joint venture to build the US$480 million China World Trade Centre in Beijing (offices, shops, hotels and residences).[11] Robert Kuok himself moved to Hong Kong with his sons, and from there, he has focused increasingly on developing hotels around the region and especially in China, on property development and on the media group he is building up with Sir Run Run Shaw. His most prominent current development project in China is the US$590 million Everbright City in Shanghai. In this he has linked up with Cheung Kong (HK) of Li Ka-shing and Top Glory of Singapore. His brother, Philip Kuok, has taken charge of the family's Malaysia- and Singapore-based companies and his businesses continue to expand. His son Khoon Ean is heavily involved in the Malaysia- and Singapore-based companies. A cousin, Chye Kuok, is involved in managing the Group and its TVE interests.

The Kuok-controlled Shangri-La Asia has two major hotels in Hong Kong. In China, it has major stakes in hotels in Beijing, Shanghai, Hangzhou, Xian and Shenzhen, and in November 1993, it announced the purchase of interests in another twelve hotel and associated mainland projects, including plans to construct on Hainan Island. There are also Shangri-La hotels in Bali, Fiji, Jakarta, Kota Kinabalu, Kuala Lumpur, Penang, Singapore, Taipei and Vancouver. There are reportedly plans for a US$100 million hotel in Fuzhou; a Shangri-La in Yangon (Myanmar) is underway; and the feasibility of one in Mandalay (Myanmar) is being assessed. In addition, the Group controls the three-to-four star Traders Hotel chain. The chain has hotels in China and is building one in Yangon.

Robert Kuok is an almost equal shareholder with Run Run Shaw (the Hong Kong and Singapore film producer and distributor) in TVE and Television Broadcasts (TVB) which operate two Hong Kong TV channels and are the world's largest producers of Chinese language TV programs. They dominate Cantonese and Mandarin programming and have a large number of viewers in south-eastern China who can receive Hong Kong television. They also sell dubbed and subtitled programs throughout Asia and are the main rivals to Star TV, now controlled by Rupert Murdoch. This competition is likely to increase as TVB received approval from the Hong Kong government in October 1994 to set up a

11 Plans are now underway to expand the Trade Centre.

regional satellite TV service. This is in addition to the current satellite service to Taiwan. They have recently expanded their reach to Mandarin speakers in North America with stakes in a Canadian cable TV service that also reaches 52 000 viewers in Los Angeles and San Francisco. In 1993, Kerry Media bought Murdoch's controlling share in South China Morning Post Holdings, the publisher of the leading English-language newspaper in Hong Kong, and also a Chinese-language newspaper (*Wah Kiu Yat Po* - since closed) in Hong Kong and 15 per cent of the *Bangkok Post*. The Wee family of Singapore's United Overseas Bank took a minority stake. The purchase has caused some concern about editorial independence in Hong Kong, in the run up to 1997, as Kuok has close relationships with China's leaders and is an adviser to China on Hong Kong affairs.

There are other diverse activities. Kuok's Kerry Group recently took a 15 per cent stake in Hong Kong's new Western Harbour Tunnel project, and has 13.5 per cent of Citic Pacific, the overseas arm of China's state-owned China International Trust and Investment Corporation (CITIC).

The Kuok Group (Singapore) moved into property development in the Philippines in 1988 and had a leading position within three years. It built and now operates a toll-road in Thailand. With Li Ka-shing and the Japanese Yaohan Group (a family business whose owner spends half the year in Hong Kong), Kuok is in a joint venture for a major commercial and shopping complex in Japan. In China, there are projects to develop a major commercial complex in Shanghai, an oil refinery and petrochemical complex in Behai, a flour and feed mill, a US$100 million investment in Coca Cola bottling plants, and an investment of US$100 million in vegetable oil plants. In March 1993, Kouk pulled Kerry out of a US$130 million project to redevelop Beijing's Wangfujing shopping district reportedly because of differences with the local partner, but insisted on his continuing commitment to China investment.

Currently, the Kuok Group is leading the way for investment into Myanmar, now a priority market. This compares with Vietnam, where the Group has deliberately avoided any significant investments to date, preferring to wait instead for the current investment bubble to burst and for assets to cheapen. The Group also is expanding its vegetable oil interests in China, complementing the Group's large oil palm interests in Malaysia. As for succession, it is not clear who is going to takeover when Robert Kuok moves aside; this issue is yet to be resolved.

QUEK/KWEK FAMILY[12]

Family Head and Founder: Kwek Hong Png in Singapore (retired 1984, deceased 1994)

Singapore Branch: Kwek Leng Beng (son of Kwek Hong Png, head of Hong Leong Group, Singapore); Kwek Leng Joo (son of Kwek Hong Png, head of the Singapore Chinese Chamber of Commerce)

Malaysian Branch: Quek Leng Chan (son of Kwek's brother Kwek Hong Lye, died 1973; Kwek Leng Hai (brother of Quek Leng Chan)

Singapore Branch, Main Companies:

Hong Leong Group (Singapore)

Managing Director: Kwek Leng Beng
Main Companies: City Developments; Hong Leong Finance (Singapore); Hotel Properties; King's Hotel Group; Quality Hotels; Manila Plaza (Philippines); Grand Hyatt (Taipei); CDL Hotels (HK Capitalised at US$560 million); Hong Leong International (HK)
Main Activities: Real estate, hotels, finance
Location of Main Activities: East Asia

Malaysia Branch:

Hong Leong Company (Malaysia) is a general holding company for companies in Malaysia and around the region.

Group Head: Quek Leng Chan

Assets in Malaysia, 1993: US$1.18 billion

a) **Hong Leong Credit (Malaysia)** and seven associated companies

Main Activities: Finance

b) **Hong Leong Bank (Malaysia)** (35 branches and Hong Leong Finance)

Main Activities: Retail banking, finance

c) **Hong Leong Industries (Malaysia)** and 15 associated companies

Main Activities: Manufacture of building materials, motorcycles, steel, electronics, packaging

d) **Hume Industries (Malaysia)** and five associated companies, including Nanyang Press

Main Activities: Construction, daily Chinese newspaper

....

12 See *Corporate International's Company Handbook*, Hong Kong (various issues); *Dun's Asia Pacific Key Business Enterprises*, 1993/4; *Far Eastern Economic Review*, various issues; *Forbes Magazine*, 18 July 1994; *The Financial Times*, 11 January 1994, p26; *The Straits Times Weekly*, various issues; *Straits Times Weekly Edition*, 'Hong Leong group's founder dies at 83', 12 November 1994; Suehiro, A., 'Family business reassessed: Corporate structure and late-starting industrialization in Thailand', *The Developing Economies*, December 1994, p. 383; *Australian Financial Review*, 'Landcorp assets sold to Hong Leong family', 3 November 1994.

e) Guoco Group (Hong Kong)

Market capitalisation June 1994: US$1.686 billion
Main Shareholders: Hong Leong Co. (27 per cent); Kuwait Investment Office (17 per cent)
Chairman: Quek Leng Chan
Managing Director: Kwek Leng Hai

f) Dao Heng Bank (Hong Kong)

Market capitalisation June 1994: US$1.888 billion
Main shareholder: Guoco Group
Chairman: Quek Leng Chan
Managing Director: Kwek Leng Hai

Dao Heng Bank, listed in 1994, is the third largest bank in Hong Kong in terms of branches and the fifth largest in assets. Guoco's acquisition of Overseas Trust Bank in 1994 increased the Dao Heng group's branch coverage to 97 in Hong Kong.

The Group has a further 33 associated companies including 14 in Hong Kong; two in London, including Benchmark Bank; five in Singapore (amongst which Guoco Investment, First Capital Corp); six in the Philippines, including the First Lepanto Group; six in China; and a regional merchant bank, Hoare Govett Asia.

Main Activities: Banking, finance, manufacturing (engines, construction materials), property development

Location of Main Activities: Malaysia, Hong Kong, China, Singapore, Philippines

The Kwek family migrated from Fujian to Singapore in the 1920s. After saving his earnings as a shop assistant working for his brother-in-law, Kwek Hong Png started a small machinery shop in 1941. In 1963, he sent his brother Kwek Hong Lye to Malaya (from which Singapore was soon to separate) to extend the family's operations there. When Hong Lye died in 1973, his son, Quek Leng Chan then aged 30, took over the Malaysian business. Relations between the two branches have been strained at times, as the junior branch has grown bigger than the senior one. Those in Malaysia sought and obtained control over their own operations, and their purchase (via their Hong Kong Guoco Group) of First Capital Corporation in Singapore, in 1988, was seen as a hostile act, encroaching on the other branch's territory. Despite some family differences, there has been no split and ownership of the Malaysian holding company, Hong Leong Company (Malaysia), is fairly evenly spread between both sides of the family. Family members exclusively control the Group through a series of family-owned holding companies and interlocking directorates. The Group has the appearance of being quite Western in its outward appearance, but decision making is still tightly controlled by a small circle of family members. The Kuwait Investment Office and the Italian Agnelli family are long-term minority shareholders in the Malaysian branch's operations.

Hong Leong (Malaysia) has grown into one of the biggest conglomerates in Malaysia. Its ten companies listed on the Kuala Lumpur Stock Exchange, the most by any group, have an annual turnover of US$1.3 billion and are involved in everything from the manufacture of roofing tiles and semi-conductors to property and the largest circulation Chinese daily newspaper. Hume Industries is one of Malaysia's biggest construction companies and is expanding rapidly in tandem with a massive infrastructure development program being undertaken in Malaysia. Hong Leong Industries produces building materials, steel and electronic products and components, and assembles Yamaha motorcycles (supplying 50 per cent of the Malaysian market). Through Hong Leong Credit, Quek has interests in finance companies, insurance and stockbroking, and in 1993, he finally acquired a commercial bank in Malaysia, MUI Bank, which has been renamed the Hong Leong Bank. Quek is well connected to senior members of Malaysia's Government and has a close relationship with companies controlled by Malaysia's dominant political party UMNO.

Like a number of South-East Asian conglomerates, Malaysian Hong Leong's regional and China activities are carried on from a Hong Kong-based company. Since 1983, this has been through their Guoco Group, which is run by Quek Leng Chan's brother, Kwek Leng Hai. Guoco merged three Hong Kong banks, Dao Heng and Hang Lung in 1990, and the Overseas Trust Bank in 1993, producing the fifth largest banking group in Hong Kong with 97 branches. Dao Heng's original client base was the Hong Kong Teochiu business community, notwithstanding the fact that Quek is Hokkien. It faced liquidity problems in the mid 1980s, and was subsequently passed into government receivership before being acquired by Guoco. This was also the fate of the Overseas Trust Bank. Through subsidiaries, Guoco is engaged in securities broking, insurance, property, manufacturing and trading in the region, especially in the Philippines and Singapore. Non-financial diversification in Asia is mainly through Guoco's Singapore-listed, First Capital Corporation.

Both branches of the family are involved in China. Quek, through Guoco, has a hotel in Fuzhou, and motorcycle assembly and garment factories (Heshe and Benefashions). The Singapore Kweks have announced a US$150 million plan to build a chain of budget hotels in China; US$10 million to set up a plastics packaging plant in Qingdao; and US$52 million (with other Singapore and Hong Kong partners) for a 51 per cent stake in a diesel engine manufacturing joint venture in Guangxi. The Singapore Kweks have also invested heavily in real estate in Australia, New Zealand and the United States.

Kwek Leng Joo, Managing Director of Hong Leong International (Singapore) and the current president of the Singapore Chinese Chamber of Commerce and Industry, presented a plan to the World Chinese Entrepreneurs Convention in Hong Kong in November 1993, for co-operative investment in China and elsewhere by investors from Chinese Chambers of Commerce in Singapore, and also in countries like Malaysia, Taiwan and Hong Kong.

Appendix 8

AN OVERVIEW OF MALAYSIA'S NEW ECONOMIC POLICY

The main aspects of Malaysia's New Economic Policy (NEP) are set out below. The NEP is discussed in Chapter 3.

- Firms were required to establish plans for employing, training and promoting Malays at all levels of operations. Such plans were prerequisites for government contracts and licences. Malay employment quotas varied according to the size of a firm. Larger firms were required to achieve a 40 per cent quota.
- Twenty per cent of all loans made by commercial banks were to be made to *bumiputeras*.
- *Bumiputeras* were given price preferences for all government tenders ranging from two to ten per cent and additionally, 30 per cent of the contracts were reserved for *bumiputeras*.
- Preference was to be given to *bumiputeras* in the issue of new licences or permits pertaining to logging, sawmilling, timber exports, vehicle import, mining, banking, finance, insurance, transport, and tin and rubber dealing.
- A preferential share allocation scheme was introduced whereby all companies listing on the KLSE must offer at least 30 per cent of their shares to *bumiputeras*. This is often achieved by having two floats - a 30 per cent tranche is available only to *bumiputera* applicants, and then a 70 per cent tranche is made available to all share applicants including *bumiputeras*.[1]
- In 1975, the Government introduced the Industrial Coordination Act (ICA) requiring every manufacturing firm with shareholders' funds in excess of M$250,000 or employing more than 25 full-time workers to apply for a manufacturing licence. The Act specified that firms covered must organise in a way which would further the 'national interest', which subsequently was defined by regulation, giving the responsible Minister enormous powers to regulate all aspects of firms' operations. Regulations thus imposed have included: requiring respondent firms to put aside at least 30 per cent of their equity for Malay interests; requiring non-Malay firms to employ and train Malaysian citizens to reflect the multiracial composition of the country's population in all grades of appointment up to managerial level; and requiring firms to adopt real measures over a reasonable time to use Malay distributors to the maximum extent possible, the minimum being 30 per cent of turnover.

---

1 The first tranche often sells below the listing price or even the offer price, meaning that those *bumiputeras* investors who might acquire shares in the first offer are able to later 'stag' or sell their shares on the open market and realise potentially sizeable capital gains.

- In a further effort to expedite Malay ownership and control of the economy, the government formed public corporations, known as *bumiputera* trust agencies, to buy corporate shares in select companies on behalf of Malays.[2]
- For a time, the Government pursued what has been termed 'ethnic by-pass', by which joint ventures between the *bumiputera* holding companies and government-linked companies have looked beyond local, Chinese joint-venture partners to Japanese partners for heavy investment projects.[3]
- Ethnically-based quotas were introduced for local universities. Currently, the official quotas for all local universities stand at 55 per cent for *bumiputeras*, 35 per cent for Chinese, and ten per cent for Indians and those of mixed race.

---

2 One of these, Pernas Trading, was awarded control of the Malaysia-China trade. Malaysian Chinese traders were then required to pay a commission to Pernas if they wanted to trade with China. This caused much resentment in Malaysia's Chinese community and was ultimately abandoned. (See Jesudason, J. V., *Ethnicity and the Economy: The State, Chinese Business, and Multinationals in Malaysia*, Oxford University Press, Singapore, 1989, p. 132).

3 See Jomo, K. S., 'Is Chinese capital in Malaysia 'progressive'?', Unpublished paper, 1994.

Appendix 9

LIST OF ACRONYMS USED

A$	Australian Dollars
ACAHK	Australian Chinese Association of Hong Kong
ACCCIM	Associated Chinese Chambers of Commerce and Industry of Malaysia
ACT	Australian Capital Territory
ADFA	Australian Defence Force Academy
AGPS	Australian Government Publishing Service
AMA	Australian Medical Association
ANZ	Australia and New Zealand Banking Group
ASEAN	Association of South-East Asian Nations
ASX	Australian Stock Exchange
Austrade	Australian Trade Commission
BAKOM-PKB	Agency for the Communication of Comprehension of National Unity (Indonesia)
BCA	Bank Central Asia (Indonesia)
BDNI	Bank Dagang Nasional Indonesia
Bhd	Berhad (Malaysia)
BII	Bank International Indonesia
BPT	Barito Pacific Timber (Indonesia)
BULOG	National Logistics Board (Indonesia)
Can	Canadian
Can$	Canadian Dollars
CASH	Construction and Supplies House Berhad (Malaysia)
CBD	Central Business District
CD	Compact Disc
CEDA	Committee for the Economic Development of Australia
CEO	Chief Executive Officer
CEPA	Consolidated Electric Power Asia Limited (Hong Kong)
CIML	China Industrial Management Limited (Hong Kong)
CITIC	China International Trust and Investment Corporation
CNFI	Chinese National Federation of Industries (Taiwan)
Co.	Company
Corp.	Corporation
CP	Chareon Pokphand (Thailand)
CPBA	Chinese Professional and Business Association (Melbourne,

	Australia)
CSH	China Strategic Holdings (Hong Kong)
CSIS	Centre for Strategic and International Studies (CSIS)
DAP	Democratic Action Party (Malaysia)
DBS	Development Bank of Singapore
DC	District of Colombia (United States)
DTC	Deposit-taking Cooperative
Ed.	Editor
EDB	Economic Development Board (Singapore)
Eds	Editors
FBT	Fringe Benefits Tax
FCGCC	Filipino Chinese General Chambers of Commerce (Philippines)
FDI	Foreign Direct Investment
FFCCC	Federation of Filipino Chinese Chambers of Commerce (Philippines)
FIE	Foreign-invested Enterprise
FMM	Federation of Malaysian Manufacturers
FPB	First Pacific Bank (Hong Kong)
FPC	First Pacific Company (Hong Kong)
FPI	First Pacific Investments (Hong Kong)
GDP	Gross Domestic Product
GNP	Gross National Product
HK	Hong Kong
HK$	Hong Kong Dollars
ICA	Industrial Coordination Act (Malaysia)
IMT-GT	Indonesia-Malaysia-Thailand Growth Triangle
Inc.	Incorporated
JEE	Jurong Environmental Engineering (Singapore)
JSE	Jakarta Stock Exchange
KFM	Kuantan Flour Mills (Malaysia)
KLSE	Kuala Lumpur Stock Exchange
KMP	Kabila Mandiri Persada (Singapore)
KMT	Kuomintang
KSM	Koperatitif Serbaguna (M) Berhad (Malaysia)
LFA	Lippo Finance Australia
Ltd	Limited
M	Malaysia
M$	Malaysian Dollars or Ringgit
MABC	Malaysia-Australia Business Council (Malaysia)
MBAM	Master Builders' Association of Malaysia

MCA	Malaysian Chinese Association
MCCC	Myanmar Chinese Chamber of Commerce
MCP	Malayan Communist Party
MIC	Malaysian Indian Congress
MICCI	Malaysian International Chamber of Commerce and Industry
MNC	Multinational Corporation
MOU	Memorandum of Understanding
MPHB	Multi-Purpose Holdings Berhad (Malaysia)
MPR	Majelis Perwakilan Rakyat (Indonesia)
MSG	Monosodium Glutamate
MUI	Malayan United Industry (Malaysia)
NEP	National Economic Policy (Malaysia)
NIE	Newly Industrialising Economy
NRC	National Registration Cards (Myanmar)
NSW	New South Wales (Australia)
NT	Norhern Territory (Australia)
NT$	Taiwan Dollars
NTUC	National Trades Union Congress (Singapore)
NYSE	New York Stock Exchange
OUB	Overseas Union Bank (Singapore)
OUP	Oxford University Press
P	Philippine Peso
PAP	People's Action Party (Singapore)
PKI	Communist Party of Indonesia
PKR	People's Republic of Kampuchea
PNG	Papua New Guinea
PO	Post Office
PRC	Peoples' Republic of China
PVC	polyvinyl chloride
Pte	Proprietary (Singapore)
Pty	Proprietary
Qld	Queensland (Australia)
R&D	research and development
Rp	Indonesian Rupiah
S$	Singaporean Dollars
SA	South Australia (Australia)
SCCCI	Singapore Chinese Chamber of Commerce and Industry
SCMP	South China Morning Post (Hong Kong)
SEZ	Special Economic Zone (China)
SFCCA	Singapore Federation of Chinese Clan Associations

SLORC	State Law and Order Restoration Committee (Myanmar)
SPHC	Southern Pacific Hotels Corporation (United States)
STIC	Singapore Technologies Industrial Corporation
Tas	Tasmania (Australia)
TCCC	Thai-Chinese Chamber of Commerce (Thailand)
TDB	Trade Development Board (Singapore)
TSE	Taiwan Stock Exchange
TV	Television
UIC	United Industrial Corporation (Singapore)
UK	United Kingdom
UMNO	United Malays National Organisation (Malaysia)
UNTAC	United Nations Transitional Authority in Cambodia
UOB	United Overseas Bank (Singapore)
UOL	United Overseas Land (Singapore)
US	United States
US$	United States Dollars
USSR	Union of Soviet Socialist Republics
Vic	Victoria (Australia)
WA	Western Australia (Australia)

BIBLIOGRAPHY

A Statistical Survey of China 1994.

Allen, N., *Allied Group Limited, Allied Properties (HK) Limited, Crusader Holdings Limited, Paragon Holdings Limited, Wai Yick Limited: Investigation under S.143 (1)(c) of the Companies Ordinance, Chapter 32 of the Laws of Hong Kong*, Abridged Version, Vol. 1, Office of the Financial Secretary, Hong Kong, 1993.

ANZ Panin Bank, *Banking services in Indonesia*, promotional brochure.

Asia Cement Corporation, *An Introduction to the Hualien Plant of Asia Cement Corporation*, Taipei, 1994.

Asia Pacific Foundation of Canada, *Asian Canadians: Canada's Hidden Advantage*, 1994.

Asia Today, 'Sinar Mas: Building a global empire in agribusiness, finance', May 1994.

Asia Today, 'Lippo leads equity stake in major China projects', May 1994.

Asian Development Bank, *Annual Report*, 1993; 1994.

Asian Wall Street Journal.

Asiaweek.

Australian Business Asia.

Australian Business Monthly, 'Chinese on the rebound', March 1993.

Australian Financial Review.

Baldinger, P., 'The birth of greater China', *The China Business Review*, May-June 1992.

Bangkok Post.

Barraclough, S., *A Dictionary of Malaysian Politics*, Heinemann Asia, Singapore, 1988.

Barton, C.A., 'Trust and credit: Some observations regarding business strategies of overseas Chinese traders in South Vietnam' in L.Y.C. Lim and L.A.P. Gosling (eds), *The Chinese in Southeast Asia*, Vol. 1, Maruzen Asia, Singapore, 1983.

Basu, E.O., 'Profit, loss and fate: The entrepreneurial ethic and the practice of gambling in an overseas Chinese community', *Modern China*, Vol. 17, No. 2, April 1991.

BHP, *BHP Report to Shareholders 1994: Financial Statements*, Melbourne, 1994.

Biggart, N.W. and G.G. Hamilton, 'On the limits of a firm-based theory to explain business networks: The Western bias of neoclassical economics', Unpublished paper, Research Program in East Asian Business and Development, Institute of Governmental Affairs, University of California, Davis, 1990.

BII, *1993 Annual Report*, Jakarta, 1994.

Bradley, D., 'Chinese, Thai and other languages of wider communication in the Golden Triangle', a paper delivered to the Thailand's Circles of Growth Conference, Chiangmai, northern Thailand, March 1994.

British Columbia Business, 'Two solitudes', April 1994.

Brudvig, L, 'The fifth dragon', *The China Business Review*, July-August 1993.

Bureau of Immigration, Multicultural and Population Research, *Immigration Update*, December Quarter 1994.

Burma Alert, No. 10, Vol. 5, October 1994.

Business Review Southeast Asia, *Southeast Asia Business Omnibook*, Options Publishing, 1995.

Business in Thailand, ' "Nok Kaew": No soap operas please!!', June 1994.

Business Review Southeast Asia, 'CP group', 16 November 1994.

Business Review Southeast Asia, 'Joint ventures', 14 December 1994.

Business Review Weekly, 'Rich 200', 21 May 1993.

Business Review Weekly, 'China without boundaries', 25 July 1994.

Business Times, SCMP deal: Who's doing whom a favour', 22 April 1994.

Business Traveller, 'Xiamen plays the waiting game', September 1994.

Business Week, 'The Chinese dealmakers of Southeast Asia', 11 November 1991.

Carnegie, G. and D. Sharpe, *Singapore*, Asia Australia Briefing Paper, Vol. 2, No. 10, 1993, The Asia-Australia Institute, University of New South Wales, 1993.

Cazenove & Co., *First Pacific* (research report), Hong Kong, 28 November 1994.

CERD Consultants, 'Past, present and future trends - Taiwan-China relationship as reflected by Taiwan's foreign investment', (by Chan Man-hung and Zhu Wenhui), Hong Kong, 1994 (in Chinese).

Ch'ng, D., *The Overseas Chinese Entrepreneurs in East Asia: Background, Business Practices and International Networks*, CEDA Monograph M100, 1993.

Ch'ng, D., and K. Ross, 'Growth strategies of the Charoen Pokphand Group, Thailand', *Swinburne University of Technology Faculty of Working Papers*, Serial No. 102, 1993.

Chan, K.B. and C. Chiang, *Stepping Out: The Making of Chinese Entrepreneurs*, Prentice Hall, Singapore, 1994.

Chan, M.H. and W. Zhu, 'The Hong Kong-Taiwan-South Korea factor in China's exports and its impact', China Business Centre, Hong Kong Polytechnic, Working Paper No. 2, 1994 (in Chinese).

Chang, C., 'Aliens in their adopted land', *Free China Review*, July 1989.

Chantavanich, S., 'From Gonsi to business corporatism: Socio-cultural and political conditions of ethnic Chinese big business families' success', a paper presented to the Fifth International Conference on Thai Studies, School of Oriental and African Studies, London, 1993.

Chen, G., *Getting Your Way with the Chinese*, Nolan Project Services, North Sydney, 1994.

Chen, T.J., 'FDI by small- and medium-sized enterprises from Taiwan', *CIER Newsletter*, November 1994.

Chen, H.M. and D.N. Liu, 'Taiwan's FDI in Thailand', *CIER Newsletter*, November 1994.

Cheng, L.K., 'Reflections on the changing roles of Chinese clan associations in Singapore', *Asian Culture*, April 1990.

Chew, R., 'Local Chinese banks in Singapore' in L.Suryadinata, (ed.), *Chinese Adaption and Diversity: Essays on Society and Literature in Indonesia, Malaysia and Singapore*, Singapore University Press, Singapore, 1993.

Chia, F., *The Babas Revisited*, Heinemann Asia, Singapore, 1994.

China Business Review.

China Statistical Yearbook 1993.

China Trade Report, May 1993.

Chinese General Chamber of Commerce, Hong Kong, *The 2nd World Chinese Entrepreneurs Convention: Commemorative Album*, 1994.

Chinese National Federation of Industries, *Chinese National Federation of Industries 1994-1996*, Taipei, (promotional brochure).

Chong, C., 'Making it in Japan', *Free China Review*, July 1989.

Chu, T.C. and T. MacMurray, 'The road ahead for Asia's leading conglomerates' *The McKinsey Quarterly*, No. 3, 1993.

Commercial Atlas of Guangdong, 1992.

Corporate International's Company Handbook, Hong Kong.

Courtland, C., *Collins Illustrated Guide to Burma*, William Collins Sons & Co. Ltd, 1988.

Crimson, L., G. Beattie and J. Selby, 'The segmentation and integration of the Chinese in Brisbane, Australia', *Journal of Comparative Family Studies*, Vol. 16, No. 2, Summer 1985.

Department of Foreign Affairs and Trade, *Country Economic Briefs*.

Department of Immigration, Local Government and Ethnic Affairs, *Directory of Ethnic Community Organisation in Australia 1992*, AGPS, 1992.

Department of Immigration and Ethnic Affairs, 'Community Information Summary: Chinese in Australia', November 1994.

Deyo, F.C., 'Chinese management practices and work commitment in comparative perspective, in L.Y.C. Lim and L.A.P. Gosling (eds), *The Chinese in Southeast Asia*, Vol. 2, Maruzen Asia, Singapore, 1983.

Dobbs-Higginson, M.S., *Asia Pacific: Its Role in the New World Order*, William Heinemann Australia, Port Melbourne, 1993.

Dun's Asia Pacific Key Business Enterprises, 1993-94.

Durack, T., 'Hot in Hong Kong', *Australian Gourmet Traveller*, October 1994.

Economic and Business Review Indonesia, Salim: Phones in Manila - flour in Malaysia', 10 December 1994.

Economic and Business Review Indonesia, 'China or Indonesia? The pros and the cons', 13 August 1994.

Economic and Business Review Indonesia, 'Indonesian-Chinese see prospects in "old country"', 13 August 1994.

Economic and Business Review Indonesia, 'The Gemala Group: Bad debt? Not true, says Sofjan Wanandi', 13 August 1994.

Economic Development Board, *Singapore Unlimited: Economic Development Board Yearbook 1992-93*, Singapore, 1993.

Far Eastern Economic Review.

Far Eastern Economic Review, *All Asia Travel Guide*, 16th edition, Review Publishing Co. Ltd, Hong Kong, 1993.

Far Eastern Textile Ltd, *Annual Report 1993*, Taipei, 1994.

Faulding, *Annual Report 1994*, Adelaide, 1994.

Federal Department of Muticulturalism and Citizenship Canada, *Multiculturalism Means Business 1993: A Directory of Business Contacts*, Minister of Supply and Services Canada, 1993.

Feng, C. and D. Goodman, 'China's Hainan Province: Economic development and investment environment', unpublished paper, University of Technology, Sydney, 1994.

First Pacific Co Ltd, *Annual Report 1993*, Hong Kong, 1994.

First Pacific Co Ltd, *Interim Report 1994*, Hong Kong, 1994.

Fortune, 'Billionaires in the making', 18 July 1994.

Fujian Province, *Statistical Yearbook*, 1993; 1994.

Godley, M.R. and C.A. Coppel, 'The Indonesian Chinese in Hong Kong: A preliminary report on a minority community in transition', *Issues and Studies: A Journal of Chinese Studies and International Affairs*, Vol. 26, No. 7, July 1990.

Gomez, E. T., *Money Politics in the Barisan Nasional*, Forum, Kuala Lumpur, 1991.

Gomez, E.T., *Political Business: Corporate Involvement of Malaysian Political Parties*, James Cook University of North Queensland, Townsville, 1994.

Goodman, D., *Deng Xiaoping*, Cardinal, London, 1990.

Guangdong Province, *Statistical Yearbook*, 1993; 1994.

Hafner, J.A., 'Market gardening in Thailand: The origins of an ethnic Chinese monopoly', in L.Y.C. Lim and L.A.P. Gosling (eds), *The Chinese in Southeast Asia*, Vol. 1, Maruzen Asia, Singapore, 1983, p. 36.

Hall, T.D., 'Ethnicity and economics', *International Economic Insights*, July/August 1993.

Hamilton, G.G., 'Overseas Chinese capitalism', Working Paper No. 42, Research Program in East Asian Business and Development, Institute of Governmental Affairs, University of California, January 1992.

Ho, W. M., *Straits Chinese Silver: A Collector's Guide*, Times Books International, Singapore, 1984.

Hofstede, G. and M.H. Bond, 'The Confucius Connection: From cultural roots to economic growth', *Organizational Dynamics* (details unknown).

Hong Kong Government Secretariat, Economic Services Branch, *Quarterly Economic Reports*.

Ip, D. and C. Lever-Tracy, 'Trailblazing into China: Networks and linkages of smaller diaspora firms', *Working Paper No. 33*, Asia Research Centre, Murdoch University, 1994.

Jakarta Post, 'Salim, two foreign partners get piggish in Singapore', 17 June 1994.

Jakarta Post, 'Analysts uncertain over Barito-CASH transaction', 18 June 1994.

Jennings, B., 'HK partner can be first step into China market', *Asia Today*, October 1994.

Jesudason, J.V., *Ethnicity and the Economy: The State, Chinese Business, and Multinationals in Malaysia*, OUP, Singapore, 1989.

Jetro China Newsletter.

Jiangsu Tongjinianjian, 1994.

Jomo, K.S., 'Is Chinese capital in Malaysia 'progressive'?', Unpublished paper, 1994.

Jones, E., L. Frost and C. White, *Coming Full Circle: An Economic History of the Pacific Rim*, OUP Australia, Oxford, 1993.

Kao, J., 'The worldwide web of Chinese business', *Harvard Business Review*, March-April 1993.

Kasper, W., 'Cultural community, liberty and prosperity: Twelve hypotheses', Unpublished paper, December 1993.

Kasper, W., 'Accelerated industrial evolution in East Asia: Some lessons', Economics and Management Discussion Paper, Department of Economics and Management, University College, The University of New South Wales, Australian Defence Force Academy, July 1989.

Kasper, W., 'Global competition, institutions and the East-Asian ascendancy', Unpublished paper, 1993.

Kiernan B., 'Kampuchea's ethnic Chinese under Pol Pot', *Journal of Contemporary Asia*, Vol. 16, No. 1, 1986.

Kotkin, J., *Tribes*, Random House, New York, 1993.

KPMG Asian Business Group, *Australian-Asian Alumni Network Report*, August 1994.

Kraar, L., 'The wealth and power of the overseas Chinese', *Fortune*, March 1971.

Kraar, L., 'Merill Lynch's Asian thriller', *Fortune*, 8 July 1985.

Ku, Y.H., 'Taiwan's FDI in Indonesia', *CIER Newsletter*, November 1994.

Kua, K.S. (ed.), *Polarisation in Malaysia: The Root Causes*, K. Das Ink, Petaling Jaya, 1987.

Kunio, Y., *The Rise of Ersatz Capitalism in South-East Asia*, Oxford University Press, Singapore, 1988.

Lardy, N., 'Chinese foreign trade', *The China Quarterly*, 131,1992.

Lever-Tracy, C. and Tracy, N., 'The dragon and the rising sun: Market integration and economic rivalry in East and South-East Asia', *Policy, Organisation and Society*, No. 6, 1993.

Lim, L.Y.C. and L.A.P. Gosling (eds), *The Chinese in Southeast Asia*, Two Vols, Maruzen Asia, Singapore, 1983.

Lim, L.Y.C., 'Chinese business, multinationals and the state: Manufacturing for export in Malaysia and Singapore' in L.Y.C. Lim and L.A.P. Gosling (eds), *The Chinese in Southeast Asia*, Vol. 1, Maruzen Asia, Singapore, 1983.

Lim, M.H., 'The ownership and control of large corporations in Malaysia: The role of Chinese businessmen', in L.Y.C. Lim and L.A.P. Gosling, *The Chinese in Southeast Asia*, Vol 1, Maruzen Asia, Singapore, 1983.

Limlingan, V.S., *The Overseas Chinese in ASEAN: Business Strategies and Management Practices*, Vita Development Corporation, Manila, 1986.

Ling, A., *Golden Dreams of Borneo*, Singapore, 1993.

Linge, G. and D. Forbes, *China's New Spatial Economy*, OUP, 1990.

Lip, E., *Feng Shui for the Home*, Times Books International, Singapore, 1986.

Lippo Group of Companies, *Lippoworld*, November 1994.

Lippobank, *Annual Report 1993*, Jakarta, 1994.

Mackie, J.A.C., 'Overseas Chinese entrepreneurship', *Asian-Pacific Economic Literature*, May 1992.

Mackie, J.A.C., 'The ethnic Chinese economy in Southeast Asia', paper presented to the International Conference on Southeast Asian Chinese Culture, Economy and Society, Singapore, 21-23 January 1994.

Mackie, J.A.C., 'Changing economic roles and ethnic identities of the Southeast Asian Chinese: A comparison of Indonesia and Thailand' in J.W. Cushman and Wang Gungwu *Changing Identities of the Southeast Asian Chinese since World War II*, Hong Kong University Press, 1988.

Marco Polo Pacific Dynasty Fund (prospectus summary), Hong Kong.

Margaret Gee's Australian Media Guide, November 1994-March 1995, 47th Edition, Melbourne, 1994.

Maruya, T. (ed.), *Guangdong: "Open Door" Economic Development Strategy*, Institute of Developing Economies, Tokyo, 1992.

Master Builders Association Malaysia, *Master Builders*, 2nd Quarter 1994.

Minchin, J., *No Man is an Island*, 2nd Edition, Allen and Unwin, North Sydney, 1990.

MOFTEC, *International Trade News (ITN)*, Beijing, various issues.

Mya Maung, 'On the road to Mandalay', *Asian Survey*, May 1994.

News Corporation Ltd, *The News Corporation Ltd: Financial Report 1994*, Adelaide, 1994.

Nikkei Weekly.

Ningbo Economic and Technical Development Zone, *Investment Guide to Ningbo Economic and Technical Development Zone*, Ningbo, 1995.

North, D.C. 'Transactions costs, institutions and economic performance', Occasional Paper No. 30, San Francisco, International Centre for Economic Growth, 1992.

Numazaki, I., 'Networks of Taiwanese big business: A preliminary analysis', *Modern China*, Vol. 12, No. 4, October 1986.

Numazaki, I., 'The Tainanbang: The rise and growth of a banana-bunch-shaped business group in Taiwan', *The Developing Economies*, December 1993.

Oetomo, D., 'Multilinguism and Chinese identities in Indonesia', in J.W. Cushman and Wang Gungwu (eds), *Changing Identities of the Southeast Asian Chinese since World War II*, Hong Kong University Press, 1988.

Office of Multicultural Affairs, 'Winning new sales with ancient symbols', Canberra, (Productive Diversity information brochure).

Olson, M., *The Logic of Collective Action: Public Goods and the Theory of Groups*, Harvard University Press, Cambridge, 1971.

Osborne, M., *Sihanouk: Prince of Light; Prince of Darkness*, Allen and Unwin, 1994.

Overholt, W., *The Rise of China: How Economic Reform is Creating a New Superpower*, Norton, 1993.

Overseas Chinese Affairs Commission, *We Always Stay Together*, Taipei, June 1991.

Pan, L., *Sons of the Yellow Emperor: The Story of the Overseas Chinese*, Mandarin, 1991.

Pandey, B.N., *South and South-East Asia 1945-1979: Problems and Policies*, Macmillan, London, 1980.

Panin Bank, *1993 Annual Report*, Jakarta, 1994.

Perkins, F., 'Export performance and enterprise reform in China's coastal provinces', *Economics Division Working Papers*, 95/2, Research School of Pacific and Asian Studies, Australian National University, 1995.

Peters, J., *Lonely Planet Travel Survival Guide: Philippines - A Travel Survival Kit*, Lonely Planet Publications, Hawthorn, 1991.

Prospek, 'Mereka Bukan Shang Hui', 16 January 1994.

PT Indah Kiat Pulp and Paper Corp., *Annual Report '92*, Jakarta, 1993.

PT Pabrik Kertas Tjiwa Kimia, *1992 Annual Report*, Jakarta, 1993.

PT Smart Corp., *Annual Report 1993*, Jakarta, 1994.

Pusat Data Business Indonesia, *Conglomeration Indonesia*, 2nd edition, Jakarta, 1994.

Raybeck, D., 'Chinese patterns of adaption in Southeast Asia' in L.Y.C. Lim and L.A.P. Gosling (eds), *The Chinese in Southeast Asia*, Vol. 2, Maruzen Asia, Singapore, 1983.

Redding, G.S., *The Spirit of Chinese Capitalism*, Walter de Gruyter and Co., Berlin, 1990.

Republika, 'Peraup dana publik terbesar (The biggest holders of public funds)', 10 August 1994.

Salim Group, *An Overview of the Salim Group*, Jakarta, 1993.

Sato, Y., 'The Salim Group in Indonesia: The development and behaviour of the largest conglomerate in Southeast Asia', *The Developing Economies*, December 1993.

Sender, H., 'Inside the overseas Chinese network', *Institutional Investor*, August 1991.

Schwarz, A., *A Nation in Waiting: Indonesia in the 1990s*, Allen and Unwin, 1994.

Shari, M., 'Selling family secrets', *Asia, Inc.*, December 1994.

Shirk, S., *The Political Logic of Economic Reform in China*, University of California Press, 1993.

Sinar Mas, *Sinar Mas Group*, promotional brochure.

Singapore Chinese Chamber of Commerce and Industry, *1st World Chinese Entrepreneurs Convention: A Global Network*, Singapore 1992.

Singapore Chinese Chamber of Commerce and Industry, *Singapore Chinese Chamber of Commerce and Industry: Directory of Members of the 47th Council*, March 1993-March 1995, Singapore, 1993.

Singapore Chinese Chamber of Commerce and Industry, *Singapore Chinese Chamber of Commerce and Industry Annual Report* '93, Singapore, 1994.

Singapore Business Times.

Singapore Trade and Investment Mission to Myanmar, 22-26 August 1994, Singapore, 1994, mission handbook.

Singapore-Suzhou Township Development Pte Ltd, *Singapore-Suzhou Township*, promotional brochure.

Siow, M., 'The problems of ethnic cohesion among the Chinese in peninsular Malaysia: Intraethnic divisions and interethnic accommodation' in L.Y.C. Lim and L.A.P. Gosling (eds), *The Chinese in Southeast Asia*, Vol. 1, Maruzen Asia, Singapore, 1983.

Skinner, G.W., *Chinese Society in Thailand: An Analytical History*, Cornell University Press, Ithaca, New York, 1957.

South China Morning Post.

South China Morning Post International Weekly.

South-East Asian Monitor, 'Foreign Competition to Spur Bank Sector', Vol. 5, No. 11, November 1994.

Sowell, T., 'Middleman Minorities', *The American Enterprise*, May/June 1993.

Sowell, T., *The Economics and Politics of Race*, Quill, New York, 1983.

State Commercial Bureau, *FDI in China: Analysis of Trends and Future Directions*, Beijing, 1993.

Studwell, J., 'Sweet and sour times for a sugar king', *Asia, Inc.*, December 1994.

Suehiro, A., 'Bangkok bank: Management reforms of a Thai commercial bank', *East Asian Cultural Studies*, Vol. 28, 1989.

Suehiro, A., 'Family business reassessed: Corporate structure and late-starting industrialization in Thailand', *The Developing Economies*, December 1994.

Sunday Times (Singapore), 'Chinese Indonesians reaffirm national identity', 26 June 1994.

Supang Chantavanich, 'Refugee flows from Indochina: Mass movements and challenges for the 1990s', *Occasional Paper Series No. 006*, Indochinese Refugee Information Center (IRIC), Institute of Asian Studies, Chulalongkorn University, Bangkok, 1993.

Suryadinata, L., 'Introduction' in L. Suryadinata (ed.), *The Ethnic Chinese in the ASEAN States: Biographical Essays*, ISEAS, Singapore, 1989.

Suryadinata, L., 'Chinese economic elites in Indonesia: A preliminary study', in J.W. Cushman and Wang Gungwu *Changing Identities of the Southeast Asian Chinese since World War II*, Hong Kong University Press, 1988.

Suryadinata, L., 'The Xinghua community in Singapore: A study of the socio-economic adjustment of a minority group', in L. Suryadinata, (ed.), *Chinese Adaption and Diversity: Essays on Society and Literature in Indonesia, Malaysia and Singapore*, Singapore University Press, Singapore, 1993.

SyCip, W., 'Role and prospects for developing countries', presented to an Asialink seminar, Melbourne 1992.

Sydney Morning Herald, 'Hidden side of the resurgent dragon', 28 April 1993.

Tan, C.B., 'Acculturation and the Chinese in Melaka: The expression of Baba identity today' in L.Y.C. Lim and L.A.P. Gosling (eds), *The Chinese in Southeast Asia*, Vol. 1, Maruzen Asia, Singapore, 1983.

Thai-Chinese Chamber of Commerce, *14th Board Executive Committee 1994-1995 of Thai-Chinese Chamber of Commerce, Bangkok, Thailand*, Bangkok, 1994.

The Australian.

The Bulletin, 'Backdoor bonanza', 14 June 1994.

The Chinese General Chamber of Commerce, *The Chinese General Chamber of Commerce*, Hong Kong 1990, Chamber brochure.

The Chinese General Chamber of Commerce, *1993 Annual Report*, Hong Kong, 1994.

The Economist, 'A bruiser from Bangkok', 26 November 1994.

The Economist, 'Singapore: Giant leaps', 2 April 1994.

The Federation of Hokkien Associations of Malaysia, *Handbook, 1993*, Kuala Lumpur.

The Irrawaddy, 'City Realty plans hotel in Burma with Thai Cont', 15 December 1994.

The Straits Times.

The Straits Times Weekly Edition.

The Weekend Australian, 'The Thakral Group gets an instant hotel chain', 26-27 March 1994.

The World Bank, *China: Foreign Trade Reform*, Washington DC, 1994.

Time, 'The secret weapon', 10 May 1994.

Tracy, N., 'The making of a new little dragon: The overseas Chinese and the transformation of Guangdong', *Working Paper No. 36*, Asia Research Centre, Murdoch University, 1994.

Tran Khanh, *The Ethnic Chinese and Economic Development in Vietnam*, Institute of Southeast Asian Studies, Singapore, 1993.

Tseng, Y.L., 'Survival of the persistent', *Free China Review*, July 1989.

Verchere, I., The Changing World of Robert Kuok', *Insight*, August 1978.

Waldron, S., 'Indonesian Chinese investment in Indonesia: Magnitude, motivations and meaning', *Australia-Asia Papers No. 73*, Centre of the Study of Australia Asia Relations, Griffith University, March 1995.

Washington Post, 'Relative success story', 11 September 1994.

Washington Post, 'A maze of family connections complicates succession', 11 September 1994.

Weidenbaum, M., *Greater China: The Next Superpower*, Georgetown University Press, 1993.

Willmott, W.E., *The Chinese in Cambodia*, University of British Columbia, Vancouver, 1967.

Wong, S.L., *Emigrant Entrepreneurs: Shanghai Industrialists in Hong Kong*, OUP, Hong Kong, 1988.

Wu, David Y.H., *The Chinese in Papua New Guinea: 1880-1980*, The Chinese University Press, Hong Kong, 1982.

Wu, Y.L. and C.H. Wu, *Economic Development in Southeast Asia: The Chinese Dimension*, Hoover Institute Press, Stanford, 1980.

Xu, X.Q. and S.M. Li, 'China's open door policy and urbanisation in the Pearl River Delta region', *International Journal of Urban and Regional Research*, 14(1), 1990.

Yamaguchi, M., 'The emerging Chinese business sphere', *Nomura Asian Perspectives*, Vol. 11, No. 2, July 1993, Nomura Research Institute.

Yellow Pages Corporation, *1995 Taiwan Yellow Pages*, Taipei, 1994.

Yeo Hiap Seng Ltd, *YHS: Annual Report 1993*, Singapore, 1994.

Yong, P., *A Dream of Feedom: The Early Sarawak Chinese*, Pelanduk Publications, Petaling Jaya.

Zhang, C., 'A memorandum on the workers' situation in foreign capital enterprises', *Chinese Industrial and Commercial News*, 24 June 1994.

Zhang, X. and N. Tracy, *The Third Foreign Investment Wave in Mainland China: Origins, Features and Implications*, Asia Research Centre, Murdoch University, Working Paper No. 34, 1994.

INDEX

A

Acer 101
Alien Registration Tax 75
Allied Banking Corporation 67
Amnuay Viravan 77
AMP Panin Life 257
AMP Society 257
An Dong shopping centre 85
Ansett Australia 283, 312
Anwar Ibrahim 237
Aquino, Corazon 65, 66
Argo Manunggal Group 47
Asia Financial 91, 141, 321, 322
Asia Pacific Foundation of Canada 87, 340
Asia Property Australia 255
Associated Chinese Chambers of Commerce 53, 59, 276, 289, 336
Astra Group 145, 146, 172, 245
astronaut effect 113
Austrade 258, 259, 263, 274, 278, 280
Australia and New Zealand Banking Group 257
Australia Taiwanese Chamber of Commerce 276, 293, 296, 297, 300
Australia-Brunei Chamber of Commerce 276, 282, 292, 297, 300
Australia-China Business and Trade Association 292, 297, 302
Australia-Shanghai General Chamber of Commerce 282, 293, 296, 297, 300
Australian Chamber of Manufacturers 258
Australian Chinese Association of Hong Kong 98, 296, 307
Australian Chinese Medical Association 292, 304
Australian Chinese Teo-Chew Association 309
Australian Mainland Chinese Association 307
Australian Stock Exchange 254
Aw, Sally 92, 283

B

babas, the 17, 18, 37, 48, 55, 69, 70, 71, 81, 121, 136
backdoor listing 159
BAKOM-PKB 37, 39, 284
Bakrie Group 143, 145
Ballarat 111
Ban Hin Lee Bank 58, 141
Bangkok Commercial Bank 79
Bangkok Metropolitan Bank 138, 156
Bank Bumiputera 33, 56
Bank Central Asia 33, 135, 148, 160, 163, 165, 172, 174
Bank Dagang Nasional Indonesia 160
Bank International Indonesia 146, 160
Bank Nusa 178
Bank of Ayudha 79
Bank Summa 46, 151
Barito Group 47, 145, 172
Barito Pacific Timber 159
Basic Law of Hong Kong 98
Bathurst 111
Bendigo 111
Berjaya Group 199, 237
Berli Jucker 167
Binh Tien Imex Corporation 85
Bogasari Flour Mill 164
Bong Son An 30
Boonchu Rojanasatien 77
Boonsong Srifeungfung 78, 286
Brashs 253
Brunei Chinese Chamber of Commerce 35
Bulam complex 166
BULOG 152, 164
bumiputeras 53, 54, 55, 56, 57, 59, 183, 334, 335
Bunge Group 168, 256
Burmese Chinese 91, 92, 100, 179, 185

C

Calcutta 88
Cambodiana Hotel 180
Campos, Jose 68
cemeteries, Chinese 51, 310
Central Group 75, 155, 257

Centre for Strategic and International Studies 46
Chan, Bernard 117
Chan, Sir Julius 88
Chan, Raymond 87
Chan, Robin 91, 141, 320, 321, 322
Chareon Pokphand (CP) 159, 162, 241, 246, 247, 313, 323, 324, 325, 326
Chearavanont family 120, 159, 325, 326
Chen, Daniel 117
Chen Hsong 217
Chen Teh Shu 30
Cheng Ho 13
Cheung Kong 93, 96, 154, 242, 315, 329
Chia, Jack 253
Chien Tai Cement Company 164
Chien Thang Agricultural Processing Company 85
China Banking Corporation 67
China Industrial Management Holdings 242, 243
China Mercantile Bank 177
China Pacific Group 236
China Strategic Holdings 97, 198, 242, 243, 256, 317
China Town Business Association 303
China Travel Services 235
Chinese Chamber of Commerce of South Australia 24, 178, 297, 299
Chinese Chamber of Commerce of Victoria 292, 297, 298, 301
Chinese Chamber of Commerce of Western Australia 297
Chinese Club of Queensland 282, 305
Chinese Community Cultural Centre 308
Chinese Community Society of Victoria 295, 306
Chinese Fellowship of Victoria 282, 305
Chinese General Chamber 66, 92, 195, 283, 288
Chinese Masonic Society 283, 294, 308
Chinese National Federation of Industries (CNFI) 106, 336
Chinese Nationalist Party 308
Chinese Professional and Business Association 292, 301
Chinese Restaurateurs Association of Victoria 304
Chirathivat family 75, 257
Cholon 15, 81, 85
Christiani & Nielsen 248, 249
Chuan Hauy Group 28
Chuan Leekpai 74, 77, 241
Chulachomklao Military Academy 74
Chun King Corporation 249
Chung Po Investment Company 235
Chung Shing Textile Group 137
Ciputra (Chia Ching Hwa) 172
CITIC 175, 252, 317, 330
Citra Caraka 245
clan associations 2, 7, 17, 58, 65, 67, 71, 72, 73, 74, 79, 122
Clinton, President Bill 151
Cold Rolling Mill Indonesia Utama 45, 165, 174
Commercial Bank 30, 79, 91, 120, 141, 184, 320, 321, 322, 333
Confucianism; Confucius 122, 123
Cultural Revolution 62, 124, 182, 186, 242, 243

D
Darmadi, Jan 148, 247
Darya Varia Laboratoria 167
Davids Holdings 257, 258
decision making 3, 132, 133, 142, 203, 260, 332
Delta Group 31
Democratic Action Party 52, 284
Democratic Progressive Party 36
deposit-taking cooperatives 58
Development Bank of Singapore 70, 240
Dharmala Group 42, 145, 160, 199, 320, 322
dialect associations 16, 17, 22, 23, 33, 46, 51, 59, 61, 63, 71, 83, 177, 185
Dickson Concepts 248
Djajanti Group 30
Djuhar, Tedy 166, 171, 251
doi moi 81, 85
due diligence 94, 277, 278

E
East Meets West 10, 258, 278
Economic Development Board 70, 169, 188, 189, 239, 286
Ekran Bhd 31

Equitable Bank 67
Ethnic Communities Program 10, 258, 278
Evergreen 101, 120
Export Development 10, 258, 278, 281

F

face 123
Far Eastern Group 104
Faulding 256, 257
Federation of Filipino Chinese Chambers of Commerce 66, 276
Federation of Hokkien Associations of Malaysia 22, 58, 60
Federation of Malaysian Manufacturers 59
feng shui 51, 76, 306, 310, 311, 312
Filipino Chinese General Chambers of Commerce 276
First Pacific Bank 167, 175
First Pacific Company 97, 163, 166, 172, 173, 175, 283
First Pacific Group 166, 167, 175, 254
First Pacific Investments 166
Formosa Plastics 101, 106, 107, 120, 154, 157
Fosters Brewing Group 257, 319
Fringe Benefits Tax 255

G

Gadjah Tunggal Group 42, 145, 160
Geelong Grammar 251
Gemala Group 42, 45, 254
Genting Group 60, 154
Gerakan 52, 53, 184, 284, 285
Goh Chok Tong 192
Goh Keng Swee 70, 285
Goh Tjoei Kok 181
Gokongwei families 65
Gokongwei, John 68, 120
gold fields 110
Golden Key Group 30
Gotianum, Andrew 68, 161
Government-linked companies (Singapore) 169, 170, 335
Gow Swie Kie 152
Great Wall Business Association 280, 297, 302
GSS Electronics 248, 249
Guangdong Trade Fair 238
Guangzhou Television 261
Gudang Garam Group 47
guilds (Chinese) 16, 17, 50, 51, 54, 59, 63, 71, 78, 92, 122, 276, 294

H

Hagemeyer 166, 170, 175, 248
Hainan 1, 14, 22, 23, 24, 25, 58, 199, 200, 201, 208, 216, 237, 238, 239, 316, 329
Hainanese 2, 14, 22, 24, 25, 26, 27, 35, 37, 47, 49, 52, 58, 69, 82, 83, 112, 199, 237
Halim, Andree 172
Harapan Group 30
Hard Rock Cafe 150
Harian Indonesia 38
Haw Par 135
Heineken 247, 325
Henderson Land 120, 140, 317
Hendra Rahardja 30
Henghua 16, 23, 26, 27, 28, 29, 30, 32
Hii Yu Peng 31
Hip Hang Trading 261
Ho Chi Minh City 9, 81, 82, 85, 113, 170, 193, 321
Ho, Halpin 186
Ho Whye Tong 252, 267, 270
Hock Hua Bank 31, 58, 141
Hokchia 2, 23, 28, 29, 30, 50
Hong Kong Business and Professionals Association of Queensland 280
Hong Kong Club 98, 281, 296, 307
Hong Kong Cotton Spinners' Association 95
Hong Leong Group 33, 120, 137, 140, 146, 157, 176, 331
Hopewell Holdings 93, 96, 120, 313
Hour Glass 178
Hua-qiao 12, 14, 108
Hua-ren 12
Huachiew Chalermprakiet University 76
Huachiew Foundation 75, 76, 78
Huang, John 151
Huang, SC 181
Hume Industries 56, 331, 333
Husky Oil 248, 249, 316
Hutchison Whampoa 120, 248, 249, 315, 316

I

Imagineering Technology Ltd 254
Imora Group 245
in-house lending 103, 161

India 9, 88, 184, 186, 188, 192, 217, 262, 275, 314
Indocement 45, 151, 164, 172, 174
Indofood Sukses Makmur 166
Indonesian Chinese living in Hong Kong 91, 182
Indosiar Visual Mandiri 166
Industrial Coordination Act 54, 334, 337
information leakage 160
inheritance practices 137
internal financing 3, 93, 134
International Maritime Carriers 96
International Society of Fuzhous 31, 33
Internet 193

J
Jaguh Mutiara Bhd 56
Jakarta Land 174
Jakarta Stock Exchange 146, 164
Jasper Group 258
Java 13, 18, 37, 45, 163, 169, 171, 314
Jurong Environmental Engineering 169, 170, 285

K
Kabila Mandiri Persada 168
Kao Chin-yuan 106
Kayin Holdings 58
Kazakhstan 89
Kerry Financial Services 33, 185, 186
Kerry Group 97, 120, 157, 327, 328, 330
Kerry Investment Management 138, 283
Khmer Rouge 35, 36
Khoo Kay Peng 32, 55, 139
Khoo Kongsi 50, 58
kidnappings (Philippines) 68
Kobe 89, 288
Kong Lee Bank 58, 141
kongsis 50, 58, 72
Koo family 120, 174
Koperatitif Serbaguna 57
Kota 46, 289, 329
Kotjo, Johannes 142
Krakatau Steel 45, 165, 174
Krama Yudha Group 245
Kuala Lumpur Stock Exchange 58, 168, 332
Kuantan Flour Mills 32, 161, 168
Kuok, Robert 2, 31, 32, 56, 57, 68, 97, 120, 138, 139, 146, 157, 161, 172, 174, 186, 197, 213, 248, 313, 317, 321, 327, 328, 329, 330
Kuok Philippines Properties 32
Kuomintang 184, 219, 228, 294, 308
Kwan, Perry 88
Kwek family 120, 157, 332
Kwek Leng Joo 186, 331, 333
Kwok Brothers 96, 120

L
Lamsam family 79, 120, 156, 322
Laos 25, 28, 47, 182, 183, 192, 237, 300
Lee, Tun Sir Colonel Henry H.S. 184
Lee Kuan Yew 70, 178, 188, 195
Lee Shau-kee 140, 317
Lend Lease 257
Li Ka-shing 90, 96, 99, 120, 146, 178, 213, 242, 243, 248, 313, 315, 316, 317, 329, 330
Liem Investors 166, 171
Liem Oen Kian 30, 31, 164, 171
Liem Sioe Hie 163, 172
Lien Ying Chow 72, 140
Ling Beng Siew 31
Ling Liong Sik 31, 57
Lippo Finance Australia 97, 254, 255, 280
Lippo Group 30, 42, 97, 140, 145, 147, 151, 160, 171, 176, 177, 247, 254, 255, 283, 317, 322
Lippobank 45, 97, 160, 177, 251, 255
locality associations 16, 17, 50
Loh Boon Siew 51, 60, 244, 269
Lon Nol 35
Los Angeles 33, 60, 85, 88, 97, 100, 321, 330
Low Yow Chuan 251, 267

M
Ma, C.K. 113, 267
Macau 6, 12, 13, 60, 90, 99, 100, 178, 182, 184, 194, 198, 202, 209, 212, 221, 222, 288, 313, 315, 321, 322
Mahathir, Prime Minister 49, 237
Majelis Perwakilan Rakyat 46
Makati business district 32, 68, 161, 169
Makro Holding 247
Malacca 13, 18, 48, 50, 58, 70, 121
Malayan Communist Party 48
Malayan United Industries (MUI) 32, 33, 55, 139, 269, 333
Malaysia-Australia Business Council 251, 284
Malaysian Chinese Association 52, 184, 284
Malaysian Chinese students 51
Malaysian Indian Congress 52
Malaysian International Chamber of Commerce 59
Man Po Holdings 254
Mandalay 61, 62, 63, 64, 186, 238, 329
Mandalay Beer 185
Mandarin 19, 21, 22, 55, 60, 61, 69, 78, 88, 90, 135, 178, 188, 191, 206, 235, 239, 273, 282, 296, 308, 328, 329, 330
Mandarin Association of Melbourne 282, 308
Manila 32, 33, 65, 68, 97, 158, 161, 177, 183, 289, 320, 323, 331
Marco Polo Dynasty Fund 138
Marcos, President 65, 152
market niches 5, 29, 126, 127, 128, 150, 152, 153, 250, 261
Matahari Department Store 42, 157, 181
Mauritius 89, 178
Mawei Economic and Technological Development 213
Mayflower Bank 187
MBf 178, 272
Medan 22, 39, 40, 184
Mega 164
Metro Bank 67
Metro Department Store 42, 157, 181
Metro Pacific Corporation 32, 68, 161, 169
Minbei 23
Minh Phung Garment Factory 85
Minnan 23
Montana 36
Moran Group 132, 133, 260, 282
MUI Bank 33, 139, 333
Multi-Purpose Holdings 57
Myanmar Chinese Chamber of Commerce 63, 285, 289
Myanmar Fund 185, 186
Myanmar Oriental Bank 187
Myanmar Seafoods 185

N
Nagasaki 89
National Cheng-Chi University Alumni Association 307
National Development Policy 53
National Registration Cards 62
National Trades Union Congress (NTUC) 240
New Economic Policy (NEP) 39, 53, 54, 55, 183, 334
Ne Win 62, 63, 185, 186
New Order Government 38, 39, 40
New South Wales Lotteries 312
New Villages 50, 53, 57
New World Developments 317
New York Stock Exchange 243, 325
Ngee Ann City complex 72
Ngo Dinh Diem 83
Nguyen dynasty 15
Ning Yung Society 282, 296, 305
Ningbobang 96
nonya 69, 70
North Point 91, 92
NSW Indo-China Chinese Association 306

O
Occupation-dialect links 275
Oceania 13
Oei Hong Leong 97, 168, 213, 242, 256, 317
Ometraco Group 42, 145
Ong Beng Seng 150, 253, 270, 271
Ong Teng Cheong 188
Ong Tjoe Kim 157, 181
Ongko Group 164
Oriental Travel Agencies Consortium 281, 293, 304
Osaka Foreign Trade Association 246
Overseas Chinese Affairs Commission 107, 286, 308

Overseas Chinese Credit Guarantee Fund 108
Overseas Union Bank 72, 140, 184, 269

P
Pacific Bank 58, 141, 167, 175
Pacifique Sino 262, 263, 264, 265, 283
Palang Dharma Party 74
Pangestu, Prajogo 42, 46, 47, 120, 146, 172
Panin Bank 42, 148, 257, 283, 340
Pao, YK 95, 96, 136, 318
Papua New Guinea 31, 88, 110, 117
Parsons Galloway Foundation Pty Ltd 260, 282
PB Com 67
Penang Chinese Chamber of Commerce 59, 183, 238, 284, 285, 289
People's Action Party 70
People's Republic of Kampuchea 35
Phaya Taksin 74
Philippine Banking Corporation 67
Philippine Trust 67
Philippines Chinese 92
Pico Far East 177
Pinyin 12, 23, 287
Pipat Tantipipatpong 30, 213
PL International 185
Pol Pot 35
Pornpat Group 30, 241
Prasetiya Mulya Foundation 46, 47
President Group 106, 109
Pribadi, Henry 171
pribumis, pribumi 16, 32, 39, 40, 41, 42, 45, 46, 47, 160, 165, 171, 172
Producers Bank 67
Productive Diversity program 259
Putian 14, 28, 29, 177, 211, 235
Putonghua 90

Q
Qing Dynasty 14, 17, 294, 305, 308
quadrangle trade 79

R
Ramos Administration 236
Republic Act No. 3018 67
Riady, Mochtar 30, 32, 33, 37, 45, 97, 135, 148, 151, 155, 165, 171, 172, 177, 178, 213, 235, 236, 255, 317
Riady family 251
Rimbunan Hijau Group 30, 162
Rizal Commercial Banking Corporation 67
Robe 111
Robinson Department Store 257
Ruby Holdings 243

S
S.E.A. Food International 261
Sabah 50, 51, 58, 289
Saha Group 156, 245
Saha Union Group 156
Salim, Anthony 46, 132, 136, 141, 163, 166, 171, 172, 174
Salim Economic Development Corporation 166, 172
San Francisco 25, 88, 97, 123, 185, 321, 322, 330
Security Bank and Trust 67
See Yap districts 111
Semen Cibinong 143, 145
Shan State 64
Shanghainese 19, 21, 26, 88, 90, 95, 96, 100, 101, 103, 104, 148, 264, 300
Shangri-La hotels 97, 329
Shangri-La Properties 33
Shantou 14, 15, 24, 79, 90, 91, 117, 127, 156, 191, 206, 209, 210, 241, 242, 287, 309, 316, 320, 321, 323
Shaw, Sir Run Run 96, 99, 248, 327, 328, 329
ShoeMart 158
Siam Motors 178, 245
Sibu 14, 29, 30, 31, 50, 214, 238
Sihanouk, King 37
Sin, Cardinal 65
Sin Ban Group 168, 256
Sinar Mas Group 47, 120, 136, 137, 145, 155, 160, 171, 172, 198, 255, 283

Sing Tao Holdings 97
Sing Tao Jih Pao 254
Singapore Chinese Chamber of Commerce 69, 72, 73, 170, 177, 186, 239, 240, 246, 285, 289, 298, 331, 333
Singapore Federation of Chinese Clan Associations 72, 338
Singapore Land 140, 168, 169, 170
Singapore Technologies Industrial Corporation 170, 178, 339
Singapore World Trade Centre 99
Singapore-Suzhou Industrial Township 240, 241, 275
sinkehs 18
Sino-Burmese 9, 185, 186, 187, 238, 275
Sino-Vietnamese 9, 80, 85, 92, 100, 107, 113, 117, 273
Smart Communications 166
Social Development Unit 70
Soeharto, President 40, 42, 46, 163, 164, 166, 171, 174
Soeryadjaya, William 45, 46, 146, 151, 317
Somsavad Lengsavath 47
Son Hoa Plastics Enterprise 85
Sophonpanich, Chatri 320, 321
Sophonpanich, Chin 145, 164, 251, 320, 321, 322
Sophonpanich, Chote 251
Sophonpanich family 77, 120, 141, 321, 322
South China Morning Post 31, 32, 33, 140, 151, 157, 163, 202, 205, 217, 242, 313, 315, 317, 319, 323, 327, 328, 330
South Korea 86, 186, 197, 262, 263, 320, 342
Southern Pacific Hotels Corporation 339
Southern-California Fukienese Association 33
Speak Mandarin campaign 239
Special Economic Zones (SEZs) 199, 206, 213, 219, 220, 226, 229, 230
State Law and Order Restoration Committee (SLORC) 238
Subic Bay development 190
Sudwikatmono 42, 166, 171, 172
Sukarno, President 38, 164
Sumampouw, Robbie 31
Sumatra 17, 22, 32, 37, 39, 40, 42, 45, 184
Sun Chua Luen Professional Chefs Association 303
Sun Hung Kai Group 96
Sun Yat Sen 17
Sung, Peter 134, 285
Surya Hidup Satwa 162
Sy, Henry 68, 120, 136, 158, 161
Sydney Chinatown Chamber of Commerce 281, 291, 303

T

Tahiti 89
Tainanbang 102, 106, 107
Taishan Cantonese, Taishan 14, 15, 23, 25, 61, 88, 287
Taiwan Stock Exchange 101, 339
Taiwanese Association of Australia 281, 307
Taiwanese Australia Business Association 291, 303
Tan, Lucio 67, 68, 97, 120, 152, 161
Tan, Vincent 33, 56, 139
Tan Koon Swan 57
Tan Siew Sin 48, 55, 70
Tan Tjoe Hing 30
Tang, Henry 96
Tao, SP 92, 97, 185, 254, 283, 322
Tat Lee Bank 181
Tat Lee Company 181
Tati Group 235
Tay Son rebellion 15
Tech Pacific 167, 254
Tejaphaibul family 138, 156
Thai Farmers Bank 79, 120, 156, 322
Thai-Chinese Chamber of Commerce 76, 77, 78, 156, 286, 290, 298
Thang Loi Machine Rice Mills Factory 85
The Ning King 47
Tiger Balm 92, 135, 185
Ting Pek Khiing 31
Tiong Hiew King 30, 31, 60, 162
Tomei Group 95, 313
Tongnian 107
tontine system 117, 134
Toronto 86, 97
totok 18, 37, 45, 46, 181, 235
Townsend Chemicals 262, 263, 264, 265, 274, 282
Trade Development Board 70, 186

Traders Hotel 186, 329
transactions costs 5, 123, 128, 129, 132, 346
Treaty of Nanking 14
Treaty of Shimonoseki 100
Tsao, Frank 96
Tuan Sing Holdings 21, 134, 285
Ty, George 67, 68, 161

U
Unicord 80, 249
United Engineers 56
United Hokkien Cemetery Committee 51
United Industrial Corporation 168, 175, 242
United Malays National Organisation (UMNO) 52, 56, 57, 333
United Nations Transitional Authority in Cambodia 36
United Overseas Bank 140, 170, 266, 267, 330
United Overseas Land 170, 269
United World Chinese Commercial Bank 30
USSR 89

V
Vancouver 35, 86, 87, 97, 316, 329
Vichit Suraphongchai 77
Victorian Chinese Chamber of Commerce 178, 298
Viet Huong Instant Noodle Processing Company 85
Viet-Hoa Bank 85
Viet-Hoa Construction Company 85
Vietnamese Chinese 81, 84, 92, 100, 112, 113, 114, 179, 193
VTech Holdings 218
Vuu Khai Thanh 85

W
Wade-Giles 12, 23, 111, 287
Wah Tung International 254
Walmart 8, 246
Wanandi, Sofyan 45
Wang-lee family 156
Wesfarmers Ltd 256
Wheelock Pacific Group 257
Widjaja, Eka Tjipta 37, 47, 120, 136, 155, 168, 172, 213, 236, 242
Wong Nai Siong 29
Wong Soon Kai 31
Wong Tuong Kwang 31
Woo, Peter 96, 136, 257, 317, 318
World Trade Centre 99, 138, 329
WTK Group 31
Wu, Gordon 96, 120, 197, 313, 314, 317

X
Xu Xi Min 92

Y
Yaohan Group 330
Yaowarat 26
Yeo Hiap Seng Ltd 139, 249, 350
Yokohama 288
Yuan Hong Industrial Park 168, 169, 170
Yuchengco, Alfonso 67, 68
Yunnanese 27, 61, 62, 63, 74, 192, 241

Z
Zeta Holdings 142

Also by the EAST ASIA ANALYTICAL UNIT

Australia and North-East Asia in the 1990s: Accelerating Change
Published February 1992 (AGPS Cat No. 92 1073 6), 320 pages, A$29.95

Australia's Business Challenge: South-East Asia in the 1990s
Published December 1992 (AGPS Cat No. 92 2863 9), 380 pages, A$34.95

Grain in China
Published December 1992 (AGPS Cat No. 92 2820 5), 150 pages, A$19.95

Korea to the Year 2000: Implications for Australia
Published November 1992 (AGPS Cat No. 92 2818 5), 150 pages, A$19.95

Southern China in Transition
Published December 1992 (APGS Cat No. 92 2821 7), 150 pages, A$19.95

Changing Tack: Australian Investment in South-East Asia
Published March 1994 (AGPS Cat No. 94 1579 8), 110 pages, A$19.95

ASEAN Free Trade Area (AFTA): Trading Bloc or Building Block?
Published April 1994 (AGPS Cat No. 94 1816 3), 180 pages, A$26.95

India's Economy at the Midnight Hour: Australia's India Strategy
Published April 1994 (AGPS Cat No. 94 1818 7), 260 pages, A$34.95

Expanding Horizons: Australia and Indonesia into the 21st Century
Published June 1994 (AGPS Cat No. 94 20224), 350 pages, A$34.95

Subsistence to Supermarket:
Food and Agricultural Transformation in South-East Asia
Published August 1994 (AGPS Cat No. 94 2419 3), 376 pages, A$37.95

The Unit also produces a range of Working Papers, also available from AGPS, for A$15 each.

All reports can be obtained from Commonwealth Government Bookshops or from:

AGPS MAIL ORDER SALES
GPO BOX 84
CANBERRA ACT 2601
AUSTRALIA
To order by phone: (008) 02 0049 or (06) 295 4861.